SUMMER
in the
SHADOW
of BYRON

D0755781

521 436 37 5

Also by Andrew McConnell Stott

The Pantomime Life of Joseph Grimaldi: Laughter, Madness and the Story of Britain's Greatest Comedian

SUMMER
in the
SHADOW
of BYRON

ANDREW McCONNELL STOTT

CANONGATE
Edinburgh · London

This edition first published by Canongate Books in 2015
First published in Great Britain as *The Vampyre Family* in 2013
by Canongate Books Ltd,
14 High Street, Edinburgh EH1 1TE

www.canongate.tv

1

Copyright © Andrew McConnell Stott, 2013

The moral right of the author has been asserted

British Library Cataloguing-in-Publication Data
A catalogue record for this book is available on
request from the British Library

ISBN 978 1 84767 872 0

Typeset in ITC New Baskerville Std by Palimpsest Book Production Ltd,
Falkirk, Stirlingshire

Printed and bound in Great Britain by Clays Ltd, St Ives plc

For Josie, Frances and Floyd

Why do you make a book? Because my Hands can extend but a few score Inches from my body; because my poverty keeps those Hands empty when my Heart aches to empty them; because my Life is short, & my Infirmities; & because a Book, if it extends but to one Edition, will probably benefit three or four on whom I could not otherwise have acted . . . O but think only of the thoughts, feelings, radical Impulses that have been implanted in how many thousands of thousands by the little Ballad of the Children of the Wood! The sphere of Alexander the Great's Agency is trifling compared with it.

– Notebook of Samuel Taylor Coleridge, May–July 1811

Who would write, who had any thing better to do?

– Journal of Lord Byron, 24 November 1813

CONTENTS

LIST OF ILLUSTRATIONS

PRELUDE

Dr Polidori stood by the side of the grave. At his feet lay his only patient.

Lord Byron was not dead, merely trying it for size. His exile had begun the day before and, although only twenty-eight years old, the question of the afterlife weighed heavily on his mind.

Their departure for the Continent had been delayed by contrary winds, and Byron, John Polidori, and Byron's two closest friends from university, John Cam Hobhouse and Scrope Berdmore Davies, had spent the day in Dover procuring last-minute items left in London and seeing the carriage stowed safely from bailiffs. After a dinner at the Ship Inn, the four men had set off in search of the tomb of Charles Churchill, a poet who had enjoyed a brief but brilliant celebrity more than fifty years before. Polidori had led the way, walking a mile uphill to Cow Lane and the near-derelict church of St Martin-le-Gran, where children played among the weathered graves, heedless of what they trampled on. An old sexton pointed to the poet's terminus, a plain headstone indistinguishable from those of the tradesmen and mariners surrounding it that read, 'Here lie the remains of the celebrated Charles Churchill.'

'What was he celebrated for?' asked Byron.

'I cannot tell,' replied the sexton. 'I had not the burying of him.'

It was the perfect answer, ideally complementing Byron's sense of futility and loss. As the sun began to set, seemingly amplifying the nearby waves, he tossed the old man a crown to tidy the plot, got down on his knees and laid himself across its uneven sod.

Polidori said nothing, but inwardly, he was thrilled. 'What a lesson,' wrote the young doctor in his diary, for those 'ambitious of literary distinction'.

1

ST GEORGE'S DAY

No one had slept well the night before. Hobhouse, Byron's staunchest ally through the preceding months of acrimony and accusation, had succumbed to the stress and retired with an acute pain that shot up his shoulder. Polidori, Byron's private physician, in service for barely a week, had not been offered a bed in the vast and unwelcoming house at 13 Piccadilly Terrace, and had to make do with a couch, keeping vigil over two empty bottles of champagne and a platter of cake crumbs, the earthly remains of a farewell gift from Douglas Kinnaird. Byron had stayed up writing letters: one to the composer Isaac Nathan, thanking him for the matzo bread, 'a charm against the destroying Angel', and a second to his dear half-sister Augusta Leigh, commanding her to 'never mention nor allude to Lady Byron's name again in any shape – or on any occasion'.

The false quiet was broken by the rattling of servants busying themselves with breakfast. The men rose at six intending to make an early start, but the bustle and confusion that inevitably accompanied Byron meant that no one was ready until half past nine. A clamour could be heard outside, and by the time the coaches came around at ten o'clock, an angry crowd had assembled that was large enough to block the street. Fletcher and Rushton,

Byron's long-time servants, were the first out of the door, followed by a Swiss named Berger, all hurrying down the steps to keep the passage clear. Hobhouse, pug-featured and barrel-chested, came next, pushing his way to the first coach with Polidori and pulling away as bodies closed up their wake. Now Scrope Davies appeared, and with him Byron. The crowd found its voice, barracking the poet with shouts and threats, calling him traitor and repeating the insults of that day's *Morning Post*, which had mocked his '*clump foot*'. They climbed into their carriage as the shouts grew louder and fiercer. Hobhouse turned backwards, imagining 'all sorts of accidents', until at last the dark green livery of his friend's coach emerged from the scrum.

Within minutes the bailiffs arrived to empty the house in lieu of a half-year's rent, giving the crowd the chance to ogle Byron's furniture, paintings, his birds and pet squirrel. His library had already been auctioned, the proceeds hardly making a dent in the thirty thousand pounds he owed in debts, including five hundred to the coach-maker for the vehicle in which he was making his escape, an exact replica of the coach Napoleon had used at the Battle of Waterloo. Emblazoned on its side was a scrolled Latin crest that read 'Trust Byron'. It was St George's Day, 23 April 1816.

That Byron should be jeered and jostled on his own doorstep was testament to the extent to which popular feeling about him had undergone an almost total reversal in a matter of weeks. The cause was the break-up of his marriage to Annabella Milbanke, and the unpleasant battle of their separation. Byron had been distant, even cruel, during the fifteen months of their marriage, behaviour that had only worsened following the birth of their daughter, Ada, just four months earlier, although the precise reasons for their separation remained vague and uncertain, even to themselves. Concerned that Byron would be granted custody of their child, Lady Byron's legal advisers had incubated a lurid silence from which a host of monstrous rumours had been birthed: that Byron was a lunatic and a drunkard, that he had committed incest with his half-sister Augusta, that his politics were treasonous and, most damning of all, that he was guilty of the capital crime of sodomy. The reaction had been savage. The 'lion of 1812', the '*hot-pressed* darling', a man so famous that they even wrote about him in Javanese newspapers, found himself cursed in the streets and abused in the press. Concerned friends warned him not to attend the theatre, or use his carriage in daylight lest he be assassinated.

It was only fitting that rumour and insinuation should play such a powerful part in Byron's fall, as so much of his ascent had been predicated on the careful cultivation of a protean fiction named 'Byron'. Although he had claimed that he simply 'awoke one morning and found myself famous', Byron's rise to celebrity had been calculated and incremental, the attainment of a dream he had craved since childhood. From his élite boarding school in Harrow he had written to his mother to tell her that 'however the way to *riches* or *Greatness* lies before me, I can, I will cut myself a path in the world or perish in the attempt', a steaming ambition that arose from a number of insecurities that accumulated around the congenital dysplasia that had deformed his right leg, the death of his profligate father, Captain 'Mad Jack' Byron, and a title he had inherited unexpectedly by way of the death of a great-uncle's grandson, only to find it encrusted in nuisance and debt.

Byron's ambitions were initially focused on public life. But while his parliamentary career would prove brief and undistinguished, by the age of twenty-one he was eager to see himself as 'a *Man* whose works are praised by *Reviewers*, admired by *Duchesses* and sold by every Bookseller of the Metropolis'. By this time he had published four volumes of poetry, although none had met with much success. His first publicly circulated volume, *Hours of Idleness* (1807) had been savaged by the lawyer Henry Brougham in the *Edinburgh Review*, who called it 'stagnant water', 'stupid and tiresome', and encouraged its author to 'forthwith abandon poetry'. The review drove Byron to down three bottles of claret and threaten to blow his own brains out. He stayed his hand and retaliated instead in verse, composing a long, caustic satire entitled *English Bards and Scotch Reviewers* that excoriated the editors of the *Edinburgh Review* and found a way to insult every contemporary writer of note, calling Sir Walter Scott 'stale', Wordsworth an 'idiot', and Coleridge an 'ass'. Conciliation was not in his nature.

In the summer of 1809, shortly after the publication of *English Bards*, Byron borrowed money from Scrope Davies and left England to travel through Portugal, Spain, Albania, Greece and Turkey in the company of Hobhouse. It was an unorthodox Grand Tour, one necessitated by the Continental armies that obstructed the time-worn procession through the ruins of Italy and the brothels of France. It proved to be the formative experience of the young man's life. After two years of adventure, Byron returned on a ship heavy with Lord Elgin's Grecian plunder, and a portmanteau of manuscripts he had written while abroad. Among these was a long autobiographical poem he called *Childe Burun*, which his cousin and business adviser, Robert Dallas, declared 'one of the most delightful poems I have ever read'. Byron was himself indifferent to it, preferring instead another comic satire he had written in the style of *English Bards*, and it was only when Dallas insisted that he be allowed to shop the poem around that Byron relented. Many rejections followed until the poem at last found a home with John Samuel Murray, the ambitious son of an established publisher who was actively trying to transform the nature of his business from bookseller and stationer to deal-maker and trend-setter.

It was Murray's vision that largely shaped what happened next. Employing a canny sense of marketing, the publisher solicited the help of Tory writer William Gifford, the editor of his literary journal, the *Quarterly Review*, to make a series of cuts that smoothed out the politics of the poem and made it palatable to the broadest audience possible. Then, in March 1812, having whetted the public's appetite with advance publicity that emphasised the poet's aristocratic title, he published the poem in two cantos in a small run of expensive quartos. By charging fifty shillings for a book that could appeal only to the wealthiest clientele, Murray hoped to capture the fashionable set, whose leisure habits set the agenda in all matters of taste. It worked, for in three days, the poem, now titled *Childe Harold's Pilgrimage*, sold out entirely, and Byron found himself fêted by the most powerful families in the land, a 'circle of star-gazers' that included powerful Establishment luminaries such as Lord Holland, the Cowpers, Lady Jersey, the Marquess of Lansdowne, and the Prince Regent himself. Five years after announcing that he wanted to be 'admired by *Duchesses*', Byron had attained his wish. 'This poem appears on every table,' wrote the Duchess of Devonshire, 'and himself courted, visited, flattered and praised wherever he appears . . . he is really the only topic of almost every conversation – the men jealous of him, the women of each other.' 'The genius which the poem exhibited, the youth, the rank of the author, his romantic wanderings in Greece,' wrote the poet Samuel Rogers, all 'combined to make the world stark mad about *Childe Harold* and Byron.'

Having made Byron fashionable, Murray proceeded to make

him profitable, permitting anybody with twelve shillings the chance to experience the poem for themselves. By September, *Childe Harold* had already reached a fourth edition, and over the next three years, more than thirty thousand copies would be sold. Yet however shrewdly Murray had brought the poem to market, the strong attachment readers felt for it was derived from the text itself. *Childe Harold* was eminently accessible, rich in incident and exotic scenes that maintained their momentum with short stanzas and a jogging rhythm stripped of the obfuscating metaphysics of poets like Wordsworth and Coleridge. Its narrative of a young man scouring the mysterious East offered fantasies of boundless movement and sensuous possibility that were avidly consumed by a readership dispirited by war, a deranged monarch and foolish Prince Regent, and the confinements of industrial culture. The real key to Byron's success, however, was the finely tooled sense of introspection his poem conveyed, laying bare a private soul in turmoil through a prematurely jaded protagonist 'sore and sick at heart':

> Yet oft-times in his maddest mirthful mood
> Strange pangs would flash along Childe Harold's brow,
> As if the memory of some deadly feud
> Or disappointed passion lurk'd below:
> But this none knew, nor haply car'd to know;
> For his was not that open, artless soul
> That feels relief by bidding sorrow flow,
> Nor sought he friend to counsel or condole,
> Whate'er this grief mote be, which he could not control.

Byron, in the words of Sir Walter Scott, was 'the first poet who, either in his own person, or covered by no very thick disguise, has directly appeared before the public, an actual living man expressing his own sentiments, thoughts, hopes and fears'. No poet before had so intimately drawn readers into his private world, or done so much to plot the landscape of the inner life as richly as the external scenes through which he passed. New poems consolidated this idea of a man among the multitude, excluded from fellowship by grief, as in the seven enigmatic sonnets addressing a dead lover, titled 'To Thyrza', which were appended to later additions of *Childe Harold*:

> Then bring me wine, the banquet bring;
> Man was not form'd to live alone:
> I'll be that light unmeaning thing
> That smiles with all, and weeps with none.
> It was not thus in days more dear,
> It never would have been, but thou
> Hast fled and left me lonely here;
> Thou'rt nothing – all are nothing now.

The appeal of personality had never been so strong as in this revolutionary age in which fame had been uncoupled from notions of high birth and piety, to be replaced by more entrepreneurial definitions of success. No one exemplified the idea of the career open to talent like Napoleon Bonaparte, who had risen from Corsican obscurity to an imperial throne seemingly by force of character alone. Byron, who had cherished a bust of Bonaparte since his schooldays, similarly put passion and struggle at the heart of existence. Having stood uncloaked before his readers in *Childe Harold*, the following year Byron introduced a more urgent note of danger and erotic charge to his protagonists through a series of 'Eastern tales' that began in 1813 with *The Giaour* and *The Bride of Abydos*, and continued into 1814 with *Lara* and the swashbuckling *The Corsair*, which sold fourteen thousand copies on its first day.* These long narrative poems, heavily seasoned with jasmine and brine, created a succession of solitary anti-heroes, men of 'loneliness and mystery', made of equal parts passion and cruelty, and tormented by a secret past. Even in such ostentatiously melodramatic settings, readers under the spell of Harold's sincerity continued to see Byron in his creations, a phenomenon the author did not try particularly hard to refute – Harold was not a 'real personage', he wrote in the preface to the poem, but 'the child of imagination'. 'In some very trivial particulars, and those merely local, there might be grounds for such a notion; but in the main points, I should hope, none whatever.'

It was one of the great ironies of his success that such intimate poetry should rely so heavily upon the anonymous cogs of industrialisation to attain its widespread appeal, as advances in publishing, marketing and distribution made Byron's work available to a greater number of readers than at any time in history, while simultaneously placing the author at a further remove. It was only natural that excited consumers should fill this empty space with gossip and speculation, the effect of which was not lost on his contemporaries. As early as 1800, William Wordsworth had complained about the damaging effect consumerism was having on literary production, claiming in the Preface to *Lyrical Ballads* that it had produced a thirst for 'outrageous stimulation' that was stupefying the masses and reducing culture to 'a state of almost savage torpor'. When he came to read Byron's work, he found it 'coarse' and 'epigrammatic', telling the diarist Henry Crabb Robinson that 'there is insanity in Lord Byron's family'

---

* Even with the enormous success of these poems, Byron was studiously nonchalant about their creation, later boasting, '*Lara*, I wrote while undressing after coming home from balls and masquerades in the year of revelry, 1814. *The Bride* was written in four, *The Corsair* in ten days.'

and that he believed Byron himself 'to be somewhat cracked'. (For his own part, Byron referred to the Lake Poet simply as 'Turdsworth'.)

There was substance to Wordsworth's warnings. Rarely had an author been so talked about without being known, and as Byron's star ascended, it became progressively difficult to view him outside the distortions of his celebrity. With the line between the poet and the poem increasingly indistinct, Byron obliged his readership by consciously inhabiting a kind of double identity: 'the impersonation of myself', he called it, which 'made every one curious to know me'. Performing his moody solitude for the masses, he toyed consciously with a bespoke persona, presenting himself at one minute as an artist who wrote poetry to 'withdraw myself from myself' and at the next as a man of deed: 'I prefer the talents of *action* – of war – or the Senate – or even of Science,' he said, 'to all the speculations of these mere dreamers of another existence.' New poems appeared with coy prefaces disavowing any autobiographical content – 'I must admit Childe Harold to be a very repulsive personage,' he wrote, in the preface to *The Corsair*, 'and as to his identity, those who like it must give him whatever "alias" they please' – while elsewhere he became adept at exploiting what the Irish poet Thomas Moore, his close friend and earliest biographer, called 'the alleged singularities of his mode of life, which kept curiosity alive and inquisitive'. From 1812 to 1815, a period that would become known as the 'years of fame', Byron teased the line between the real and fictive worlds by generating rumours about his atheism and sexual appetites, and by appearing dressed as a monk or in flamboyant Albanian robes, hosting orgiastic parties in which wine was drunk from a carved skull. The key to it all was constant change. 'The mobility of his nature is extraordinary,' remarked Lady Blessington. 'Everything by turns,' said Byron, 'and nothing long.' Meanwhile, in the privacy of his own home, he dieted furiously, put his hair in curlers, fussed over his complexion, and paid his fencing master to lose.*

In time, the Byronic double came even to stalk his marriage. Byron had enjoyed a series of affairs with prominent society women, including Lady Caroline Lamb, Lady Frances Webster and the Countess of Oxford, all married, and all allies in wit and transgression. When it came to the question of finding his own bride, however, he was insouciant, only agreeing to consider marriage after pressure from his confidante and co-conspirator, Lady Melbourne, who thought that some stability might help to quash some of the more unsavoury rumours, and curb his worst excess. In the question of marriage, Byron shared the prejudices of his class, considering less the qualities of the woman herself than the spotlessness of her reputation and her family's rank. There were several candidates, but it was to Lady Melbourne's niece Anna Isabella (known as Annabella) Milbanke that Byron eventually became engaged. Because Annabella and Byron moved in the same social circles, she had already witnessed much of the hysteria that trailed in his wake, and had chosen to decline the first opportunity she had to be introduced rather than be thought to be 'absurdly courting him' like her peers. Highly intelligent and coolly aloof, Annabella was proud of her imperviousness, even writing a poem in which she coined the phrase 'Byromania' and appealed for immunity against the nonsense and the strength 'to be an anything – except an Ape!!' That Byron should choose Annabella struck many as odd – Caroline

---

* 'Having a *daily* scholar, far more lucrative than any of the others,' wrote Byron's fencing master, Henry Angelo, 'I took care to make the assaults the more satisfactory to him; keeping always on the defensive, retreating on his attacks; now and then receiving a stroke: not like the clowns for a gold-laced hat, or broken head, mine was a gold half-guinea each lesson.'

Lamb, for example, said that he would 'never be able to pull with a woman who went to church *punctually*, understood statistics and had a bad figure' – but as their relationship developed, both felt invested in the promise of its redemptive power.

Although Annabella held herself above the Byromania, she could not necessarily see through it, believing that he really was a tortured soul who had stumbled onto a wayward path, and exulting in the role of the ministering angel who would restore him to hope and religion. Byron encouraged her in this, writing long, apologetic letters in which he promised to reform, while claiming that poetry was not his vocation but 'the result of temporary solitude and accident'.

After an unsteady engagement, the two were married on 2 January 1815. Even as they embarked on their honeymoon, the extent of their mistake was clear. Byron was needling and offhand, becoming unkinder by the day as he found that, instead of soothing him as he had hoped, his wife's patrician reserve incited him to ever greater heights of provocation and melodrama until she became convinced that he truly was tormented. By the time she was pregnant, he was bingeing on brandy and falling into 'paroxysms of rage', in which he would ask if the child she carried was dead, goad her by intimating incestuous infidelities with Augusta, and make dark allusions to appalling crimes committed in his youth. Young and sheltered, Annabella was understandably terrified and, unable to comprehend his meaning, allowed her imagination to run wild. She became suspicious of his friends, Hobhouse in particular, believing that he held horrible sway over her husband through some secret in their shared past, writing to Byron's childhood physician that '*Murder* was the idea suggested to my mind.' He was convinced, she wrote, that he *must* be wicked – is foredoomed to evil – and compelled by some irresistible power to follow his destiny, doing violence all the time to his feelings. Under the influence of this imagined fatalism he will be most unkind to those whom he loves best, suffering agonies at the same time for the pain he gives them. He then believes the world to be governed by a Malignant Spirit, and at one time conceived himself to be a fallen angel, though he was half-ashamed of the idea, and grew cunning and mysterious about it after I seemed to detect it.

Searching for evidence to confirm her fears, she riffled through his private things and discovered a small bottle of laudanum and an illustrated copy of the Marquis de Sade's pornographic novel, *Justine*. Certain that Byron was insane, she took their four-week-old daughter and left London. He would never see either of them again.

Rather than solving his problems, Annabella's departure made Byron worse. Hobhouse rushed to London, where he found him in the midst of blackouts and crying fits that would transmute into bouts of extreme narcissism in which he would wrap himself in his parliamentary robes and begin 'strutting about . . . saying he was like Bonaparte, and the greatest man in the world' – mood swings made all the more worrying by Augusta's discovery of a pistol on his mantelpiece. Hobhouse's response was to stay close, and with the assistance of Scrope Davies, attempt to lift their friend's spirits. In practice, this meant reverting to the youthful dissipations of their days at Cambridge, and long nights at the Cocoa Tree club that were less than medicinal. One morning, Byron's servant Fletcher came down to find that they had come in drunk and left the street-door wide open at three in the morning. It was 'lucky we had not all our throats cut', he said.

Understanding that his daughter's marriage could not be repaired, Annabella's father, Sir Ralph Milbanke, had written to Byron to propose an amicable separation, which may have been attainable, were it not that Annabella was acutely aware that the law gave men inalienable rights in the question of custody. 'Loneliness and mystery' became the weapons she used to keep her child. With the help of her friends and advisers, she mounted a campaign of rumours that placed him under increased pressure. As the private life of the Byrons became national news, the poet's many enemies leaped at the opportunity to tarnish his name as recompense for his radical politics and literary success. Even so, his allies still hoped that things would come to correct themselves, but by the time Caroline Lamb had spread rumours that he had slept with boys and tried to sodomise his wife, the situation had finally deteriorated to a point which, in the words of Tom Moore, 'could not be considered otherwise than disastrous and humiliating'.

The Byromaniacal spell, unravelling at speed, came fully unstrung in the spring of 1816, following the unauthorised publication of two poems Byron had written for private circulation. The first, titled 'Fare Thee Well', was a parting address to Annabella, expressing tenderness and deep regret; the second, 'A Sketch from Private Life', was a sneering and ungenerous attack on his wife's retired governess, Mrs Clermont, whom he accused of poisoning Annabella's thoughts. When both poems somehow found their way into the pages of the *Champion* newspaper, leaked by Byron's enemy, Henry Brougham, they were published as evidence of their author's deep hypocrisy, an impostor who performed remorse to conceal a thwarted, vengeful heart. Believing, according to his own grandiose logic, that the entire nation had dishonoured him, Byron prepared to turn his back, travelling to Geneva where he would spend the summer recovering his health, before moving on to Italy, and ultimately Venice, the city he would call 'the greenest island of my imagination'.

Exile did not mean disgrace, but something akin to the fate of his idol, 'poor dear Bonaparte!!!', a great man levelled by an illiberal enemy and sent where the blaze of his genius could do no harm. That he travelled in a replica of Napoleon's coach only served to reinforce his sense that their fates were somehow aligned. Yet even this gesture of contempt was not indemnified from the power of his own fiction: he 'Childe Harolded himself,' said Sir Walter Scott, 'and outlawed himself, into too great a resemblance with the pictures of his imagination'.

Safely past the crowd, the two carriages hurried through the Haymarket before crossing the river at Westminster Bridge and escaping the city at the top of the Kent Road, marked by the mute bricks of the Asylum for the Deaf and Dumb and the Institution for the Cure of Cancers. From the elevation of Shooter's Hill, they took a last look at London squatting in its miasma as the Thames coiled back in fat bends. The pace was quick, although the scenery offered little to lift the spirits with spring barely in evidence due to hard frosts and unstinting rains that had caused nationwide flooding. At Sittingbourne they were met by a lunch of cold meats, stopping later at Canterbury to take a turn around the cathedral and view the high altar and tomb of Thomas Becket.

Byron recorded nothing of the journey, while in the other coach, John Polidori and Hobhouse also had little to say. Hobhouse was almost ten years older than the doctor, and could not have contrasted more with the spider-limbed young man who sat across from him. Polidori was strikingly handsome, though he smiled only rarely, possessed of a remarkable profile that teenaged girls sketched dreamily on the back of letters. Like so many of his peers, Polidori adopted the Byronic style, dressing mostly in black and going about bare-necked with his shirt collars down in a study of artistic dishevelment. Indeed, he looked more Byronic than Byron, who, it was said, 'barely escaped being short and thick'.

Hobhouse, pragmatic, self-assured and habitually condescending, eyed the doctor with distaste, considering him a most undesirable companion for his friend. He disliked the way he had become so familiar so quickly, inviting himself along as he called in on news-papers to air their side of the story, and making himself 'cavalierly at home' at Piccadilly Terrace, drifting about and calling 'in a strange manner for water and a towel'. Not only was he a mere twenty years old, he had never worked in professional practice, and Hobhouse, who had been caring for his adored friend for the past three months, thought him woefully under-prepared.

Even as Hobhouse objected to the physician's 'damned Italian polysyllabic name', there was no question that if Byron was going to travel, it was necessary he take a doctor with him. The poet had been under medical supervision of one kind or another his entire life, suffering a compendium of maladies from his deformed leg to the 'dreadful and most periodical headaches' he suffered until he was fourteen. As an adult, he had been prescribed special diets, endured kidney stones and episodic bouts of a sickness he had first contracted in Greece, where a naval surgeon had treated him for gonorrhoea, tertian fever and haemorrhoids all at the same time. In 1816 alone, he had been diagnosed with a 'torpid liver', as well as chronic constipation caused by dieting, the symp-toms of which he tried to ease with a compound of mercury and a cocktail of magnesia, Epsom salts, syrup of ipecacuanha and calomel – a neurotoxin used as a laxative. 'He was very ill,' recalled his friend the journalist Leigh Hunt, who saw him just before he left, 'his face jaundiced with bile'. When the decision was made to leave that spring, Polidori was recommended because of his facility with languages. Still Hobhouse remained uncertain. He is 'an odd dog', he told Byron, possibly suggesting that he suspected him of homosexuality, adding, 'I don't like his *ori*.' Byron agreed, but said that his employment was 'inevitable'.

The travellers arrived at Dover late in the evening, retiring to bed at the Ship Inn only after having to deal with much fuss at the hands of the captain of their packet ship. The following day was one of delay and the visit to Churchill's grave, but also the final opportunity for Scrope and Hobhouse to give their friend a proper farewell. Both planned to join him later that summer, but for now they toasted their loss, taking a table back at the inn that became quickly loud and convivial under the auspices of Scrope, who often captained their worst excesses. Onlookers fogged the windows of the lounge and peered through doorways to get a glimpse of Byron, one man even reporting that ladies had come dressed as chambermaids 'for the purpose of obtaining under that disguise a nearer inspection'. One or two were permitted to approach, including Thomas Wildman, an old school-fellow and veteran of the Battle of Waterloo, who recounted the final moments of Byron's cousin who had died there. His companion, Sir Nathaniel Wraxall, introduced himself as a friend of the family, his voice shaking as he spoke and 'knocking his feet in rattattat, all the while oppressed by feeling very awkward' (said Polidori). Even in disgrace, Byron retained the power to awe.

As Scrope continued to ply them with what he protested were merely 'light wines', Polidori produced a sheaf of papers, three plays he had written as a medical student, all much dearer to him than his profession. He well knew that Byron's position on the sub-committee of management at Drury Lane Theatre gave him considerable influence, but what he didn't know was that Byron hated the endless solicitations that this entailed and petitions from hat-makers and 'wild Irishmen' and 'Miss Emma Somebody, with a play entitled "The Bandit of Bohemia".' Nonetheless, he selected a work and began to read aloud. But instead of having his work critiqued by a discerning audience, Polidori found himself roundly mocked. Early passages were greeted with sniggers that grew into loud barks of laughter as Byron contorted the lines, hovering over their infelicities and chewing them beyond all sense. Polidori first went pale, and then became visibly angry, but this only served to make the others laugh harder and widen the gulf that lay between the three old university friends and a mere employee.

Sensing that the sport had gone too far, Scrope picked up the play 'to smooth, I suppose, my ruffled spirits', said Polidori, and began to 'read on with so much attention that the others declared he had never been so attentive before'. But the damage had been done. Furious and humiliated, Polidori stormed out to stalk the streets of Dover, his fury driving him to commit what he called 'a very absurd thing'. Shame prevented him from recording exactly what it was – an act of vandalism, perhaps, or an assault – but it calmed him sufficiently to return and, overcome by remorse, he sought out Byron and Hobhouse to confess. Both were livid, joining together to deliver a strong reprimand before sending him to bed. 'Doctor Polidori committed a strange solecism tonight,' wrote Hobhouse in his own journal, 'and had the naïveté to tell us of it. His attachment to reputation and his three tragedies, is most singular and ridiculous.'

With more than eight hundred miles of uneven road ahead of him, Byron already had a premonition of how this might end. '[I] shall have the reputation,' he told his friend, 'of having made a sober commonplace fellow quite mad.'

DIRECTIONS FOR JOHN

John Polidori was used to being treated as an outsider. Born in London on 7 September 1795, just a few weeks before another aspiring author, John Keats, his father's high expectations often set him at a distance from his peers. His father, Gaetano, was a Tuscan writer who had arrived in London in 1789 to settle in Soho's Golden Square, a neighbourhood long colonised by well-heeled *émigrés,* and notable for its piano-makers and a small community of Italian writers and artists who heard Mass at the nearby Sardinian Embassy. From a house at 42 Broad Street, Gaetano had set himself up as a literary jack-of-all-trades, making translations of English and Italian literature that he sold to the booksellers in Carnaby Market, teaching Italian to wealthy clients, among them the Duke of Sussex and the illustrious actor, John Philip Kemble, and working on his own compositions, poems, plays and 'moral tales', in such prolific number that he set up a printing press in his house to manage them all. In 1793, Gaetano started a family with an English governess named Anna Maria Pierce, the daughter of a writing master. Their first child was a girl, Maria, known as Margaret, and prone to fits of nervous giggles. Next came John, a dainty boy whose dark eyes and thick black hair contrasted strongly with the pale northern complexion he inherited from his mother. Another brother followed who survived only a day, then two more sisters: Frances in 1800, and Charlotte in 1802.

The family was comfortable, although Gaetano proved an austere parent, 'a sworn enemy to pretence and frivolity of all sorts', who insisted upon a tone of frugal sobriety throughout his house, even to the extent of forbidding his daughters dancing lessons. Yet as a man of letters and a child of the Enlightenment, Gaetano believed passionately in the capacity for moral and intellectual improvement through liberal education, and John, as his eldest boy, was valued exorbitantly in the ledger of fatherly ambition. First John imbibed languages, a household mix of English and Italian, which soon grew to include French, followed by immersion in the political history of Greece and Rome. The curriculum revealed much about Gaetano's own preoccupations, as eight months after John was born, Napoleon had marched into Milan with a promise to liberate the Italian people, only to plunder the country of its cultural treasures and liberate fifty-eight million francs from its exchequer. Helpless in exile, Gaetano embraced a brand of Italian nationalism that held republican Rome as its example, feeding his son a historical diet that concentrated on anti-imperial heroes, such as Lucius Junius Brutus, founder of the Roman republic and slayer of the last king of Rome, and his famous descendant, Marcus Brutus, who ended Caesar's imperial ambitions with a dagger to the neck. As John would later recall, 'The Roman and Greek historians were always given to me as the Bible, according to which I should order myself.'

John devoured his studies, demonstrating, in the words of his father, 'a remarkable talent and a lively and very ready ability to understand and retain even the most difficult things' – such as reading a French translation of Dante's *Divine Comedy* in a single sitting before the age of eight. Such precocity did not come without difficulties, as John's talents were hampered by temper and impatience. Having inherited his father's inability to be idle, he would rise before dawn and pace his room until the weak city sun provided enough light to read by. Boredom turned quickly to anger, and to keep him busy, Gaetano set him thought experiments intended to sharpen the accuracy of his language and enlarge his powers of description. 'Let us suppose,' Gaetano would say to his boy, 'that I had never seen a carriage and that you wished – with words – to make me understand what one was.' John pondered, and offered 'an explication of it that was so exact and true, that it would not have been easy for anyone, even by means of study and observation, to make one any plainer and clearer'.

At the age of seven, John was sent to study at a small Catholic charity school in Somers Town, a half-built suburb two and a half miles north-west of Soho that had been settled by French refugees attracted by low rents and the belief that the nearby St Pancras Churchyard would provide them with Catholic burial rites. This was his first brush with organised religion since his father, though nominally a Catholic, followed no liturgy and partook of no rituals. His mother, by contrast, was a devout Anglican. As was the tradition in mixed-faith families, boys were to be raised in accordance with their father's religion and girls in line with their mother's (Mrs Polidori's great piety would later earn her girls a reputation for always seeming 'out-of-the-world'). For Gaetano, sending John to a Catholic school was a cultural choice rather than a spiritual one, yet it would prove to be the most influential decision he would make in his son's life. Legal toleration of Catholics was still a very recent phenomenon in Britain, and while the second Relief Act of 1791 had removed some of the most oppressive obstacles to Catholic worship, religious bigotry remained so entrenched that the king himself had preferred to accept the resignation of his most capable prime minister rather than allow him to permit Irish Catholics to serve in parliament. Catholicism meant being set apart.

John did not study in Somers Town for long, as Gaetano soon decided that the school was unsuitable due to the 'bad company' his boy was falling into, and the 'ill effect' and 'bad example' of the other children. He remained at home, only venturing out for lessons in astronomy and geography with an exiled priest named Abbé Marty, who was amazed at both the child's mathematical ability and the intensity with which he studied. 'My boy,' prophesied Marty to his student, 'thou wilt be nothing insignificant, but something great . . . either for good or evil.' His words made a great impression on Gaetano, who realised that his exceptional child required not only a good education, but also a less frenetic place than London in which to study. Thus, in 1804, just a few months after Napoleon had been declared Emperor of France, John was set into a coach and driven more than two hundred miles into the deep Yorkshire countryside where, for the next seven years, he would be a student at a newly established boarding school for Catholics named Ampleforth Lodge.

To an eight-year-old boy raised in London's most cosmopolitan precinct, Ampleforth must have seemed as barren as the penal colony in Van Diemen's Land. The school was desperately remote, nestled in the woods and hollows of the Vale of Mowbray, an area that had sheltered recusant Catholics since the Reformation. Even getting there was a trial of faith. First, John and his father had to travel to York, a journey that took three days and cost seven pounds. There, they had to find a local carriage to take them thirteen miles north to the small market town of Easingwold, from where they had to walk two miles across the fields to the tiny village of Crayke and either pick up a footpath and walk the final eight miles, or wait to be collected by the school cart. Approaching the Lodge, they descended into a low valley in which stood a spare rectangular building of white stone, three storeys high, behind which fields fanned out in all directions. In summer it was an Eden; in winter, a frosty basin of mud and caws.

When John arrived at Ampleforth, the school was home to twelve boys and twenty-four Benedictine monks. Tuition cost forty pounds a year, which was not inconsiderable given that Byron's school, Harrow, one of the élite 'inner five', cost fifty. Not a penny was spent on luxury. The Lodge in which the boys ate and slept consisted of seven rooms including a dormitory lined with thin flock mattresses, a chapel and a refectory, all of it draughty and crumbling, although not especially old. Lessons were conducted in an outhouse that leaned against the kitchen wall, behind which was a walled garden where the boys tended plots of basil, carnations and Venus's looking-glass. Leaving was discouraged: 'It is wished that the parents would avoid, as much as possible, taking their children home,' read the prospectus, 'and, on this account, there will be no additional charge for those who leave them at the College during the vacation.' Seclusion suited the monks who ran the school, for whom the memory of persecution remained fresh. Chased from their European abbeys by French Revolutionary forces, the headmaster, Richard Marsh, had only narrowly escaped the guillotine by swimming across the Mosel river in the dead of night.

As he prepared to leave his son, Gaetano handed him a lengthy memorandum. Titled 'Directions for John', it offered reminders to rise early and clean his teeth, but also not to repeat 'past faults'. 'Remember,' it said, 'that I would rather see you an idiot than a learned rogue . . . Truth, Truth, Truth.' But there were few temptations here. Asceticism was key to the school's monastic principles, yet its intimacy and the kindliness of the monks meant there was little of the casual viciousness and sadistic ritual that preserved order in most nineteenth-century schools. Daily life was overseen by the 'First Prefect', a monk with responsibility for setting the day's schedule and maintaining discipline through the threat of additional chores rather than the more common methods of flogging and fagging, public-school traditions from which no one was exempt, however grand (Byron's fag at Harrow had been George Sackville, 4th Duke of Dorset).*

A sense of how life in a bleak monastery might play on the imagination of a nine-year-old child comes from the very first letters John wrote home. It tells of an 'accident which befell us on monday night', just as the boys were settling down to study. It was dark, and the weather was terrible. 'We heard a knock at the door,' John told his father:

> one of the boy's went to open it and a poor old woman asked for some money. Iorang gave her a penny and i a shilling and then she asked for some Bear and we gave some to her and she went and seet down on the stairs we asked the boys what they said she was going to kill a live child which she had in her hand or how is all.

Choosing to ignore the fact that a distressed infanticide seems to have stepped into a roomful of little boys, Gaetano scolded his

---

* Hobhouse's school, Westminster, had a reputation for being the most brutal in Britain, where it was not unheard of for children to be so badly bullied they were permanently maimed. Sexual exploitation was also commonplace. When the *Vanity Fair* author William Thackeray arrived at Charterhouse, the first instruction he received from the boy he fagged for was 'Come and frig me.'

son for the illiteracy of his account, calling the letter 'foolish' and insisting that he confine himself to the facts. 'Now tell me!' he wrote,

> Is your health good? Do you find yourself comfortable? Do you behave with respect to your Masters? Are you obedient to them? Do you learn the principles of the Religion which you are to follow? What are the studies you make, and which do you like best? Answer all these questions one after the other. You make many faults in your English. I am afraid you neglect your language. Think, my dear John, that to know foreign languages is an ornament, but it is a shame not to know one's own. As you are born an Englishman, you must know English well.

But even as Gaetano exhorted his son to consider himself English, the size, solitude and, above all, Catholicism of Ampleforth, served to instil in its pupils a strong sense of their separateness from the general run of society. John flourished in this closed community, excelling in its full curriculum of Latin, Greek, French and Hebrew, learning the flute, studying botany, history and geography, and playing battledore and shuttlecock with his friends. The topic that most seduced him, however, was religion, from four a.m., when he rose for matins, through to the final service of the day.

At least half of John's classmates went on to become monks, and after two years of assimilating the rhythms of devotion, John wrote home seeking permission to be allowed to enter the noviciate, 'for I have thought for a great while that it was my calling . . . what I think God calls me to'. Gaetano refused, and the question of the boy's future went unresolved until, at the age of thirteen, John was unexpectedly contacted by his uncle, Frederick Pierce, a major in the Fifth Regiment of Native Infantry stationed at Madras, who invited him to India to enrol in the army. The prospect of soldiering horrified John. The dangers of military service were well known, as aside from the prospect of violence, there was the risk of disease. Of the four hundred young men who made up the 51st Regiment stationed in Ceylon in 1803, for example, nearly three-quarters died within the first three months, killed by tropical illnesses. Yet the dangers John feared most were spiritual, not physical. 'I have learned that in choosing a state of life,' he wrote to his father,

> greater attention must be paid to the means each state affords of attaining happiness in a future world than to the temporal advantages, which it may promise. Now as far as I have been able to learn, there is great reason to apprehend that I should not have it in my power to practice my religion were I to go to India as a Cadet, I should most probably have only Protestant companions, and these perhaps of not the most moral character. And it is much to be feared that bad example together with ridicule would soon deprive me of the Religious sentiments, which I have imbibed since I came to Ampleforth Lodge.

But there was no cause for alarm, as Gaetano considered soldiering as inadequate to his son's 'genius' as becoming a monk, brushing the suggestion aside with so little regard for his brother-in-law's feelings that the offended major subsequently cut all ties. With the question of John's 'state of life' now squarely set before them, Gaetano announced that his son must prepare himself to enter the University of Edinburgh, where he was to study to become a doctor. This was hardly news – the 'Directions for John' had told him to pay special attention to his Latin and Greek 'as indispensable things for the studies of higher sciences to which you will pass as soon as you are qualified for them' – but John still found the proposition as troubling as being billeted with a squad of Protestant recruits. 'Do you not think,' he wrote anxiously to his father, 'that . . . I should be exposed to very great danger of having my morals corrupted by bad example? Are not the young men in these Universities generally rather dissolute, and would it not be too dangerous to expose me while young to their infectious society?' It was the prologue to a final impassioned plea: 'As far as my youth and inexperience will enable me at present to judge: I think that I have a vocation for the Ecclesiastical life.'

Gaetano would hear no more, and John was recalled to London.

The city of Edinburgh strained under the weight of its population – a hundred thousand people stacked into buildings on volcanic crags that rose in tiers and swept into the black waters of the Firth of Forth. At its centre ran a long ridge that carried the high street all the way from the castle to the ancient abbey of Holyroodhouse, from whose sides ran a series of tributary wynds that jutted out like ribs, 'so that its general appearance,' remarked the *Traveller's Guide to Scotland*, 'has been, not unaptly, compared to that of a turtle'. To the traveller Louis Simond, it appeared as 'a confused heap of ancient houses, one over the other, very dingy and high . . . with windows innumerable', its sense of teetering profusion compounded by the new buildings and half-finished edifices erected everywhere throughout the town. Filth and overcrowding were the 'dirty and detestable way in Old Edinburgh' where it was not uncommon to find '7, 8, or 10 families inhabiting the different floors of the same building and having a common staircase'. Even 'people of fashion were obliged to submit to small, dull and unhealthy habitations', wrote the *Traveller's Guide*, echoing the complaint of a bemused English student who said that it was 'strange that the people here cannot learn to be a little more neat and cleanly'.

John had arrived four weeks after his sixteenth birthday, taking rooms in Buccleuch Place, the same long street of tenements that housed the offices of the *Edinburgh Review*, bordered by the flat granite of Salisbury Crags at one end and the parkland of the Meadows at the other. Proceeding to the university library, he joined a line of 450 other young men who queued for the privilege of handing over a half a crown and signing the matriculation album that would officially make them students of medicine. It was the largest intake of any university course in Britain, and also the most diverse: students from Russia, Canada, Brazil and the Azores were attracted by Edinburgh University's reputation as one of the finest medical schools in the world, and because, unlike Oxford and Cambridge, it did not prohibit Catholics.

It was hard to adapt to student life, and with no Mass to anchor his day, or prefects to assign him tasks, John found his sudden independence disorientating, especially as the university offered no set curriculum or prescribed route of study. Direction came from handbooks such as Johnson's *Guide For Studying Medicine at the University of Edinburgh*, and from the explicit marketing of the professors themselves who were not paid a salary by the university but took their income directly from students, they charged them three guineas apiece to attend their courses. The first two weeks of term were chaotic, as students considered a rialto of possibilities, dropping in to sample the lectures of professors like Thomas Charles Hope, who would punctuate his chemistry classes with colourful phosphoric displays to maximise his income.

John signed up for classes in anatomy, *materia medica*, and the Institutions of Medicine, which, according to Johnson's *Guide*, 'is to explain the principles on which the study of physic is founded'. But the most important class John took was undoubtedly 'Practice of Medicine', a class that imparted all the indispensable skills of a nineteenth-century physician, taught by Professor John Gregory, a popular eccentric who began each class by bowing and begging leave to wear his hat. Thanks to a long career, and students who had fanned out across the globe, Gregory had become one of the most influential medical educators alive by virtue of a class that focused almost exclusively on ridding the body of noxious substances in the briskest manner possible by means of blood-letting, plunge baths, blisters, enemas and vomiting. Out in the field, this 'antiphlogistic' regime, as it was known, produced remedies such as that used to treat a soldier named Walter Henry, who developed malaria during the Peninsular Campaign. His treatment began by having thirty-six leeches applied to his shaven head, after which he was carried into a yard and stood up while twenty-five buckets of cold water were poured on him from a third-floor window. It didn't work, so Henry devised his own plan to 'outrun' his fever by drinking hot, spiced wine and galloping across the Spanish plain.

Under Gregory, John learned how to administer all the major classes of such remedies – purgatives, emetics, cathartics, tonics, stimulants, astringents and sudorifics – and to apply its powerful pharmacy: opium for sedation, rhubarb, magnesia and senna for laxatives, Peruvian bark for fevers, and calomel for gripes and worms. He learned phlebotomy (blood-letting), the physician's stock-in-trade, drawing blood with a lancet from the arm, neck or, for women, the ankle, taking anywhere between 40 and 72 ounces (between 2½ and 4½ pints), or through the application of leeches to the temples, ears and anus. Opportunities to practise these skills on sick people, however, were severely limited, and John's sole chance to walk the wards was confined to a single course of clinical lectures at the infirmary, where students formed unruly 'shoals' and 'pushed and jostled, and ran and crowded round the beds, quite regardless of the patients' feelings or condition'. 'Certainly not much was to be learned at these "goings round",' recalled one eminent professor, 'they were mostly occupied with chattering and playing, and making extra-hospital arrangements'. Students keen for additional clinical experience could pay a guinea and buy a ticket to visit the wards at noon, an hour set aside specifically for this purpose. Few took it up, since not only was it expensive, it flew in the face of the assumption that physicians were gentlemen who should not demean themselves by unnecessary proximity to sickness, and what Sir Robert Christison, who briefly overlapped with John at Edinburgh, called 'the emanations . . . of the human "subject"'.*

---

* Such diffidence need not always be taken as a lack of empathy, as it may have been the only way students and professors were able to cope with their constant exposure to suffering in the days before asepsis and anaesthesia. Viewing an open corpse was harrowing enough, and, having once seen one, Christison could never forget his 'repugnance' and 'constant disgust at the odour of the anatomical theatre'. Similarly attending a surgical demonstration on a live patient could be profoundly traumatic. Needless to say, it was exponentially worse for the patient, strapped to the table in the middle of a stifling lecture theatre whose walls bent closer with every ululating scream, yet students also recorded them being 'a very hard trial'. The famous London surgeon John Flint South had to draw on all his reserves just to stay in the room: 'So long as the patient did not make much noise I got on very well,' he wrote, 'but if the cries were great, and specifically if they came from a child, I was quickly upset, and had to leave the theatre, and not infrequently fainted.' Charles Darwin, sent by his father to study medicine at Edinburgh in 1825, had a similar experience. 'I also attended on two occasions the operating theatre in the hospital at Edinburgh and saw two very bad operations one on a child,' he wrote in his *Autobiography*, 'but I rushed away before they were completed . . . The two cases fairly haunted me for many a long year.'

The neglect of practical studies was responsible for some of the worst abuses at the university, specifically in the case of anatomy. Edinburgh's professorship in this key area had been occupied for a total of 126 years by three men, all of whom had been named Alexander Munro: father, son and grandson. This was not unusual in a nepotistic age when, of the ten professors hired in the two decades prior to John's arrival, eight were the sons of professors already in residence. By sheer good fortune, the first two Alexander Munros had been men of parts, but by the time John was there, the post had devolved to Alexander Munro III, who treated it as a tiresome inheritance. Appearing in class with his clothes in runkled disarray, Munro mumbled through the notes his grandfather had written almost three-quarters of a century before without even bothering to omit such obvious anachronisms as the phrase 'when I was a student in Leyden in 1714' – a passage that took on such a mythic status that its annual utterance became something of a *fête*, the students showering the professor with peas when they heard it while Munro sputtered on.

To supplement his anatomical studies, John would have paid an extra guinea to attend either the demonstrations of the chief dissector, Andrew Fyfe, a curious old relic and the last man in Scotland to wear a pig-tail wig, or those of John Barclay, a freelance anatomist so popular with the students that he taught twice a day to accommodate them. Even with these extra classes, practical anatomical experience fell short as the law forbade dissecting any bodies except those of executed criminals, and while cadavers were shipped from London, they were expensive and the supply was unreliable. With upwards of five hundred students a year taking private lessons just to pass anatomy, the university authorities turned a blind eye as the ghoulish practice of 'resurrection' began to take hold. Body-snatching, which would become murderously professionalised under Burke and Hare in the 1820s, was largely carried out during John's residence by anatomists' assistants and their students, who, according to Robert Christison, considered it the ultimate student spree. Alerted to a fresh burial, they would enter the churchyard on dark winter afternoons before the church or city Watch began their rounds. Setting a canvas sheet at the head of the grave to protect the grass, they attacked the dirt with wooden trowels to avoid the sound of metal hitting stones. There was no need to dig everything out, as a small, rectangular hole at the head of the coffin would suffice. Having dug down to the coffin top, iron hooks attached to a rope were positioned under both sides of the lid and, with the hole covered to muffle the crack, the rope was given a sharp pull, snapping off enough of the wood to allow the body to be dragged out by the armpits. The 'thing', as they referred to their treasure, was stripped, its clothes and effects reburied, and the earth scrupulously replaced so as not to betray the least sign of disturbance. When performed by experienced resurrection men, the operation took less than an hour.

In spite of its many shortcomings, medical education at the turn of the nineteenth century was at the leading edge of scientific innovation, as the fields of biology, psychology, comparative anatomy, botany and pharmacology succeeded physics as the key sites of discovery that challenged humanity's relationship to history, nature and God. In comparison with Byron's education at Cambridge, John's studies at Edinburgh were positively complex. Even though Byron claimed to have read four thousand novels and countless volumes of law, history, biography and poetry by the time he was nineteen, his formal education did virtually nothing to improve him.* Going up to Trinity College in the autumn of 1805, he entered what his friend Edward Noel Long called 'the headquarters of Dullness', an institution embalmed in the past that required its students and faculty to wear gowns denoting their social rank, and where his own aristocratic status exempted him entirely from participation in lectures or exams. 'College improves in everything but Learning,' Byron had written to the son of his solicitor, 'nobody here seems to look into an author ancient or modern if they can avoid it.' Whereas John would dress before dawn, sit all day in lectures and walk home in the dark to spend his evening bent over a candlelit text, of the three years of his enrolment at Cambridge, Byron spent less than ten months in residence, and most of that he passed in larking with Scrope and Hobhouse, swimming in the weir above Grantchester or parading with Bruin, a pet bear he lodged in the stables of Ram Yard. The rest of the time was lost in country houses or dallying in London, where he was said to have learned more from his boxing lessons with Gentleman John Jackson than he did from his college tutor, Thomas Jones. What Jackson couldn't teach him, he sought in the arms of the *corps de ballet.* 'I am buried in an abyss of Sensuality,' he told Hobhouse, from his suite at Dorant's Hotel where he had retreated with some students of Drury Lane's dancing master, James D'Egville. 'I am given to Harlots, and live in a state of Concubinage,' he said, 'I have some thoughts of purchasing D'Egville's pupils, they would fill a glorious harem.'

The fleshpots of Scotland were of a flintier hue. Medical students had a reputation for solemnity and discipline, which was reflected

---

* Sir Walter Scott commented on meeting him in 1815, that 'Lord Byron's reading did not seem to me to have been very extensive either in poetry or history. Having the advantage of him in that respect . . . I was sometimes able to put under his eye objects which had for him the interest of novelty.' 'His acquaintance with books was very circumscribed,' added Leigh Hunt.

in their sober recreations: shopping for hand-made trinkets sold through the palisades by prisoners at Edinburgh Castle, or taking rambles out to Craig Cooke and the medieval chapel at Rosslyn, mantled with ivy and in a picturesque state of ruin. In winter, they went ice-skating and in summer stirred with their boots the gravel paths of the Botanical Gardens, whose five acres of plantings were strictly arranged according to the Linnaean system. There were some moments of intemperance – taverns commandeered for all-night games of billiards, and visits to brothels, which were so numerous in Edinburgh that even a particularly pious student named Sylas Neville visited three on his last day of term, 'not with any bad intention, but merely from curiosity'.

John did not socialise. He hated medicine and, as he had predicted, failed to mix with the other students, whom he found dull, provincial and devoid of intellectual curiosity. 'They are autom-atons,' he complained to his father. 'They have no enthusiasms, nor other vivid passion.' The restless intensity he had shown as a boy had moved on from the religiosity of Ampleforth to embrace new obsessions with politics and current affairs, topics on which he clumsily tried to debate his peers only to have them withdraw after a series of what John called 'petty bickerings which arose from [my] enlivened discussions'. 'They always think me mad,' he told his father, 'and I can never say what I feel for fear that they should treat me as crazy if I talk of liberty, war, Literature. Whatever object I begin discussion, I get interested in it, and forthwith they conclude I am angry, and hold their tongues.' In time he avoided the company of British students entirely, preferring that of two Germans, Mathias Thierens and Alex Ziegler. 'As soon as I am in company with a foreigner, what a relief!' he told his father. 'I see that *they* feel like myself: we dissent, we talk of all things with enthusiasm . . . But, when I am with these Scotchmen, I drone, one leg crossed over the other, and they think me a pedant.'

Ignoring Gaetano's injunction to consider himself an Englishman, John sought refuge in his foreignness by emulating his father's nationalism, referring to himself as '*Italo-Anglus*', and hungrily consuming news from abroad. The heralds of war had attracted many of his classmates who had signed up as military surgeons or recruits to the Royal Army Medical Service, and soon John was begging Gaetano to be given leave to help in Italy's struggle for freedom. 'If that is my country,' he wrote, 'why should I not go and lend a hand in saving it? . . . I hope therefore that you will not hesitate in allowing me to respond to the cry of my country, which now calls me to arms.' Patriotism and the love of liberty were not the sole motivations behind John's desire to thrust himself into battle. There was also the lure of fame. 'Besides,' he told his father, 'ambition, and the love of glory, which consumes me, call me to action.' 'No doctor ever acquired glory,' he added. 'My ambition aims at *general* fame: for this I would give life and all. I have but life to sacrifice: and this who would hesitate to hazard for so noble a prize?'

Gaetano's response was terse. 'I *will* answer you immediately,' he wrote from London, 'but only to tell you that you are a madman fit for a strait waistcoat'. He threatened to break off their correspondence entirely, 'for your madness pierces my heart, and has increased to such an extent that I myself am at the point of losing my senses by reason of your presumptions, conceited, empty, and silly notions.' 'Return to your reason,' he wrote, 'if you *will* be mad, wait until I am dead.'

Once again John stood down in the face of his father's rebuke and, turning back to his studies, found himself unprepared for his final exams. Rather than risking failure, which 'would be a shame for the rest of my life', he decided to stay in Edinburgh for an extra year. The abdication of Napoleon in the spring of 1814 had dampened his desire for war, and he found himself instead nurturing a love of literature, especially what he called 'the bliss of touching that more than heavenly lyre – poetry; which gives no insensate sounds, but, with its harmonious notes, breathes into vivid flames the irritable sparks of enthusiasms and hope'. It was around this time that he wrote the first of his tragedies, 'Count Orlando', a short drama of jealousy, disguise and revenge that drew heavily from Samuel Taylor Coleridge's play, *Remorse*. He also began to attend literary salons he called 'half literary, half bacchanalian meetings', when he would stay up 'whole nights to drink wine, or the more intoxicating draught of poetry'. He made a rare friend in an alumnus named Robert Gooch, a slight individual thirty years of age 'with a marked disposition to melancholy', who had overcome poverty and a fear of skeletons to become London's leading expert in midwifery and post-natal medicine. With a practice in Berners Street, just a short walk from the Polidori home, Gooch enjoyed considerable prosperity thanks to the overflow of trade from his patron, Sir William Knighton, physician to the Prince Regent. Gooch had many literary friends, including Coleridge, and in 1814 he was able to introduce John by letter to William Taylor, a prolific writer who had played a pivotal role in the introduction of German Romanticism to Britain through a series of essays he had written for the *Monthly Review* that had been praised for pioneering a new school of 'philosophical criticism'. Soon, Taylor and John were corresponding regularly.

At fifty years old, William Taylor was the same age as John's father, though in his temperament and liberality he could not have been more different. He lived in Norwich, where he sat at the head of a large group of talented literati known as the 'Speculative Society', which he warmly invited John to attend. A visit was arranged in early 1815, and John found that not only did the Speculative Society offer the kind of animated and uncensored discussion he sorely craved, but he was respected as a writer and much admired for his romantic good looks. When it was time to leave, the portrait painter Mr Sharpe presented John with a sketch of himself as Apollo, his brow adorned with laurels, above the lines 'Apollo here his every gift imparts/His form, verse, brilliance, and his healing arts.' Excited by his triumph, John wrote to his favourite sister, Frances, 'See how I must have caught them.'

In truth, by the time John arrived in Norwich, both William Taylor and the Speculative Society were in decline. Riddled with gout and general ill-health, Taylor was reeling under severe financial losses, and had become an unbiddable procrastinator who had largely abandoned writing in favour of heavy drinking and surrounding himself with an inner circle of 'ignorant and conceited young men, who thought they could set the world right by their destructive propensities', according to the writer Harriet Martineau, whose surgeon father had once been a member. Their meetings now consisted primarily of Taylor baiting his sycophantic audience with blasphemous comments. Polidori, said Martineau, was just another 'handsome, harum-scarum young man – taken up by William Taylor as William Taylor did take up harum-scarum young men'.

Norwich so energised John that he determined to settle there after graduation, although first there was the question of exams and a dissertation to contend with. This last was a long Latin essay that set out all the available knowledge on a given medical subject but without the expectation of novel argumentation or even original research – indeed, most were heavily plagiarised, or even entirely written by a hired tutor called a 'grinder'. Most students chose well-worn topics like pneumonia or the circulation of the blood, but John sought to differentiate himself by writing on the self-consciously Gothic phenomenon of sleep-walking, a subject that reflected his poetic interest in the moonlit motivations of the mind. But aside from the topic, there was nothing especially innovative about John's work. Instead it quoted at length from a case history his Uncle Luigi had presented to the Royal College of Physicians in 1793 that dealt with the violent nocturnal outbursts of a twelve-year-old boy, and a second involving a Burgundian priest who wrote detailed sermons in his sleep, which had been suggested by William Taylor who had himself read it in Diderot's *Encyclopédie*.*

Just as he was finishing the piece, John received discouraging news. Taylor had written to say that the chances of practising medicine in Norwich were slight due to the monopoly of Drs Martineau and Rigby, and another man, Dr Wright, who was waiting in the wings. John was downcast. He considered moving to Italy, but revealed the extent of his cooling revolutionary fervour when he told his sister Frances that it was 'in too convulsed and precarious a state' to visit. His landlady encouraged him to consider the Indian Medical Service, but John merely complained that without money and the support of his estranged Uncle Frederick he would have 'no interest to push me on when arrived'. As he told Frances, 'I really see obstacles every way I turn.'

On 24 June 1815, John returned to the university library along with eighty-three other hopefuls assembled for their examinations in a room that buzzed with news of Napoleon's capture and defeat at Waterloo, as it was told in the pages of the *Caledonian Mercury* that were passed around containing the first full accounts of the battle. A week later, he was back again, ready to undergo final scrutiny before being asked to leave the room, change into an academic gown, 'and was by the imposition of the velvet cap raised to the degree of Doctor of Medicine'.

---

* John elected not to include another of Taylor's examples, that of a woman whose sleep-walking led her into unplanned sexual encounters with a variety of men.

The reward for four miserable years in Edinburgh, however, was the discovery that his degree was virtually useless. When John returned home and tried to acquire a licence to practise medicine in London, he encountered a problem that no one had ever thought to check when the beadle of the College of Physicians told him that 'No man was allowed to practise until he had passed their examinations.' To sit the London examination, candidates had to be at least twenty-six years of age. There were no exceptions, and anyone who flouted the injunction would be prosecuted. Dr Polidori was still only twenty.

THE FOOTING OF AN EQUAL

After a day of idleness in Dover, things were as rushed and chaotic as they had been when the group left Piccadilly. The captain called the tide and demanded everyone get on board even though it was a bad time to leave for Ostend, as it would mean arriving in darkness and having what one traveller referred to as 'an ugly coast to tamper with'. Hobhouse had advised Byron repeatedly against the port. Only six months earlier, bad weather had run the *Sir William Curtis* aground just fifty yards from the pier-head, smashing it against the pilings and pulling it under before a crowd of onlookers powerless to help. Among the dead were the mother and sister of Lord Dorchester.

Byron was not ready and neither was Berger, the Swiss, who was still in bed. At nine, Hobhouse collected his friend and hurried him down the wooden dock as the last of the luggage was lowered from the quay. Byron appreciated the haste, but fretted about what he had left behind, and specifically the question of whether or not he should answer his accusers in print or, 'at any rate, be ready for them'. He had spoken before of returning in a year or two but now told Hobhouse he had 'a presentiment his absence would be long'. Berger appeared with moments to spare before the packet slipped its mooring and churned into a rough, disagreeable sea.

'The wind was completely in our teeth,' wrote John, as they heaved off and turned before coming back for a second pass past the pier where Scrope and Hobhouse stood waving. 'God bless him for a gallant spirit – and a kind one,' wrote Hobhouse, having watched his friend disappear over the horizon, and with him, months of his own ferocious, maternal care.

Byron sought the shelter of the cabins while the servants secured the baggage and checked the fastenings that kept the coach from rolling around the deck, before finding their own spot to wait out the voyage. John remained at the taffrail, watching Dover's 'stern white cliff' receding and finding himself powerless against the melancholy of departure. 'The sea dashed over us, and all wore an aspect of grief,' he wrote in his diary, with no particular reason to be sad, before turning his thoughts to an unnamed lady left ashore – 'her who bade me join her remembrance with the last sight of my native soil'. Contemplating women would be a feature of John's travels, although whether this remark referred to an actual lady or a poetic shade summoned to suit the mood is unclear. He maintained his watch for much of the crossing, marvelling at the sight of the French coast and becoming ever more lyrical with the setting sun. 'The stars shedding merely a twilight enabled me to see the phosphoric light of the broken foam in all its splendour,' he wrote.

> But the most beautiful moment was that of its first appearance: no sound around save the sullen rushing of the vessel, and the hoarse cries of the heaving sailor; no light save a melancholy twilight, which soothed the mind into forgetfulness of its grief for a while – a beautiful streak following the lead through the waves.

Below deck, Byron was throwing up.

They made good progress, tacking and turning in spite of the winds, and spotting the lights of Ostend some time after midnight. Having braced themselves for the customary swindling from the green-uniformed Customs officials, they were pleasantly surprised to find them honest and polite, and even the scrum of men who met each boat with their solicitations had not bothered them unduly. The only disappointment of their arrival was the tea at the Cour Impériale, which was unpleasantly perfumed. Byron had consoled himself by going straight to his room where, John fancied, he 'fell like a thunderbolt upon the chambermaid'.

The next day, John awoke with a headache from the smell of fresh paint in his hotel room. He rose and went to his desk to write letters announcing his safe arrival, while further down the hall his patient did the same, including one to Hobhouse with the instruction 'Don't forget the Cundums.'

John's letter to his father was particularly difficult. After Edinburgh, John had gone to live at 36 Great Pulteney Street, a four-storey London terrace house that Gaetano had purchased in Soho to accommodate his growing family – two young sons, a baby daughter, and John's godfather, John Deagostini, who occupied the top-floor flat. Living there felt much like being a child again, so when Robert Gooch appeared in March 1816 with the unlikely news that Sir William Knighton had asked him to recommend a physician to accompany Lord Byron on his expedition to Italy, John, faced with protracted unemployment, did not hesitate to accept. Immediately, he and his father argued, Gaetano fiercely opposing his son working for such an '"atrabilious" man' and demanding that he withdraw his application. John agreed, but regretted his decision and fell sighing into a copy of George Wheeler's *Journey Into Greece.* The promise of travel, Gaetano told his brother Luigi, had got 'his youthful fancy so excited that, in that heat, he ran off to Lord Byron, and re-spun the broken thread, contrary to my advice'. Thus, John drew up a will, collected a passport signed by a minister of the King of Sardinia, and joined his master in Piccadilly.

It wasn't merely that Gaetano objected to Byron's notoriety, although he certainly did. Rather, he had his own experience of what it meant to be a famous writer's companion, an experience he did not wish his son to repeat. As a young man, Gaetano had studied law at the University of Pisa but, like John, had truly wanted to pursue his passion for literature. In 1785, he had abandoned his studies to take up a position as secretary to the Italian tragedian, Count Vittorio Alfieri. For four years, Gaetano was to be found at Alfieri's side as the writer moved between villas in Rome, Piedmont and Alsace, compiling and revising a definitive edition of his collected works and shepherding it through the press. It was the perfect apprenticeship for the life Gaetano would later lead, yet Alfieri was far from an ideal employer. Dogged by depression since childhood, his first suicide attempt had come when he tried to poison himself at the age of seven, and he compensated for a life of unhappiness and insecurity with bullying and disdain. He was as 'proud as Milton's Satan, and more choleric than Homer's Achilles', recalled Gaetano, and 'esteemed himself far beyond his real worth'. Show was everything: he maintained 'a fine and speckless apparel', a carriage with sixteen horses, and a mane of long red hair, which he wore 'studiously curled and tended'.

The tragedian also fancied himself as a lover, which led him into a variety of misadventures, the most dangerous of which resulted in a duel with the renowned swordsman Earl Ligonier, who graciously decided not to kill the Italian after he discovered that his wife was being unfaithful to them both with one of her grooms. Alfieri's women would also prove a source of discomfort for Gaetano, who was careful and meticulous, and shared none of his master's swank. He was particularly wary of the young, beautiful and vexatious Louisa Stolberg, Countess of Albany and the estranged wife of the pitiful alcoholic Charles Edward Stuart, the 'Young Pretender'. Louisa and Alfieri had a volatile relationship, and Gaetano often found himself the target of Alfieri's jealousy after Louisa had made one of her comments about the young man's looks, or the firmness of his thighs. More troubling still was the writer's idealistic embrace of revolutionary politics. In 1788, Alfieri moved to Paris to be closer to Louisa despite declaring it 'a filthy sewer', arriving just as the French Revolution began to unfold. Alfieri had nurtured a profound hatred of French royalty ever since Louis XV had once looked upon him 'as if he were Jupiter and Alfieri an ant', and he exulted in the mayhem he found, leaping with joy 'upon the ruins of the Bastille' while his young secretary was filled with horror at the bloodlust that seemed to have infected even the most elderly Parisian. Peering through the rhetoric of freedom to the carnage that lay beyond, Gaetano abandoned Alfieri and left for London, counting himself lucky to be free of such a demanding and capricious master.

The parallels between Byron and Alfieri were so plain to see that even Byron had made the comparison, pointing out the habits he shared with the Italian, and finding 'so many points of resemblance,' wrote Lady Blessington, 'that it leads one to suspect that he is a copy of an original he has long studied.'

It was a Friday, and Byron, believing that Fridays brought ill-luck, was in no hurry to travel, so John breakfasted alone and took a stroll, noting the odd little carriages, women in their clogs, and shiftless peasants 'basking in the sun as if that would evaporate their idleness'.

Ostend had flourished in wartime, heavily garrisoned and

profiting from the shutting up of Calais, but its air now hung with the tallage of brackish water and its long, empty streets were fringed with the debris of two and a half decades of war. The fortifications, which John thought 'miserable', were little more than a series of dirty sluices and broken poles sharpened into points, while its dockyard was crammed with rotting vessels, many of them the remains of barges amassed for a mooted invasion of England, their decks broad enough to mount a two-pound cannon. At the shoreline stood a solitary bathing-machine, ignored by the impoverished shrimpers wading chest-high in seawater, their skin the colour of mercury. 'A few hours at Ostend are likely to exhaust a traveller's patience,' said one guidebook. A British soldier put it this way: 'Were I to be banished among the Algerins, I could not feel more reluctance, than on entering this place, in which there can be nothing to prevent the grass growing in the streets, but the irreclaimable sterility of the soil.' It reminded John of Scotland, 'only not quite so filthy'.

One curiosity of the town was the open display of erotic literature, volumes 'of the most obscene nature', exhibited in the window of every bookshop. Entering one to take a closer look, John found himself so captivated by the sight of the pretty shop girl that he accidentally knocked a quarto onto her head 'while looking at her eyes' and had to buy two books to cover his embarrassment. It was his second mortification of the morning. He had already tried out his French only to find that no one spoke it and, undeterred, had ventured some German, at which point 'half-a-dozen women burst out laughing'. 'Luckily for myself,' he told his diary, he was able to master his temper: 'in a good humour; laughed with them'.

It was three o'clock by the time Byron was ready to undertake the thirty-five-mile trip to Ghent, the first leg of an unnecessarily long and circuitous journey to Geneva that would take them eastwards through Flanders to Liège, and from there to meet the Rhine at Cologne, which they would follow south before crossing into Switzerland by the Jura mountains. Such an itinerary, studiously avoiding even a kilometre of French soil, was intended as an expression of contempt for the newly restored Bourbon monarchy and especially its first minister, Charles-Maurice de Talleyrand-Périgord, whom Byron denounced as the 'living record of all that public Treason private Treachery and moral Infamy can accumulate in the person of one degraded being'. He had, he had told Hobhouse, 'no desire to view a degraded country – and oppressed people', and rejected France for rejecting Bonaparte just as he rejected England for rejecting him.

There were other benefits to travelling through Flanders. Its officials were less corrupt than the French, and its political climate much less oppressive than that of the Bourbons, for whom merely carrying a sealed letter was enough to get a man thrown into prison and subject to a crippling fine. Even so, a number of precautions had to be taken for a long trip of this kind, especially in a country where many suffered from the privations of war. Local servants had to be selected with great care, and loaded pistols carried at all times. It was also essential that they refrain from picking up any travellers along the road, which 'has been the cause of many murders and assassinations', according to Charles Campbell's *Complete Guide Through Belgium, Holland and Germany*, although the same guide was happy to report that accounts of '*zielverkoopers*', Flemish kidnappers who murdered victims to drain and sell their blood, 'are very much exaggerated', even if they were not 'altogether void of foundation'. Of course the primary hazard of travel remained the relentless chiselling of the posthouses and innkeepers that stood along the road. This was where Berger came in. One of the many foreigners who hung around London's Panton Square offering themselves as couriers,

Berger had been hired for his knowledge of local languages and roads, enabling him to find good rooms and fresh horses, and grease palms with small bribes known as '*frais du grassage*'.

The stale-breathed dereliction of Ostend abated as they moved into the countryside, travelling along roads lined with beech trees and through farmland flat as a fishpond, or, as John put it, 'as unchangeable as the Flemish face'. Pretty villages appeared on either side, their plain churchyards marking graves with simple wooden crosses in keeping with the neatness and regularity in evidence all around them. Even small huts perched on the banks of damp canals were spotlessly clean and hung with signs that translated as 'Country Pleasure' or 'My Delight' and adorned with thick hedges cut into fantastical shapes by master topiarists.

Progress, however, was slow. John had brought little luggage with him besides clothes, a satchel filled with privately printed copies of his dissertation, and a medicine chest equipped with the oddments of his profession: scales, flasks, a spring-loaded bundle of needle-points, known as a scarificator, and remedies such as manna, worm cakes and turkey rhubarb. Byron, by contrast, had packed far too much and, without the benefit of Scrope's coach to carry the load, had been obliged to hire an additional *calèche* for the servants and freight. His own carriage, with its grooved leather interior, escritoire for writing, 'a library, a plate-chest, and every apparatus for dining' and a curious coffin-like bulkhead that jutted out under the driver's seat allowing its passengers to sleep at full stretch on a '*lit de repos*', was, as they soon discovered, not built for Flemish roads. Unlike Britain, where charging mail coaches and fashionable young men inspired to recklessness by membership of carriage clubs had made speed customary, Belgian postilions rarely spurred their horses beyond a dilatory trot on deserted roads that, while paved in the centre, consisted principally of potholes and sand, punctuated by toll booths placed every mile and a half. People here preferred to travel by water, using the large black and green barges called *Treckschuyts* that traversed the canals so gracefully 'that a person may read, write, or even draw' on them. To Britons, they were deathly: 'Nothing but the patience of a Dutchman could stand the *ennui* of the *coche à l'eau*,' wrote one British traveller, glancing with horror at decks filled with passengers indulging their national pastime of smoking 'or doing nothing at all; perfectly silent, and moving at the rate of about three miles an hour'.

The afternoon light had faded, and the carriage lamps had been lit by the time they reached Bruges, a city John described as 'one of the most beautiful towns I ever saw', with its ornamental canals and gabled mansions, many of which had forty or fifty windows, evoking a lavish translucence unimaginable to Britons still used to the window tax. But Bruges was another ghostly relic, having ceded its economic importance to the modern efficiencies of Brussels and Antwerp, leaving many of its grandest houses either shut up or converted into warehouses for corn. 'Twilight softened all the beauty,' wrote John, seized once more with the poetic melancholy he had experienced on the crossing, 'and I do not know how to describe the feeling of pleasure we felt going through its long roof-fretted streets, bursting on to spots where people were promenading amidst short avenues of trees.' At the city gates, their coach passed a boy playing in the dirt and watching it run 'through his fingers laughingly, heedless of the myriads whose life hung upon each sand'.

Once more in open country, they came upon an inn from which streamed a robust but skilful music. Enquiring about its source, Byron, who disliked all but quick, lively tunes, was invited in by the innkeeper, who showed them an orchestra of farm labourers tackling a series of difficult marches with great aplomb.

John was particularly impressed to see farmhands doing something other than drinking for amusement and, as a physician, was especially taken with one player who blew on an enormous trombone despite being 'manifestly consumptive'.

Leaving the inn, they continued on their way. By now, they had been travelling for almost ten hours, much of it in the dark, their slow procession lulling John in and out of sleep. Dreaming of an English fireside, he was jolted awake by Byron, who announced that they had lost their way. Their postilion had been acting strangely, driving over the same bridge multiple times before coming to a complete halt. A savage-looking man in an ill-fitting jacket, thigh-high boots and 'a most rascally face', he had whipped the horses without mercy and overcharged his passengers at every barrier, and now, John feared, had led them into a trap. They stopped near some houses, where the postilion had climbed down as if he were going to knock at one of them, before suddenly running off. John also got down, approached a cottage and found it deserted. Suspecting an ambush, he fetched a pistol and knocked at another door, but found that house, too, was empty. By now, even Byron's valet, Fletcher, who had tangled with bandits in the mountains of Albania, was starting to worry, and he ran back to find sabres for himself and the other servants, Rushton and Berger. But there was no need, as out of the shadows came the postilion, who announced that they simply had to continue straight on the same road. Byron, who had not even bothered to get down from the carriage, claimed to find the entire episode absurd. Did they not know, he later wrote to Hobhouse, 'that four or five well-armed people were not immediately to be plundered and anatomised by a single person fortified with a horse-whip to be sure – but nevertheless a little encumbered with large jack boots – and a tight jacket that did not fit him'? They arrived at Ghent at three in the morning to find the city gates shut fast, gaining admittance only after much knocking and fuss. The next day, Byron decreed, would be a day of rest.

Ghent was a fine city, with wide squares and avenues, that John thought superior even to London. As the capital of Flanders and home to many of the Belgian nobility, there was much to see, including a famous library and botanical garden, a prestigious art school, literary societies, an eighteen-foot cannon named La Folle Marguerite, and an élite college that had its own private prison for mischievous boys ('For slighter offences, one day may be enough; but three, five, ten, or fifteen days are sometimes necessary.') The streets were perfectly primed for tourists, with women selling little rolls and slices of cold baked eel on sticks, and gangs of 'Cupids' offering to act as tour guides. These young idlers crowded around strangers the moment they appeared and had to be watched at all times: if a traveller 'is not on the alert', wrote one British visitor, 'his baggage will soon disappear, and while bustling about to find it, they would steal the very spectacles from his nose'.

Even prosperous Ghent exhibited the scars of war, and everywhere visitors would go, its citizens volunteered their grievances about the French. A huge new church stood half finished after Napoleon had looted its funds, and much of its art still remained in Paris as Bourbon ministers did all they could to stall its repatriation. The situation had exasperated the allies so much that the previous September, 150 British riflemen had entered the Louvre and begun systematically to strip the walls, inciting the anger of a Parisian mob, who had to be held back by Austrian cavalrymen. The Prussians secured their treasures, and the government of Rome had dispatched the sculptor Antonio Canova to supervise the return of theirs, yet the Flemish could not seem to locate many of their artworks. Dominique Vivant, the frustrated leader of the Flemish delegation, went to see the head curator of Napoleon's museums, the man who had personally overseen the looting of conquered territories, and threatened to attack him with a detachment of three hundred soldiers if the pictures were not immediately produced. Many came forward, but more remained lost that only began to trickle back after several were discovered in the private palaces of the Prince of Orange, and yet more in the home of a notorious art-collecting cleric named Cardinal Fesch.

John and Byron forwent the Cupids and toured the city by themselves, beginning with the cathedral, whose decorations John considered the ideal compromise between Catholic tinsel and Presbyterian sobriety. Having poked through its catacombs, they next climbed the 450 iron-plated steps to its spire, from which they could enjoy a view of the flat countryside they had driven across, with the spires of Bruges in the distance and, beyond them, the sea. At the École de Dessin, they elbowed past art students to view paintings by Rubens, Van Eyck and Krüger, the latter's *Judgment of Solomon* containing an image of a dead child that so disturbed Byron he was forced to turn away. In the church of St Bavon, they saw some Van Dycks, and so many other paintings that John had a hard time keeping track. Of all the pieces on view, those that attracted him most were two statues of young Englishwomen.

At eight the following morning, they set off for Antwerp but, two hours into the journey, were stopped by a long, rasping scrape that brought the coach to a halt. One of the front wheels was frozen and refused to turn. John hailed a passing carriage and rode back to Ghent to return with a farrier, who removed the wheel and took it to a local blacksmith. They were marooned in the tiny hamlet of Lochristi, where the entire village was dressed for Sunday Mass, the men in three-cornered hats, 'capacious breeches', buckles and greatcoats, and the women wearing clogs, enormous gold earrings and dresses that reminded John of a 'bed-gown, like the Scotch'. It was not an appealing image. 'Indeed,' he lamented, 'I have not seen a pretty woman since I left Ostend.'

The blacksmith invited John and Byron to wait in his house, providing them with a further opportunity to marvel at the taste and cleanliness of even the meanest habitations. He was an elderly man and suffering from a fever, and as he hammered at the wheel, John pulled down his medicine chest to provide the man with some relief – 'Physicked him,' Byron told Hobhouse. 'I dare say he is dead by now.'

The delay meant returning to their hotel in Ghent, where an article in the town's *Gazette* revealed that Byron's brief appearance had already been noted. With nothing to do but wait, John inspected the canal and promenade, while continuing to search in vain for a pretty face – 'Many ladies,' he wrote, dejectedly, 'all ugly without exception – the only pretty woman being fat and sixty' – before stumbling inadvertently into a café full of prostitutes on the way back. In the morning, they made their second attempt at departure for Antwerp, this time arriving without incident, and immediately proceeded to indulge in more sightseeing and more art, including the cathedral's famous Rubens altarpieces, newly returned from Paris after the French had first tried to pass them off with counterfeits. Art, however, was beginning to wear on Byron. He took no great pleasure in viewing paintings and refused to believe that other people did. 'As for churches – and pictures,' he wrote to Augusta, 'I have stared at them till my brains are like a guide-book: – the last (though it is heresy to say so) don't please me at all – I think Rubens a very great dauber – and prefer

Vandyke a hundred times over – (but then I know nothing about the matter) . . . It may all be very fine – and I suppose it must be Art – for I'll swear – 'tis not Nature.'

The following day they were off, through a landscape that John, his style increasingly adopting a Byronic indifference, described as 'tiresomely beautiful' and full of 'fine avenues, which make us yawn in admiration'. The carriage continued to give them trouble, breaking down twice more, the second time so badly that they were forced to get out and walk to the village of Malines. An angry meeting with a farrier resulted in the unwelcome news that the carriage's large curvilinear cee springs had to be replaced, a big job that would require removing the entire body from its wrought-iron frame. Their best hope was to have it repaired at Simon's, the Brussels manufacturer that had built the chassis for Napoleon's original, and so, hiring another *calèche*, they embarked upon an unscheduled detour. In Brussels, they learned that the wheels kept freezing because the front end of the carriage had been badly built, and that the whole body required work, which would result in a lengthy delay. Ensconced in the Hôtel d'Angleterre, Byron wrote to Hobhouse exhorting him to vent his spleen on Baxter the coachmaker – 'I beg that you will abuse him like a pickpocket,' he wrote, failing, of course, to mention the matter of his own unpaid bill.

The enforced stop provided John with an opportunity to write to his sister Frances for the first time since leaving England. 'I am very pleased with Lord Byron,' he told her, the spat at Dover seemingly forgotten. 'I am with him on the footing of an equal every thing alike at present here we have a suit of rooms between us. I have my sitting room at one end he at the other.' 'He has not shown any passions,' he continued, 'tho we have had nothing but a series of mishaps that have put me out of temper tho they have not ruffled him.' On the contrary, said John, Byron had been in high spirits, belting out songs as they inched across the pavement, and indulging his doctor's literary ambitions by discussing his writing and earnestly insisting that he 'continue being a tragedian'. Best of all, John said, Byron had extended an offer of five hundred guineas from John Murray to publish two of his dramas, and £150 for his journal of their tour.

Byron, however, would remember none of this, and recalled their conversations taking quite a different tack. 'He was,' he said of his doctor, 'always talking of Prussic acid, oil of amber, blowing into veins, suffocating by charcoal, and compounding poisons.'

4

THAT ODD-HEADED GIRL

As John composed letters in a Brussels hotel, a second party was on the move, making its own more rapid progress towards Geneva. They travelled at the insistence of a determined young woman who had celebrated her eighteenth birthday only days before. She was small and beautiful with dark hair and a name that kept changing, although for now she was known as Claire Clairmont. Crowded beside her into a dainty and ill-provisioned post-chaise was her step-sister, Mary Godwin, tired, fair-complexioned and also eighteen, and Mary's lover, a twenty-three-year-old poet of some obscurity named Percy Bysshe Shelley. Three-month-old William, Mary and Shelley's son, lay swaddled and fumbling in Mary's arms.

All three had their reasons for leaving England. Shelley and Mary were exhausted by financial struggles and the hostility their relationship had aroused, especially from Mary's father and Shelley's wife. Europe, they hoped, would allow them to live both freely and cheaply. Claire also sought to take possession of the life she craved, although her hopes did not reside in a place but in a person – Lord Byron.

Although Claire had met Byron only a handful of times, her future, she believed, lay interleaved with his. It was this conviction that had led her to write to him in March 1816, during what were the darkest days of his separation. 'An utter stranger takes the liberty of addressing you,' she had said, 'my feet are on the edge of a precipice; Hope flying on forward wings beckons me to follow her and rather than resign this cherished creature, I jump though at the peril of my Life.' All that determined whether she would soar or die was his answer to the simplest of questions:

> If a woman, whose reputation has yet remained unstained if without either guardian or husband to control she should throw herself upon your mercy, if with a beating heart she should confess the love she has borne you many years, if she should secure to you secrisy and safety, if she should return your kindness with fond affection and unbounded devotion could you betray her, or would you be silent as the grave?

As an invitation to intrigue, it could not have been more direct, and Claire was impatient for an answer 'because I hate to be tortured by suspense'. She signed the letter 'E. Trefusis' and sealed it with an elegant, aristocratic seal, although this in itself was not enough to catch Byron's attention. His home besieged by emissaries bearing armfuls of correspondence, he had little patience for anonymous mail, and no longer took much interest in the entreaties he had received from female readers in the years since *Childe Harold*. The poem had resonated strongly with women who identified with Harold's need to construct an interior life as a defence against domestic isolation, and who found in the text a form for their own feelings. Such was the view of the admiring 'MH', who wrote to say 'That upon perusing "Childe Harold" and its accompanying poems I became as it were animated by a new soul, alive to wholly novel sensations and actuated by feelings till then unknown'.

Byron's verse not only fed 'intellectual understanding' and the yearning soul, it also inspired sexual desire for its author. It was, according to the Scottish novelist Susan Ferrier, enough 'to make a woman fly into the arms of a *tiger*'. Many women, like Claire, wrote to him under assumed names with the intention of establishing a more intimate relationship. 'Rosalie' declared her love and asked him to place a note in the classified columns of the *Evening Star* or *Sunday Observer* under the name 'Antonio' if he wished to meet. 'Echo' asked him to come to her in Green Park 'on that side . . . that has the gate opening onto Piccadilly, and leave the rest to Echo'. 'Henrietta' engaged in a long, one-sided correspondence, in which she unpacked her heart and confessed to hiding in the shadows outside his bachelor apartment at Albany in hopes of seeing him alight from his carriage. When his engagement to Annabella Milbanke was announced, she resigned her love in a lengthy letter whose last page was extravagantly blotted with real or simulated tear-stains. Forgoing a pseudonym, the expensive society courtesan Harriette Wilson simply invited him to bed, while from all across the country he was petitioned for verses, locks of hair, samples of handwriting and even 'an occasional place in your lordship's thoughts'.*

Claire was not deterred by his silence. Having received no answer, she wrote a second, more measured letter asking whether he would be at home to 'receive a lady to communicate with him on business of peculiar importance'. It was a third of the length of her previous note and signed with the initials 'G. C. B.', no

---

* Popular legend has it that Byron responded to requests for his hair by sending clippings from his dog, Boatswain. This is unlikely to be true, as the Newfoundland died in 1808, four years before the full onset of his master's celebrity (he is honoured with a prominent memorial at Newstead Abbey, Byron's ancestral home until debt forced its sale in 1817). Byron did, however, send Lady Caroline Lamb a lock of Lady Oxford's hair in response to a request for one of his own.

doubt to give the impression that it came from a different author. This at least piqued the poet's curiosity. 'Ld. B. is not aware of any "importance" which can be attached to an interview with him,' he replied, 'and more particularly by one with whom it does not appear that he has the honour of being acquainted. He will however be at home at the time mentioned.'

This was all the encouragement Claire needed, and while the exact sequence of their initial meetings is difficult to establish, she was granted an audience at Piccadilly Terrace some time in March, where she revealed to Byron her 'utmost secrets'. She also appears to have sung for him, displaying a beautiful voice that her music teacher, Dr Corrie, likened to 'a string of pearls, each note was so perfect', and which became the inspiration for one of Byron's best short lyrics, 'Stanzas for Music', dated 28 March 1816:

> There be none of Beauty's daughters
> With a magic like thee;
> And like music on the waters
> Is thy sweet voice to me:
> When, as if its sound were causing
> The charmed ocean's pausing,
> The waves lie still and gleaming,
> And the lulled winds seem dreaming:
>
> And the midnight Moon is weaving
> Her bright chain o'er the deep;
> Whose breast is gently heaving,
> As an infant's asleep:
> So the spirit bows before thee,
> To listen and adore thee;
> With a full but soft emotion,
> Like the swell of Summer's ocean.

In the fullness of time, the combination of summer, infancy and moonlit water would prove unnervingly prescient, but in that stressful season in the spring of 1816, it merely expressed gratitude for being momentarily relinquished from the tortures of his predicament.

Byron was far from smitten. Although rumour attached him to the Drury Lane actress, Mrs Mardyn, he was in fact sleeping with her colleague, Susan Boyce, and seems to have shown little interest in seducing Claire as well. She called twice at Piccadilly Terrace in the following days only to be told that the master was busy or not at home, but still she persevered. Her next letter acknowledged his 'affairs and cares' and promised to refrain from empty praise and ask merely for advice: 'May I beg of you,' she wrote, in a letter she signed 'Clara Clairmont', 'to procure some of your theatrical friends an account of what instructions are necessary for one who intends entering that career.' Byron duly referred her to his friend Douglas Kinnaird, chairman of the Drury Lane Theatre subcommittee, with permission to use him as a reference, at which point Claire altered her approach, telling him that in fact she was unable to decide between the theatre or a literary life, and seeking to impress him by transcribing an Italian sonnet by Dante from memory, discussing the merits of Shelley's poems *Queen Mab* and *Alastor*, while also telling him that for the past two years she had been working on a novel she called 'The Ideot'.

In discussing her work, Claire revealed just how different she was. Its plot concerned a woman 'committing every offence against received opinion', a noble savage, 'educated amidst mountains and deserts', with no acculturation beyond her own untutored thoughts and impulses. On a superficial level, she told Byron, it was a cautionary tale, a warning to follow 'Mama and Papa's good advice'. More astute readers, however, those she called 'Atheists', would divine its true subtext as a radical critique of slavish orthodoxy and the institutions that enforced it. Having shown her dissident side, Claire began to reveal, little by little, more of her unusual 'theories', a series of unorthodox, almost heretical, opinions that were all the more exceptional for being advocated by a seventeen-year-old woman, as well as 'the ill humour I feel for every thing by which I am surrounded'. Byron, however, declined the invitation to read her work-in-progress, and instructed her to write shorter letters, before he stopped answering altogether.

Still Claire refused to be ignored. By 9 April, she had dropped all pretence at soliciting advice, and despite Byron's attempts to convince her that her attachment to him was pure 'fancy', she openly declared her feelings:

> I do not expect you to love me, I am not worthy of your love – I feel you are superior – yet much to my surprize, more to my happiness you betrayed passions I had believed no longer alive in your bosom . . . I may appear to you imprudent vicious; my opinions detestable, my theory depraved, but one thing at least time shall show you that I love gently and with affection, that I am incapable of any thing approaching to the feeling of revenge or malice; I do assure you, your future will shall be mine and every thing you shall do or say, I shall not question.

More appointments came and went until Claire eventually took the affair into her own hands, telling him flatly, 'If you stand in need of amusement and I afford it you, pray indulge your humour.' Proposing a plan for them to escape somewhere outside London where they might spend the night together, 'free and unknown', she suggested a date and waited around the corner for his servant to bring the reply: '*Certainly*,' said his note, on which she scrawled at the bottom, 'God bless you – I *never* was so happy.' When the appointed evening came, Byron made her wait in the hall for more than a quarter of an hour before rescheduling their assignation for the next Saturday. Then, on 20 April 1816, Byron and his 'little fiend' slept together. The following day, he signed the papers that officially separated him from his wife.

Now that they were lovers, Claire told Byron of her intention to follow him to Geneva. At first he did not believe her and thought she was merely romancing, but having sensed her determination he warned her he would be angry if she tried to travel alone. But while Byron assumed this would scupper her plans, Claire interpreted it as an invitation to bring Mary and Shelley along, as both were keen to leave England and meet Lord Byron. Waiting only to discover the verdict of a legal case Shelley was involved in, they made their way to Switzerland as quickly as they were able, travelling from Dover to Calais and ploughing a straight line through France, stopping only when necessary and wasting no time on the sights. They were much faster than Byron, but also much less comfortable. Shelley's carriage was cramped with a baby and three adults, whose shared intimacy was often oppressive. Claire and Mary's relationship was especially tense, with its roots in a family of five children all jostling for position, none of whom shared the same two parents.

The step-sisters had grown up in London above a shop at 41 Skinner Street known as the Juvenile Library, a children's bookshop and publishing house run by Mary's father and Claire's mother. It specialised in textbooks, fairy-tales, parenting manuals, and retellings of Biblical stories and classical myths.

Although the shop was remarkable, Skinner Street was an unfortunate location for such an enterprise. The road, newly constructed to relieve the dense traffic of Holborn, was unforgivingly steep, clogged with carts and lined with malodorous warehouses wholesaling cheese, oil, oysters and oranges. The Library was one of only a handful of retailers, set between a hat shop and a haberdasher, and subject to the fly-blown stench of Smithfield cattle market from one direction, and the potent miasma of London's principal sewer, Fleet Ditch, from another. It also stood at the crossroads of the city's penal system, with Newgate Prison at the bottom of the road and Fleet Prison just around the corner. Even closer was the New Drop, the site of public executions since 1783, and barely a hundred yards from their doorstep. Just weeks before Claire and Mary moved in, four thousand people had come to witness the hanging of the murderers Owen Haggerty and John Holloway, the crush causing a stampede in which almost forty people lost their lives.

In spite of their surroundings, 41 Skinner Street remained a busy and social household with a constant stream of visitors who shook the beams as they stumped up and down all five storeys of the 'crazy and ill-built' house. As children, Claire and Mary were used to seeing the study and dining room filled with garrulous adults engaged in free and fierce debate, their passions jostling without fear of censorship. Exceptional visitors were a daily occurrence, and those passing through included William Wordsworth, the writers Thomas Holcroft and Maria Edgeworth, and the artists James Northcote and Henry Fuseli. Both girls remembered well the night that they had crept out of bed to sit on the stairs and listen to Coleridge recite 'The Rime of the Ancient Mariner' in their parents' sitting room.

This unique domesticity had been carefully cultivated by Mary's father, William Godwin, who considered it his duty to maintain one of the fullest social lives in literary Britain. Raised in a Dissenting tradition, where frequent visits were exchanged to bolster a sense of fellowship and solidarity, Godwin had applied the same principle to his adult life as a way of promoting the strain of radical politics and Jacobin philosophy he had fostered in the late eighteenth century. Although now somewhat anonymous, for a period in the 1790s he had been considered one of the most dangerous men in Britain, thanks to a series of successful novels, most notably *The Adventures of Caleb Williams* (1794), his tale of secrets and pursuit, and an uncompromising work of philosophy entitled *An Enquiry Concerning Political Justice* (1793). It was *Political Justice* that set Godwin squarely at the head of radical culture by not only calling for greater personal liberty and the end of monarchy ('a species of government unavoidably corrupt') but by extending his attack to include every institution that sought to impose on individual freedom. For centuries, Godwin argued, the human mind had been steadily evolving according to the principle of 'perfectibility'; that is, it possessed an infinite and unfolding capacity for improvement that would eventually lead to wholesale enlightenment and the redundancy of all external laws and systems. Human beings, he believed, were naturally benevolent creatures who could not fail to act virtuously once they had attuned their minds to reason and were free from hypocrisy and the pressures exerted by self-interested bodies like the Church or state. To be truly liberated, Godwin claimed, humanity must see all the instruments of government, privilege and legal coercion fully dismantled, replaced instead by an earnest commitment to self-improvement, virtuous action and the moral courage to tell the truth, irrespective of another's feelings.

Unvarnished candour lay at the heart of all Godwin's interactions, and when combined with the profound personal awkwardness that was the inheritance of his austere, religious childhood, it is unsurprising that he should have remained a virgin until the age of forty. In 1796, however, he embarked upon a life-altering relationship with Mary Wollstonecraft, the brilliant and iconoclastic author of *A Vindication of the Rights of Woman*, who was herself remarkable for her self-sufficiency and decision at fifteen years of age 'never to endure a life of dependence'. Wollstonecraft had only recently survived a suicide attempt yet found in Godwin a sympathetic friend. Theirs was a wonderfully academic romance – they shared newspapers, read by the fire together, critiqued each other's writing, and bothered each other for stationery ('Pray *lend* me a bit of indian rubber,' she wrote to him, 'I have lost mine.') It was a flirtatious relationship as well, and a sensual one. 'What say you,' Mary would write, arranging an assignation, 'may I come to your house, about eight – to philosophise?' It was Wollstonecraft who introduced Godwin to sexual pleasure, and found herself rather encouraged with the results: 'Seldom have I seen such live fire running about my features,' she wrote to him one morning, 'when recollections – very dear; called forth the blush of pleasure, as I adjusted my hair.'

Godwin and Wollstonecraft married after discovering that she was pregnant, and on 30 August 1797, she went into labour. 'Mrs Blenkinsop tells me that I am in the most natural state,' she wrote to Godwin that day, 'and can promise me a safe delivery.' It was the last sentence she would ever write. At 11.20 p.m., she gave birth to Mary but survived only eleven days before succumbing to a slow death from septicaemia and a puerperal fever that could have been wholly avoided if the attending physician had acted quickly to remove the placenta. Her passing put Godwin into deep mourning, but now he was the father of a newborn baby and also guardian to Wollstonecraft's first daughter, three-year-old Fanny, her child from an unhappy dalliance with an American adventurer named Gilbert Imlay. Wollstonecraft had been careful to cultivate the relationship between Fanny and Godwin and, aware that paternal instincts did not flow through him naturally, had coached him in how to give her a biscuit or a piece of cake to make sure that she always enjoyed seeing him. It had worked and Fanny loved him. But without his wife's intelligent prompts, Godwin found himself poorly equipped to fashion a suitable environment for two small girls. For long months, their house at the Polygon in Somers Town was sombre and sepulchral. Calling in one day, Samuel Taylor Coleridge described it as 'catacombish', reverberating with the 'cadaverous silence' of Fanny and Mary, then aged five and two respectively.

In April 1801, Claire's mother appeared, moving into the Polygon with two small children of her own. According to family legend, Mary Jane Clairmont, 'a handsome, fantastic woman', whose particular dress, Catholicism and foreign manners spoke of mysterious origins, introduced herself to Godwin either by leaning over her balcony and openly declaring her interest, or by pacing the length of their adjoining wall and murmuring, 'You great Being, how I adore you.' However she gained his attention, it worked, for having made his acquaintance she was pregnant within weeks (the child was stillborn), and by December they were married.

Little was known of Mary Jane's background, and she volunteered even less, saying only that she had been born in England, the daughter of one Andrew Peter Devereux, and had spent a considerable portion of her childhood in France before fleeing the Revolution for Cádiz. There she had met and married a member of a prominent Swiss family named Charles Abram Marc Gaulis, before settling in Bristol, where the couple Anglicised their name to 'Clairmont' and had two children – Charles in 1795, and Clara (Claire, who was known throughout her childhood as 'Jane') on 27 April 1798. Shortly afterwards, Gaulis died during a cholera epidemic while on a trip to Hamburg.

Almost none of this was true. The seigniorial Andrew Peter Devereux, for example, was entirely imaginary, his name chosen, like 'Clairmont', for its air of baronial dash. Mary Jane's real father was in fact a bankrupt Exeter merchant named Pierre de Vial, who seems to have indentured his daughter at the age of sixteen to an Exeter milliner, and while she did spend some time in Europe, her version of those travels appears as fictional as that of her parentage. Similar lies were invented for her children, for although Charles Gaulis, whom she had initially met in Bristol, was in all likelihood the father of Claire's brother, Charles, he and Mary Jane were never married. Neither could Gaulis have been the father of Claire, as he had died two years before she was born.

Claire's father was in fact a fifty-two-year-old landowner named John Lethbridge, whose family held considerable estates in Devon and Somerset, and who had met Mary Jane at a point in her life when she was tackling the world with all the energy and resourcefulness of one of Daniel Defoe's venture-heroines. She was in her late twenties, attractive, and not only possessed many of the accomplishments that allowed her to pass in provincial society, but also understood the value of discretion, telling the admiring Lethbridge, 'I have the means of concealing my Engagements from the world.' When their brief affair resulted in pregnancy, Lethbridge initially refused to acknowledge the child as his, accusing Mary Jane of entrapment and sleeping with a man in Barry Island: 'I will not be *bullied* by any *Man*, nor will I become a *Dupe* to any *woman* under the Canopy of Heaven,' he wrote to his solicitor, Robert Beadon, denouncing her as 'a person of first Rate Ingenuity' and an 'artful Harpey'.

As the epitome of county respectability, Lethbridge had much to lose. A former Sheriff of Somersetshire, he lived in the stately mansion of Sandhill Park with his wife and three children, the eldest of whom, Thomas, was expecting his own first child. He refused to see Mary Jane, but she was dogged in pursuit, attacking his innuendo and citing the fact of baby Claire, who looked, in the words of one who knew them both, 'as much like him as I ever saw a Child like a Father'. At first, Mary Jane pushed for Lethbridge to take sole custody of their child, but added that if the thought 'is highly disagreeable to you, I am ready to keep her on certain conditions': a financial settlement and a promise never to trouble him again, to which Lethbridge reluctantly agreed, noting that 'If some step of this kind is not taken, I shall have a child to maintain for 20 years at least.' Lawyer Beadon was instructed to pay Mary Jane a stipend or, if she preferred, she could hand the child over and have her brought up on the parish. 'She is an extraordinary production in Nature,' wrote Lethbridge, ruefully. 'I had no business to have anything to do with her.'

Mary Jane took the money, but Claire's first year remained precarious. She was sick, her mother wavered on the question of whether or not to keep her, and when, in April 1799, Mary Jane was arrested for debt and imprisoned in Ilchester for six months – where she went by the name of 'Mrs St Julian', suspecting Lethbridge of having orchestrated the whole affair – Claire and her brother were placed with a local widow. Having secured her release thanks to the intercession of friends in the local gentry, she continued to petition for her allowance, did some piecework for a mantua-maker, and posed as 'Mrs Jones', a respectable widow in 'reduced circumstances'. Next, she took her children to London, where they were reinvented as Clairmonts, and proclaimed an ambition to work 'in the literary line'.

Few of Godwin's friends took to the second Mrs Godwin. They laughed at her fat bottom and the green lenses in her spectacles, and considered her petulant, untrustworthy and, worst of all, a fount of prosaic thoughts and old-fashioned prejudices. The writer

Charles Lamb labelled her an 'infernal bitch' and the 'bad baby', while the lawyer John Philpot Curran (whom Byron considered the wittiest man of his day) called her 'a pustule of vanity'. What was more, their gossip skirted perilously close to the truth, accusing her of being a cast-off convict, washed up and hiding out amid the Somers Town French. How much she told her new husband was unclear, although something of the past must have lain behind the dual wedding ceremonies they had on 21 December 1801 – the first so that she could be married as Mary Clairmont in Shoreditch, and a second in Whitechapel an hour later, where she was married as Mary de Vial.

The newly constituted Clairmont-Godwin house was a full and complicated one, as Charles and Claire became step-siblings to Fanny and Mary, and then, in 1803, after Mrs Godwin gave birth to a baby boy, half-brother and -sister to William Junior. The children were expected to emulate the adults around them and, from the outset, played an important role in the social life of the house, singing, dancing and delivering cups of leathery tea. The lonesome American-in-exile Aaron Burr, for example, a former vice-president of the United States and the man who killed Alexander Hamilton in a duel, was particularly grateful for the welcome. He flirted with Mrs Godwin, one of the few people who seemed genuinely to like her, and brought the girls, whom he styled '*les* goddesses', gifts of silk stockings, which he ultimately proved too shy to give. Burr, who had raised his own daughter, Theodosia, according to Wollstonecraftian principles, felt comfortable in a home where even the youngest were required to contribute to the elevated debate, and was present one Sunday lunchtime when Willie, then nine years old, 'having heard how Coleridge and others lectured', mounted a purpose-built podium in the sitting room and began to orate. The lecture, written by Mary, was delivered with 'great gravity and decorum', Burr said, its subject, 'the influence of governments on the character of a people'.

That a nine-year-old should deliver a lecture on political theory was normal for Skinner Street. 'All the family worked hard,' recalled Claire, 'learning and studying':

> we all took the liveliest interests in the great questions
> of the day – common topics, gossiping, scandal, found
> no entrance in our circle for we had been brought up
> by Mr Godwin to think it was the greatest misfortune
> to be fond of the world, or worldly pleasures or of luxury
> or money; and that there was no greater happiness than
> to think well of those around us, to love them, and to
> delight in being useful or pleasing them.

Godwin made no distinction between the sexes in terms of education, following the dictum of his first wife, Mary Wollstonecraft, that if a woman were to avoid becoming the imbecilic 'toy of man' she must be provided with a 'well-stored mind'. To this end, Fanny, Claire and Mary were granted an uncommon independence for girls of the early nineteenth century, keeping the second floor of the shop for themselves, where they had bedrooms and a large school-room that they could also use as a sitting room to entertain friends. It was here they went through lessons in geography, mathematics and chemistry with their governess, Maria Smith, and their master, Mr Burton, as well as tutors who taught them French and Italian. Fanny and Mary also learned to draw, although Claire had to give it up due to her short-sightedness and, with her mother's encouragement, focused instead on the piano and singing. It was Godwin himself who instructed them in literature, mythology and ancient history, through a curriculum intended to make them to think critically and comparatively across languages, cultures and eras, and to cultivate a reflective inner life.* They were encouraged to debate one another according to his belief that philosophical truth was best arrived at through the open and contending 'collision of mind with mind', and they read the books he published, many in proof, and were taught to cross-reference and undertake research, according to his principle that it was childish to read a book without simultaneously having two or three others open beside it. Godwin was intellectually generous, but also strict and demanding, a pedantic pedagogue undeviating in his demand for excellence and scathing in his criticism of imperfect work. The extent of his influence over the children was enormous, and his works became a central pillar of who they were. 'They totally annihilate me,' said Charles Clairmont, of Godwin's novels. 'I can neither walk, nor read, nor write, nor do anything but shut my eyes and think and be sorrowful after them.' Many times in life, they would cast events through the prism of one of his narratives, and even the passage

---

* Many books published by the Juvenile Library emphasise stoicism, reflection and the importance of critical thinking. For example, a volume by W. F. Mylius (one of the many pseudonyms Godwin wrote under to avoid public censure of his children's books), entitled *The First Book of Poetry*, was intended for children under ten, and blended playful poems such as 'The Life of a Fairy' and 'Cheerful Thoughts and Gooseberry Pie' with others that had unapologetically Romantic themes – 'Self-Examination' and 'Hymn on Solitude'. Mary Lamb's *Mrs Leicester's School; or, the History of Several Young Ladies, Related by Themselves* consisted of fictional accounts of girls' problems through which young readers might be prompted to reflect upon challenges of their own. Given Mary's personal history, some of these must have struck close to home, such as the story of Elizabeth Villiers, who learns to write her name by tracing the letters on her mother's gravestone (the inspiration for the opening scene in Charles Dickens's *Great Expectations*), before ultimately coming to understand that she must always be kind to those she loves in the event that death may suddenly take them. In another, Elinor learns to love the step-mother she initially resented, while in a third, the neglected Margaret Green reads herself into a dangerous fever and convinces herself she is a 'Mahometan', having embarked on a course of unsupervised reading without first having learned the value of maintaining critical distance.

in Claire's letter to Byron announcing that 'my feet are on the edge of a precipice' was a direct echo of a similar passage in Godwin's novel *St Leon*.

Even though both parents took care to expose them to the more parochial aspects of their surroundings – 'to bring us up in respect for all conventionalities', as Claire put it – taking them to weekly sermons at St Paul's Cathedral and getting them to cook, clean, sew and compile laundry lists, the emphasis on study came with an implicit pressure to succeed. Godwin had experienced celebrity at first hand, and long admitted to being driven by a 'liberal passion' for fame, even as his religious upbringing and deep stoicism made this a site of conflict for him. From her earliest years, wrote Mary, 'I was nursed and fed with a love of glory. To be something great and good was the precept given to me by my Father'; 'In our family,' echoed Claire, 'if you cannot write an epic poem or novel that by its originality knocks all other novels on the head, you are a despicable creature, not worth acknowledging.'

An iron band of competition ran throughout the house, which, when combined with their unfastened blood-ties, grew into fierce rivalries, which Godwin seemed happy to nurture. Answering a curious correspondent who had asked for descriptions of Mary Wollstonecraft's daughters, Godwin had replied characteristically without reserve:

> Of the two persons to whom your enquiries relate, my own daughter is considerably superior in capacity to the one her mother had before. Fanny, the eldest, is of a quiet, modest, unshowy disposition, somewhat given to indolence, which is her greatest fault, but sober, observing, peculiarly clear and distinct in the faculty of memory, and disposed to exercise her own thoughts

and follow her own judgment. Mary, my daughter, is the reverse of her in many particulars. She is singularly bold, somewhat imperious, and active of mind. Her desire of knowledge is great, and her perseverance in everything she undertakes almost invincible. My own daughter is, I believe, very pretty; Fanny is by no means handsome, but in general prepossessing.

The keenest competition, however, was reserved for Mary and Claire. Only eight months apart in age, both were intelligent, engaging and lively, although Claire, with her talent for languages and music, was the more confident and voluble, although she could be sullen and suffered from nightmares. Mary, with her long, brown-bronze hair, pale English complexion and 'calm, grey eyes', inherited not only her father's looks, but also his scholarly caution and subterranean levels of introspection, as well as a literary talent that revealed itself early in many poems and stories.

Although Claire and Mary had been close as children, their intimacy became more precarious as they entered puberty. Claire freely acknowledged Mary's superior scholarship, but was guarded about her accomplishments, and both were touchy about their place in the family, leading them into fantasies about alternative kinfolk and more auspicious estates. Claire knew nothing of her mother's early years, or of her true paternity, even though Mary Jane received intermittent payments from Lethbridge until at least 1813, and maintained throughout her life that her father was Charles Gaulis and that 'blessed Switzerland' (as she would tell Byron) was 'the land of my ancestors'. Mary's impeccable Jacobin pedigree, meanwhile, had made her something of a curiosity, and she was used to being treated as a spectacle by the old radicals and young romantics alike, who came for 'pleasure in contemplating the daughter of Mary Wollstonecraft'. Her attachment to

her parentage ran deep, calling her father 'my God' and vener-
ating the memory of her dead mother, whose large, imposing
portrait still hung in her father's study. This ethereal divinity stood
in sharp contradistinction to all-too-tangible Mrs Godwin, the evil
step-mother she claimed to 'detest'. Such high-handedness
annoyed Claire, who made her own pointed effort to outdo Mary
in the emulation of Wollstonecraft by being the first of the girls
to refuse to wear whalebone corsets and laced stays. They would
quarrel, and Mary would call Claire 'stupid', leading Claire to
retaliate by invoking her mother's favouritism, and sulking in
what Mary called the 'Clairmont style'.

Claire and Mary's struggles played themselves out as the family
business experienced turbulent fortunes. Godwin had worked
hard at the Juvenile Library and, contrary to the expectations
of his friends, his wife had proven to be a resourceful partner,
constitutionally more dependable than her indigestive husband,
and ably marshalling the family, running the shop, keeping
accounts and translating books from French. Sadly, the business
had been hobbled from the start, and the Library failed to thrive.
Soon the costs of running a shop, a family, and servicing the
large debts they had taken on to set themselves up pulled them
into a demoralising cycle of last-minute loans that merely
deferred the ultimate day of reckoning. As debt and uncertainty
became an everyday reality, the entire household felt the strain,
even to the extent that, in 1810, Mrs Godwin gathered up Claire
and Charles and left, and though she soon returned, the pressure of never having enough remained. In 1811, family tensions
again came to a head, when at the age of thirteen, Mary suffered
a sudden and unexplained outbreak of eczema on her face and
arm. Mrs Godwin decreed that this would be best treated by
sending her to the coastal town of Ramsgate, where Mary
remained for eight months, much of it alone. Mary never forgave

Mrs Godwin for sending her away, and felt the bitterness of it for many years. It was the first in a series of exiles both girls would have to endure, establishing a theme of expulsion and return they would be condemned to repeat for the rest of their lives.

HERE IS A MAN

The first time Claire set eyes on Byron it is unlikely that she even registered him at all. It was a cold Monday evening in January 1812, when Godwin had taken her, Fanny and Mary – returned from Ramsgate but not fully recovered – to hear one of Coleridge's lectures at the London Philosophical Society. The audience was particularly thin, discouraged, or so Coleridge believed, not by the dismal weather and inconvenient narrowness of the lane in which the venue stood, but by the pervasive smell of 'pork and sausages' that emanated from the local butcher's. Coleridge was an unusual speaker, reliant for the past twelve years on what he described as 'enormous doses' of daily laudanum; 'the worst and most degrading of Slaveries', he called it, its narcotic yoke apparent in the wheezing and unsteady figure he cut, clinging to the lectern flanked by the taciturn busts of Newton and Locke. As he spoke, his thoughts wandered through the magic glass of his 'opium-poisoned imagination', priming him to deliver not so much a lecture, but what one friend described as an 'immethodical rhapsody' that steered an uncertain course through a squall of paradoxes before casting his audience up on curious shores. The diarist Henry Crabb Robinson was particularly irritated by this 'desultory habit', recalling that in four lectures on *Romeo and*

Juliet, Coleridge had barely mentioned the play at all, delivering instead a series of exponential digressions that included a 'rhapsody on brotherly and sisterly love' and 'a dissertation on incest'. The lecture Claire attended was on Milton, also 'not one of Coleridge's happiest efforts', according to Robinson. When – rather than if – her attention wandered, she would have seen Byron, as yet largely unknown, seated with the poet Samuel Rogers and muffled against the cold.

It was not Byron who would alter their lives that winter but another young man, who had written to Godwin just two weeks earlier from Keswick, the Lake District village he had travelled to in the hope of (coincidentally) meeting Coleridge. Coleridge was not in residence, so the young man had to satisfy himself with the poet Robert Southey, a former radical who had once conspired to emigrate with Coleridge and set up a Utopian community in Pennsylvania governed by a system of communal ownership they called 'Pantisocracy'. Southey regarded the pale, excitable, round-eyed apparition before him as if he were a time-traveller: 'Here is a man,' wrote Southey to a friend, 'who acts upon me as my own ghost would do. He is just what I was in 1794.'

This was Percy Bysshe Shelley, a willowy nineteen-year-old who burned with fervour for the revolutionary generation to which Southey had once belonged. Shelley was searching for a master to guide him, and in this respect, both Southey and Keswick proved a disappointment. The village was contaminated with tourists and manufacturers, and the old revolutionary had chosen a different path in middle age. Fearing that, with a mad King George III and a strong Bonaparte, the country could be saved only by a return to the Tory eternals of Church and state, Southey had 'sold himself to the Court', said Shelley, and become a staunch reactionary. He did, however, pass on the news that another old radical whom Shelley had thought to be long dead was alive and well and selling children's books. The young man fell upon the news, and wrote to London immediately.

'I am young,' Shelley told Godwin in his very first letter, 'I am ardent in the cause of philanthropy and truth', admitting freely that he hoped Godwin 'should be my friend and adviser, the moderator of my enthusiasm, the personal exciter and strengthener of my virtuous habits'. A father figure was important to him: he had rejected his own, not for any mistreatment or neglect but simply for the crime of deathly conventionality. Sir Timothy Shelley, MP for New Shoreham and master of the weathered stone and ancestral plantings of Field Place, Sussex, was a perfectly decent if unremarkable baronet, assiduously concerned for his son's reputation, and utterly baffled by his insistence that inherited wealth was 'an evil of primary magnitude'.

Godwin was not keen to accept the role. He had a history of attracting earnest young men who sat at his feet and overstayed their welcome, the most recent of whom was an impoverished and melancholic young man named Proctor Patrickson, who longed to go to university against his father's wishes. Yet whereas Patrickson was bondsman to morbid intensity, Shelley had intelligence and infectious zeal. Other letters followed in which he displayed himself to be a true acolyte, telling Godwin that 'I did not truly *think* and *feel* however, until I read *Political Justice*.' Slowly, Godwin warmed to the young man's enthusiasm, but it was only after Shelley announced that he was 'heir by entail to an estate of 6000£ per an.' that he really began to take notice.

An entail was a legal device that meant that no individual could break up a family estate, thereby virtually guaranteeing inheritance through a line of descent, and making it impossible, absent a parliamentary decree, for Shelley ever to be entirely disinherited. This intrigued Godwin, who was putting together a patchwork of loans to fund the three thousand pounds he needed to refinance the bookshop and free it from unfavourable terms. He was still short by a considerable sum when Shelley appeared as a saviour, and Godwin felt no compunction in adopting the role of mentor in order to groom his new prospect. After all, had it not been set down in *Political Justice* that a man of property had 'no right to dispose of a shilling' of his money 'at the will of his caprice' but was under an obligation to spend it only where it 'may best be employed for the increase of liberty, knowledge and virtue'? For Godwin, who had spent his life in the service of mankind only to be rewarded with threats of penury and debt, nothing could be more virtuous than relieving his own distress.

'You cannot imagine how much all the females of my family, Mrs G. and three daughters, are interested in your letters and your history,' Godwin told Shelley, as Skinner Street buoyed with the promise of him. That history told of a boy's rebellion against his genteel education, first at Syon House, where he had cut a miserable figure, and then at Eton, where his resistance to fagging and refusal to bow to tradition made him a target for endless bullying, and earned him the nickname 'Mad Shelley' for pinning one tormentor's hand to a table by stabbing it with a fork. Already far advanced in science and languages, he found his lessons without substance and his masters pedantic. 'I have known no tutor or adviser,' he told Godwin, 'from whose lessons and suggestions I have not recoiled in disgust' – befriending instead a Fellow of the Royal Society named James Lind, a tall, emaciated magus resident in Windsor, who was fascinated by eastern curiosities, scientific instruments and 'tricks, conundrums and queer things'. With Lind as his guide, Shelley dived into a self-devised curriculum that burrowed deep into Gothic romances and occult 'books of Chemistry and Magic', before leaving Eton early to enter the University of Oxford.

At Oxford, he continued to stand apart, refusing to souse himself in claret and gamble at faro like his peers, devoting himself instead to 'Classical reading and poetical writing' with 'the voracious appetite of a famished man' in rooms said to resemble an alchemist's laboratory. His career there was brief, as he was sent down in the first year after collaborating with his friend Thomas Jefferson Hogg on a pamphlet entitled 'The Necessity of Atheism' that sought to prove the non-existence of God. Expelled from Oxford, Shelley continued his programme of self-education. By the time he approached Godwin he had already written two novels, three political pamphlets and a great deal of poetry, and was on the verge of mastering six languages. He had also eloped with a beautiful sixteen-year-old named Harriet Westbrook, whom he had married at Edinburgh, conducting all the while a running battle against his long-suffering father, with whom he tussled through a series of squabbles and excommunications, Sir Timothy wielding the only weapon he could use to curb his wayward son, his money.

Shelley and Godwin corresponded for ten months. During that time Shelley left Keswick for Dublin where he and Harriet agitated for Catholic emancipation and political reform, campaigning that concerned Godwin, whose method had always been contemplative rather than practical, and who believed that political groups ran counter to the dictates of personal liberty. 'You are preparing a scene of blood,' warned the older man, advice that, when combined with the muscular deterrence of his political opponents in Ireland, soon persuaded Shelley to retreat from direct action. He and Harriet returned to England and spent the following months moving between Devon and north Wales, funding philanthropic projects, searching for the ideal spot to study and reflect, and disseminating political pamphlets like 'vessels of heavenly medicine' that he rolled up and dispensed by way of paper balloons, or bottles pitched into the Bristol Channel.

It was to Devon that Godwin went in search of Shelley in

September 1812 when, unable to pay one of his debts and likely to be arrested, he hoped to secure a loan. After a gruelling and expensive journey, he arrived in Lynmouth only to find that the restless Shelleys had already gone up to London. It was another month before they would finally meet in person, but at that first dinner, both families were as delighted with one another as they had hoped they would be. For a period of about five weeks, they saw each other almost every other day, the Godwins lavishing Shelley with attention and introducing him to their impressive friends, while Shelley presented his wife Harriet, her sister Eliza, and their school-teacher friend Elizabeth Hitchener. 'I love them all,' wrote Harriet, who was determined to move to London to be near them, especially Fanny and Mrs Godwin, whom she called 'a woman of great fortitude' with 'a great sweetness marked in her countenance'. Even Claire, then at boarding school in Walham Green, a pretty hamlet of Elizabethan houses on the Thames beyond Fulham, was called back to pay court.

The only one missing was Mary. That spring, she had suffered a second bout of eczema, serious enough to incapacitate her entire right arm, and her father had arranged for her to stay with the family of William Baxter, friends who lived near Dundee. Liberated from the Clairmonts and the toxic communications of Skinner Street, she flourished, becoming inseparably close with Baxter's daughters, Christy and Isabel.

In Skinner Street, Godwin and Shelley spent long hours in the older man's study under the beneficent gaze of Wollstonecraft's portrait, debating philosophy, religion, literature and 'prejudice' – the term Shelley applied to every orthodox opinion or commonly held belief. Godwin pored over the pages of Shelley's latest, most ambitious, poem, an intergalactic vision he called *Queen Mab*, that lamented the miseries inflicted by priests, kings and gold, taking Godwin's theories and animating them with his own sprawling, prophetic, allegorical recklessness, as in this section on the 'venal interchange' of commerce:

> The harmony and happiness of man
> Yields to the wealth of nations; that which lifts
> His nature to the heaven of its pride,
> Is bartered for the poison of his soul;
> The weight that drags to earth his towering hopes,
> Blighting all prospect but of selfish gain,
> Withering all passion but of slavish fear,
> Extinguishing all free and generous love
> Of enterprise and daring, even the pulse
> That fancy kindles in the beating heart
> To mingle with sensation, it destroys, –
> Leaving nothing but the sordid lust of self,
> The grovelling hope of interest and gold,
> Unqualified, unmingled, unredeemed
> Even by hypocrisy.
>
>   And statesmen boast
> Of wealth! The wordy eloquence that lives
> After the ruin of their hearts, can gild
> The bitter poison of a nation's woe,
> Can turn the worship of the servile mob
> To their corrupt and glaring idol, fame,
> From virtue, trampled by its iron tread, –
> Although its dazzling pedestal be raised
> Amid the horrors of a limb-strewn field,
> With desolated dwellings smoking round.

It was a remarkable achievement, but so 'Anti Christian' that Shelley was dissuaded from publishing it after it had been printed.

In the end, only 250 copies saw the light of day, disguised as a dainty quarto that Shelley hoped might be mistaken for a fairy tale, 'so as to catch the aristocrats: They will not read it, but their sons and daughters may.'

Harriet, meanwhile, sat in the parlour with Mrs Godwin and Fanny, whom she now began to think 'very plain'. Her initial enthusiasm was starting to wane under the weight of endless dinners with old men, Mrs Godwin's abrasiveness, and what she perceived as Mr Godwin's demand for deference from 'all persons younger than himself'. Through a decrescent aura, Harriet began to see Godwin for the bald, constipated narcoleptic that middle age had made him, and to Skinner Street's dismay, the prospective donors escaped to Wales and stopped answering his letters. Nor did they make an effort to call when they suddenly reappeared in London the following March. When Godwin eventually caught up with him in the summer, Shelley confessed that they had stayed away because his wife could not stand Mrs Godwin, at which point Mary Jane was dispatched to smooth things over for the good of the business.

Relations were restored between the two families just as Harriet was on the verge of giving birth to a daughter, Ianthe, in the summer of 1813. Shelley began to spend more time alone in London after the birth as his wife nursed the baby in a house they had rented in Bracknell in Berkshire, attempting to raise cash to pay the considerable debts of his own he had allowed to accrue. Even revolutionaries found it hard not to exercise the privileges of rank when necessary, and Shelley had happily passed through the world on a whim, leaving behind a trail of unsettled accounts with solicitors and tradesmen. Raising cash meant endless visits to lawyers and bankers, who would scrutinise the terms of his inheritance before furnishing meagre loans. It was tedious and frustrating work, and with few friends in London, Shelley called at Skinner Street almost every day, taking his meals there and staying long into the night.

This time, Godwin was impressed by what he considered to be Shelley's growing intellectual maturity, and a set of principles he had refined through his exposure to a circle of radicals that had assembled around the Newtons and Boinvilles, an extended family he had been introduced to by Godwin, and whom Harriet and he had gone to Bracknell to be near. The family revolved around two sisters, Harriet and Cornelia (née Collins), the wealthy daughters of a West Indian planter who were both exponents of Godwin's theories and of the 'return to nature'. Both were quick to recognise Shelley's intelligence, and Shelley considered Harriet Boinville in particular, the wife of a Napoleonic officer campaigning in Russia, 'the most admirable specimen of a human being I had ever seen'.* He enjoyed flirting with this intelligent and uninhibited woman who, when not practising the 'nakedism' central to her beliefs, wore a red sash around her slight waist to signify that she was a revolutionary. Her sister Cornelia and her five children all indulged in their own 'air bathing' for three hours a day, while Cornelia's husband, John Frank Newton, 'the primate of all vegetables', was a Zoroastrian who read portentous acrostics into the signs of the zodiac, and promoted vegetarianism through his belief that meat-eating was the cause of syphilis. Shelley, already a vegetarian and the author of a pamphlet allying carnivorousness to war and insanity, also found himself in sympathy with the group's philosophy of free love. Inspiration was drawn from the work of Madame de Boinville's friend, the 'Chevalier' James Lawrence, whose novel *The Empire of the Nairs* imagined a sexual

---

* In 1813, Madame de Boinville's husband, Jean-Baptiste Chastel de Boinville, had already been killed in the Moscow retreat, although his wife would not find this out until the following autumn. He had been aide-de-camp to the Marquis de Lafayette.

paradise among the Indians of Malabar, who selected partners only for the duration of their attraction. A second authority was William Godwin, and his markedly un-erotic argument that marriage was incompatible with personal freedom as it enforced legal obligations. 'Marriage is law,' Godwin had written in 1793, 'and the worst of all laws,' for when acting in consideration of our husbands and wives, 'we are obliged to consider what is law, and not what is justice.'

Delighted by Shelley's return, Godwin began to press him seriously on the matter of a loan, pushing him to extend the full three thousand pounds he needed to refinance his debts. But while Shelley accepted the philosophical obligation to help Godwin, he disliked his persistence, and was soon off again and out of touch, travelling to Edinburgh and the Lake District on another round of his unstinting scavenger hunt. There was a brief reappearance in December at which point Godwin seems to have secured the promise he craved, personally agreeing to take on all the tortuous legal details that were involved in raising money against the income from Shelley's future estate. By March 1814, he was finally ready to advertise the auction of a 'post-obit', a bond that could be bought for three thousand pounds and paid back at eight thousand when Shelley finally came into his inheritance.

That spring, Shelley was back, dividing his time between London and Bracknell, the Godwins and the Boinvilles. Harriet, pregnant again, was staying at her father's house in London and, although it was not far away, she and Shelley spent almost two months apart, months he called 'the happiest of my life: the calmest the serenest the most free from care'. With Claire at school, Mary in Dundee, and Charles studying in Edinburgh, the only young people in residence were eleven-year-old Willy and the 'quiet, modest, unshowy' Fanny, the daughter of Mary Wollstonecraft, who was almost Shelley's age. She and Shelley became increasingly friendly, and as his visits increased, she fell in love. Shelley was unlike any other visitor she had ever met, neither bent and bookish like the old Jacobins, nor depressed and stammering like the wayward souls. Thin as a stripling and as pale as blue-veined marble, he had large, bulging eyes, long, wild, unmanaged curls and a high-pitched voice that would rise to an avian screech when he became agitated. His clothes hung on his body as if they had been left to dry, and with his neck bare, his shirt undone, and refusing to wear anything made from wool or animal skin, he went about perpetually underdressed. So immersed in his thoughts was he that he frequently forgot appointments and prior engagements, yet his gentleness, his faultless aristocratic manners and serene deportment meant that few could stay angry, even Godwin, who thought he had the sexless beauty of a Miltonic angel.

Shelley had become dissatisfied with Harriet, whom he claimed did not understand him, and must have said as much at Skinner Street. Having grown up with three fond sisters and a doting mother, he was extremely comfortable in the company of women, which he greatly preferred to that of men, and conversed with them freely. Although he was interested only in being a friend to Fanny, his effect on her did not escape the vigilance of Mrs Godwin, who observed certain 'looks and sighs', and noted how she had become suddenly 'sad and absent'. Knowing from experience where exactly this could lead, she packed Fanny off to stay with an aunt in Pentredevy, but before she could get her through the door, a more pressing problem arose. Mary had returned from Scotland, sixteen years old and in rude health as she settled back into a house that she had not lived in for two of the previous three years. Shelley, who probably met her for the first time around Godwin's dinner-table on 5 May 1814, was smitten.

At the beginning of June, Shelley engaged lodgings in Hatton

Garden and started dining with the Godwins daily, spending as much time as he could with Mary, who was quick to respond to his attentions. Bringing Claire along as a chaperone, she would take long walks around Marylebone, and 'in the wilderness of the Charterhouse', Claire recalled, as well as Mary Wollstonecraft's tomb in the churchyard of St Pancras where they would find Shelley waiting for them. It was a sacred site for courtship, for in this exalted daughter of Jacobin royalty, Shelley had finally found the partner he felt he deserved, one who shared by birth the preoccupations of his soul. As he told his friend Thomas Love Peacock, 'Everyone who knows me must know that the partner of my life should be one who can feel poetry and understand philosophy. Harriet is a noble animal, but she can do neither.' Once again, Mrs Godwin raised the alarm, but with Godwin on the verge of securing his loan, he was loath to cause trouble. As they spent more time together, Shelley and Mary became increasingly intimate, and looked for ways to rid themselves of Claire. 'They always sent me to walk at some distance from them,' Claire remembered, 'alleging that they wished to talk over philosophical subjects and that I did not like or know anything about those subjects I willingly left.' On 26 June, the couple declared their mutual love, consummating their devotion behind a veil of willow branches in the St Pancras churchyard as Claire loitered some way off.

A week later, the loan to Godwin came through, though it proved to be much less than the three thousand pounds he was relying on. The post-obit sold for just £2593.10s. at auction, of which Shelley decided to keep half for himself, which meant that after fees and expenses, Godwin's share was a mere £1,120 – nowhere near enough to solve his financial problems. That same day, while out walking in Spa Fields, Shelley confessed to Godwin that he was in love with Mary and was planning to take her abroad.

A stunned Godwin railed against 'licentious love', urging him to 'return to virtue' and to his wife, but now it was Shelley's turn to be shocked by what he saw as Godwin's hypocrisy. Even in the midst of his emotional unrest, he had felt certain that his actions were supported by the principles of *Political Justice*.

Things became worse when Mrs Godwin received a visit from a distraught Harriet, who arrived at Skinner Street to plead with her never to allow Mary to see her husband again. Shelley had told Harriet everything, explaining his passion in the spirit of Godwinian candour, with the expectation that as a rational, enlightened soul she would understand perfectly. He appealed to their shared past, telling Harriet that, just as she had needed rescue, so Mary needed to be saved from the great suffering she experienced at the hands of her family, 'and the tyranny which has been exercised upon her'. Although terrified of being abandoned, Harriet was aware that Shelley had been trying to loosen their bond for some time. In Bracknell the previous winter, he had fallen in love with Mrs Boinville's married daughter, Cornelia Turner. Cornelia's appeal was plain to see: she was attractive, intelligent and spent her days absorbed in poetry, reading from the volume of Petrarch she carried in her pocket, which rendered her 'fair prey to a kind of sweet melancholy'. Shelley maintained that his interest in her was more virtuous than sexual – 'The contemplation of female excellence,' he said, 'is the favourite food of my imagination' – but his advances were conspicuous enough for her jealous husband, Thomas, another of Godwin's students, to send her to Devon and earn Shelley a rebuke from the free-spirited Madame de Boinville.

Mrs Godwin dispatched Mary and Claire to call on Harriet at her father's house in Chapel Street so that Mary might provide her personal reassurance that there was nothing amiss. She kept her promise not to see Shelley and tranquillity was restored until a week later when the door flew open at three o'clock in the afternoon. Shelley barged past the counter and ran up the stairs towards the schoolroom where Mary and Claire were studying. According to Claire, who recalled the event in much later life, Mrs Godwin ran to intercept him, having seen him approaching from her counting house, but was pushed aside as Shelley, with a wild look, rushed to Mary and pressed a phial of laudanum into her hand. 'They wish to separate us, my beloved,' he reportedly said, 'but Death shall unite us' – at which point he pulled out a pistol and turned the muzzle on himself. The blood drained from Mary's face and Claire filled the room with screams until Mrs Godwin pushed her out to get help. Shelley seemed crazed. He had been using laudanum heavily, telling his friend Peacock that he never parted from it. Only Mary's sobbing entreaties pacified him, and the situation calmed until a few days later when the Godwins were woken by a violent ringing of their doorbell. It was Shelley's Hatton Garden landlord who, hearing groans emanating from his tenant's room, had discovered him on the verge of death. When Mrs Godwin arrived, he was already with a doctor, who was walking him up and down the room, trying to keep him conscious until the drugs wore off. It is unclear whether this was an overdose or a suicide attempt, although it would not have been the first time Shelley had poisoned himself for love. In any event, it increased the pressure on Mary, to whom he continued to pass illicit notes through the shop's porter. Weeping bitterly, she confided to Claire that Shelley claimed no longer to love Harriet, whom he believed to be pregnant by another man, and that he would finish the job of killing himself unless she agreed to elope.

At four o'clock in the morning, on 28 July 1814, Mary woke her step-sister with a whisper. It was such a beautiful morning, she said, that they should take an early walk. Attempting to diminish her own role in the affair, Claire told her mother that she had no idea what Mary had planned until they were walking up Holborn Hill in the direction of Marylebone Fields, where they found Shelley waiting in a hired carriage at the corner of Hatton Garden. At this point Mary confessed that they were eloping to the Continent and that Claire had to come with them as she was fluent in French. Claire refused and demanded to be allowed home, but Shelley was adamant, saying 'they should be ruined and discovered and lost if she made them lose a moment'. Pulling her into the carriage, he told the driver to head directly to Dover, stopping only to take on extra horses in order to 'outstrip pursuit'. Both girls were sixteen, the same age Harriet had been when Shelley had eloped with her. Mary was in tears for the duration of the journey, her head in Shelley's lap, unable to believe what she had done. Neither spoke a word to Claire until the following day – this, at least, was what she told her mother, although it should be mentioned that her version fails to account for the fact that both she and Mary carried bundles of clothes on their walk, and that both were wearing their black silk travelling dresses.

The trip was a disaster. At Calais, they were chased down and harangued by Mrs Godwin, whom Shelley imperiously dismissed, but when the Paris bankers refused to advance him any money, they were forced to continue their journey on foot, buying first a sickly donkey and then a mule that Mary and Claire took turns to ride until Shelley sprained his ankle and could no longer walk. Following back roads to avoid detection, they still managed to cover 120 miles in four days, passing through a landscape razed by war: 'village after village,' wrote Shelley, 'entirely ruined and burned; the white ruins towering in innumerable forms of destruction'. Among famished and inhospitable peasants they slept outdoors or on dirty floors where Claire felt rats scampering across her face. Mary was frequently unwell, suffering from spasms that they attributed to sea-sickness until it became clear she was pregnant. By the time they reached Neuchâtel, all three were hungry and exhausted, subsisting on a meagre diet of vegetables and Shelley's daily curriculum of Shakespeare, Tacitus, Wollstonecraft and Jean-Jacques Rousseau.

As with their later journey in pursuit of Byron, their destination was Switzerland, specifically the town of Uri, a place described in William Godwin's novel *Fleetwood* as a spiritual paradise nestled in the 'wild and entire solitude' of the Alps. Godwin had never left Britain, but in both *Fleetwood* and *St Leon*, he had represented Switzerland as the cradle of morality and the manufactory of noble thoughts, a place of enlightenment and sensibility presided over by the idols Voltaire and Rousseau. Rousseau in particular had drawn up this blueprint of an unpolluted homeland, whose clean air and spectacular scenery were conducive to honesty, simplicity and virtue. 'By rising above the habitation of men,' he had written in his best-selling novel, *Julie; ou La Nouvelle Héloïse* (1761),

> one leaves all base and earthly sentiments behind, and in proportion as one approaches ethereal spaces the soul contracts something of their unalterable purity. There, one is grave without melancholy, peaceful without indolence, content to be and to think: all excessively vivid desires are blunted; they lose that sharp point that makes them painful, they leave deep in the heart nothing but a light and sweet emotion, and thus it is that a favourable climate causes passions to contribute here to man's felicity which elsewhere make for his torment.

In reality, Uri was a rainy town packed with people Claire described as 'immoderately stupid and almost ugly to deformity'. With nearly all their money gone, they rented a house for six months that turned out to be little more than a cabin, so cold that their laundry refused to dry. After two days, Mary insisted they return home – 'Most laughable,' mocked Claire. 'All because the stove don't suit.' The tensions between them were as raw as ever, as Claire remained committed to the principles of the adventure, despite its hardships, while Mary lost patience with her step-sister's repeated attacks of the 'horrors'. To save money, they decided to return to London by boat via the Rhine, the entire endeavour proving a triumph for stomach-churning reality over the promises of Rousseau. The ordeal did nothing to stop them experiencing the world through fiction, but as even Mary would later admit, this particular episode had been 'acting a novel, being an incarnate romance'.

The effect of the elopement on those left behind was grievous. Godwin and Mary Jane were frantic, and their anxieties were magnified when the uproar caused young Willy to run away for two days. Harriet, meanwhile, let it be known that she held Godwin personally responsible for the damage done to her family. She inveighed against Shelley's transformation under the effects of his philosophy, singling out *Political Justice* for particular abuse and angrily condemning 'the very great evil that book has done'. When Shelley's friend Thomas Love Peacock asked her what she thought Shelley saw in Mary, Harriet replied, 'Nothing, but that her name was Mary, and not only Mary, but Mary Wollstonecraft.' Shelley was in love with a fantasy, she believed, and the desire to possess a republican ideal which had distorted him beyond all recognition.

'The man I once loved is dead,' she wrote to a friend. 'This is a vampire.'

6

AN EMPIRE'S DUST

Flanders was beginning to bore. 'It is a perpetuity of plain and an eternity of *pavement*,' Byron wrote to Augusta, after a week of edging along flat, featureless terrain. 'Level roads don't suit me,' he told her. 'It must be up hill or down – and then I am more au fait.' The enforced stop in Brussels offered some relief, although the city was ugly when compared with the elegance of Antwerp, Bruges and Ghent. Clues to a mysterious diluvian prehistory could be found in the coral and fossils of its sandy hills, but its cramped and narrow streets left little room for wonder, filled as they were with aggressive teenage soldiers, stray bulldogs and raw sewage. At one point, John even ran into a goat harnessed to a baby's pram.

Having returned their hired *calèche*, John was sent to buy a new one, disorientated by a town whose clocks struck the same time twice (both on the hour and thirty minutes beforehand), by yet more erotica displayed in the bookshops, and the 'beastliness publicly exhibited on the public monuments – fountains with men vomiting with effort a stream of water – and still worse', a reference, no doubt, to the city's infamous *Manneken-Pis*. A visit to the century-old playhouse in the Place de Monnaie did nothing to elevate his mood. Sitting in a box so filthy it reminded him of a London slum, he watched a farce that failed to make him laugh, with an actress who spoke French 'like a base pig', and whose portrayal of polite society appeared to be 'copied from the waiting-maids of butchers' ladies'. A second piece was hissed off before it even had a chance to begin, and when the police insisted that the show must go on before suddenly shutting it down, a violent shoving match began that afforded John's cue to leave.

Brussels had a strong Anglophone presence, thanks to an expatriate colony that had been established following Napoleon's abdication in 1814. Anchored by a brigade of English foot-guards, it had grown to accommodate almost two hundred families, drawn by the low cost of living and stylish houses close to the park. Having conducted a survey of faces, John concluded that the only attractive women in Brussels were British.

No British tourist could visit without making the short trip to the battlefield of Waterloo, a site of pilgrimage since news of the victory had first reached home in July 1815. The battle itself had been the definitive action of a four-day campaign that also featured significant engagements at Quatre Bras, ten miles to the south, and Ligny, fifteen miles to the south-east. Around 185,000 men had fought in a battle so angry that the slaughterous drone of artillery could be heard 'as one uninterrupted peal of thunder' as far north as Le Havre. Almost fifty thousand were killed or wounded, among them Byron's cousin, Frederick Howard, and Hobhouse's brother, Benjamin. The number of dead was matched only by the number of the living who succumbed to 'the travelling fit' that followed, to the extent that when John Scott, the editor of the *Champion* and another of Byron's avowed enemies, arrived at Waterloo only weeks after the battle, a quick perusal of the hotel's register showed that it was already filled with compatriots 'of each sex and every age, profession, residence, and condition, all on the swarm . . . Johnsons, Robertses, Davises, and Jacksons, coupled with Highgate, Pancras, Camberwell, and even some of the streets of London such as the Strand, Oxford Road, and Charing Cross, as the places of their respective domiciles'. Such pleasure tripping appalled the Duke of Wellington, who felt that the carriage-loads of visitors reduced his great victory into an excursion for picnickers. Yet still they came, not only the Johnsons and Robertses of Highgate and Camberwell, but the great and the good, all eager to commune with the spirit of the place that had presided over Napoleon's last stand. By the time John and Byron arrived, this list already included Sir Walter Scott, Robert Southey, the architect Sir John Soane, the diarist Henry Crabb Robinson, and the artists Charles Eastlake and David Wilkie.

John and Byron visited on the morning of 4 May, Byron and his valet Fletcher travelling in the new *calèche* that John had been talked into buying at an inflated price, while he himself rode horseback beside them. The road took them south from Brussels through the forest of Soignies, a six-mile band of beech trees where many had died or fled, their remains buried in weathered mounds dotted among the trees every hundred yards or so and through which 'hoofs, and even limbs' might occasionally be seen. When the writer Charlotte Waldie strayed into this murderous thicket, she was horrified to find a human hand, half decomposed, reaching out from the ground as if imploring her to 'take me with you'. They emerged from the forest into the tiny village of Waterloo, composed of a few brick buildings and single-storey cottages made of thatch and daub, one of several undistinguished hamlets that might equally have given their names to the battle that had taken place over many miles of farmland. An innkeeper appeared, pressing them to order dinner so that they would not leave hungry when their visit was done, followed by a row of merchants hawking memorabilia, all of it scavenged from the bodies of the dead. The looting of the battlefield had been extraordinarily rapid, with witnesses claiming that most of the bodies had been stripped and a hundred thousand horses skinned and unshod within twenty-four hours. Looting remained such a problem that even in April 1816 the mayor of the nearby town of Ohain had to send gendarmes to patrol the site, complaining that 'every day there still arrive on the battlefield a large number of people, some of them drawn by greed; these latter go so far as to dig up corpses, in the hope of discovering some who, having been buried before the battlefield had been completely looted, had retained their clothing and whatever might be in their pockets'. For sale were helmets, hats, pistols, cannonballs, bullets, insignia and huge sheaves of paper. In the wake of battle, the field was said to be so littered with the 'books, and letters of the dead' that it looked 'like the rubbish of a stationer's shop'. Sir Walter Scott's favourite souvenir was a book of French songs saturated in blood. Nothing was too gory or too trivial to be taken. In January 1816, when Henry Crabb Robinson was fitted with a false tooth, his dentist 'assured me that it came from Waterloo, and promised me it would outlast twelve natural teeth'. 'I know one honest gentleman,' joked the satirist Eaton Stannard Barrett, 'who has brought home a real Waterloo thumb, nail and all, which he preserves in a bottle of gin, for the purposes of transmitting, to the most remote posterity.'

A number of men offered themselves as escorts to point out the principal places of engagement, and John and Byron hired their acknowledged leader, Jean-Baptiste La Coste, a local who claimed to have served as Napoleon's scout throughout the battle, although some suggested that his stories were inventions intended to gild a business worth up to four thousand francs a year. There were even suggestions that La Coste – also known as Dacosta – was less of a man than a franchise, with several people claiming to be him at any one time. However unreliable, he at least brought some life to a spectacle that was itself notably anti-climactic. Those who visited Waterloo in the immediate aftermath of the battle described a sight that was truly shocking. Sir Walter Scott's friend, James Simpson, wrote, 'The field was so much covered with blood, that it appeared as if it had been completely flooded with it; dead horses seemed innumerable', with so many caps and helmets on the ground that 'it appeared as if the field had been covered with crows'. Ten months on, the feculent mulch nourished a sea of innocuous green. Tilled, sown and restored to the sovereignty of rye and barley, it was as yet unadorned with the many monuments that would come to pepper it, and without 'the importunity of boys, and the glitter of buttons in their hands,' said John, 'there would be no sign of war'.

The itinerary of their visit deviated little from the standard tour, beginning at the hamlet of Mont St Jean, where boys again tried to sell them relics from the field, before moving to inspect hawthorn hedges that marked the point of several important cavalry charges, and a sapling willow planted to connote the burial site of Lord Uxbridge's hastily amputated leg. The first substantial building they came across was Château Hougoumont, a rather pompously titled collection of outhouses bounded by a walled garden that had been one of the most strategic positions in the battle, and had seen some of its bloodiest hand-to-hand fighting. There, they inscribed their names in a visitors' book and viewed a small chapel with a crucified Jesus whose toes had been burned off. Five hundred British soldiers had died there, taking with them close to three thousand French.

Byron was in low spirits throughout the visit, showing little interest in the narrative of the battle or the positions of troops, and asking only after the resting places of the dead. He spoke little except to say that he thought the field a fine one, although nothing compared to the ancient battle sites of Marathon and Troy he had visited on his travels. 'Perhaps there is something of prejudice in this,' he later admitted to Hobhouse, 'I detest the cause and the victors

– and the victory – including Blücher and the Bourbons.' He was most animated when asking to see the spot where his cousin, Frederick Howard, had fallen. Byron had quarrelled with this branch of the family several years before, and the death of Howard, whom Byron acknowledged as 'the best of his race', was yet another reminder of the severed ties that could not be re-bound. The spot was marked by two trees, a stump, and a hollow where Howard's body had lain before its return to Britain. Having silently paid their respects, John and Byron rode twice across the battlefield as dusk began to fold around the forest of Soignies, John going first, Byron following behind singing a Turkish song on a Cossack steed.

There was still time for souvenirs before they left, Byron selecting a plumed brass helmet, a packet of Eagles tricolours, a cuirass authentically 'marked with bullets, lance, and sabre-cuts', priced at fifteen francs, plus a sabre chosen from a clutch of swords that ranged in price from five francs to twenty. Like Sir Walter before him, he was also drawn to a book, a regimental pocketbook stiff with the blood of a dead infantryman named Louis Marie Joseph Mounsigny. According to this *livret*, Mounsigny was a twenty-four-year-old farmer from Dondouville, near Calais, who had joined Napoleon's army in 1814, and had recently been issued with a new pair of *pantalon de tricot*. John was charged with the job of parcelling the whole lot up and sending it off to John Murray for safe-keeping. 'By Lord Byron's desire,' he wrote, 'I wish you would take this heap of trophies under your care paying . . . what is due for customs etc.'

On the way back to Brussels, it became clear that the new *calèche* was jogged – 'so much so,' said John, 'that it would not allow us to put confidence in it'. To add to his frustration, the coachmaker he had bought it from refused to take it back without the forfeiture of three-quarters of the deposit, roughly six hundred francs. The annoyance was so intense that he began to get pains in his stomach.

Fortunately they were called upon by an expatriate who was happy to take on the problem. His name was Pryse Lockhart Gordon, a writer in his mid-fifties who had been a friend of Byron's mother in Aberdeenshire, and whose eldest son had briefly been the young poet's schoolfellow. Gordon was one of those who had come to Brussels after Napoleon's first peace, arriving in Flanders from Sicily in order to recover from life-threatening sunburn, and remaining there throughout the 'Hundred Days' following Bonaparte's escape from Elba, in which the deposed emperor had led his reassembled army into its last campaign. He had stayed on throughout the culminating battle of Waterloo, even when many were evacuating Brussels in the belief that the French would murder them all, and was among the first civilians to witness the full extent of the horror when a tilting wagon stopped outside his house the following dawn. It was carrying sixteen men whose legs or arms had been amputated in the field. As that gruesome day wore on, Gordon pitched a marquee in his garden for the use of John Thomson, professor of military surgery at Edinburgh University, helping him in whatever way he could, from assisting with amputations and dressing wounds, to cradling his dying friend, Lieutenant Colonel Mills, a captain of the Guards, who had been shot in the lungs and lain naked on the battlefield for thirty-six hours after looters had stripped him of his clothes.*

---

* A similar fate befell Frederick Cavendish Ponsonby, the brother of Byron's former lover, Caroline Lamb. Wounded in both arms and lanced in the back, he fell off his horse and spent most of the battle lying helpless on the field where he was robbed, used as cover by a rifleman, trampled under the hoofs of Prussian cavalry, and robbed again. Despite lying out all night and suffering seven major wounds, he lived for another twenty-two years.

It was generous of Gordon to take the coach off their hands, especially as the affair soon ended up in both the newspapers and the courts, with the carriage-maker seeking eighteen hundred francs for the broken contract, and the Brussels *Courier* editorialising against famous poets and untrustworthy liberals. John and Byron, meanwhile, took themselves off to nearby Laeken, the elegant palace in which Bonaparte had drafted a premature proclamation of victory on the eve of Waterloo, and where they shocked the custodians by making obsequious bows before a chair in which the great man himself had sat.

John's next meeting with Gordon was less favourable. Gordon and his wife had invited them to dinner, an invitation that Byron declined, claiming that he ate only biscuits and drank green tea, and loathed above all to watch women eat. He did, however, condescend to appear for coffee and ices once the plates had been cleared away. It was an evening that Gordon would recall with pleasure. Byron 'was in high spirits and good humour', he claimed in his memoirs, regaling the company with anecdotes of Albania, Greece and Sir Walter Scott and leaving with Mrs Gordon's album under his arm, which he later returned inscribed with verses. John was cordially received, but the egalitarian idyll in which he considered himself and Byron to be 'perfectly on the footing of an equal' evaporated the instant Gordon announced Byron with great ceremony, and himself as a mere afterthought – 'a tassel to the purse of merit', as John put it. Years later, when Gordon came to write a rapturous account of the evening, he not only recounted his dinner party in fulsome detail, but falsely claimed to have accompanied Byron across the field of Waterloo. John he condemned as a 'venomous Bat'.

John and Byron left Brussels on 6 May, the carriage finally repaired. They drove east, passing from Flanders into Francophone Wallonia, where at last the relentless prostration of the earth gave way to occasional swells and thick forests that still harboured bears and wolves. Though they were relieved to be away from the 'eternity of pavement', the towns and villages became steadily more ruinous with each passing mile, the roads so sandy and rutted that the newly sprung coach rolled like a ship in trouble, certain to throw another spring. Their first night back on the road was spent at St Trond in the midst of farmland, which, said John, revealed 'more squalid misery than I have seen anywhere', mud houses with 'dunghills at their doors, and ditches with black foetid water before their first step'. Approaching the coal-blackened city of Liège, the hills became steeper, but the territory even more distressed, with dirty villages, deserted roads and impoverished inhabitants. Outside Battice, a flock of ragged children ran alongside the coach, the girls begging for a *sou* and hailing Byron as '*Monsieur le Général en chef*'. '*Vive l'Angleterre*,' called the boys, '*vive Lord Wellington et cela pour Napoleon*' – '*cela*' was accompanied by a thumb drawn sharply across the throat. The town itself was even worse – 'beggars, beggars', wrote John – a far cry from comfortable Flanders, where begging was permitted only on Fridays. The locals had their liberators to thank for their poverty, specifically the flood of British goods that had entered Europe with the end of Napoleon's 'Continental System' that had embargoed British trade, as the efficiencies of Birmingham, Manchester and Wakefield throttled Flemish and German manufacturing. As one irate landlady said to the tourist Charles Dodd, 'Why can't they keep their manufactures to themselves instead of ruining others? When the French were here we had twenty or thirty manufacturers who employed all the people in the town – now they are all out of work and begging – we must starve that they may get rich – and then they come abroad proud of their money.'

Crossing an invisible frontier, they entered the dominions of Frederick William III, King of Prussia, although the change did little to alleviate the squalor. Having procured fresh horses, John insisted they push on to the spa town of Aix-la-Chapelle in spite of Byron's objections, and although he prevailed, Byron made sure to berate his doctor roundly when the roads became clogged with wet sand, delaying their arrival until midnight. The following morning, John asked a local boy the way to the mineral baths, and was led straight to a brothel. When he eventually found the baths, he thought them 'not very clean-looking'.

They left Aix after lunch, driving through steep wooded valleys, on a road marked with all manner of shrines, crucifixes and makeshift piety. Passing through the fortified town of St Juliers, they descended down a long hill onto a wide plain of sands where the pavement ran out entirely as the jostling spires of Cologne rose in the distance. It was another long slog, and almost midnight by the time they drew up to the black eagle of Prussia that hung over the locked gates of the city. A bribe gained them entry, after which they endured the tedium of being turned away from several inns before finally finding rooms at the Hôtel de Prague.

All travellers were under surveillance in post-Napoleonic Europe, but being English was often enough to ensure free passage, and thus far, their passports had been asked for only once. In Prussia, however, a royal decree not only made it compulsory for visitors to employ the local *valets de place* while they stayed, but to write their names, ages, destination and route in a police book that was then published in the local papers. Working for the police afforded innkeepers and servants a sense of impunity that encouraged them in their roguishness, and travellers found the inns south of Cologne to be some of the most inhospitable in Europe. Having checked in, they would be met with mysterious tariffs as changeable as desert sands, and housed in Spartan rooms where the bed sheets were damp, curtains 'a luxury known only in palaces', and a request for soap was met with a hard stare for all save the especially persistent, for whom a small, gelatinous blob might make its way grudgingly from the kitchen. More seriously, it was widely rumoured that innkeepers tipped off thieves. Personal security was a priority: 'If you cannot padlock your door,' wrote Campbell's *Guide*, 'you may at least barricade it with the chairs and tables in your bed chamber.' On no account, it added, must one be forced into sharing a bed, 'as he cannot be too much upon his guard against becoming the dupe of a bedfellow'.

Danger appeared at the Hôtel de Prague, though of a different kind, as Byron had the pleasure of being woken by the innkeeper standing at his door and swearing 'like a Squadron of Cavalry', believing that the poet was in bed with his wife. In fact, Byron was in bed with one of the chambermaids, 'whose red cheeks and white teeth', he told Hobhouse, 'had made me venture upon her carnally'. The situation resolved itself only when the innkeeper's wife ventured out of her own room to see what the noise was about.

After a late breakfast, and a serenade from a trio led by a pretty harpist whose Scottish ballad sent John into a fleeting reverie, John and Byron mounted a *voiture* to take a tour of yet another city smutted by the imperial paw. Cologne, once an important seat of ecclesiastical power and home to almost seventy separate religious orders, had become, in the words of the tourist Charles Dodd, 'beyond question, the dirtiest and most gloomy city of its size in Europe', fallen to the same eyeless anti-clerical violence that had made refugees of John's Benedictine masters at Ampleforth. The evidence lay before them as they rode through basalt-paved streets given over to dogs and thistles, and lined with mouldering churches recommissioned as warehouses, and empty convents that had become public promenades or barracks for Prussian troops.

Their sightseeing began with the cathedral, half built since the sixteenth century, and now also partly demolished, its roof replaced with wooden boards. From there, they saw the tomb of the Three Kings, supposedly the resting place of those who had bestowed gifts on the infant Jesus, a relic of shimmering gaudiness and bejewelled skulls said to be worth countless millions. Stumbling on a step, John broke a glass, and while the custodians at first refused to take any compensation, they eventually extorted three francs. 'Kept countenance amazingly well,' John told his diary, once again impressing himself with his self-control. From there they went to the church of St Ursula to see the remarkable 'Golden Chamber', a chapel decorated with the bones of eleven thousand virgins said to have travelled from Britain to Cologne to convert the Huns only to be martyred for their trouble. Byron asked for a keepsake from the jumbled remains arranged in glass cabinets around the walls, but his request was politely refused. After lunch, John paid a call on the elderly art historian and collector Ferdinand Wallraf, and went shopping for books, admiring the dark-eyed women who carried brass pitchers in their hands and baskets on their heads. At last, John decreed, they might finally be considered beautiful.

Cologne also provided them with their first glimpse of the Rhine, 'a fine mass of water', its broad flood marking a welcome relief from the urban dereliction of the past two days. The river was a prologue to scenery that would become more spectacular the further south they travelled, as the road climbed and they drove in the shadow of perpendicular rocks of blue-black slate, and past vineyards where peasants in great buckles and cocked hats toiled at precipitous gradients. At Bonn, the river expanded to a width of more than two thousand feet, with banks that rose like mountains on both sides, intersected by a stately procession of skiffs and canoes paddled by salmon fishermen. They might even have seen one of the enormous floats of timber, constructed from fully grown trees lashed together to make rafts that could be a thousand feet in length and ninety feet wide. These huge wooden juggernauts were crewed by five hundred oarsmen who propelled them hundreds of miles downstream to be sold at Dordrecht in Holland. Having watched one pass, the novelist Ann Radcliffe described it as a 'floating island', a Neolithic settlement complete with livestock and huts for the crew. Soon they were among the Siebengebirge peaks, from whose wooded tops jutted the walls of ancient castles. The road clung above the river like a cornice, taking them through walled towns and half-ruins and groves of apple, cherry, pear and walnut. 'The whole way,' wrote John, 'one of the finest scenes, I imagine, in the world.'

At the confluence of the Rhine and Mosel rivers, they reached Koblenz, a handsome town saddened by the now-familiar air of desertion, its prominent palace converted into stables and a guard-room for troops. The outstanding beauty of the place could not distract from the fact that the entire area was a military zone, garrisoned with an intimidating mix of Bavarian, Austrian and Prussian soldiers, who kept a surly watch over this strategic bottle-neck facing French soil. The Austrians were 'brutes', said one local merchant, who bought nothing but beer and tobacco; the Prussians '*faquins*' – scoundrels – 'so proud there was no speaking to them without the chance of being knocked down'. At least 'The French knew how to spend their money,' he said. The wisdom of barracking so many different soldiers together also had to be questioned. The Austrians and Prussians fought constantly, and everyone was scared of the Cossacks.

The proximity of the enemy at Koblenz was evinced by the prominent ruin of Ehrenbreitstein that stood across from the town, an enormous fortress besieged by the French three times during the Revolutionary wars, and which finally fell at their hands as they blew it up as they fell back from the Rhineland in accordance with the 1801 treaty of Luneville. To reach it, John and Byron used a 'flying bridge' – a floating platform attached by a long chain to a boat moored in the middle of the river, which shoved off from the quay and carried them to the far bank like a swinging pendulum. The foot of the castle was being refortified by Prussian engineers, but at its summit it remained a giant muddle of shapeless black rocks, 'immense masses of solid stone and mortar,' wrote John, 'thrown fifty yards from their original situation; ruined walls, gateways, and halls'. The view it offered over the white streets of Koblenz, the rivers and vineyards beyond was sublime.

They rolled through the Rhine valley for five days, travelling from St Goar, where the mountains subsided into hills, and enjoying a fine, wide Napoleonic road that led to Mainz, which John considered 'the best town we have seen since Ghent'. Moving on to Mannheim, however, he began to feel weak, the stomach pains he had been experiencing since Waterloo erupting into vomitous migraines, which he treated with the emetic ipecacuana root and fifteen grams of opium. Having struggled as far as Karlsruhe, they were forced to stop. 'Poor Polidori is devilish ill,' wrote Byron to Hobhouse, 'I do not know with what – nor does he – but he seems to have a slight constitution – and is seriously laid up – if he does not get well soon – he will be totally unfit for travelling – nor has he had any patients, except a Belgian Blacksmith . . . and himself.'

If there was a note of impatience in Byron's letter, it arose not from the delay but rather from the emerging question of the doctor's utility. While the road had begun to disagree with John's temper and digestion, travel made Byron stronger. With no one to minister to, John's role became increasingly unclear. John admitted as much to Hobhouse, to whom he had written from Koblenz having promised to send regular medical dispatches, which he delivered with an unconvincing chumminess. His employer's health, he reported 'is greatly improved, his stomach returning rapidly to its natural state':

> Exercise and peace of mind, making great advances towards the amendment of his *corps délabre* [dishevelled body], leave little for medicine to patch up. His spirits, I think, are also much improved. He blithely carols through the day, 'Here's to you, Tom Brown': and, when he has done, says, 'That's as well as Hobhouse does it.' You and his other friend, Scrope Davies, form a great subject of conversation.

Byron always claimed to be happiest when travelling, but this rejuvenation was equally attributable to his deep absorption in a new work. The visit to Waterloo summoned a surge of creativity from which had emptied a torrent of verse now taking shape as a third canto for *Childe Harold's Pilgrimage*. He had begun it on the crossing from Dover, opening with an invocatory vision of his infant daughter Ada, from which he awoke to find himself 'Once more upon the waters! yet once more!' But it wasn't until they had surveyed the blood-soaked battlefield, grassed over with promiscuous corn, that the canto's themes presented themselves in their full panoramic array. Not the kind of poet to knot himself up in the particles of language, or to turn a solitary concept over and over in his brooding hand, he began to chart grand symmetries between his own fate and that of the ruined land. On the night of their visit alone, he blazed out twenty-six stanzas – some 234 lines – that dealt with his wounded retreat from fame and the impermanence of all things discarded in an 'Empire's dust'.

Byron's work was frequently about departure and rarely about arrival, and from that moment on, the poem and the road became contiguous, unfolding together as the present-day sights shared his imagination with a dilating sense of history and place, the past lying thick and sedimentary about him. For Byron, there was no such thing as a silent ruin, and each tombstone and battlefield they passed spoke to him both as a testament to the feats attainable under the force of human will, and as a fingerpost pointing to their inescapable futility. Above it all glowered the Corsican shade, Napoleon Bonaparte, analogous to Byron himself, proud, ambitious, emotionally isolate, the thunderbolts wrung from his hand. 'He who ascends to mountain-tops, shall find,' wrote Byron in his new poem,

> The loftiest peaks most wrapt in clouds and snow;
> He who surpasses or subdues mankind,
> Must look down on the hate of those below.
> Though high *above* the sun of glory glow,
> And far *beneath* the earth and ocean spread,
> *Round* him are icy rocks, and loudly blow
> Contending tempests on his naked head,
> And thus reward the toils which to those summits led.

So riant was he in this process that he even shared his work with John, showing him stanzas as they were written and promising to make him a gift of the completed manuscript. Yet rather than inspiring John's own ambitions, Byron's vigour only prompted jealousy. Vomiting and dizzy, John prescribed himself a diet of stewed apples and magnesia to little effect, and between fits of sleep he would try to get up and, almost fainting, fall back to the mattress. During one such episode, Byron came into John's room and took a gold-plated candlestick from his hand and swapped it for a brass one. Though feverish, John was conscious enough to consider this an affront, especially as Byron seemingly had second thoughts and sent one of the servants back with the original. It was another reminder of his place, although not as bad as the one that had occurred just a few days before. At an inn overlooking the Rhine John, who had been reading a review of Byron's works, turned abruptly to the poet and said, 'Pray, what is there excepting writing that I cannot do better than you?' There were three things, answered Byron, calmly. 'First,' he said, 'I can hit with a pistol the keyhole of that door – secondly, I can swim across that river to yonder point – and thirdly, I can give you a damned good thrashing.'

7

YOUNG TAHITIANS

'So far am I on my Journey,' wrote Claire to Byron from a hotel room on the rue Richelieu. 'Now will you believe?' Although they had left London ten days later than Byron, Claire, Mary and Shelley were already in Paris, albeit subject to a delay of their own as sullen officials pondered their incomplete documents. Forced to take apartments for two days, Claire sat around reading all of Byron's poems and writing to reassure him that she was no lovesick child but a progressive woman, devoid of sexual envy. 'Do not fear I will prove troublesome to you,' she told him, reinforcing her point by professing the charms of Mary:

> You will I dare say fall in love with her, she is very hand-some and amiable and you will no doubt be blest in your attachments. If it should be so I will redouble my attentions to please her; I will do everything she tells me whether it be good or bad for I would not stand low in the affections of the person so beyond blest as to be beloved of you.

Such sophistication befitted the new identity she had selected for herself, 'Madame Clairville', as she wished to be known on the road, on account of the fact that 'Madame's have their full liberty abroad'. But such spiritedness also revealed persistent insecurities. This was her elopement, one she had engineered entirely alone, telling no one of her correspondence with Byron or her visits to Piccadilly, and only confiding in Mary that she had made a 'friend', while scrupulously avoiding the fact that she had slept with him. Basking in her step-sister's astonishment, Claire had taken Mary to meet Byron shortly afterwards. 'How mild he is! How gentle!' Mary thrilled. 'How different from what I expected.' But having enjoyed her coup, it was not long before Claire was tormented by the thought of being passed over for the Jacobin princess. For all her philosophical bravado, Claire could not avoid a simple, revealing fact: 'I almost fear to think of your reading this stupid letter but I love you.'

Claire had experience when it came to picking through difficult emotional entanglements, having remained with Mary and Shelley following their return from the Continent in September 1814, as they spent uncertain months dodging bailiffs and living like a fugitive sect.

Godwin had convinced himself that the pregnant Mary was guilty of a grave treason and severed all links, commanding Fanny to do the same under threat of excommunication, a threat Mary attributed entirely to the malignancy of Mrs Godwin. Of Shelley, he sighed, he was 'so beautiful it was a pity he was so wicked'. Other friends followed suit, including the Newtons, the Boinvilles, the Lambs and, most hurtfully, Mary's dear friend Isabel Baxter, whose husband wrote to say that she could no longer be associated with a woman ruined by a married man. Harriet Shelley helped to stoke the anger, appearing at Skinner

Street heavily pregnant to spread the news that 'It was reported about town that Mr Godwin had sold the two girls to Mr Shelley, Mary for eight hundred pounds and Claire for seven hundred.' Mrs Godwin resigned herself to the loss of Mary while still holding out hope that Claire would come to her senses and return home, trying every ruse to extract her from Shelley's influence, from claiming to be on her deathbed to scheming to have her daughter locked in a convent. Claire was determined to remain an outlaw, and told her mother that she would come back to Skinner Street only on condition that she should always be allowed to see Shelley, and 'in all situations openly proclaim and earnestly support, a total contempt for the laws and institutions of society'.

Ostracism had made them bolder, strengthening their resolve and affirming their belief that prejudice and ignorance were the root of their misfortune. As the world turned its back, they fell upon their books like hungry mendicants, determined to justify their actions by perfecting the philosophy that Godwin and his generation had too easily abandoned, energised by the thought that they were living a life that was vital, authentic and true. Shelley felt himself renewed, 'a more ardent asserter of truth and virtue', he said, 'more consistent, more intelligible, more true', exulting in the role of preceptor as he tutored the women like 'a sparrow educating the young of the cuckoo', instructing them in Greek, and guiding them through thousands of pages of philosophy, history and political theory.

It was in those initial exhilarating weeks, as Claire read Gibbon's *History of the Decline and Fall of the Roman Empire*, and set to daily translations of Dante, Tacitus and La Boétie's *Discourse on Voluntary Servitude*, that she began to reinvent herself, dropping 'Jane' and asking to be known as 'Clara'. It was Shelley who first began to call her Claire, 'for her transparency', she said, although his fancy may also have been prompted by the parallels between their situation and the romance of the young gentlewoman, Julie, and her tutor, St Preux, in Rousseau's *Julie*. In Rousseau's text, Claire is Julie's devoted friend, an adviser and go-between who helps to facilitate a love forbidden by parental injunction. Not only did it acknowledge the complex triangulation of their circumstances, it transported them back to the philosophical Alps, and the Swiss heritage Claire claimed as her own.

How best to live became the constant topic of their conversation, speaking often of expanding their trio into an entire tribe of 'Otaheite philosophers', so-called after the South Sea islanders, popularly believed to live in one large, communal marriage. Claire envisaged them founding a Pantisocratic community, similar to that imagined by Coleridge and Southey. Located in the west of Ireland, it would be 'an Association of philosophical people', to include Shelley's publisher friend Thomas Hookham and Thomas Love Peacock, two of the few who had remained loyal to him in the fall-out of the elopement, as well as Peacock's betrothed, and Shelley's younger sisters, Helen and Eliza. As the girls were still at school, this required fomenting an additional plan for their 'carrying off', providing Shelley with another chance to deploy his not-inconsiderable skill at kidnapping schoolgirls, experience that led Mary to nickname him 'the Elfin Knight'.

Shelley also held out hope for Harriet and his daughter Ianthe, trusting that his wife would come to see the political justice of his actions and even join them. He had made several intimations on this front already, writing from France to ask her to meet them in Switzerland and, when back in London, taking a set of lodgings near her father's house, where he wrote to her inviting her to place herself once again 'within the influence of my superintending mind'. Harriet refused, and countered with threats to set the law on him, which disappointed Shelley greatly.

'I was an idiot to expect greatness or generosity from you,' he wrote to her,

> that when an occasion of the sublimest virtue occurred, you would fail to play a part of mean and despicable selfishness. The pure and liberal principles of which you used to boast that you were a disciple, served only for display. In your heart it seems you were always enslaved to the vilest superstitions, or ready to accept their support for your own narrow and worldly views. You are plainly lost to me for ever.

A subsequent letter was less ambiguous: 'I am united to another,' he told her, 'you are no longer my wife.'

In his blank refusal to entertain Harriet's fury, Shelley stood hard by his convictions, although no amount of philosophy could silence such emotions entirely. Free love made demands of its disciples that were hard to endure, requiring them to cast aside a lifetime of conditioning and resist the impulses of jealousy. Shelley had encountered this with Harriet before when, in 1812, the couple had lived briefly with Harriet's sister Eliza and Elizabeth Hitchener, whom Shelley had invited into their household as a fellow traveller, only to see her banished amid Harriet's claims that she was trying to seduce her husband. And even now, with Harriet snarling from the sidelines, Mary found that neither was she immune, passing mocking and uncharitable remarks about the 'abandoned wife', and getting annoyed at the obvious pride Shelley took in the birth of his son, Charles, delivered to Harriet at the end of November 1814. An even closer cause for concern was Claire, whom Mary resented for the demands she made on Shelley's time. With Mary pregnant and rarely well, it was Claire who accompanied him on their foraging missions and almost daily visits to the 'lawyer's holes' from which he hoped to extract settlements on the family estate. And it was Claire who stayed up talking to him on the many occasions Mary felt too tired or ill to sit up late.

There is no question that Claire, like Fanny, was in love with Shelley. She called him 'the exotic', told her mother that she thought him 'absolutely perfect', and later described him to Byron as 'the man whom I have loved, and for whom I have suffered much'. During the elopement, she had shared a bed with him and Mary, and was sufficiently demonstrative for a number of Shelley's friends simply to take it for granted that he was sleeping with her, while making jocose remarks about his 'two wives'. Her enthusiasm for free-love communities and Wollstonecraftian militancy suggest she was more ideologically in tune with Shelley than Mary ever was – or at least more eager to appear so – and Shelley certainly acted as if she were his, occupying a contorted position as tutor, older brother and consort. Claire was undoubtedly the lesser member of his triad – the girl worth seven, rather than eight hundred pounds – thought to be far less mature than Mary ('for as you know,' Mrs Godwin purportedly wrote, 'though she is nearly sixteen she is as much a child as if she were only twelve'), and possessing talents that were the least valued of the three. As much as Shelley privileged imaginative writing, he condemned theatricals for their artificiality. Her singing lessons were discontinued, because Shelley forbade it, said Claire, although it is just as likely to have been for want of money, and her attempts to emulate their literary endeavours saw her half-heartedly labouring away at 'The Ideot', which, judging from what she showed Byron, never evolved much beyond an initial plan. 'What shall poor Cordelia do?' wrote Claire in her journal, quoting *King Lear.* 'Love and be silent – Oh this is true – Real Love will never shew itself to the eye of broad day.'

As winter set in, the first flush of rebellion gave way to a dull and penurious routine. Forced again to change lodgings to dodge Shelley's creditors, they moved to Church Terrace, close to Claire and Mary's early home in Somers Town, and the grave of Mary Wollstonecraft. With no money to go out and few friends to visit, Claire stayed in, listening to Shelley and Mary call each other 'Pecksie', 'Dormouse' and 'Maie', pet names, which, like the constant studying, made the time pass slowly. 'Very philosophical way of spending the day,' she complained, 'to sleep and talk – why, this is merely vegetating.' Boredom and ambiguity created a tension between her and Shelley that skirted at the edge of hysteria. Having one night sat at the fireside debating until one in the morning, Shelley asked Claire if 'it is not horrible to feel the silence of night tingling in one's ears'. Shelley had never entirely lost his youthful fascination with the Gothic, and retained a strong belief in the supernatural throughout his life. Under his influence, Claire pondered the darkness and felt it flooding in, becoming gradually more terrified by Shelley's look of 'deep and melancholy awe' until, 'hardly daring to breathe', she retired to her room. Shelley also went to bed, lying beside Mary to read, 'when rapid footsteps descended the stairs' and Claire reappeared with eyes 'wild and starting: drawn almost from the sockets by the convulsion of the muscles'. Convinced that a pillow which had been on her bed had moved under the influence of super-natural agency, she was in a state of near panic. Shelley tried to calm her, sitting and reading in an attempt to keep her mind from the horrid associations of night, but 'Just as the dawn was struggling with moonlight,' he wrote in his journal, Claire,

> remarked in me that unutterable expression which had affected her with so much horror before. She described it as expressing a mixture of deep sadness and conscious

power over her. I covered my face with my hands and spoke to her in the most studied gentleness. It was ineffectual . . . her horror and agony increased even to the most dreadful convulsions. She shrieked and writhed on the floor.

Two days after her fit, Claire was still sick and in low spirits, unable to sleep without 'thinking of ghosts'. Later that week, she and Shelley quarrelled, with Claire admitting she was motivated by 'the bitterness of disappointment'. Shelley accused her in turn of being 'unformed' and 'insensible' to the nuances of true friendship and philosophy, shutting her out as he made a note in his journal to 'never suffer more than one even to approach the hallowed circle'. That evening, as if unconsciously protesting her exclusion, she walked in her sleep and for two hours was heard throughout the house as she 'groaned horribly'. For weeks afterwards, she remained bad-tempered and depressed. There were violent arguments, emotional stand-offs, and below it all a constant, circling gloom. 'I weep yet never know why,' Claire wrote in her diary, 'I sigh yet feel no pain.'

Though Shelley had chosen Mary over Claire, their relationship also existed within the context of his principles concerning the confinement of marriage, and what he called the 'indisciplinable wanderings of passion'. In the autumn of 1814, he seems to have set Mary a test, putting her in the way of Thomas Jefferson Hogg as a means of establishing both her commitment to the new philosophy and Hogg's loyalty to his friend. Shelley and Hogg had explored this path before after Hogg had made advances to Harriet around the time of her and Shelley's marriage. Harriet had rebuffed him, causing Shelley to reprove his friend for the indelicacy of his approach, while also admitting that Harriet was 'prejudiced'. Mary was horrified at first, with Claire recalling that her step-sister had come to her 'crying bitterly saying Shelley wants her to sleep with Hogg', having explained that the Jacobean playwrights Francis Beaumont and John Fletcher 'had one mistress'. Over the course of several weeks, however, Mary's aversion diminished as she and Hogg spent more time together and she found him to be a sympathetic and amusing friend. Hogg declared his love on New Year's Day 1815, and through a series of affectionate letters, Mary reciprocated, all the while insisting that he be patient due to her advanced state of pregnancy. 'My affection for you although it is not now exactly as you would wish will I think dayly become more so,' she wrote to him in January 1815, 'then what can you have to add to your happiness – I ask but for time – time which for other causes beside this – physical causes – that must be given – Shelley will be subject to these also – and this dear Hogg will give time for that love to spring up which you deserve and will one day have.'

Although Shelley referred to Mary as their 'common treasure', subsequent events prevented Hogg and Mary from ever becoming closer. On 22 February 1815, Mary gave birth, two months early, to a little girl. Twelve days later, her diary notes, 'Find my baby dead', the poor thing twisted in her cradle, killed in the midst of a convulsion. The bereavement devastated Mary, and the child haunted her thoughts both waking and asleep. 'Dream that my little baby came to life again,' she wrote two weeks after the child's death, 'that it had only been cold, and that we rubbed it before the fire, and it lived. Awake and find no baby.' Denied her father's consolations, Mary had to rely solely on Shelley to lift her spirits. He tried his best, taking her on outings to the British Museum, the zoo at Exeter Change, and to sail paper boats on the

Hampstead ponds, but as so often happened when he was called upon to lend support to others, his own health faltered and he succumbed to a sequence of mysterious 'spasms'. The surgeon William Lawrence diagnosed an abscess in the lungs, which, he told Shelley, would lead to his imminent death.

In early January 1815, Shelley's grandfather died leaving an estate valued at around £220,000, thus placing Shelley second in line to a substantial baronetcy. One week later, and to Mary's continued annoyance, Claire accompanied Shelley to Sussex for the reading of the will. The prospect of one day becoming a fully fledged member of the landed aristocracy appalled Shelley, and he sought instead to disinherit himself by resigning the succession and ceding the title to his younger brother in exchange for immediate liquidity he could use in the service of study and philanthropy. His father was sympathetic to the idea, although the moment Shelley realised this he began to drag his heels, convinced that his tardiness would only make Sir Timothy more impatient to settle on favourable terms. Their patrimonial games would continue for months, though in the meantime, Shelley's improved prospects and increased security put him in a position to borrow more and raise the money he needed for himself and Godwin.

The loss of her baby had persuaded Mary that she wanted no further part in any Utopian community. She was tired of their continual struggle, of estrangement from her father, and the nomadic life she had led since the elopement. 'Here are we three persons always going about,' she had written in her journal, 'and never getting anything. Good God, how wretched!!!!!' Access to money not only afforded a chance to end the rift with Godwin, but also to find a way to dispose of Claire. Soon, the question of her departure became a topic of almost obsessive regard: 'Talk about Clara's going away,' wrote Mary in her diary for 11 March, 'nothing settled. I fear it is hopeless. She will not go to Skinner Street; then our house is the only remaining place, I see plainly. What is to be done?' Shelley promised to see to it, although he spent just as much time with Claire throughout the spring as he had during Mary's pregnancy. 'The prospect appears to me more dismal than ever,' wrote Mary. 'This is, indeed, hard to bear.'

It was suggested that Claire might become a schoolmistress, just as Fanny intended to be, or perhaps find a place as a paid companion. To this end, an advertisement was placed in *The Times*, purporting to be from 'An English young LADY, who is now in France', seeking a position. Nothing came of it, so Shelley next tried to persuade a friend of Godwin's to take her, although that, too, came to nothing. Shelley and Mary entered tense negotiations, although how aware Claire was of these conversations or how serious she thought them is difficult to determine, for when in April she won a prize on the lottery, she used the money to buy two writing desks for the house – an unlikely gesture, surely, for someone on the verge of eviction.

Yet Mary's desire to be rid of Claire was unrelenting, and in early May, in what appears to have been a last resort, Shelley arranged for her to lodge in the village of Lynmouth on the Devonshire coast, staying in the same jasmine- and honeysuckle-clad cottage in which he had spent the summer with Harriet in 1812, and where Godwin had once fruitlessly searched for him. Claire left London on 13 May, the same day that Shelley reached an agreement with his father that would bring him a quarterly allowance, a lump sum and relief from his debts. By this time, Mary could hardly bring herself even to name her step-sister, referring only to 'the lady' or 'Shelley and his friend'. When she was finally gone, Mary and Shelley wrote an incantation together in their shared journal: 'A table spoonful of the spirit of aniseed, with a small quantity of spermaceti / 9 drops of human blood, 7 grains of gunpowder, ½ oz. of putrified brain, 13 mashed grave worms. The Pecksie, Dormouse. / The Maie and her Elfin Knight.' The book was then put away and another begun. They called it 'our regeneration'.

Why Claire consented to the Lynmouth plan is a mystery. She may have preferred the option of solitude to the ignominy of a return to Skinner Street or the boredom of being a widow's companion, or she may simply have had no choice. Still, its suddenness and secrecy were unusual. Not even Mrs Godwin was informed of it, and when she did at last learn the news, she scrambled for an excuse, first passing it off as Claire's wish, and then her own plan to prise her daughter from 'Mr Shelley's clutches'. They may have persuaded her it was medically advantageous, a cure for the irritability and depression she alluded to when describing to Byron a 'nervous disorder, the effects of which [I] still retain'. She may even have been pregnant. Certainly, the arrangements fit the profile of many such discreet sendings-away although, if this were the case, it is odd that no hint of it should remain in any of the thousands of pages of letters, diaries and journals that survived this logolatrous crew.

Whatever the reason, Claire experienced her departure as a humiliating and involuntary expulsion. She tried her best to conceal her upset, channelling the same spirit Mary had drawn on when sent to Dundee by writing to Fanny that 'After so much discontent, such violent scenes, such a turmoil of passion and hatred you will hardly believe how enraptured I am with this dear little quiet Spot.' Far from feeling lonely, she said, she found

solitude to 'concentre round the soul and teach it the calm determined path of Virtue and Wisdom'. But after one effusive letter,
Claire wrote no more, refusing to contact her mother or her
brother Charles, and sorely pining for London and Shelley. Shelley
missed her too. He continued to send her money and may even
have encouraged her to come and see him in July after he had
left Mary in Bristol following a tour of the south coast. This was
certainly Mary's suspicion, and reveals the extent of the unease
she felt whenever she thought Claire and Shelley might be
together. 'Pray is Clary with you?' she wrote from Clifton, 'for I
have enquired several times and no letters – but seriously it would
not in the least surprise me if you have written to her from London
and let her know that you are there without me that she should
have taken some such freak.'

Claire stayed in Lynmouth for almost nine months, brooding
over her mistreatment and promising herself that she would never
become so dependent again. Mary was pregnant once more, and
in August, she and the now-affluent Shelley had gone to settle in
a square, brick cottage with 'odious curtains' in Bishopsgate on
the edge of Windsor Great Park, not far from Windsor Castle, Eton
and Bracknell. It was an idyllic spot, as Claire was to learn from
her brother, who had visited and taken a boat excursion up the
Thames with Mary, Shelley and Peacock. The news did not comfort
her in the least, and years later, she would come to complain angrily
of being 'driven from all I loved' to sit 'companionless upon that
unfrequented sea-shore, mentally exclaiming, a life of sixteen years
is already too much for me to bear'.

In the first week of January 1816, Claire's exile ended with a
call to Bishopsgate to assist at Mary's lying-in where, three weeks
later, she gave birth to a boy they called William, the third child
Shelley had fathered in just over a year. Return failed to assuage
Claire's bitterness, and as soon as the baby was born, she left for

London with the express desire to 'vex' Mary and Shelley, taking lodgings first at Foley Place, Marylebone, and then at one of Shelley's old rooms in Arabella Row, Pimlico. Telling no one where she was going, not even her mother, she was missing for almost a month between February and March, weighing the impossibility of her position and scrupulously avoiding all the people sent in search of her.

It was then that Claire decided to contact Byron. This was not an impulsive act, but the culmination of an idea she had been considering even in Lynmouth – as she told him, 'You have been for the last year the object upon which every solitary moment led me to muse.' The public disintegration of his marriage and talk of imminent departure made the need to act more pressing, but so had the birth of the baby that cemented Shelley's bond to Mary and underlined the fact that if Claire were to avoid the fate of Fanny and become a school-teacher or a governess, she needed a saviour of her own. It was Byron himself who had suggested he might suit such a role, albeit unwittingly. Earlier that year, having heard of Godwin's financial difficulties, he had planned to make a considerable gift, instructing John Murray to divert the proceeds from his poems *The Siege of Corinth* and *Parisina* to relieve the philosopher's debts, an idea that the Tory Murray had ultimately vetoed. Byron would be her own Elfin Knight: poet, benefactor and, even better, a prize to flaunt before Mary.

Claire, Mary and Shelley entered Switzerland through the mountain pass at Nion, having had to bribe their way on to this better road. The route was shorter, but steep, and with spring unaccountably late this year, the snow still lay thick in places, requiring their *voiturier* to find the way using roadside poles first put in place by the Romans, and whose height was a reminder of how completely a path might be obliterated by blizzard, even in summertime. Four horses and a gang of ten men were needed to push them up towards the summits where their tilting carriage melded with clouds and was pelted with snow, out of whose smur would appear boys leading herds of goats along invisible tracks. The higher they rose, the colder it became, gaps in the mist revealing desolate rocklands and unfathomable drops towards a patchwork of pasture below. In the face of such unreal terrain, the barrier of the mountains, with its curtain of haze and drizzle, seemed to mark the line between theirs and a different world entirely, one that rose to meet the mental and spiritual clarity promised by Rousseau.

On Monday, 13 May, ten days after sailing from Dover, they reached the Lausanne road, which carried them down to the basin of Lac Léman, as Lake Geneva was locally known. Wild mountains gave way to smooth rocks covered with dark woods of spruce, fir and juniper, providing a panorama of the richly culti-vated Pays de Vaud and the plain of Geneva, along a lakeshore thick with literary and historical associations. A mile and a quarter outside the city, they stopped at the Hôtel d'Angleterre in the suburb of Sécheron. This fashionable *auberge* was known as 'one of the best inns on the Continent'. From the road it looked like a quaint two-storey inn, but at the back it went down for several more floors to form an imposing bulk surrounded by a huge cobbled forecourt and two enormous covered sheds, from which was run one of the most impressive and efficient transport busi-nesses in Europe, stabling horses, selling and repairing vehicles, and hiring out drivers to ferry tourists hundreds of miles. As its name suggested, its proprietor, Monsieur Dejean, was a committed Anglophile who had fitted out his establishment in the style of the English manors in which he had once served. 'The house is not only *à l'Anglais,'* wrote one bemused British visitor, 'but *à l'Anglais* to a defect,' with 'little tent beds, white wooden floors, low roofs, and small-paned windows'. Despite its imported inconveniences, the setting was majestic, with rooms that looked across the broad scimitar of Lac Léman, arcing fifty miles from Geneva at one end to Montreux at the other, and almost as deep as the Baltic Sea. On the opposite bank stood vineyards dotted with the elegant chalets of wealthy Genevese, behind which rose the black wall of the Alps and, in the distance, Mont Blanc.

Byron was nowhere to be found. By using the faster route, Claire, Mary and Shelley had overtaken him a day after leaving Paris, taking the road through Troyes and arriving at the foot of the Jura while John Polidori lay ailing in Karlsruhe 250 miles to the east. Claire tried not to show her disappointment, joining Shelley and Mary as they began to explore. Geneva was a fortified city, whose walls served rather to keep its inhabitants in than its enemies out, with gates that opened at five in the morning and closed promptly at ten at night, thus forcing many residents who would have preferred to stay in their Genevan homes in the summer months to repair to the countryside rather than risk being locked out. The town itself was compact, irregular and busy, twenty-six thousand people crammed into a series of hilly, rough-stoned streets intersected by the fast-running Rhône, which remained silt-free and shone emerald blue despite the mills and factories that lined its banks, and the quay piled with 'offals and wood'. The most peculiar feature of the city was the preponderance of domed arcades that roofed its principal shopping streets, held up by slender wooden props to the height of four or five storeys to provide shelter from the snow, making the streets dark and murky. To the south was the grassy plain of the Plainpalais, where Genevans took their constitutionals, and where an obelisk had been erected to the memory of Rousseau. A botanical garden was being built on the site the French had used for executions.

Shelley was unmoved by the town, which he called 'far from interesting', yet drew inspiration from the scenery, and best of all was able to indulge his lifelong passion for boats. From six to ten each night they went out on the lake, letting their craft float across water that was the colour of iodine, driven by small waves the locals called '*moutons*' past banks clothed in sweet and wild chestnut, walnut, magnolia, and cedar of Lebanon. Of Lac Léman, Rousseau had written, 'Give me here an orchard, a true friend, an amiable wife, a cow, and a little boat, and my happiness will be perfect.' Of the three of them, Mary had taken these words closest to heart. In love with her new baby and devoted to Shelley, she was delighted to be away from the oppressive gloom of London, and settled quickly into a blissful routine, reading Latin and Italian, writing and sketching until lunchtime, and taking long walks to enjoy the lizards that hid in the garden walls, and the pair of monogamous Chamois that grazed on the hotel lawn. When a twenty-one-year-old seamstress named Louise (Elise) Duvillard was engaged as William's nurse, Mary had even more time for her pursuits. She and Shelley stayed out late, watching the sun set on the Alps, their yellow tops melting into rose while their bases turned a rich violet. Mary Wollstonecraft had once described the May sunlight as 'balsamic', and this was exactly the effect it had on her daughter, soothing her, just as it softened the rock's appearance. 'I feel as happy as a new-fledged bird,' she wrote to Fanny in London, 'and hardly care what twig I fly to, so that I may try my new-found wings.' Years later, she would recall this as a transformative moment, the time 'when I first stepped out from childhood into life'.

But there was no Byron. Having rushed to Geneva, Claire found herself waiting for a lover who did not arrive. In London, she claimed to be tranquil, 'like my native mountains', but now that she was among them, sitting in her room at the top of the building and watching every coach that clattered into the yard, the Hôtel d'Angleterre had become a hell. Days passed in which she started to believe that Byron had 'purposely deceived' her, and was not coming to Geneva at all. At the post office, she saw her letter from Paris sitting uncollected, and the fact that she saw another addressed to Polidori '*à poste restante*' reassured her only slightly.

A whole week passed in the crook of this anxiety, and another began.

A STAR IN THE
HALO OF THE MOON

The acid and magnesia John had dosed himself with in Karlsruhe had a properly antiphlogistic effect – violent, but restorative – and by 18 May he was well enough to get back on the road. Byron had also regained some patience with his young doctor, telling Hobhouse, 'a little experience will make him a very good traveller – if his health can stand it'. A day later, they got their first view of Switzerland, crossing the river to enter the neat city of Basel in the foothills of the Jura mountains, and beyond it, the Alpine source of the Rhine. In Basel there were more paintings to visit, most notably Holbein's famous *Dance of Death*, but the real attractions lay further along a road that climbed skyward through swathes of dark pine, skirting chasms that required John to reach for a specialised vocabulary: 'To the right, beautiful,' he wrote, 'to the left . . . tendency to sublimity.'

At Murten, they stopped to visit another battlefield, the site at which the Swiss Confederation had defeated the army of Charles the Bold. A chapel here had once held the bones of ten thousand slain Burgundians, since scattered by French soldiers keen to obliterate the dishonour of their forebears. A few relics remained to which Byron helped himself, 'a leg and a wing', he told Hobhouse; 'as much as may have made the quarter of a hero', justifying the theft by saying that he had saved them from the 'less sordid purpose' of the locals, who sold them for use as knife handles. The nearby Roman ruins of Aventicum afforded a second tour, its streets and amphitheatre still discernible through the thin grass. A trace of mosaic was visible on the floor of a barn, while a second outhouse stored a jumble of marble columns, carved heads, capitals and plinths, all 'heaped promiscuously', said John, indicting the locals for being so 'shamefully negligent of the antiquities of their forefathers'. The site was also associated with the tale of Julia Alpinula, a Roman priestess who been slain while trying to save her father from a false accusation of treason. John and Byron searched for an inscription or epitaph that might support this story, but found nothing, although this did not prevent Byron from fabricating one and putting it in the notes of his evolving poem. Moved by the idea of a daughter's sacrifice, he again wrote himself into the landscape and its history.

On 25 May 1816, seven days after leaving Karlsruhe, and a month after sailing from Dover, the travellers finally reached the outskirts of Geneva and the Hôtel d'Angleterre. Byron, exhausted, entered his age in the hotel register as 100, and immediately took himself up to bed, but within minutes was disturbed by the arrival of a note from Claire. If he was amazed, he didn't show it, although John thought it 'a thing that seems worthy of a novel'. 'I am sorry you are grown so old,' Claire had written, after spying his name in the register, 'indeed I suspected you were 200 from the slowness of your journey. I suppose your venerable age could not bear quicker travelling. Well, heaven send you sweet sleep – I am so happy.' In a postscript, she added, 'Direct under cover to Shelley for I do not wish to appear either in love or curious.'

Byron did not reply, but simply put himself to bed. The following morning, he and John took a stroll, and finding a rowing-boat moored at the bottom of the hotel garden, they decided to take an inaugural trip on the lake. Out on the water, a hotel waiter leaned out of a ferry and scolded them for taking someone else's boat, so they returned it for another, and rowed back out to bathe. Byron's love of swimming was legendary, but on this occasion John was the first one in, a small instance of pre-eminence he felt worth recording in his diary: 'I *rode* first with LB upon the field of Waterloo; *walked* first to see Churchill's tomb; *bathed and rowed* first on the Léman Lake.'

News of Byron's arrival in Geneva circulated quickly, and his first caller was announced the moment he and John stepped back on shore. It was Professor Marc-August Pictet, director of the Geneva Observatory, a Fellow of the Royal Society in London and acquaintance of Hobhouse. Byron let it be known that he was 'not at home'. A second note, written on the hotel's thin light-blue paper and sealed with a sigil of entwined Cs, also lay in wait. 'How can you be so very unkind,' it read,

> I did not expect you to answer my note last Evening because I supposed you to be so tired. But this morning; I am sure you can't say as you used in London that you are overwhelm'd with affairs and have not an instant to yourself. I have been in this weary hotel this fortnight and it seems so unkind, so cruel, of you to treat me with such marked indifference.

But Claire was unable to sustain her anger, and the rest of her note laid the ground for a reunion. 'Will you go straight up to the top of the house this evening at ½ past seven,' she wrote:

> and I will infallibly be on the landing place and shew you the room. Pray do not ask any servants to conduct you for they might take you to Shelley which would be

very awkward. I will be sure to be waiting for you and nobody will observe you walking up stairs.

Byron, however, rarely went anywhere unobserved. 'They tell a strange adventure of his,' wrote the Englishman Lord Glenbervie, 'at Dejean's Inn.'

Geneva was lousy with English. Lady Frances Shelley, a distant and unacquainted relation to Percy Bysshe, put the number of British visitors that summer at somewhere over a thousand. The Swiss had traditionally held Britons in high esteem, but this most recent generation of tourists, rolling down the slopes to take the air, was a different breed entirely, comprised not merely of the gentry 'but all classes,' sniffed the traveller Louis Simond, 'and not the best of all classes either'. New detachments disembarked from Dejean's coaches every Wednesday, a curiously uncurious gaggle who harangued the locals in impatient English, haggled over every penny, and let it be known that the local cheese was the cause of diarrhoea. They yawned at salons, were champions of belligerent politics, and loved only dancing: 'At the sound of the fiddle,' said Simond, 'the thinking nation starts up at once . . . you may know the houses where they live by the scraping of the fiddle, and shaking of the floor, which disturb their neighbours.' John discovered as much when venturing out to a musical evening within the city walls, where he had been appalled by the 'quantities of English' there, speaking only 'amongst themselves, arms by their sides, mouths open and eyes glowing, might as well make a tour of the Isle of Dogs'.

That Dejean's hotel was popular with Anglophone tourists made Byron particularly uncomfortable. There were a few, like the

Rawdons, Mrs and Miss, to whom he was happy to pay his respects, especially as they were about to leave and he hoped they would carry his letters back to England and spare them from being opened by the French. The vast majority, however, appeared as boorish caricatures, filling the inn with 'the discordant and unceasing cries uttered in honest English accents from the garret to the cellar', cutting him in public, and spying on him behind his back.

Desirous of solitude, Byron and his doctor cast off on their second morning at Dejean's, John rowing the mile and a half across the lake to the hamlet of Bellerive where they had their first appointment to view a house. The meeting proved fruitless, and for the return journey Byron took the oars himself. As they neared Sécheron, three figures became slowly apparent on the bank, descending from the hotel lawn and watching them from the jetty. Byron, who had his back to them, was unable to see that it was Claire, and with her, Mary and Shelley. These three, seeing only Byron's back in the distance and a striking figure seated in the stern, initially mistook John for Byron, Mary and Shelley even remarking on 'how handsome he was'.*

By the time Byron would have realised what was happening, an encounter was inevitable. Claire came to him as he climbed ashore, feverish with excitement at finally being able to make the introductions she'd dreamed of since Lynmouth, and full of pride at her accomplishment. Byron and Shelley met for the first time, the two poets exchanging greetings before the newly constituted group turned together and walked back across the lawn towards the hotel.

All except John. It was the most auspicious literary meeting

---

* Shelley was not the most observant of people. In France, he had mistaken an old woman for a nine-year-old child.

since a puzzled Wordsworth had stood at his kitchen window and watched Coleridge pass up a perfectly good footpath to go crashing through the corn to reach his front door, yet John remained unnoticed in the boat throughout. Having watched the excited party leave, he pushed off silently and rowed out into the middle of the lake where, far from land, he pulled his oars in, climbed into the hull and looked up at the sky – 'and there lay my length, letting the boat go its way'.

John had the opportunity to meet Shelley that evening at a dinner to which Claire and Mary were not invited in accordance with Byron's proscription against watching women eat. The doctor's first impressions of the newcomer were largely accurate, even if his diagnosis was not: he saw a young man who looked slightly older than he was, 'bashful, shy, consumptive', and with an unconventional lifestyle. 'Keeps two daughters of Godwin who practise his theories,' he wrote in his diary, noting what either Claire's behaviour had made transparent or what Byron had expressly told him, 'one LB's'.

John was properly introduced to Claire and Mary (known here as 'Mrs Shelley') the following day, meeting all three of them at breakfast again two days later, and subsequently accompanying them as they rowed across the lake to view a cottage for themselves. Out on the water, Shelley volunteered a potted account of his marriage to Harriet, his elopement with Mary and their treatment at the hands of Godwin, which John summarised neatly as 'paid Godwin's debts, and seduced his daughter; then wondered that he would not see him'. In Mary and Claire, John had been prepared to meet a pair of infamous women, creatures of the *demi-monde*, but was surprised to find not only 'no meretricious appearance' in them whatsoever, but propriety and intelligence in both. He was similarly impressed with Shelley, who recounted his story freely and without the slightest hint of embarrassment, although John was clearly more interested in his literary successes than his life: 'Published at fourteen a novel; got £30 for it; by his second work £100,' he wrote, noting, perhaps, how lucrative defying one's father could be.

John returned to the lake with Claire and the Shelleys later that evening, boating until nine, and spending a further two hours chatting over tea as they explored some of their mutual connections. John and Mary's fathers had known each other for many years after Gaetano had assisted Godwin on a biography of Chaucer published in 1803. The Polidoris had also been part of the same Somers Town congregation in which the infant Claire and her mother had worshipped when they first moved to London, and had socialised with many of the same *émigrés*. At Edinburgh, John's studies had overlapped with those of Shelley's cousin, John Grove, and he had been in residence when Shelley came up to visit in 1813 with some faint notion of pursuing a career in medicine. Given John's preference for foreigners, there is also a chance he knew Shelley's friend, Joachim Baptista Pereira, 'a frank, warm-hearted, very gentlemanly young man' from Brazil, who, like John, had studied medicine at his father's behest while nursing a lambent desire for poetry. The Brazilian had been devoted to Shelley, translating his poetry into Portuguese and emulating him in every aspect from politics to vegetarianism, until his precipitate death from lung disease. At this point in their acquaintance, John was similarly drawn to him, finding much to admire in both the man and his work: 'The more I read his *Queen Mab*,' he wrote, 'the more beauties I find.'

It was perhaps inevitable that, of all the newcomers, John should be most taken with Mary, and he spent the entire next day alone in her company, reading Italian with her, and taking her out on the lake before returning to the hotel where they 'tea'd together'. Possibly he was attracted by the same philosophical pedigree that had enticed Shelley or, as another driven child of a dreaming scrivener, he felt an affinity for the disproportionate apportioning of wealth and ambition that had coloured her childhood. Whatever her appeal, John was assiduous in the attention he paid to 'Mrs Shelley', even taking baby William to be vaccinated after news arrived that an eighteen-year-old girl in Geneva had died of a sudden and mysterious contagion, receiving from the child's mother a gold chain as a token of her gratitude. This was in marked distinction to Claire, whom he barely mentioned at all, perhaps aware of the dangers inherent in tarrying with his master's mistress.

These early days of friendship were pleasant for John, and trips on the water became an evening ritual, passing among the lateen sails and rocky islands filled with nesting birds to watch the sunset and talk intently 'until the ladies' brains whizzed with giddiness, about idealism', said John, significantly underestimating Claire and Mary's capacity for speculative conversation. Other times, they sat in silence, the moon on its back, listening to the lap of water and the convivial chirrups of Swiss frogs. When Byron began to accompany them, the dynamic changed as he monopolised their outings with the brutal comedy of his worldliness, and uncensored views on the literary and political figures of London. Others rose to the occasion – Mary recited Coleridge so well that a smitten John became a convert to his poetry, and Shelley amused them with the insults he had received on account of his atheism, the crimes of William Godwin, and the time his father had tried to disinherit him by having him committed to an asylum for the insane at Eton. The weather was unpredictable, and cold, sharp winds shot suddenly across the lake from the mountains. One night, as they drifted on deep in conversation, a strong north-easterly wind blew them towards the mouth of Rhône, where strong currents threatened to drive them against the pier. Grabbing the oars, it took all their strength to control the boat against waves that were 'high and inspiriting', recalled Mary. 'We were all animated by our contest with the elements,' she remembered, when Byron suddenly offered to sing an Albanian song. 'Now, be sentimental and give me all your attention,' he said, but instead of singing a tune, it was 'a strange, wild howl that he gave forth; but such as, he declared, was an exact imitation of the savage Albanian mode, – laughing, the while, at our disappointment, who had expected a wild Eastern melody.' And so Byron asserted himself while also making sure to stand aloof, screaming and laughing in the face of the wind, sure enough of his audience that he could delight in disappointing them.

John tried to contribute, but lacking Byron's authority or Shelley's unique perspective, his actions were tangled in uncertainty. He was the only paid employee among them and, though clearly apart from the servants, an uncomfortable ambiguity lingered about his caste, providing Byron with licence to treat him as he wished, cracking jokes at his expense and watching him bristle as he nicknamed him 'Pollydolly', a sobriquet lifted straight from his Harrow schooldays where any fair or mannered child was given a girl's name. To further sour John's mood, it was clear that Mary had an eye for Byron, whom she found 'capricious, fascinating' and beautiful. On the rare occasions he managed to assert himself, his efforts emerged misshapen. One evening while they were all out boating, he happened to strike Byron violently on the kneecap with his oar, 'and the latter', as Mary told Tom Moore, 'without speaking, turned his face away to hide the pain':

After a moment he said, 'Be so kind, Polidori, another time, to take more care, for you hurt me very much.' – 'I am glad of it,' answered the other; 'I am glad to see you can suffer pain.' In a calm suppressed tone, Lord Byron replied, 'Let me advise you, Polidori, when you, another time, hurt any one, not to express your satisfaction. People don't like to be told that those who give them pain are glad of it; and they cannot always command their anger. It was with some difficulty that I refrained from throwing you into the water; and, but for Mrs Shelley's presence, I should probably have done some such rash thing.'

He was, said Byron, 'exactly the kind of person to whom, if he fell overboard, one would hold out a straw, to know if the adage be true that drowning men catch at straws'. For his part, John was beginning to feel frustrated by boating and all that it offered. 'Pains in my loins,' he wrote, 'and languor in my bones.'

At the beginning of June, Mary, Claire and Shelley moved out of Dejean's hotel and rented a two-storey villa at Montalègre known as Maison Chappuis. The cottage, hidden from the road and separated from the water by an overgrown garden of trees, provided the privacy they were looking for, as well as a small harbour in which to moor a boat.

Byron was also anxious to move as the gossip from Dejean's grew more incredible with each passing day. His departure from Britain had made him a universal object of speculation, with each anonymous squib attributed to him, and every preposterous lie believed. His stock, said John Murray, had never been higher. 'I have some delectable things to tell you when we meet,' Hobhouse wrote to him, of 'that phantom which passes for yourself'. 'Be assured that whatever you do comes so distorted through the prism of prattling ignorance and the fogs of the Jura,' he continued, 'that it will require some efforts of credible eye witnesses to put it into the straight line of truth.'

There were few credible witnesses in Geneva, for whom having Byron among them was like having a panther at large in the hills, the reputed appetites of 'his Satanic Majesty' growing more depraved as he was accused of luring pages into his carriage and 'corrupting all the *grisettes* [shop girls and seam-stresses] in the Rue Basse'. Lord Glenbervie, building on what had been gleaned of Byron's nocturnal travels up the stairs, had identified his mistress as 'Mrs Shelley, wife to the man who keeps the Mount Coffee-house'. Glenbervie was not entirely misinformed – it was Harriet's father, John Westbrook, who owned the fashionable Mount Coffee-house in north London. It was Lady Frances Shelley who got closest to the mark: 'Lord Byron is living near here with Percy Shelley,' she wrote in her diary, 'or rather, with his wife's sister, as the *chronique scandaleuse* says.' The worst of the rumours was attributed to Robert Southey, the poet who had once seen himself reflected in the youthful Shelley. It was said that Southey had claimed that Byron had formed a 'League of Incest' with Claire and Mary, who had been mistaken for consanguineous sisters. Southey turned out to be innocent of the charge, although Byron never forgave him nonetheless. The true culprit was Henry Brougham, the lawyer who had plagued Byron since authoring the abusive review of *Hours of Idleness* that had sent the poet reaching for a bottle and a gun.

Byron sent John out to scour the local properties, travelling as far as the Rhône valley with Charles Hentsch-Chevrier, a well-connected young banker recommended by Hobhouse, who had himself been persuaded to consider Byron a 'madman'. A house was found that had belonged to the father of the famous author Madame de Staël, who still spent much of the year at her family estate on the north shore of the lake. Four days after agreeing the lease, however, Byron pulled out after learning that the house he and John had seen on the morning they had met Shelley had suddenly become available. This was the Villa Diodati, a house that claimed an auspicious literary connection by belonging to the ancestors of the theologian Jean Diodati, a friend of John Milton and the first man to translate the Bible into Italian. Hentsch arranged a six-month lease at a fee roughly equivalent to £125, and John and Byron moved in on 10 June after a fortnight at Monsieur Dejean's. The hotelier was sorry to see them go although, ever enterprising, he continued to profit from his famous guest by setting out telescopes in his garden and renting them to anyone who wished to peer across the lake and mistake Byron's drying linen for 'petticoats' and 'certain robes and flounces'. He also had a second spectral villain in the form of Joseph Bonaparte, Napoleon's elder brother and one-time King of Naples and Spain. Though supposedly in exile in Baltimore, he was said to be hiding in the neighbourhood, a fact confirmed by Dejean, who claimed to have seen him in his kitchen ordering a glass of kirsch.

Villa Diodati was on the southern shore of Lac Léman, sitting high in a sloping garden amid orchards and terraces in one of the most picturesque sites outside Geneva, where city spires rose from the west, and a fine view looked across the water to graceful villas and the snow-capped wall of the Jura. It was a relatively modern house, tall, square and spacious, although smaller than Byron preferred, with a mansard roof, colonnaded patio, and a balcony that went around three sides. Inside was a picture gallery, hung with portraits of French kings, and a saloon that ran the length of the house, its large windows opening out onto the lake, bringing light to an interior dimmed by heavy shutters and parquet floors. Less than ten minutes away, separated by vineyards and a narrow path, were the Shelleys, and the harbour where Byron and Shelley shared a small-keeled boat.

Having at last come to rest, Byron wanted only to retreat into himself, and daily life at Diodati was marked by his conscious inertia. While to his new friends, 'Albé', as they had christened him, seemed flamboyant and companionable, the ordeal of his marriage and exile had left him in 'unequal spirits'.* 'The Separation – has broken my heart,' he confessed to Augusta. 'I feel as if an Elephant has trodden on it – I am convinced I shall never get over it . . . I breathe lead.' He rose at two in the afternoon and dined alone, confining himself to thin slices of bread and 'a vegetable dinner' of *petits pois*. Despite suppressing his appetite with cigars and soda water, he could rarely stick to his diets. His boatman, a vain little Swiss named Maurice, recalled being once summoned to take his lordship out to swim in the early hours as Byron breakfasted on cold duck and four bottles of wine, then lobbed the empties into the lake. In the evenings, Claire, Mary and Shelley would climb up from their cottage to spend long nights talking around the fire at Diodati, after which Byron would retire to his small room off the *grand salon* to write

---

* The pet name that Claire, Mary and Shelley gave to Byron that summer was characteristically intertextual, containing as it did the sound of his initials 'L.B.', but also a reference to his Albanian travels and Sophie Cottin's scandalous novel, *Claire D'Albe* (1799), whose eponymous heroine succumbs to forbidden passion.

until three in the morning, then go to bed, never sleeping, or so the rumour went, 'without a pair of pistols and a dagger by his side'.

John was hoping for something livelier. He had found the house, arranged the move and supervised the packing of 'linen and plate', but settling into Diodati had left him under-employed. It was a situation that had worsened the further south they had travelled as his duties became almost entirely secretarial, balancing the books and the daily accounts, writing inventories, paying the servants' wages, and arguing with coachmen over drink money. Now he was reduced to writing to Murray and asking him to send Byron's 'common red tooth powder from Waithe the dentist', and ordering books by Coleridge, Maturin, Scott and others, as well as three volumes of Thomas Crabbe's poetry for Shelley. Even this he failed to dispatch to Byron's satisfaction, adding in a subsequent note that 'Lord Byron desires me to say that it was my neglect from having his writing in my last that hindered me repeating to you his comp[liments]which he now sends you thrice repeated.'

Sitting in his closet rooms, reading Lucian, doing some writing, and poking at the corrections to an essay he had written against the death penalty, John was impatient to experience Genevan society. To satisfy this desire, Byron agreed to broker his introduction to some company on the understanding that he would then withdraw and leave John to himself. The doctor agreed, eager to avoid a repeat of a recent scene when he had again felt the force of Byron's obliterating fame at a visit to the house of Madame Eynard-Châtelain: 'LB's name was alone mentioned; mine, like a star in the halo of the moon, invisible.' This would be Byron's sole appearance at a large social gathering all summer, save for a visit to Lady Dalrymple Hamilton he abandoned at the doorway having seen how full her house was, and realising how much the

English would 'dog his footsteps'. 'The expression on his face was somewhat demoniacal,' said Lady Frances Shelley, who had spotted him there. 'What a strange person!'

John sought out the company of medical men, aiming to culti-vate relationships among the leading Genevan professionals, of whom at least eight had taken their degrees at Edinburgh. Gravitating to the older physicians who might dispense the kind of paternal affirmation he instinctively favoured, he first made the acquaintance of a Dr de Roche, who invited him to breakfast and proved 'acute, sensible', despite being a Bourbonist and displaying too much curiosity about Byron to be truly endearing. A more generous friend was Louis Odier, 'a good, old, toothless, chatty, easy-believing man', an expert on public health and another Edinburgh alumnus who invited John to attend his weekly musical evenings where, aside from tea, cakes and politics, medical lectures were regularly presented. Topics included the ethics of informing loved ones about a terminal illness, and sleepwalking, on which John and Odier exchanged manuscripts. Of them all, John was most drawn to Pellegrino Rossi, 'a shrewd, quick, manly-minded' Italian exiled for his patriotism, who had previously been a professor of law and economics at the University of Bologna, and whose first words were to warn John that Genevan women were 'amazingly chaste even in thoughts'. The advice may have had a bearing on another of John's adventures. One night, coming home from the city, he got lost in the rain and lightning, and had to be shown the way by Genevan constables. The evidence suggests that he had been leaving a brothel – although the page of his diary that said as much was carefully destroyed by his sister, Charlotte.

Summer was yet to arrive in Geneva, and by mid-June, it looked as if it would never come. 'Such stupid mists – fogs – rains – and perpetual density,' complained Byron, as the damp of Britain found him out in his new home. Temperatures in London had barely reached 40 degrees Fahrenheit by May, and crops had already drowned under swollen rivers that had swept livestock away. Until now, the agriculture in the Pays de Vaud had proceeded according to the almanac, although thick snow could still be seen on the lower slopes of the Jura. But the blue skies that had first greeted them in Switzerland were themselves quickening to a thunderous black, sending the tourists running to the shelter of their houses where they remained confined by what Mary called 'an almost perpetual rain', punctuated by vast, orchestral storms that they watched roll over the mountains from the windows of the saloon, streaking the lake with lightning. 'How the lit lake shines, a phosphoric sea,' wrote Byron in *Childe Harold*, 'and the big rain comes dancing to the earth!' Over the coming weeks, the rain would cause both the lake and the Rhône to rise and creep onto the land, threatening the crops and forcing the magistrates to prohibit the baking of white bread. From the steps of the Hôtel de la Couronne, on the quai du Rhône, one man hooked a fifteen-pound trout.

Astronomers blamed the downpour on an ailing sun, specifically two mysterious sunspots that could be seen with the naked eye. Concerned citizens observed them through smoked glasses, worrying that a chunk might shear off the weak disc and incinerate the Earth. In fact, the unwholesome weather was caused by a series of volcanic eruptions in the Caribbean, the Philippines and, most catastrophically, Indonesia, where the eruption of Mount Tambora in April 1815 had discharged twenty-five cubic miles of debris into the air, sending it up into the high stratosphere where it circled the Earth and reflected sunlight back into space.

John was another victim of the rain. On 15 June, as they sat out on the balcony of Diodati, Byron saw Mary coming up the slippery hill and, turning to John, said, 'Now, you who wish to be gallant ought to jump down this small height, and offer your arm.' John leaped, but landed awkwardly, spraining his left ankle so badly that he had to be carried into the house; Byron fetched him a pillow to prop up his leg. 'Well, I did not believe you had so much feeling,' snapped John. The following day, Mary made a comment that caused his spirits to sink even further: 'Mrs S. called me her brother,' he confided in his diary, '(younger).'

There were further mortifications in store. That same evening, John produced 'a tragedy of his own writing', insisting that Byron, Shelley, Mary and Claire 'should undergo the operation of hearing it'. Byron offered to read it aloud, just as he had done in Dover, but 'In spite of the jealous watch kept upon every countenance by the author,'

> it was impossible to withstand the smile lurking in the eye of the reader, whose only resource against the outbreak of his own laughter lay in lauding, from time to time, most vehemently, the sublimity of the verses; – particularly some that began ''Tis thus the goitr'd idiot of the Alps,' – and then adding, at the close of every such eulogy, 'I assure you, when I was in the Drury Lane Committee, much worse things were offered us.'

The details of the play, its Alpine setting and unfortunate reference to the goitre, a malady prevalent in Switzerland, suggests that this was new work, but even so, John had failed to learn his earlier lesson.* This was the second time Byron had ridiculed his

---

* Shelley's friend and publisher, Thomas Hookham, in his *Walk Through Switzerland*, (1816) writes of 'persons called *Goitres* and *cretins*: the disorders of both are considered epidemical'.

writing in front of others, even after encouraging him in private, but John decided to let the incident pass, making only a demoralised note in his diary: 'talked of my play, etc. which all agreed was worth nothing'. The rest of the evening he sat with Shelley, having what he described as 'a conversation about principles, – whether man was thought to be merely an instrument'.

The following evening the pattern was repeated. The rain descended in sheets, John was 'laid up' with his ankle, and the others came up to sit at Byron's fireside. The gloom turned their amusements ghostly, and they passed the time by reading aloud from a collection of German tales translated into French as *Fantasmagoriana; ou Recueil d'Histoires d'Apparitions, de Spectres, Revenans, Fantômes, etc.*, a pageant of grotesque stories replete with poisoned kisses, deadly portraits, fatal contracts and headless brides. The tales moved Byron to propose a competition that would make an icon of Mary and set John on an altogether more complicated path: 'We will each write a ghost story,' he declared.

Literary history has made much of this announcement, which would ultimately inspire the creation of Mary's *Frankenstein*. Yet on those wet summerless nights, the appetite for competition was remarkably short-lived. John began his story 'after tea', but only after first attending a ball at the Odiers' where he met the Polish Countess Potocka, a woman of forty who still possessed much of the beauty that had once moved Napoleon to court her, returning to Diodati against his will when the pain in his ankle prevented him from dancing. He wrote until midnight, at which time the company 'really began to talk ghostly', as Byron entertained them by reciting verses from Coleridge's poem *Christabel*. Reaching the point at which Christabel sees the witch's withered breast – 'a sight to dream of, not to tell' – Shelley emitted a sudden scream and, putting his hands to his head, ran from the room. John followed him, bringing him to his senses by throwing water on his face and administering ether, while a pale and sweating Shelley babbled of a horrible vision that had come over him as he looked towards Mary and saw a woman with eyes in her nipples. Having calmed himself, he opened up to John once more, telling him of his relationships with Harriet and Thomas Jefferson Hogg, and lamenting the vampiric associates 'who feed upon him, and draw upon him as their banker'.

Shelley's fit, along with the improving weather, cooled the enthusiasm for ghost stories, especially among the two most fancied contenders. Byron stopped writing after a day, his unfinished piece totalling just eight leaves he had torn from an old account book he carried with him because it contained the only scrap of his wife's handwriting he had besides her signature on the Deed of Separation. His creation, steeped in magic, featured an unnamed narrator setting out on a journey with an older man named Augustus Darvell, a rich, mysterious fellow, 'deeply initiated into what is called the world'. After a tour of southern Europe, the two men turn east towards Smyrna, at which point Darvell succumbs to such a sudden and rapid deterioration in his health that they are forced to halt in a Turkish cemetery that sits on the way to the ruins of Ephesus. Darvell tells his friend he is about to die and enjoins him to perform meticulous rituals after his death while not revealing his passing to any human being. Having extracted this oath, his skin turns black and he is buried in a shallow grave at the exact point at which a stork is seen to seize a serpent in its claws and fly into the heavens.

Though only a fragment, Byron's effort was far more substantial than Shelley's, who left no trace of a story whatsoever, a tale he had intended to base 'on the experiences of early life', unless, that is, a ghostly lyric in his Genevan notebook reflects his thoughts in that direction:

John Polidori at twenty-one, around the time he entered Byron's employ. 'He was a handsome, harum-scarum young man', wrote Harriet Martineau.

Claire Clairmont, also twenty-one. Claire sat for this portrait by the Irish painter Amelia Curran while travelling in Rome. Curran painted portraits of Claire, Mary, Shelley, and four-year-old William Shelley, although none were considered successful. 'Claire is not yet reconciled to hers', wrote Mary in 1820.

*Lord Byron in the first flush of fame, posing in the Albanian dress he
purchased while travelling in 1809. Having seen the finished painting,
Byron decided he didn't like the nose and directed the artist, Thomas
Phillips, to re-do it.*

Percy Bysshe Shelley, after the portrait by Amelia Curran.

No contemporary images of the young Mary Shelley have survived, although this portrait of a woman in her mid-forties, painted around 1843, has recently been identified as her. By this time, Mary had been a widow for more than two decades.

Ampleforth Lodge as it appeared in 1804. John was nine years old when he arrived at this isolated school of twelve boys and twenty-four Benedictine monks, located over two hundred miles from his home in London.

William Godwin's Juvenile Library, the children's bookshop where Claire and Mary grew up.

'Dirty and detestable' Old Edinburgh, home to the university where John studied medicine from 1811–1815.

The village of Lynmouth in Devon. Shelley had spent the summer of 1812 in Lynmouth with his first wife, Harriet, and in 1815, sent Claire to live there. Alone for almost nine months, she hated it. 'Day after day I sat companionless upon that unfrequented sea-shore,' she wrote, 'mentally exclaiming, a life of sixteen years is already too much to bear'.

Byron's 'Fare Thee Well'. This satirical cartoon depicts Byron's departure for the Continent accompanied by a cargo of women and booze. With his arm around 'the beauteous Mrs Mardyn', he versifies in the direction of the white cliffs of Dover, where his estranged wife Annabella Milbanke can be seen holding baby Ada.

Byron travelled abroad in a carriage based on Napoleon's campaigning coach, seen here being captured at the Battle of Waterloo. The carriage was brought to London where it was put on display at William Bullock's Egyptian Hall, and became a major attraction. In 1816, Byron commissioned a copy from Baxter the coachmaker. By 1823, Baxter was still waiting to get paid.

A nineteenth-century medical chest of the kind John would have carried in his role as Byron's personal physician.

The field of Waterloo as it appeared the morning after the battle, 18th June 1815. Almost fifty thousand combatants were killed or wounded, and their bodies stripped by local scavengers.

Monsieur Dejean's Hôtel d'Angleterre, in the Genevan suburb of Sécheron. Dejean's hotel was considered to be one of the best in Europe, host to an impressive trans-continental coaching operation housed in a pair of giant sheds.

Villa Diodati on the southern shore of Lac Léman.

> A shovel of his ashes took
> And from the hearth's obscurest nook
> With a body bowed and bent
> And tottering forth to the paved courtyard
> She followed – muttering mysteries as she went
> Helen and Henry knew that granny
> Was as much afraid of ghosts as any
> And so they followed hard –
> But Helen clung to her brother's arm
> And he over shadow made her *shake*.

The only ones who persevered were Mary, who would continue to work on her story for the next eighteen months, gripped by the power of her own Diodati visions and motivated by Byron's promise that he and she would publish theirs together, and, much less diligently, John.

With the weather improving slightly, Byron hatched a plan for himself and Shelley to make a pilgrimage in honour of Rousseau, following as closely as possible Rousseau's own 1754 excursion around Lac Léman, while also visiting the sites most closely associated with his novel *Julie*. The trip addressed the same questions of legacy and influence that had dogged Byron since he had lain across Churchill's grave at Dover. But it was also a piece of pure literary tourism that afforded him the chance to experience the pleasures of admiration. Byron felt an affinity for Rousseau, with whom he had often been compared for his ability to capture the essence of emotions in works that were considered highly autobiographical. Rousseau had also had an awkward relationship to his celebrity, even going to the extent of building a trap-door in his study to escape unwanted sightseers. In addition, the journey was an expression of the fondness Byron was developing for Shelley, whom he had nicknamed 'Shiloh' after the messianic infant to whom the apocalyptic prophet Joanna Southcott had claimed she would give birth in 1814 at the age of sixty-four – an affectionate dig at the younger man's ethereal nature. Byron generally tried to avoid writers, but it helped that he and Shelley shared a similar social background, with Byron nesting comfortably on a higher perch, and that Shelley was an acolyte just like everyone else. Having read the third canto of *Childe Harold* in manuscript, Shelley told Hogg that, 'It infinitely surpasses any poem he has yet published, with the exception perhaps of *Lara*, which is of another character.'

Boatmen were hired and the two men left Diodati on Saturday, 22 June. Naturally, the women were excluded from the trip, but so was John. The reason was his twisted ankle, but even John knew this was a pretext, and his anger boiled out. There was a violent argument in which he accused his employer of bullying and mistreatment, aiming at him a series of 'intemperate remonstrances' that set Byron in a fury. The doctor's immediate dismissal seemed inevitable, and faced with the thought of ruin, he limped upstairs, determined to destroy himself. Byron followed, finding him decanting poisons from his medicine chest and hesitating over whether or not to leave a suicide note. Offered a conciliatory hand, John burst into tears. Such behaviour was clearly untenable, but, for now, the question of his future would be deferred until Byron returned from the lake.

Both Byron and Shelley wrote a great deal about their tour and the sights that allowed them to feel a deep sense of communion with the spirit of Rousseau, whom Shelley called 'the greatest man the world has produced since Milton'. On the fourth day of the journey, having visited the castle at Chillon and toured its fêteless dungeons, they landed at the sacred ground of Clarens, where locals pointed out a wooded thicket known as the *bosquet de Julie,* the bower where Julie and St Preux had stolen their first illicit kiss. 'In the evening,' wrote Shelley, 'we walked forward among the vineyards', passing along the narrow terraces that overlooked the bower, and strolling through the aged trees that gave shade to the memory of 'that tenderness and peace' with which Rousseau had infused the scene. The place filled Byron with 'a sense of the existence of love in its most extended and sublime capacity' and of his own place in 'its good and of its glory'. Shelley, moved to the brink of tears, stood in silence and let his eyes absorb the wonder, 'even until the darkness of night had swallowed up the objects which excited them'.

It was Byron who broke the spell. 'Thank God,' he said, 'Polidori is not here.'

9

FOG OF THE JURA

The painful anticipation of Claire's stay at Dejean's did not abate with Byron's arrival, but rather drew on as he continued to deny her the recognition she desired. There was no love affair, nor even much direct interaction, as he refused to be seen with her in public, and she was once again left to trail in the wake of Mary and Shelley, waiting for a chance to see him on the lake or by the fireside at Diodati. When those opportunities did arrive, they were far from intimate, as Byron monopolised his audience, regaling them with anecdotes and expecting that they listen. On the few occasions she did speak with him, she worried that he would laugh at her in his 'little proud way' and say 'cross unkind things'. 'How contemptuously you used sometimes to speak of me little guessing the dreadful pain I endured to hear these speeches,' she told him. 'I did the greatest violence to my feelings for fear of being troublesome or disgusting to you. When I was so happy to see you again I was obliged to sit silent and only look at you . . . And when you were kindest to me I had so great a fear of offending you I dared not express half I felt.'

As was the case with John Polidori's many conflicts, Claire's reminiscences of life at Diodati offer a counterpoint to the view that the summer of 1816 was a time of mutual inspiration and collaborative creativity. According to her, the fireside salon revealed Byron at his worst. Even his friends admitted that he had little conversation beyond 'quip and crank', and on those nights he held forth, he gave full vent to his anger and despondency, indulging reckless thoughts and making wild pronouncements fuelled by the gin and wine he drank daily. He brooded on his fall from grace, claiming that it had destroyed his belief in God and made him immune to all morality beyond pleasure and self-interest: 'My will is law,' Claire records him saying, 'and so it is with every one only they are hypocrites and will not acknowledge it.' These were 'dark despairing modes of thought,' she said, 'without a glimmer of Hope or Faith in the goodness of Human Nature in them'. Even his anecdotes were cruel and nihilistic, relating 'deeds of his which, if true, indicated a savage nature not averse to deeds of darkness'. 'One evening,' she recalled,

> when we were all three with him he told us quite unexpectedly that at Constantinople he had sewn a mistress who was unfaithful to him up in a sack, and had her carried by two Greeks in the dead of the night (he walking with them) and thrown into the Bosphorus. Mary asked – did she not shriek and alarm the neighbourhood – he said – no, she was perfectly quiet and reconciled to her fate, as women expect no better treatment in that city.

On another occasion, Byron claimed to reveal the identity of 'Thyrza', the enigmatic addressee whose elegiac sonnets had caused so much speculation in the past. Today they are understood to have been written as memorials to John Edleston, a young chorister for whom Byron developed a deep sexual fascination while at Cambridge. In 1816 they were universally believed to be addressed to a woman (the name is pronounced 'Theresa', and the poems contain a reference to 'her grave'.) At Diodati, Byron told them she was a Nottingham girl who lived near his ancestral home at Newstead Abbey, and with whom he had fathered two illegitimate children before refusing to marry her due to her impossibly low birth. She had committed suicide, he claimed, and was buried at a crossroads, which, he said, explained the absence of any grave or memorial.

These stories, with their shared theme of dead and discarded mistresses, terrified Claire, and she took no heart from Shelley and Mary who laughed at them as obvious fabrications and admired his desire to provoke – a perfectly legitimate tactic, said Shelley, for 'shaking the prejudices of society'. Claire thought Shelley wilfully blind. He 'adored Genius', she said, and was so convinced that Byron possessed it he could 'think no ill of him'.

Yet, as Claire well knew, Byron's poem *The Giaour* begins with a woman sewn into a sack, an episode inspired by a story he and Hobhouse had heard in Albania. What was more, Byron might even have interceded in a similar event, and actually prevented a woman from being drowned in Athens. Byron, it seemed, enjoyed tormenting Claire, who found it difficult to separate the man from his image. Indeed, the public perception of him as a debauched seducer had reached its apotheosis that summer through the publication of a novel by one of his ex-lovers, Caroline Lamb. It was Lamb who dubbed Byron (possibly apocryphally) 'mad, bad, and dangerous to know' after they had embarked on a three-month affair in the spring of 1812. She had been intoxicated by him even before they had met, reading an advance copy of *Childe Harold's Pilgrimage* and writing an anonymous letter to its author on the eve of publication to admire his 'great and promising Genius', telling her diary after she had met him in person two weeks later,

'That beautiful pale face is my fate.' So visibly obsessed did she become that Annabella Milbanke likened her to a rabid dog: 'I really thought that Lady Caroline had bit half the company,' she wrote, 'and communicated the *Nonsense-mania.*'

To Byron, Caroline Lamb was an evil genius – '*Genio maligno*' – and a 'little volcano'. Slight, boyish, and three years older than Byron, she was the wife of William Lamb, an admired but indecisive member of the influential Holland and Devonshire House sets, whose uninspiring qualities would one day launch him into the office of prime minister. Their marriage followed the principle of reverse magnetism, uniting his respectable dullness with her unpredictability and talent for flouting convention, and they lived more or less independently of one another. The product of a privileged but chaotic childhood spent shuttling between a forbidding grandmother and running wild in a cavernous mansion, uncontrolled by absent parents, Caroline had virtually no formal schooling but possessed a powerful intellect and fertile imagination. With her mind 'heated by novel reading' (as Byron said), she was capable of so fully inhabiting a world of invention that her fantasies took on formidable form. From the outset of their affair she behaved as if they were both characters in one of his poems (fittingly, her initial letter to him was one of those that addressed him as 'Childe Harold'.) Calling herself his 'wild antelope', she established elaborate forms of courtship that included cross-dressing, sex by proxy, and gifts of her pubic hair, requesting his, commingled with blood, by return of post. By this point, Byron had tired of her intensity and begun to recoil from her histrionics, taking respite in the arms of her rival Lady Oxford, thus sending Caroline into a fit of suicidal near-insanity from which she took years to recover.

Part of her rehabilitation involved dressing as a man and retiring to a secluded attic to write a novel, which, on 9 May

1816, she published anonymously under the auspices of Henry Colburn, a publisher who specialised in novels by aristocrats that he marketed as true-life exposés. *Glenarvon* did not disappoint, and when Lady Caroline's authorship was discovered, it became a fully fledged *succès de scandale* of which Byron came to learn 'marvellous and grievous things'. In mid-July, after both he and John Polidori had read it for themselves, he decried her as a 'bedlamite', and issued through Augusta a dire warning: 'If she stirs against you,' he told his sister, 'neither her folly nor her falsehood should or shall protect her. Such a monster as that *has no sex*, and should live no longer.'

Glenarvon was a tale of erotic doom set in a lonely castle during the Irish Rebellion of 1798, which interwove breathless Gothic with thinly veiled portraits of the Holland and Devonshire House sets, and real-life documents, including the actual letter Byron had sent to Caroline ending their relationship.* Yet the most remarkable thing about the novel is its sustained emotional pitch, so over-wrought that it constantly threatens to veer into incoherence, while also enacting the shattered identity of a lover flayed by proximity to a glamorous 'spirit of evil'. Caroline is imagined as the ethereal waif Calantha (the name borrowed from a character in John Ford's Jacobean tragedy *The Broken Heart*), subject to the oppressive scrutiny of the extended clan around her and caught in an unhappy, guilt-burdened marriage. Into this life of dutiful boredom comes

---

* The note contained a particular streak of cruelty, in both form and content. 'I am no longer your lover,' it said, and 'am attached to another; whose name it would of course be dishonourable to mention . . . I shall ever continue your friend, if your ladyship will permit me so to style myself; and, as a first proof of my regard, I offer you this advice, correct your vanity, which is ridiculous; exert your absurd caprices upon others; and leave me in peace.' Lady Caroline could not fail to learn the identity of Byron's new lover, Lady Oxford, as he had made sure to compose the note on her writing-paper, and close it with her seal, both of which bore her coat of arms.

the Irish rebel, Clarence de Ruthven, Lord Glenarvon, whose face glowers 'as if the soul of passion had been stamped and printed upon every feature'. 'The hand of Heaven never impressed on man a countenance so beautiful,' says Calantha, 'so glorious.' A proto-typical demon lover, part-Vicomte de Valmont, part-Lovelace, and precursor to Emily Brontë's Heathcliff, Glenarvon dresses as a monk, stalks ruined priories, and howls like a dog at the moon. Such is his allure that even the pigs and cattle follow him from their paddocks, and once he has fixed his desires on the powerless Calantha, she becomes his slave. 'Turn from me if you can,' he challenges her, 'the heart that I have won you cannot reclaim', before drawing her into a sado-masochistic affair that results in her utter degradation: 'Weep,' he cries, binding her ever tighter to him, 'I like to see your tears; they are the last tears of expiring virtue. Henceforward you will shed no more.'

Claire did not read *Glenarvon* in Geneva, but its version of Byron informs her own memories of him as a lover. He abused her with impunity, confident that his hold over her was total, adamant that she would never forget him in spite of her efforts to break free. 'When he was savage and unkind,' she wrote,

> I often said I will go away and never see you again and then I shall forget you and perhaps be happier. He invar-iably answered: you may go away, if you like but you shall not forget me – no woman who has once loved me has ever forgotten me for I took good care to brand her with such infamy, she could not but remember me for the rest of her existence and I will do the same by you.

'Unblessed myself, I can but give misery to all who approach me,' Glenarvon tells Calantha. 'My love is death.'

Even as he kept her at arm's length, Byron continued to sleep with Claire, although their liaisons were neither planned nor regular and he took no responsibility for initiating them. 'A man is a man,' he told Douglas Kinnaird, 'and if a girl of eighteen comes prancing to you at all hours there is but one way.' Once she had spent the night, Claire said, he had a 'very impertinent way of looking in a person's face who loves you and telling them you are very tired and wish they'd go'. Though she searched for a signal that their relationship might have quickened into some- thing more substantial, he continued to keep her at a distance, allowing her to believe that their affair had to be concealed from Polidori. (Claire agreed that the doctor did seem 'so extremely suspicious'.) Nevertheless, she tried to will the affair to life with cajoling, seductive notes, and playful teasing, although this could be dangerous as Byron was said to be 'skinless in sensibility' when it came to jokes about himself. Claire's letters to him often apolo- gise for being a 'teize', and she is no doubt the 'heedless girl' Mary reports trying to make fun of Byron by saying 'that she thought he had a little of the Scotch accent', a comment that sent him into a rage in which he damned the whole of Scotland and wished it sunk to the bottom of the sea. Incidents such as these were behind Claire's comment that Byron suffered from a 'family complaint of suspicion and defence where any reasonable man would have taken no offence'. At other times it was her turn to show her anger, berating him for his 'marked indifference', although more often than not this was turned inwards as she contemplated her powerlessness, returning to the disavowal that was the constant refrain of her earliest letters: 'Were I to float by your window drowned,' she wrote to him, 'all you would say would be "Ah voilà!"' In later years, she would come to understand this as a reflection of her upbringing, and Godwin's conviction that the faults of others were actually the faults of one's own percep- tions, 'creations of our own mind [that] had no real existence'.

But Claire had another reason for not thinking the worst of Byron. By the time he and Shelley had left for the lake in search of the spirit of Rousseau, she knew for certain that she was pregnant.

With the two poets away, Villa Diodati became virtually dormant. Claire did nothing but read Byron's poems and commit her thoughts to a journal she ultimately destroyed. John, similarly aimless, went in and out of town, trying the patience of his new friend Pellegrino Rossi. The only one with purpose was Mary, who began to work at her ghost story in earnest while the Swiss nurse, Elise, looked after baby William. John came to sit with them between appointments. He continued to be wary of Claire, who was usually distant, save for one occasion when she embarked upon a speech he described as a 'soliloquy', a chance, perhaps, for this bold and usually outspoken woman to make up for the awed silences she fell into at Diodati.

After nine days away, Byron and Shelley returned on 30 June. The trip had been artistically rewarding, especially for Byron, who by now had 117 stanzas of the third canto of *Childe Harold*, as well as a new poem entitled *The Prisoner of Chillon*. Both works showed the influence of Shelley, who had transferred to the older poet some of his idealism and an appreciation for Wordsworth and the poetry of nature. The trip also cemented Byron's decision to stop seeing Claire. She had told Shelley about the pregnancy before he left. Shelley had told Byron, whose immediate reaction was to seal the doors of Diodati and forbid her entrance, refusing to believe that her feelings for him amounted to anything more than 'amusing herself'. A week later, however, when the cross-written and blotted sheets that formed the new part of *Childe Harold* were finally ready to be transcribed, he found a use for her. Byron hated making fair copies, and was always happy to palm the work off on someone else, a task for which Claire offered herself willingly, absorbed into the Byron industry as a loyal clerk making daily devotions to his words. Even when tasked in this way, she still had to beg for admittance: 'If you <u>want</u> me, or anything of, or belonging to me I am sure Shelley would come and fetch me,' she wrote. 'I am afraid to come dearest for fear of meeting any one. Can you pretext the copying . . . Everything is so awkward.'

Claire was not the only one feeling excluded, although John's upset manifested itself more explosively, specifically in a threat to shoot Shelley in the head. It had happened in a fit of irrepressible anger after the poet had beaten him in a contest of sailing or rowing, at which point John had challenged him to a duel. Shelley remained impassive, but Byron not only promised to take up the challenge on behalf of his friend, he assured the doctor that he would have no compunction in putting him in his place. Further recriminations followed: 'Had a long explanation with S and LB about my conduct,' John wrote.

Shelley had enjoyed his time with Byron, but was some distance from falling under his spell. In fact, as he told his friend Thomas Love Peacock, he had rather assumed that Byron would fall under his. 'Lord Byron is an exceedingly interesting person,' he wrote,

> and as such is it not to be regretted that he is a slave to the vilest and most vulgar prejudices, and as mad as the winds? I do not mean to say that he is a Christian, or that his ordinary conduct is devoid of prudence. But in the course of an intimacy of two months, and an

observation the most minute, I see reason to regret the union of great genius, and things that make genius useless . . . I had some hope that an intercourse with me would operate to weaken those superstitions of rank and wealth and revenge and servility to opinion with which he, in common with other men, is so poisonously imbued.

Three weeks after his tour of the lake, Shelley planned another trip, this time with Mary and Claire into the Alps to see Chamonix, Mont Blanc and Montanvert, inviting Byron, who declined, citing the imminent arrival of friends from London and the inclemency of the weather. The trip held little prospect of enjoyment for Claire, who had still not been readmitted to Diodati and could not fail to see that her relationship with Byron was about to end. 'We go I believe in two days. Are you satisfied?' she wrote angrily, before tempering her tone and offering to complete the fair copy of *The Prisoner of Chillon* before departing. 'It is said that you expressed yourself so decisively last Evening,' she wrote, 'that it is impossible to see you at Diodati':

> Remember how very short a time I have to teize you and that you will soon be left to your dear-bought freedom. Let me have Chillon then, pray do — send one of your own Servants with it and some pens. Tell me one thing else — Shall I never see you again? Not once again.
> When you had such bad news to announce, was it not a little cruel to behave so harshly all the day. Pray send me an answer directly — I cannot wait.

Claire, Mary and Shelley left Montalègre on the morning of 21 July, stuffed into Shelley's carriage while baby William stayed behind with Elise. Byron need not have feared the weather, as for once the day was cloudless and hot. Leaving the plain of Geneva, they moved into a narrow pass hollowed by the river Arve and entered the mountains to spend the first night at Sallanches. This was as far as the carriage could go, and the next morning they hired guides and mules for a second ascent. Before them rose Mont Blanc, its summit obscured by clouds. 'I never imagined what mountains were before,' wrote Shelley, 'the immensity of these aerial summits excited, when they suddenly burst upon the sight, a sentiment of extatic wonder, not unallied to madness.'

As they descended into the Vale of Chamonix, the plain widened into meadows and cottages. In one village Mary purchased a caged squirrel, which bit her immediately and ran off, only to be recaptured for a short while before Shelley decided to set it free. Elsewhere, they pored over unusual stones and geological curiosities, until high above they heard the roar of thunder and witnessed an avalanche thump into a river and send a wall of water cascading to the bottom of the mountain where it tore up the road.

A day of rain hindered their ascent of the Mer de Glace glacier at Montenvers, but when they were finally able to climb it, both Mary and Shelley were affected by the view. It was rightly called a sea of ice, petrified into cresting waves, and both marvelled at its pristine barrenness and its 'palaces of death and frost'. The impression was particularly strong on Mary, who would use 'the most desolate place in the world' as a setting in *Frankenstein*. But even in the midst of such sublimity, Shelley found himself bothered by the English and their 'melancholy exhibitions of tourism' that made the glacier 'another Keswick'. As always, when faced with the conventional world, Shelley felt compelled to make a gesture of defiance. In a stone hut on the slope, he entered their names in a visitors' book and, in Greek, the phrase 'atheists one and all' and their destination 'hell'. Similar inscriptions were left in a trail of hotel registers: at Chamonix's Hôtel d'Angleterre he signed himself in Greek, 'democrat, lover of mankind, and atheist' (beneath which, a second hand had written the Greek for 'fool'); at the Hôtel de Londres, he wrote the same again, while referring to Claire as 'Theossteique' – 'hated' or 'hater' of God. She approved the game and, as a parting shot, attempted to reproduce the word again, claiming that she was an Irish subject, travelling between Geneva and Constantinople, and adding 'These mountains are molehills compared with those of my native country, and the landlord is nothing after the one of Grenbergh.'

The rebels had fun at the locals' expense, as the Swiss yet again failed to live up to their literary image. Shelley described them as 'half deformed or idiotic and most of whom are deprived of anything that can excite interest and admiration' or, in the case of the proprietor of a provincial museum, 'the very vilest specimen, of that vilest quack that together with the whole army of aubergistes and guides and indeed the entire mass of the population subsist on the weakness and credulity of travellers as leeches subsist on the blood of the sick'.

The trip lasted a week, but Claire left no record of her state of mind, save for a letter she urged Shelley to write to Diodati when they first reached Chamonix 'fatigued to death'. It was short and deferential, describing the scenery and excellent roads and expressing twice the wish that he would come out to join them. 'Clare sends her love to you,' he signed off, 'and Mary desires to be kindly remembered.'

By the end of July, Claire's pregnancy was beginning to show, and the question of what to do with her was becoming increasingly urgent. Not only did Shelley share Claire's concern but, unknown to her, he had already made a provision for her in a will he had drawn up on the second day of his tour with Byron around Léman.

That morning, near the village of Meillerie, the two men and their crew had been caught in a sudden squall that threatened to sink them. The crewmen proved inept, and the boat struggled so badly that Byron called them to abandon it, while Shelley, who could not swim, prepared himself to drown. By good fortune they were preserved, but that night Shelley settled all his goods on Mary, William and his children by Harriet, and left a generous provision for Claire, bequeathing her six thousand pounds in the event of his death and a further six thousand to be invested for an annuity. The second sum was most likely intended for her unborn child, although Shelley was careful not to bequeath it to the child directly, lest to do so should imply that he was the father.

On 1 August, Shelley turned twenty-four. Mary gave him a telescope, and they celebrated on the lake shore, sending a paper balloon into the night with a tea-light in its gondola that caught fire and burned brilliantly in the seconds before it was consumed. The next day a summons arrived from Diodati for Claire and Shelley, but not Mary, 'for Lord Byron did not seem to wish it'. They were there to discuss the pregnancy, but the negotiations began poorly. In moments like these, Byron withdrew behind the social barriers that stood between them, refusing to offer either emotional support or hopes for the future. Shelley was determined that Byron should accept responsibility for his child, if only to assuage his own sense of guilt and responsibility for Claire. Byron, for his own part, suspected that Claire and Shelley had once been lovers, and that paternity might more properly be laid at Shelley's door. When at last he was persuaded to accept that the child was his, he insisted on the utmost secrecy. No one was to know about Claire's pregnancy, and when the baby was born, it was to be placed in Augusta's care, a solution to which Claire objected strongly 'on the ground that a Child always wanted a parent's care at least till seven years old'. Byron capitulated, offering a verbal agreement that the baby would always live with one of its natural parents – first with its mother, and then, as soon as it was weaned, with him. Claire would be known as the baby's aunt, 'and in that character I could see it and watch over it without injury to anyone's reputation', she said. He also insisted that the right to name the child and choose its education belonged to him.

Having reached this tentative settlement, Shelley took delivery of a letter from his London lawyer that would add a further complication. The letter informed him that his father was threatening to refuse his annual allowance unless he returned immediately to resolve the question of financial support for his children with Harriet, Charles and Ianthe. Given that Sir Timothy had already refused one request for an increase in his allowance and also withheld a loan, Shelley, in 'very bad spirits', realized that he had no real option but to leave. Naturally, this meant Claire would have to leave too, although what plans Shelley had for her were uncertain. Even before this news had come from his father, Shelley had been thinking of life beyond Geneva, writing to Thomas Love Peacock and instructing him to secure a furnished house in the Windsor Forest, what he called 'a fixed, settled, eternal home', for himself, Mary, William and a kitten – but no Claire.

Claire, Mary and Shelley would be leaving Geneva at the end of August, and an uneasy truce settled for what remained of their stay. Claire continued transcribing, copying almost all of the work Byron produced that summer, providing her with a greater insight into his artistic life than anybody else alive. She made fair copies of his poems on visiting Churchill's grave in Dover, a Wordsworthian meditation on 'The Glory and the Nothing of a Name'; his 'Prometheus', a poem on the unending punishment inflicted upon the Titan who stole the secret of fire; 'Darkness', a Shelleyan vision of chaos, and the world turned cannibal; and both the 'Stanzas' and 'Epistle' to Augusta, quailing pleas for understanding, muck-wet with remorse.

Claire was occasionally suffered to socialise, although there were many fewer visits to Diodati and these not always convivial – Mary describing the 13 August visit in a single word: 'War'. Instead, Byron broke the established pattern by coming down to sit with them at Maison Chappuis, but mostly spent his time with Shelley alone. On 14 August, the tenor of the house changed dramatically, as the first of Byron's London visitors arrived in the form of the writer Matthew Lewis. Lewis had become a publishing sensation in 1795 with his lurid novel *The Monk*, followed with a number of equally successful stage productions, including the outrageously melodramatic *Castle Spectre*, which, sniffed William Wordsworth, pathologically suspicious of success, 'fitted the taste of the audience like a glove'.

Lewis's writing career had recently come to a halt with the death of his father that had put him into possession of several large Jamaican plantations and nearly four hundred slaves. His arrival at Diodati followed a five-month tour of his estates, where he had been so appalled by their treatment that he had returned to Britain committed to collaborating with the abolitionist William Wilberforce. Lewis's first-hand experience of slavery may have been what persuaded Shelley to renounce sugar around this time, rejecting it on the grounds that any commodity produced by means of injustice must be avoided. Although inspired by reform, Lewis remained at heart a green-room *bon viveur*, his presence transforming the atmosphere of Byron's saloon into that of a brandy-soaked gentlemen's club. He was drawn to anyone with a title, and could talk uninterrupted for hours, Shelley recording one performance when he recited poetry and told five ghost stories from a capacious memory that also allowed him to translate Goethe's *Faust* off the cuff. He and Byron argued about almost everything, Byron calling him 'Luigi' and teasing him about his vanity and his undisguised attraction to good-looking young men.

Shortly after Lewis arrived, he and Byron went to visit Ferney, the scrupulously preserved home of Voltaire, where the main attraction was the writer's heart preserved in a box. On their return, Claire was summoned for one final audience, and while it was not the tender parting she might have wished for, she at least extracted a promise that he would write. A few days later, the full transformation of Diodati was accomplished with the arrival of Hobhouse and Scrope Davies. They had landed at Calais, where they paid a call on Scrope's old gambling friend and tsar of the dandies, George 'Beau' Brummell, who had run away to France leaving fifty thousand pounds in debts. They had followed much the same route as Byron, marvelling at much the same scenery, and cursing the criminality of many of the same innkeepers. Hobhouse brought provisions – money, pistol brushes, a sword stick to replace one that Byron had dropped in the lake, tooth powder, magnesia for his stomach, a copy of Pausanias's *Description of Greece* and, somewhat belatedly, condoms.

With Byron's friends assembled, women were excluded from the house, and neither Claire nor Mary set foot in Diodati again. There were also fewer trips on the water, as boating made Hobhouse sick, and while Shelley would go up for dinner, he had little in common with a racecourse Corinthian like Scrope, or a self-approving patrician like Hobhouse, who disliked the young poet from the start, discrediting his influence over Byron and stamping him 'lean and feeble'.

Claire, Shelley and Mary left Geneva on Thursday 29 August after a last-minute farewell from Byron and some parting words from John calculated to put Shelley on edge. William's nursemaid,

Elise, came too, leaving her own family behind to follow them to England. They travelled through France and landed in Portsmouth nine days later, having spent two days in Le Havre waiting for a favourable wind. Claire wrote to Byron from the road, full of regret that their parting had not been easier. 'I should have been happier to have seen and kissed you once before I went,' she wrote, 'it would have made me quite happy but now I feel as if we parted ill friends.'

With Claire gone and surrounded by familiar friends, Byron took stock, unburdening himself in a letter to Augusta in which he disabused her of the salacious rumours about harems of Genevese mistresses that had come her way. 'Lord help me,' he told her, 'I have had but one.'

> Now – don't scold – but what could I do? – A foolish girl – in spite of all I could say or do – would come after me – or rather went before me – for I found her here – and I have had all the plague possible to persuade her to go back again – but at last she went. – Now – dearest – I do most truly tell thee – that I could not help this – that I did all I could to prevent it – and have at last put an end to it. – I am not in love – nor have any love left for any, – but I could not exactly play the Stoic with a woman – who had scrambled eight hundred miles to unphilosophize me – besides I had been regaled of late with so many 'two courses and a *desert*' (Alas!) of aversion – that I was fain to take a little love (if pressed particularly) by way of novelty.

But where Byron acknowledged fleeting pleasure, Claire felt the forging of a bond she would nurture for ever. 'There is nothing in the world I love or care about but yourself,' she told him, as she juddered uncomfortably northwards in Shelley's carriage,

> and though you may love others better there are none
> more faithfully and disinterestedly attached to you than
> myself. My dreadful fear is lest you quite forget me. I
> shall pine through all the wretched winter months while
> you I hope may never have one uneasy thought. One
> thing I do entreat you to remember and beware of any
> excess in wine; my dearest dear friend pray take care
> of yourself . . . I am ashamed to say how much I love
> you for fear of being troublesome and yet I think you
> would be kinder to me if you could but know how
> wretched this going makes me. Sometimes I feel as if
> you were dead and I make no account of Mary and
> Shelley's friendship so much more do I love you . . . I
> am fearful of death yet I do not exaggerate when I
> declare I would die to please or serve you with the
> greatest pleasure nay I should feel as happy in so doing
> as I now feel miserable.

'Farewell then dearest,' she ended, 'I shall love you to the end
of my life and nobody else.'

10

TO DIE OF JOY

John had begun his journal with high hopes of selling it to John Murray, yet he failed to write a single entry from July until September, an omission he ascribed to 'neglect and dissipation'. Somehow he had managed to keep his job in spite of the fights and the threats of suicide, but by the time summer began to fade and he returned to his diary, his situation was hopeless once again.

He had spent the summer trying to distance himself from Diodati, dividing his time between three distinct social circles. The first was Geneva, where he was spending so much time he applied to the police bureau for a *Permission de Séjour* that allowed him to stay in the city without having constantly to show a passport at the gate. Here he socialised with the masculine patriot Rossi, Dr Odier's medical and scientific friends, and made occasional visits to the Genevan Liberal Society, a debating club patronised by mostly British visitors. The speakers included a priest called Evans, who spoke in favour of immortality and against death, and the powerful peer Lord Conyngham, whose wife was just three years away from attaining her decade-long ambition of becoming mistress to the Prince of Wales.

His second refuge was the salon of Madame de Staël, which

met at her estate at Coppet, a one-street town on the north bank of the lake close to Lausanne. De Staël was legendary throughout Europe for her writing, her eloquence and her affairs. Brought up in Paris as the only child of Jacques Necker, a devout Swiss Protestant who rose to become the finance minister of Louis XVI, her fortunes had been linked to those of France. When her father was sacked in 1789, the people rioted in a protest that culminated in the storming of the Bastille, and it was reputed that she was one of the two women Napoleon hated most in the world (the other being his brother Lucien's wife). When in 1803 he forbade her to live within forty leagues of Paris, she began extensive travels across Europe that included considerable time in London and Germany, while producing a series of influential works of fiction and criticism.

At Coppet, de Staël had established one of the most important centres of intellectual exchange in Europe, although Byron found her entourage to be 'a strange sprinkling — orators, dandies, and all kinds of *Blue*, from the regular Grub-street uniform, down to the azure jacket of the "*Literrateur*",' many of whom were old enough to summon the grave. De Staël herself was fifty years old and recently married to a Genevan named Albert Jean de Rocca who was half her age and in poor health due to wounds received in the Peninsular War that refused to heal. Their marriage was supposedly a secret, although everybody had guessed it from their physical intimacy and because she contradicted almost every word he said.

De Staël was one of the few people Byron agreed to see in Geneva, having known her since her residence in London in 1813. When she arrived at Coppet in the second week of July, he paid his respects, taking John along with him. Byron was frustrated with the visit as, on arriving at what he had been told was a small family dinner, he found 'the room full of strangers, who had come to stare at me as at some outlandish beast in a raree-show'. One of the company, Lady Elizabeth Hervey, even contrived to scream and faint as he came in. De Staël, thought by Byron to be one of the most tactless people alive, took the opportunity to lecture him before this audience on his marriage, to which Byron merely replied with a low bow. 'I admire her abilities,' he said of her, 'but really her society is overwhelming – an avalanche that buries one in glittering nonsense – all snow and sophistry.'

John dined with de Staël three times over the summer, in a house which, although large, was comprised of only small rooms filled with books, desks and billiard tables in a permanent state of chaos. He presented her with a copy of his dissertation after she refused to believe he was a physician, and met a circle that included internationally famous figures such as August Wilhelm von Schlegel ('a presumptuous literato'), and Karl Viktor von Bonstetten who had once been *protégé* to the poet Thomas Gray, author of 'Elegy Written in a Country Church-Yard'. Age had caused them all to grow a little forgetful, and even de Staël's fêted eloquence was somewhat ragged, giving her sentences a tendency to stumble into brakes and labyrinths from which she found it difficult to escape. ('This same lady writes octavos, and *talks* folios,' said Byron. 'Her tongue is perpetual motion.') She had grown heedless to convention. During one dinner, her corset burst, leaving a whalebone busk protruding from her chest that refused to return to its place, even with the help of her *valet de chambre*, who at last thrust his hand into her cleavage and pulled it out in full view of the guests. While all the English were convulsed in embarrassed laughter, de Staël remained utterly impassive. John did, however, admire her daughter, Albertine, a soft-eyed dancer of waltzes, whom he described as 'a beautiful, dirty-skinned woman' (Hobhouse preferred the word 'dingy').

Geneva was not all professional debates and improving discussions for John. The greatest portion of his time was spent more pleasurably in the neighbourhood of Genthod, where seven or eight families and their guests met twice a week under the patronage of Countess Bruce, Breuss or even Bryus, a Russian aristocrat who presided at the magnificent Maison d'Abraham Gallatin, an idyllic spot across the lake from Diodati, constructed for all the '*agrémens de la Société*'. Not much is known about the countess, although she was likely the daughter of the Russian courtier Praskovya Rumyantsev, wife of the governor general of Moscow and *femme d'honneur* to Catherine the Great. Her duties included (according to the testimony of Giacomo Casanova) testing the sexual techniques of her mistress's prospective lovers. John's countess shared some of this liberality, as she reportedly had two husbands, one in Russia and another in Venice. She was an elegant woman in her early forties, extremely good-natured and welcoming, laughing all the time and with nothing but good words for her friends. Her household, like de Staël's, boasted several unusual characters, including an attentive Brescian priest and the glassy-eyed Madame Gatelier, whom John described as 'a great lover of medicaments', but the crowd was generally much younger than Coppet's. On summer nights, the garden would be filled with young gentlemen and ladies, enjoying grounds filled with follies and bowers – a towering treehouse wrapped around the trunk of a great chestnut, a Moorish summer house, a Roman bath, a little island surrounded by a moat – all perfect settings for intrigues and banquets. Best of all, the countess loved to lead her friends in dress-up and amateur theatricals, having herself performed at the Hermitage for her mother's patron.

John visited Genthod as often as he could, rowing across in a flat-bottomed boat and staying into the early hours before rowing himself back 'often whilst the storms were raging in the circling summits of the mountains'. He repaid his hostess's hospitality with indiscretions about Byron, sitting at her feet like a favoured pet as he wrote out stories for her amusement. He made another good friend there in a Welshman named Lloyd, and with this companion and the countess's benign protection, he seems to have been able to stand down his constant vigilance against insult, smoothing his furrowed seriousness and acting his age as he played charades and games of forfeit, sang songs, danced pantaloon dances and acted in plays.

Romance thrived in such an environment, and along with his playful flirtation with the countess, John paid court to both Madame Clemann, 'who excites love in every young man's breast', and Mademoiselle Jacquet, with whom he thought he was 'half in love' – or at least with her eight thousand a year – until, that was, 'her face and bad singing . . . cured me'. In the midst of these passing fancies, there was one woman with whom he was genuinely smitten – Madame Brelaz. 'In love with her,' he told his diary, 'I think fond of me too; imprudent.' She was Portuguese, but John records little else, besides the fact that, like the countess and Clemann, she was somewhat older than him and had two pretty daughters close to adult age, neither of whom approved of him. Rivalries were common, and John got into a dispute with Madame Clemann's 'two fools'. He was especially jealous of a handsome Piedmontese officer named Foncet, whose fine embodiment of Italian masculinity bothered him greatly. He also took a strong dislike to Nicolas-Théodore de Saussure, the son of the famous naturalist Horace-Bénédict de Saussure, and a 'would-be scientific gentleman', who, John said, 'thought me a fool because I danced pantaloon and himself a wise man because he knows the names of his father's stones'.

The depth of John's affair with Madame Brelaz is difficult to determine for, although a keen observer of women, his journal shows that whenever he had the chance to interact with them, he became mannered and self-conscious, his feelings mediated by the stiff and scripted language of courtship. It must have been fairly serious, however, as Claire was able to allude to it as a means for getting him out of the way: 'Pray if you can send M. Polidori either to write another dictionary or to the lady he loves,' she wrote to Byron one evening (evidently confusing John with his father, who had published a dictionary). 'I hope this last may be his pillow, and then he will go to sleep; for I cannot come at this hour of the night and be seen by him.' Claire must have known of his affections because John had unwisely confessed them to Byron, who had announced them to the world in a series of jokes at the doctor's expense. Once again, John accused him of bullying and insensitivity. 'I never met a person so unfeeling,' he said. 'Call *me* cold-hearted – *me* insensible!' thundered the 'Lord of Feeling', 'as well might you say that glass is not brittle, which has been cast down a precipice, and lies dashed to pieces at the foot!'

Such antagonism set the real tone for the summer, with literary games and romantic interludes providing only a brief respite from the many moments of rancour and irritability that Diodati bred. Since Byron and Shelley had returned from the lake, John had been responsible for several liberties that had increasingly tried his employer's patience, such as his habit of hiring a carriage at a louis a day and charging it to Byron's account, or taking horses out on his social calls and denying responsibility when Berger accused him of returning them lame. On another occasion, he treated the house as if it were his own, taking it upon himself to invite Pictet and Bonstetten over to dine with Byron, only for Byron to refuse to appear: 'As you asked these guests yourself,' he said, 'you may entertain them yourself.'

Even worse were the flashes of anger that John still struggled to suppress. When thieves targeted the house, trying first to break in and then contenting themselves with stealing Shelley's sails and anchors, John upbraided the authorities so severely that he was forced to appear before the Syndic and apologise in person. On another occasion, while riding with Lloyd, his gig bumped against a horse tethered to a row of carts, causing an argument that resulted in the carter striking him across the back with his whip. John jumped down to retaliate, but was immediately set upon by the carter's six friends. Lloyd joined the fight, and together they were able to repel the carters after John had knocked one to the ground and flattened his nose. The men continued to pelt them with stones until the affray was broken up by a passing carriage of Englishmen. While John might not have started that particular altercation, he was less blameless in mid-August when he went to purchase some magnesia from a local apothecary named Castan. Byron was dependent on magnesia to ease his heartburn, and had been 'in a fuss' about procuring some ever since John's clumsiness had broken their last bottle in Karlsruhe. Castan's magnesia, however, was bad, becoming frothy and rose-coloured when John tested its quality by dissolving it in sulphuric acid. He summoned the apothecary to Diodati to witness the reaction and demanded a refund. Castan refused to see the demonstration or give back the money, at which point John 'collared him', pushing him and breaking his spectacles, after which Castan went outside and 'laid himself on a wall for three hours'. A few days later a 'writ of *arrêt*' arrived that read '"*cassée ses lunettes et fait tomber son chapeau*" of the apothecary'. John chose to defend himself in court in a trial before five judges, where he 'laughed at the advocate' and derided his charge 'of calumny'. The judges were not impressed, but John considered it a victory: 'Gained my cause,' he wrote to William Taylor in Norwich, 'for

I only had to pay enough to buy a pair of spectacles which were broken in the row about 4 shillings.'

The arrival of Hobhouse in August had made John's precarious position even more untenable. Hobhouse had neither time nor sympathy for truculence, and even Shelley, who had written to Byron from Dover, hoped that his presence had 'destroyed whatever scruples you might have felt, in dismissing Polidori. The anecdote which he recounted to me the evening before I left Geneva made my blood run cold.' Sadly, John's words are lost.

Byron had planned another excursion for his friends, going to see for himself the Alps at Chamonix that Shelley had viewed with Mary and Claire. He invited John along, although possibly only as a precaution against having to stop the doctor trying to kill himself again. Nevertheless, John took it as a last opportunity to win Hobhouse's favour and retain his post.

As on his flight from Piccadilly, Byron shared a carriage with Scrope Davies, while John and Hobhouse rode together in a small landaulet ill suited to such difficult roads. Driven by a local butcher, they were almost put down a ravine on the first day. The four men toured many of the same sights Shelley had visited, entering the peaks of the Bernese Oberland and passing in the shadow of Mont Blanc as they wrangled with the same English tourists and the bauble-dealers from whom Byron purchased crystals, necklaces and a granite ball to send home for Ada. Shelley's footprint was also legible at the inns at which they stopped, Byron coming across one of his atheistical entries in the register and thinking to do him a 'service' by carefully scratching it out. Curiously, at the Montenvers hut – which Byron did not visit – it was Claire's name only that had been carefully cancelled.

John tried his hardest to engage Hobhouse at every stage of the journey, pointing out curious geological formations and the 'vertical strata' of the cliffs, and with other conversational gambits clearly designed to assert his credentials as a man of science. Hobhouse, however, remained impassive. Listening to him lecture on the difference between Huttonian and Wernerian theories of geology – ideas that John seems to have picked up from Shelley, who had been studying them – he was signally unimpressed when John 'declared himself for both'. John also provided a lesson on the many goitres that they saw among the population. 'Dr Polidori says they are caused, not by bad water, but by bad air,' wrote Hobhouse, and were 'much more common, for that reason, amongst sedentary females than men who change their atmosphere' – an inaccurate diagnosis, and an unusual one for the mountains.

The trip did nothing to alter Hobhouse's opinion of John, and by the time they returned to Diodati in the first week of September, Byron had been persuaded to let his doctor go. There was 'no great harm of him', he told John Murray, except his 'alacrity of getting into scrapes' and the fact that he was 'too young and heedless'. 'Having enough to attend to in my own concerns,' he told his publisher, 'without time to become his tutor – I thought it much better to give him his Congé.' When he broke the news to John he told him that it was 'not upon any quarrel, but on account of our not suiting', handing him a payment of seventy pounds, fifty for three months' work and twenty for his passage home. John was expecting the news, and was better prepared than he had been in June, his sole retaliation being to miss the boat one afternoon after they had gone into Geneva to look at watches, and forcing them all to wait before they could sit down to dinner. And showing that he clearly understood Hobhouse's role in Byron's decision, he did not forbear to take a small measure of revenge. The next day, when Hobhouse complained of feeling 'an uneasiness in my throat and head', John was happy to give him his professional opinion: 'Polidori says I shall die of apoplexy or pneumony.'

That evening, John composed a mournful letter to William Taylor in Norwich. 'LB's conduct to me has been kind liberal and gentlemanly. Subject to bad temper it is sometimes disagreeable but that is all,' he wrote. 'I do not repent of what I have done,' he said, fearing only that his service under Byron would become an embarrassment, and 'the many who would bait me for years afterwards upon that subject'. Switzerland he described as 'magnificent scenery with petty souls' – 'Everything around me should elevate the souls of the natives liberty such as it is has debased them an attention to petty trifles with a neglect of noble ends.' 'John Bull is not wrong in preferring England,' he concluded, 'liberty only makes them insolent[,] have had more rows than in my life.'

John handed the letter to Scrope Davies, who was due himself to depart on 5 September, running home to reach Newmarket in time for the racing calendar to begin, waved off by Hobhouse who was pleased to say that he had spent six weeks in his company and 'not had even a bickering'. With Scrope went Byron's servant Robert Rushton, who had asked to be allowed to return to Nottinghamshire where he would eventually marry and settle on the Newstead estate. Scrope also bore presents for Ada, and Augusta's children, a fair copy of *Childe Harold* Canto III (made by Mary) to take to Murray, as well as Shelley's notebook containing rough copies of 'Mont Blanc' and 'Hymn to Intellectual Beauty', the two major works he had composed that summer. While Rushton and the gifts were safely delivered home, it is doubtful that John's letter ever reached its destination, for when Scrope arrived he placed his trunk and its contents in a bank vault where it lay undisturbed until 1976.*

On 7 September, John turned twenty-one, but there was no celebration. He remained at Diodati for another week with no idea what to do. He despaired of going back to London to be reliant on a father who would not hesitate to remind him of his faults, and even after Byron had paid him, he had little money, as Hobhouse made him settle his accounts, ensuring that he paid all the debts he owed the household – 'paid away a great deal', John wrote glumly. Caught between penury and disgrace, he made the decision to walk across the Alps to Italy where he would seek out his relatives and tour the medical schools in search of opportunity. On 15 September, Hobhouse bade him farewell. 'He does not answer to Madame de Staël's definition of a happy man, whose capacities are squared with his inclinations,' wrote Hobhouse in his diary. 'Poor fellow!! He is anything but an amiable man, and has a most unmeasured ambition, as well as inordinate vanity. The true ingredients of misery.'

Claire had also urged Byron to eject the doctor. 'I am sure you will be very sorry to hear poor Shelley has had dreadful violent

---

* When later asked about his friend Byron, Scrope would reply that he was 'very agreeable and very clever' but 'vain, overbearing, conceited, suspicious, and jealous . . . and thought the whole world ought to be constantly employed in admiring his poetry and himself; could never write a poem or a drama without making himself its hero, and he was the subject of his own conversation'.

spasms in the head,' she wrote from Britain, 'this all that vile and nauseous animal Polidori's doing – he will do you some mischief so pray send him away and hire a steady clever physician; with your health you must not be without one.'

The circumstances to which Claire had returned were no better than those she had left. Shelley's father continued to wield his estate as a weapon, and Godwin pressured the young man to pay his debts. Personal troubles were mirrored by the consternation of the state. Britain had triumphed over Napoleon only to find itself with an old, blind king, shut up in his palace and raving at his footmen, and a corpulent regent, who indulged himself while his detested first minister Castlereagh put down riots in the north and midlands caused by poor harvests, depressed trade and the high price of bread. Protest was met by repressive policies, most notably the suspension of Habeas Corpus, which gave the government the right to imprison its critics without any evidence of wrongdoing and at risk of entrapment by *agents provocateurs*, who incited illegal activity among working men, then denounced them. The situation would continue to deteriorate, and riots and bloodshed would eventually follow.

After landing at Portsmouth, Shelley went straight to London to deal with his father and an unfolding custody battle with Harriet, delivering Claire's copy of *Childe Harold* Canto III to Murray on the way and sleeping in old lodgings in Marchmont Street with 'no companions but the ghosts of old remembrances'. Mary, William and Elise went with Claire to Bath to find a discreet lodging where Claire might see out her pregnancy away from prying eyes, especially those of the Godwins. As with her time in Lynmouth, Shelley had once again sent Claire to a place associated with his first wife, who had been in Bath when his romance with Mary had first begun.

Life in Bath was dull. Claire and Mary shared lodgings at 5 Abbey Church Yard, a pretty lane in a pretty town, but with no friends near them and no desire to attract attention, they stayed close to their apartments and did little. Mary took drawing lessons and tried to catch up on the Latin she had neglected in Geneva, and became more absorbed in her story. Claire made clothes and played with William, who returned her affection by 'putting his heel with great composure into my eye'. When Shelley arrived in Bath, things became even lonelier for Claire, who was ousted from the lodgings and asked to take a room two minutes' walk away at 12 New Bond Street. Only the thought of Byron eased her isolation. 'I love you more and more every day,' she wrote to him. 'You can't conceive how happy it would make me only just to see your hand writing . . . I am sure I should die of joy.'

As always, the anxieties of Skinner Street found them out. Fanny wrote to inform them that Harriet had been 'very industrious in spreading false reports against you', and to warn them that they should take greater care with their letters, which she suspected were being read by the servants. In this, she was not only trying to mitigate the suffering of the Godwins but also to protect her own future: she had always been considered the obvious heir to the Dublin school run by her aunts, but their attitude to her had decidedly cooled in the midst of family scandal. Fanny, the true orphan of Skinner Street, was also feeling hurt and excluded from her sisters' lives. Mary's letters from Geneva had served only to remind her of the drudgery of her own life, and put her in an ill humour as she imagined Shelley's boat rides with Byron, about whom she asked to know 'the minutest particulars'. She was wounded by Mary's lack of candour; constrained by the secret of Claire's pregnancy, Mary had been unable to explain the real purpose of the residence in Bath. From the other side, Fanny felt undermined by Mrs Godwin, who set her against Mary by telling her that she was a 'laughing stock' and a 'constant beacon of . . . satire' between Mary and Shelley. Fanny scolded her sister for treating them all so unfairly, but Mary simply laid the letter aside, calling it 'stupid'.

Byron was not above spreading rumours of his own. While in London, Shelley had met Douglas Kinnaird, who informed him that Byron had referred to Claire as 'an Atheist and Murderer'. Claire elected to play along. His name was everywhere, and *Glenarvon* proving so popular that it was checked out from every one of Bath's circulating libraries: 'another proof of the delightful taste of the wretched mummies usually distinguished as Men and Women', Claire told him, also passing on the news that Godwin had thought the novel displayed a great deal of talent and 'every word of it true'. It was October by the time she finally read it, after which she wrote to tease him for being such a 'wicked creature to go about seducing and stabbing and rebelling', and informing him that they had started to use his portrait to 'frighten little Will when he is naughty, telling him "the great Poet is coming"'. 'With such a reputation how happy ought you not to be,' she said,

> My dearest Albe might be the most contented of creatures if other's would let him alone. You should have a nice house to live in; my nice little girl (I hope it will be a girl) to educate and all the friends you love best to visit you and we should have nice Poems written by you and copied by me to improve this vile world which always reviles in proportion to its envy.

Claire's daydreams belied the fact that she was struggling. She was feeling 'dull and heavy', suffering from rheumatism and the constant threat of being bled. 'I wonder whether you _ever_ think the least of me,' she asked him. 'I dare say not. I am melancholy and ill-humoured and low spirited.' All she wanted, she said, was

a 'consoling letter' to ease her sadness, and blaming the intermi-
nable delay on the fact that his replies had to come through
Shelley's solicitor. By early October, however, she had begun to
despair of hearing from him. 'We have been gone from Geneva
these six weeks and not one word of news have we of you,' she
wrote,

> You might be ill or you might be dead and I who love
> you as much if not more than any body living am as
> ignorant and neglected by you as if I had never heard
> your name. You treat me dear as if love and affection
> were as easy to be had as pebbles; for you, one species
> I own is; every body thinks you handsome and no woman
> would be so foolish or so stingy to herself to refuse you
> any thing but would they love you as I do through fire
> and water, and scoldings and being sent away and
> absence and contempt, indeed I may say through every
> suffering and wretchedness. And does the recollection
> of such affection give you no pleasure. If any person,
> ugly mean or contemptible were to love me as I do you,
> though I could not return it yet how pleased should I
> be to shew them kindness and satisfaction. The greatest
> misery of this world is to live unloved.

Claire knew what his silence meant for herself, yet feared what it
meant for her unborn child:

> I can not but see that if you have but little care to
> prevent any of my sufferings the chance is very small in
> favour of the affection you may shew the poor little
> Child. This above all makes me the most miserable of
> human Beings: I could take care of my Child myself

and would, but the idea of those poor little helpless
things wanting the cares of a father and being deserted
and becoming unhappy, perhaps as myself makes me
cry from hour to hour.

She would rather be dead, she said, than 'perpetually lamenting
the past and struggling with dread of the future'.

Three days after Claire sent these lines, Shelley received a note
from Fanny that made him bolt up and post immediately for
Bristol. He stayed there for hours looking for her, but returned
at two in the morning after a fruitless search. The next day, they
learned that Fanny had killed herself.

Fanny had left Skinner Street on 7 October under the pretence
of visiting her aunts in Dublin, but had gone instead to Bristol,
where she wrote to Godwin and Shelley informing them of her
intent, before boarding a coach to Swansea, where she took a
room in the Mackworth Arms, composed a note, and drank an
overdose of laudanum. Her body was discovered the following
morning dressed in her mother's stays.

Godwin rushed to Swansea when he heard the news and stayed
a night at Bath, though he refused to visit Mary and insisted on
Shelley's silence. 'Go not to Swansea,' he told him, 'disturb not
the silent dead; do nothing to destroy the obscurity she so much
desired that now rests upon the event.' Unable to deal with the
public repercussions of this latest blow, Godwin let it be known
that Fanny had gone to Dublin as planned, waiting a considerable
time before eventually telling people that she had died of influ-
enza. Not even Charles Clairmont, then travelling in France, was
told. There was no doubt in Godwin's mind where the blame for

her death should lie. 'From the fatal day of Mary's elopement,' he wrote, 'Fanny's mind had been unsettled, her duty kept her with us: but I am afraid her affections were with them.'

The death affected everyone, especially Shelley, who was unable to defray his guilt. He became sick, and each day before eating, weighed his food. Mary buried herself in her story, now four chapters long. Claire felt ever more solitary. 'Though I cannot say,' she wrote to Byron of Fanny, 'I had so great an affection for her.' Claire's anxieties about Byron were growing, exacerbated by a report in *The Times* that he had gone to Albania, which made her worry that he might die without sending her a line. 'I would do any thing, suffer any pain or degradation so I might be so very happy as to receive a letter from you,' she proclaimed to the air. 'Write me a nice letter beginning not those scanty words "dear Clare" but "My dearest Clare", and tell me that you like me that you will be very pleased to have a little baby of which you will take great care. Make as many jokes on me as you will dearest I shall be so happy to receive any thing from you.'

Nothing came, and Mary and Shelley both tried to disabuse her of her fantasies, telling her to expect nothing from Byron. Her fretfulness was wearing on them all, so much so that Shelley even wrote to Byron himself asking him to 'send me some kind message to her, which I will, to give suspicion his due, throw into the fire as a sacrifice'. Claire resented their intrusion deeply, calling Mary 'impertinent and nauseous', while Mary again began to imagine a life without her. 'A house with a lawn a river or lake – noble trees and divine mountains that should be our little mousehole to retire to,' she told Shelley. 'But never mind this – give me a garden and absentia Clariæ and I will thank my love for many favours.' Concerned, perhaps, that Claire would uncover these secrets in her journal, she began to pepper its pages with ciphers, representing her step-sister as a crescent moon.

On 19 November, a letter finally arrived from Italy, but there was no comfort to be had from it. Byron, addressing Shelley, made it clear that he had no intention of ever writing to Claire again, a letter Shelley allowed her to read as a means of confronting the truth. 'My hopes are therefore over,' said Claire. Shelley immediately regretted what he'd done.

With Fanny's death and Claire's abandonment by Byron, a funereal mood descended on Bath, yet worse was still to come. Barely a month after Fanny's suicide, Harriet Shelley, heavily pregnant, told her sister that 'I don't think I am made to inspire love', and disappeared. Fearing the worst, her family asked to have the local ponds dragged, but found nothing, until on 10 December her body was discovered floating in Hyde Park's Serpentine river. Harriet's life had unravelled steadily since Shelley had left her, with Shelley telling Mary that she had been 'driven from her father's house, and descended the steps of prostitution until she lived with a groom of the name of Smith, who deserting her, she killed herself'. No evidence supports this claim, and neither did Shelley propose his theory to anyone else but Mary. The father of Harriet's unborn child remains a mystery, and may even have been Shelley himself. 'My dear Bysshe,' her purported suicide note had read, 'I could never refuse you and if you had never left me I might have lived.' Fanny had been only twenty-two when she died. Harriet was twenty-one.

11

THE HERO OF MILAN

John left Villa Diodati at six in the morning on 16 September, carrying nothing but a clean shirt, a notebook and three letters of introduction from Madame de Staël. Intending to walk across the Alps to Milan, he struck out along the south shore of Lac Léman, heading for Montreux, into a landscape of deep precipices and rushing torrents, dark forests and glacial peaks. A dog trotted beside him that he had picked up somewhere but failed to name. The day before, he had arranged to have his baggage sent ahead and purchased a new pair of shoes at Mr Brightstone's, before rowing over to Genthod for a final night of summer theatricals. There, he kissed the hand of Countess Breuss and was gratified to see tears welling in the eyes of Madame Brelaz. Rowing back towards Diodati, he watched the lights of the Maison d'Abraham Gallatin grow dim for the last time. 'Wished nobody good-bye,' he wrote.

Fortified by his surroundings and the heroism of wild, romantic solitude, John covered ninety miles in the first three days, hiking through valleys and up steep inclines on rock-strewn paths, passing through tiny hamlets 'without a visible soul'. On the fourth day, he slowed. The new shoes had rubbed a deep cut in his left heel, and when his dog started vomiting, the thought that it might have been poisoned reduced him to tears. Overcome by loneliness, he attached himself to two Englishman at Interlaken but, believing himself to be in their way, soon made his excuses and left after a single day. On the road between Interlaken and Grindelwald, he passed Byron and Hobhouse, making a final Swiss excursion of their own. 'We saluted,' said John, although neither Byron nor Hobhouse mentioned the meeting in their own journals. It was an awkward reminder of his humiliation, feelings he recorded in a poem he composed on the dreary, ice-clad Grimsel, giving vent to the bitterness he felt towards those 'tormenting fiend-like sprites' that continued to taunt him with the desire for fame. 'The best advice to authors,' Samuel Johnson had written in his *Lives of the Poets*, would be, 'that they should keep out of the way of one another.'

It took John some time to summon the will to inform his father of what had passed between himself and Byron, and when he did, he merely told him that they had 'parted, finding that our tempers did not agree'. There was no cause, he said, beyond a 'continued series of slight quarrels' and his own ill-suitedness to service. 'I am not accustomed to have a master,' he wrote, 'and therefore my conduct was not free and easy.' It was his intention, he said, to find a job in Italy, perhaps making use of Madame de Staël's letter of introduction to the English traveller Lady Westmorland, then resident in Rome. It was speculative at best, but at least it was an excuse not to go home – 'For assure yourself,' he told his father, 'I will do all I can not to allow you to feel any inconvenience on my account.'

With fresh shoes and an apostolic staff, he pressed on, although the pain in his foot soon forced him to ride a mule. At Brig he met the Simplon Pass, the Napoleonic marvel that had taken a narrow path and carved it into a modern highway, cutting an artery through the mountains wide enough for four carriages to travel abreast. This miracle of engineering passed over some of the highest altitudes of the Alps while still maintaining a gradient that was never more than six inches in every six feet, making it, in the words of one traveller, 'as smooth as the walk of a garden'. Twenty-two wooden bridges and seven 'galleries' – open-sided tunnels that protected travellers from avalanches – connected Paris and Milan. For John, it was the realisation of a childhood dream. The border, however, was unmarked, and he had no idea he had even set foot in Italy until he spoke to a boy in German and was answered in Italian. He could have hugged the child he was so happy, and the fine blue sky and rich green countryside that greeted him as he began his descent were enough to make him forgive even the dirtiness of the inn in which he spent the night, 'where the grease might be scraped from the floor'.

Despite his joy at having arrived, it paid to be cautious in these borderlands, where bandits in the foothills between Varese and Milan were said to number fifteen hundred. By now he had been walking for twelve days with feet so painful that it now took him five hours to go a mere six miles, and having heard that a train of English carriages had been stopped by a gun-wielding gang of 'not gallant cavaliers', he decided to make the rest of the journey by haycart and barge. Floating through the rice fields that surrounded the city on one of three navigable canals, John entered Milan on 1 October.

Milan was a large city by Italian standards, home to approximately 130,000 people among the half-built marble columns and triumphal arches left by the retreating Napoleonic armies. John and his dog enjoyed it immensely, exploring its narrow backstreets with strips of raised parallel flagstones for the carriages to run along, strolling beside the fashionable promenaders along the Corso di Orientali and its adjacent garden, and browsing in its well-stocked bookshops. But what really made John feel as if his fortunes had changed was the welcome he received from Ludovico di Breme, a friend of Madame de Staël whom he had met briefly at Coppet that summer.

Breme, a Piedmontese, was the ex-almoner to Napoleon's brother-in-law, Eugène Beauharnais, even though he was only thirty years old and did not believe in God. Since ending his affiliation with the Church, Breme had become deeply involved in writing and politics, becoming a prominent ally of the leading Italian nationalist-in-exile, Ugo Foscolo, and a member of the Società Romantica, the literary wing of Italian liberalism. Both placed him dangerously at odds with the state, for even though Bonaparte was safely imprisoned on St Helena, Milan remained a city under foreign occupation. Restored to the kingdom of Lombardy-Venetia by the Congress of Vienna, it had become a possession of Hapsburg Austria and its universally unpopular monarch, Archduke Rainier, whose large empire was overseen by a class of German-speaking bureaucrats who believed that the religious, moral, and intellectual lives of the diverse peoples they governed were best administered by police and censorship offices called *Revisionsämter*. Under an expansive system of surveillance and espionage, political discussion was banned, Italian poetry suppressed (most notably that of Alfieri), and literary salons like Breme's were closely scrutinised by policemen who filed reports that described them as existing 'for the purpose of educating its members in the belief that man is subject to no religious or moral principle, but ought only to obey his natural instincts'. Liberals despised life in such a despotic state, which pandered slavishly to the hierarchies of birth while opposing virulently careers built on talent, and was so paranoid that even its tax code was secret.

Convinced that only hypocrites and imbeciles could thrive in such a place, one of Breme's friends had produced a series of guidelines for those wishing to escape the attentions of the Austrian police:

1. Must go to Mass every day, and take as his father confessor an intelligent priest devoted to the cause of Monarchy, and in the confessional avow to him only the most irreproachable sentiments.
2. Be certain to frequent no person reputed to be intelligent, and on every occasion to speak of rebellion with horror, as a thing never to be countenanced.
3. Never allow himself to be seen at the café, never read any papers but the official gazettes of Turin and Milan; and in general betray a certain dislike of reading, and above all never read any work printed after 1720 except, if need be, the novels of Walter Scott.
4. Finally . . . he must pay the most observable court to some one of the attractive women of the community, of the noble class naturally; this would show that he does not possess the grim and malcontent spirit of a nascent conspirator.

Breme greeted John as a long-lost friend, inviting him to Casa Roma, the large *palazzo* he shared with his brother, and saluting him 'with two kisses and apparent joy'. John became a regular visitor, teaching Breme English in return for help with the Italian translation of his play 'Count Orlando', the drama he had been nursing since the age of eighteen. He found his host to be studious, disciplined, charitable and, above all, a principled 'hater of all Austrians'. He was also extremely dashing, and shared John's amatory enthusiasms, telling him that that he found English women the most beautiful of all.* John adored him. 'His friendship,' he wrote, 'gratifies me more than any attentions, friendship, or any relations I had before, with my fellow companions.'

At seven each evening in Milan's La Scala opera house, Breme met a large group of friends to discuss literature, politics, and the condition of Italy. The opera was so central to Milanese social life that people rarely went anywhere else. Although three thousand people could fit into this lush and gilded space, it had the ambience of a drawing room, with patrons becoming so attached to their boxes that they spent lavishly to decorate them and fit them out with chandeliers and card tables so they could read or play, and curtains that could be drawn on occasions that required more privacy. The first two circles of boxes were generally occupied by polite society, who moved from box to box throughout the performance to make calls on one another, even unattended ladies, who moved about freely 'without the slightest chance of receiving an insult'. The next two circles were less respectable, and generally set aside for young men and intrigues. The fifth was known for sexual liaisons and the sixth *loggione*, the most boisterous, was open to anyone. At the back of the pit an enormous foyer was fitted out with gaming tables, and occupied by men doing business or loudly discussing the news, while ladies promenaded behind them. Indeed, the seats near the front of the orchestra were the only place that anybody paid attention to the stage, and performances were almost an afterthought, with the same opera shown every night except Fridays. Even so, what scant attention John paid to the performances, he still thought them the greatest he had ever seen.

Breme's circle included, among others, his brother, the marquis;

---

* Hobhouse described Breme as 'one of the most attractive men I ever saw', at least until he had fallen out with him, after which he would deride him as a 'masturbator'.

the elderly poet Vincento Monti, once acclaimed as the successor
to Dante; the author and translator Pietro Borsieri; and the whisk-
ered Marie-Henri Beyle, a self-exiled Frenchman who would
become better known by his penname, Stendhal. The group was
friendly, informal, often contentious and unashamedly gossipy.
One minute Breme would be reciting Alfieri and praising him to
the heavens, while the next he would be discussing the minutiae
of Madame de Staël's domestic affairs, and cursing the detested
Schlegel for leeching thirty-six thousand francs from her each
year. The aged and affable Monti was tolerated but not to be
trusted: he had lost all credibility over a long career filled with
Janus-like transformations, first declaiming against the Austrians
for making Italians 'the vilest slaves of Europe', then censoring
the Italians in case their talk might affect the pension he received
from the archduke. Beyle, 'a fat lascivious man', according to
John, had been a secretary to Napoleon during the Russian
campaign, and remained an ardent lover of his former master,
whom he immortalised in a series of detailed anecdotes about
his generalship, his sexual dealings, and how long he liked to
scrape his tongue in the morning. John was not sure what to
make of Beyle, but was nonetheless happy to trade some anecdotes
of his own, entertaining his new friend by freely confiding Byron's
work habits, his drinking, his diets, and the tendency of his body
to emulate that of his short, fat mother. Beyle in turn thought
John extremely handsome and was certain that he had made the
poet 'an excellent pimp'.

As if summoned by an incantation, Byron and Hobhouse appeared
in Milan on 12 October. The former had left Diodati for good,
telling his friend Tom Moore that he had been 'half mad' while

living there, 'between metaphysics, mountains, lakes, love unex-tinguishable, thoughts unutterable, and the nightmare of my own delinquencies'. He would have 'blown my brains out,' he said, 'but for the recollection that it would have given pleasure to my mother-in-law'.

Byron had also met Breme at Coppet, and it was only natural that he should enter his circle at La Scala. As always, his fame preceded him as both barrier and spectacle, his presence making everyone turn 'solemn and awkward', as they found him polite but guarded, and with the 'air of a man who finds he has to repulse an intrusion'. His brilliance charmed them, but his behaviour could be odd. He once left the box in a rage after the conversation lit on the case of a prince who had murdered his lover in cold blood – leaving the company wondering if they had sailed a little too close to the wind. Meanwhile, young women flooded into the theatre supposedly having travelled hundreds of miles to catch a glimpse of him. Beyle, who was by his own admission 'mad' about Byron's works, was moved almost to the point of tears on meeting him. As the only one among Breme's Romantici who spoke any English, he acted as his translator only to find his idol a strange mixture of poetical feeling and aristocratic vanity, as if he were so used to being looked at that he had never learned how to observe. When Byron began to complain to the Frenchman of the bitter persecutions he had endured at the hands of his countrymen, Beyle suggested that he fake his own death by interring a log and retiring to the isle of Elba or travelling the world in disguise. Byron, who had once remarked that Napoleon's biggest mistake was not killing himself and leaving 'the stage like a hero', responded with a caustic look. 'My cousin, who is heir to my title,' he told Beyle, 'owes you an infinity of thanks.' Still, the Frenchman felt sorry for the many libels his hero had been forced to endure. 'In the 19th Century,' he wrote, 'there is but one alternative, to be a <u>blockhead</u> or a <u>monster</u>.'

Byron's arrival did not unsettle John, who was secure in his new social standing as an Italian patriot. Neither was he too put out when he ran into Lloyd, the Welsh friend he had made at Genthod, who told him that Madame Brelaz was receiving the attentions of a young man named Bertolini, who, he said, 'seemed worked off his legs'. John not only shrugged it off, he was the happiest and most relaxed he had ever been, settling into a pleasant and methodical routine: he rose early and went to the hospital to study with a doctor named Locatelli, who placed a female hysteric under his care, and introduced him to a variety of interesting cases, including a rare case of pemphigus, or life-threatening blisters. In the afternoons he and Breme exchanged English and Italian, and in the evenings went together to the opera house.

Before long, the severance pay he had received from Byron was gone, spent on living comfortably and a haul of almost three hundred books, most of them by Latin authors according to the list he made on the back of his passport. Despite Lloyd's generous offer to lend him half his purse, the need for employment again reared its head. At Breme's suggestion, he considered teaching English, although the thought of emulating his father put him off, and he preferred to stay in medicine. One possibility was entering the service of Princess Caroline of Brunswick, the disgraced Princess of Wales, who was currently living on the banks of Lake Como under the watchful eye of British agents and the Milanese police. Having been ill-treated by her husband for almost twenty years, Caroline had fled to the Continent when he became regent, running a house that, according to English scandalmongers, was a court of debauchery overrun with dubious foreigners, the most prominent of whom was the strapping Bartolomeo Bergami, a *faux*-baron on whom she was said to lavish much attention. When not hosting orgies or crowning donkeys with rose diadems, said the numerous spies who clipped her hedges and hovered in her doorways, she ate beefsteaks and drank porter like a man.

A less lurid interpretation of the princess's Milanese household suggests a sportive estate in the manner of the Countess Breuss's house at Genthod, a carefree place where minor European aristocrats might come to play billiards, perform amateur theatricals and mess around in boats. In this respect, a position there would have suited John immensely, especially since his good looks would have been a useful asset in winning the princess's patronage. Hobhouse obliged him with a reference, but even with Caroline's notoriety in mind, he still felt that it was the princess who was in for the harder time. 'This night wrote a letter for Polidori,' he told his journal, 'who is going to try to make himself physician to the Princess of Wales – poor thing, she must be mad.'

Due to the hostile atmosphere surrounding the princess, her estate was forbidden to the English, and when John went to drop off his letter of introduction, he found himself barred by her current physician, Dr Mochetti, and Baron Bergami, flanked by two Austrian grenadiers. There was a discussion, 'all very civil', during which John plainly told Mochetti he was after his job. It came to nothing, and now all John's hopes rested on the answer of Lady Westmorland, still believed to be resident in Rome.

Some time in mid-October, a letter arrived from Gaetano, responding to his son's news. 'Your letter produced in me a twofold and opposite sensation,' he said,

> gratification at your having quitted a man so discredited in public opinion, and sorrow at seeing you almost a vagrant, and at the uncertainty as to your lot . . . I hope

however that mishaps, if this can be called one, will open your eyes, and that you will recognise the error of following overmuch the dictates of a warm fancy. I recommend you to be at least cautious in your travels.

Gaetano had heard rumours of a fight with an apothecary and demanded to be informed 'minutely as to this affair'. 'Look to your security in roaming here and there,' he counselled his son, 'and always remember that hint which a Sienese gave to Milton . . . "open countenance and close thoughts".'

It was practical advice for a city like Milan, but unfortunately advice that John was unable to heed. On 28 October, while watching the ballet from the pit of La Scala with Hobhouse, John ran into Pietro Borsieri, with whom he began to complain loudly about the presence of so many Austrian soldiers in the house. When an Austrian grenadier then came and stood directly in front of him, obscuring his view, John said, clearly enough for everyone to hear, 'Look at that man, with his cap on his head,' before tapping his shoulder and asking him to remove it.

'Would you wish for it?' the guardsman answered abruptly.

'Yes, I wish it,' replied John, matching his tone.

The Austrian, who turned out to be the captain on duty, asked John to accompany him outside the auditorium.

'Yes, with pleasure,' said John, and thinking he was about to be challenged to a duel, asked Hobhouse to act as his second. But instead of going out onto the street, the soldier stopped at the theatre's guardroom and ordered John to go in. He refused, at which point the captain drew his sabre until Hobhouse intervened and urged John to submit to custody, while the captain harangued him in 'Billingsgate German' and John roared back that he was every bit his equal. 'Equal to me?' replied the guardsman. 'You are not equal to the last of the Austrian soldiers in the house.'

As this was unfolding, Byron was sitting in Breme's box 'quietly staring at the ballet' until the poet Silvio Pellico entered in a hurry and, breathing heavily, asked for his help downstairs. On entering the guardroom, Byron found it filled with fifteen to twenty of Breme's friends, all demanding the release of John Polidori who sat 'begirt with grenadiers', amid 'much swearing in several languages', 'beside himself with passion', his face 'as red as a burning coal'. Byron too became angry, his face turning ashen when it became clear that the Austrians were unimpressed by his name. The captain had grown increasingly agitated at the number of people in the room, and called for his men to grab their weapons until the venerable Monti at last managed to calm the situation by suggesting that everyone depart, save those with aristocratic titles, leaving only Byron and Breme's brother, the marquis. With the two sides finally able to hear each other, the captain accepted Byron's card as bail for John on condition that the young man would answer for his conduct in the morning.

As promised, a printed order to report to the police arrived for John the following day, but when he presented himself at the police headquarters in the Via Santa Margherita, he was asked only where he would like a visa for.

'I am not thinking of going,' he told the officer.

'You must be off in four-and-twenty hours for Florence,' he was told. 'You must be off in that time, or you will have something disagreeable happen to you.'

Outraged at this sentence, Breme set out to speak with General Bubna, commandant of the Milanese police, only to be told that the matter had been settled much higher up. John called on Byron, who in turn dispatched Hobhouse to Franz Josef Saurau, the governor of Milan, who received him courteously and edged him closer to the door with each smiling compliment and friendly assurance that the matter was a 'bagatelle' until Hobhouse was finally out in the hallway. It was naïve perhaps to seek mercy from Saurau, whom John had witnessed enter the box of a man in La Scala and publicly slap him for refusing to remove his hat in the presence of the archduke.

There were those who wanted to press the issue, but neither Byron nor Hobhouse was among them, Byron even making sure to write a number of letters home to explain the incident in case 'by some kind mistake – his squabbles may be set down to me'. Both he and Hobhouse thought John 'exceedingly in the wrong' – yet another example of 'having begun a row for row's sake', said Byron, his sentiment echoed by Hobhouse, who told Scrope that 'the truth is, the delinquent wished to shew off before some Italian acquaintance'. Hobhouse even suspected that the police had long marked him down for deportation, and 'could not help thinking,' he wrote, 'that Polidori must have been talking foolishly in public somewhere'. 'I was never more disgusted with any human production,' Byron wrote to Murray, 'than with his eternal nonsense – and tracasseries – and emptiness – and ill humour – and vanity of that young person.'

John received his judgment 'foaming with rage' and swearing that 'he would one day return and bestow manual castigation on the governor who had treated him with so little respect' – although for now he could do nothing but stuff a clean shirt into his pocket and whistle to his dog. This second expulsion was even more bitter than the first, and taking his leave of Breme, he fell into his arms and wept like a child.

It was only a matter of time before John would be compelled to return to England, yet still he tried to resist it. With no clear sense of where to go, he set out for Florence, spending the entire first day of the journey so eaten with anger against Saurau and the Austrian captain that he frequently burst into tears and could think of nothing but bloody revenge. After eight days' walking with only five napoleons in his pocket, he arrived in the Tuscan capital and took shelter with an old friend of his father, the Cavalier Pontelli, who was happy to take him in so long as the young man agreed to strange house rules seemingly devised for the purpose of keeping him away from his young housekeeper, 'though she is hardly worth it', wrote John, as he was ushered out for dinner, or up to bed at six o'clock. While in Florence, he visited the tomb of Alfieri and paid court to his widowed mistress, the Countess of Albany, she who had so admired the roundness of his father's thighs. The old countess commented favourably on John's resemblance to Gaetano, and invited him to join the company in her parlour where the conversation soon turned to the virtues of republicanism over monarchy. John defended them warmly against the arguments of an old gentleman sitting next to him, whom he later discovered to be brother to the King of Prussia.

A week later, he moved on to Arezzo, walking forty-five miles in twelve hours, through thunder and lightning, where he lost his dog but found his Uncle Luigi, a tall, mild-looking man, and a successful physician decorated by the Tuscan government for his advances in the treatment of typhus, a disease particularly rampant in the marches of northern Italy. Here John enjoyed a quiet reprieve, playing cards with his cousins, seeing the sights, and being happily reunited with his dog, which appeared one day outside the Chapel of St Mary, as if waiting for him.

At his uncle's prompting, John wrote to his father for the first time in two months, studiously avoiding any reference to the tumult in Milan, and saying only that he was waiting on word from Lady Westmorland before deciding whether or not to meet her in Rome or return directly to London. His uncle added some observations of his own, telling Gaetano that he was certain John would 'secure honour and fortune in that part of the world where good qualities count for something', adding that 'I got indignant at some mention of the perversities of the nobleman he was travelling with; but he maintained much calmness – I envy him that. These people are all harsh.' At the end of the week, John refused his uncle's offer of money, as to do so would have revealed the extent of his need. By now he had only half a *scudo*. The wound in his foot had reopened, and his dog had gone missing again, this time for good.

John's next stop was Pisa, where he paid his respects to Andrea Vaccà Berlinghieri, 'the first surgeon in Italy'. Vaccà was another school friend of his father, and one of the most highly regarded men of his profession, writing and teaching through an endowed chair at the University of Pisa, and doing charitable work among the poor. Things began to improve: Vaccà invited John to share his table in the company of his beautiful wife, Sofia, 'queen of the Pisan salons', and to become his pupil, attending him at the hospital, conducting research in his library, consulting with his patients, and compiling a journal of his observations. For the first time in his life, John took pleasure in the study of medicine, all thanks to his new patron whom he considered 'more usefull than a book to me'. And through Vaccà's contacts in Pisa's English colony, John was even able to take on some paying patients, including Lord Guilford, the Whig politician Francis Horner, and the family of the novelist Thomas Hope. Whether it was through an absence of skill or sheer bad luck, however, none of them lasted long. Lord Guilford died first, falling to chronic alcoholism and such tumorous guts that John had to remove his intestines and embalm the body before it could be sent back to Britain for burial. In February 1817,

Francis Horner succumbed to a heart condition, followed shortly afterwards by Thomas Hope's young son, who died of scarlet fever.

Despondent at the loss of his patients, John became doubly miserable when twenty-five pounds arrived from Gaetano to pay for his passage home. Lloyd suggested that he try moving back to Florence and ministering to the English there, but with no letters of introduction, John saw few prospects beyond the Countess of Albany, who already retained a French physician to specialise in what he called her 'Cytherean complaints'. Vaccà, however, proposed an alternative. He had a friend named Olindo Giusto, who had recently been appointed Danish general consul to Brazil because he had married the daughter of Denmark's first minister. Giusto was due to take up his post in the coming summer, and Vaccà had recommended that John go with him to establish a practice there, thereby guaranteeing a monopoly on all the Danish and possibly even English patients in Brazil. Giusto himself was keen on the idea, but, as with his uncle's offer of India and his Edinburgh landlady's support for doctoring in the colonies, John saw only impediments, considering the scheme 'absurd' without the two or three hundred pounds he felt he would need to set himself up.

On the day Lord Guilford died, John wrote to Byron, who had at last set up home in his longed-for Venice, to explain his predicament. 'This is so much,' he told him, 'that I fear I shall have to struggle it out without hope in Europe.' It was the first time he had contacted the poet since the fracas in Milan, yet only six days later, he wrote to him again, explaining that he was determined to emigrate to Brazil, and asking for his support. The first thing he needed was a reference, 'some means of getting recommended to some one of the English who have influence at the Portuguese court', but he also hoped that Byron would intercede with John

Murray. 'I have arranged the observations I made upon different subjects in Italy,' he wrote,

> but especially medicine and surgery into the shape of a journal and I think I have got some interesting information upon the state of these two last sciences and I have at least in my own eye set it upon papers in if not an accurate at least a clear style. Might I ask your Lordship to recommend it to Murray? I have also a play . . . but I fear at this you will be more inclined to laugh than any thing else but as I wish to go to the Bresil and I do not think my father will help me might I ask your Lordship to read and judge it.

Byron did not read the play, but otherwise did as he was asked, prodding Murray to recommend the young doctor on four separate occasions, and asking him, as publisher of *The Navy List*, to use his contacts in the Admiralty as a means of setting John up. While Byron neither promised nor offered any direct help of his own, his attitude towards his ex-employee in these letters showed real benevolence: 'I know no great harm of him – and some good,' he told his publisher,

> he is clever – and accomplished – knows his profession by all accounts well – and is honourable in his dealings – and not at all malevolent. – I think with luck he will turn out a useful member of society (from which he will lop the diseased members) and the college of Physicians. – If you can be of any use to him – or know any one who can – pray be so – as he has his fortune to make.

He also pressed Murray to consider John's Pisan journal, adding that 'He has also a tragedy – of which having seen nothing I say nothing – but the very circumstance of his having made these efforts (if they are only efforts) at one and twenty – is in his favour and proves him to have good dispositions for his own improvement.' In another letter, his request was more succinct: 'If you can help him to a publisher do – or, if you have any sick relation – I would advise his advice – all the patients he had in Italy are dead.'

Having secured Byron's help, John's plans for emigration were suddenly put aside as he finally heard from Lady Westmorland and travelled to Rome to meet her. She enjoyed her liberty, having separated from her much older husband in 1811 and, though fifteen years John's senior, was known to favour handsome young men. Also, as the daughter of a doctor, she looked kindly on physicians. It was she who had first introduced Byron to Caroline Lamb, and though Byron disliked her immensely for having taken Caroline's side in their scrappy parting, he still considered this an ideal position for John: 'I think he would suit her,' he told Murray, 'he is a very well looking man.' He suggested to Hobhouse that John might be on the verge of securing his fortune, the key to which lay in his handling of 'Lady W's Clitoris, which is supposed to be of the longest', and ability to talk her into a quick marriage, 'if only to fill up the gap which he has already made in the population'.

In spite of Byron's hopes, Lady Westmorland's household did not prove a good fit for John, and he stayed with her for only a few weeks before arriving in Venice on 10 April 1817 in the entourage of the new Lord Guilford. This was another of Byron's enemies, a 'despicable old Ox and Charlatan' and, most unforgivably from Byron's perspective, a 'perambulating humbugger' – a homosexual insufficiently ashamed of himself to conceal his tastes from public view. The party was bound for London, where John hoped to revive his emigration plan and rendezvous with Giusto before committing to Brazil. For the three days he remained in Italy, he called at Byron's *palazzo* every day, even coaxing him out to tour the Manfrini Palace. 'The Doctor Polidori is here,' Byron told Scrope, 'on his way to England with the present Lord Guilford – having actually embowelled the last at Pisa and spiced and pickled him for his rancid ancestors.' Despite the joke, Byron was happy to report that he found him much improved in the six months since he had seen him in a Milanese guardroom, if not a little full of himself due to the high society he had been keeping. He was also rather too free in transmitting all the gossip he had heard about Byron as he passed through the expatriate communities of Florence and Rome, all of it similar, if not worse, than that which had dogged him at Geneva. 'It is very odd that they will not let me alone,' complained Byron to his friend. 'I make love but with one woman at a time and as quietly as possible.' To amuse him, Byron also included an account of John's Pisan career in the form of a military dispatch:

> The said Doctor has had several invalids under his proscription – but has now no more patients – because his patients are no more – the following is the Gazette extraordinary according to his last *dispatches* –

> Ld. Guildford – killed – inflammation of the bowels –
> Mr Horner – killed – diseased lungs –
> Mr Ts Hope's son – killed – Scarlet fever

> Rank and file – killed – 45 paupers of Pisa – wounded and missing (the last supposed to be dissected) 18 in the hospitals of that city. –

Wounded

Lady Westmorland – incurable – her disease not defined. But the Doctor himself is alive and well and still bent upon the Brazils – Frederic North that was and the disconsolate widow of his embalmed brother – have bodkined him homewards.

John set sail for Britain on 14 April 1817, having been abroad nine days shy of a year, during which time he had attempted suicide, been arraigned for assault, traversed the Alps on foot, threatened to kill Shelley, and been sacked by the only paying patient who hadn't died. The bourgeois pedestrianism of Great Pulteney Street he found on his return was unbearable, and with his sister Frances working as a governess in Surrey, Margaret living with a family in Gloucester, and his brothers Robert and Henry away at Ampleforth, he was alone with his parents and two young sisters he hardly knew – Charlotte, fifteen, and seven-year-old Eliza. Gaetano refused to aid his Brazilian plan, so he sent a long, complaining letter to John Taylor, receiving in reply the news that Norwich might soon have room for a new physician thanks to the current doctor, Dr Wright, having recently come into a large fortune. With that in mind, Taylor suggested that John bring as many letters of recommendation as he could muster and take lodgings in Norwich so as to be on the spot the moment Wright announced his retirement.

John decamped at once, but Dr Wright remained obstinately in post. Refusing to be idle, John made every effort to re-create his Pisan routine in Norfolk, spending mornings at the hospital, and settling into a life of study, writing and socialising as he eased back into Taylor's circle, becoming once again an object of fascination for many young ladies. These included Harriet Martineau and her sisters, who 'romanced amazingly about him – dreamed of him [and] listened to all his remarkable stories'. He opened a small dispensary by public subscription that gave medical advice to the needy, and endeavoured to knit himself closer to the local professions by joining a lodge of Freemasons and cultivating the patronage of prominent members of the Catholic gentry. Chief among these were the family of Sir George Jerningham, who resided at Costessey Hall, a large estate set in sweeping lawns bisected by the river Wensum. Costessey was a Gothic collision of manor and ruin, much of it designed by Sir George's uncle, the poet Edward Jerningham, who had looked to his friend Horace Walpole's Strawberry Hill for inspiration. Sir Edward was now deceased, to the relief of his devout family who were scandalised by his rejection of Catholicism in favour of the heresies of Voltaire and Rousseau, as well as his flamboyant enthusiasm for opera and literary salons, at which he could often be found in a pink coat, plastered in rouge and plucking a harp.

The Jerninghams were yet another surrogate family, and while they did little to advance John's career, he spent a great deal of time with them, enjoying the aristocratic comforts of Costessey, and the hospitality of Lady Jerningham, an attractive, motherly figure of whom he became exceptionally fond. There were other reasons to linger, such as the opportunity to informally tutor the Jerninghams' eldest daughter, Charlotte, in Italian, and setting her up in a correspondence course with Gaetano. Charlotte, like John's sister of the same name, was fifteen years old and, by all accounts, accomplished and pretty, which led to the inevitable rumours that the doctor had fallen in love. Whether they were true or not, he reported being always 'blissfully happy' whenever he was near her, penning a number of love poems in which the name of the beloved appears as a tantalising three-syllable blank. Not 'Charlotte', certainly, but 'Carlotta' perhaps?

This moment of happiness, too, was about to end abruptly. On the night of 20 September, while driving his gig through the grounds, John lost control behind another carriage, left the road and hit a tree with such force that it broke the chassis. The impact threw him from his seat, and his landing dealt a violent blow to the head. Help came quickly, but he was unable to move his limbs and kept slipping out of consciousness. Carried back to the house, he lay insensible for four or five days, nursed by Charlotte and Lady Jerningham, who stood over him in prayers led by the estate's chaplain, Mr Jones. It seemed certain he would die. Gaetano was summoned from London to be at his son's bedside.

After a couple of difficult weeks, the prognosis was modified to severe concussion, as John slowly regained movement and lucidity. 'They are almost all astonished to hear that you are rapidly progressing in convalescence,' wrote Gaetano, of his friends in London, 'as they had given you up for dead. For me, I seem to be dreaming when I think that you are alive and well: but this is a happy dream, and I thank Heaven for it with all my heart and all my soul.' Looking back, there would be those such as Harriet Martineau who saw it differently. 'If he had (happily) died then,' she wrote, 'he would have remained a hero.'

12

HOUSEHOLD GODS

At four in the morning on 12 January 1817 Claire gave birth to a baby girl. She named her 'Alba' – an echo of 'Albé', but also Italian and Spanish for 'dawn'. She was the embodiment of summer, 'pretty eyes of a deep dazzling blue,' said Claire, 'more like the colours of the waters of the lake of Geneva under a summer sky than any thing else I ever saw, rosy projecting lips and a little square chin divided in the middle'. She looked exactly like her father.

Both Mary and Shelley wrote to tell him the news, but received no reply. His silence had been broken only once since their departure from Diodati, but still Claire refused to believe that she had been abandoned, insisting that Byron would eventually honour his promise. He had tried his hardest to ignore the pregnancy, not even mentioning it to Hobhouse during their five months of travels through Switzerland and Italy, and only casually alluding to it when her confinement was imminent. 'I hear,' he said, 'that C. is about to produce a young "it and I".' A few weeks later, he informed Douglas Kinnaird, presumably from a sense of legal obligation, as Kinnaird held Byron's power of attorney: 'You know – and I believe saw once that odd-headed girl,' he wrote, recalling the time he had sent Claire to call on him at Drury Lane, 'but you do not know – that I found her with Shelley and her sister at Geneva':

> the suit of all this is that she was with *child* – and returned to England to assist in peopling that desolate island – Whether this impregnation took place before I left England or since – I do not know – the (carnal) connection had commenced previously to my setting out – but by or about this time she has – or is about to produce. – The next question is is the brat *mine?* – I have reason to think so – for I know as much as one can know such a thing – that she had *not lived* with S during the time of our acquaintance – and that she had a good deal of that same with me.

The moral of the story? 'This comes of "putting it about".'

Mary and Shelley had married two weeks before Alba's birth in a ceremony attended solely by Mr and Mrs Godwin. Shelley called it 'a measure of convenience' and was quick to reassure his friends 'that our opinions as to the importance of this pretended sanction, and all the prejudices connected with it, remain the same'. Godwin, however, considered it an essential step in the restoration of his family's reputation, pressing hard for the marriage the moment he learned of Harriet's death, even boasting to his brother that it was an exceptional match for his girl who had neither title nor dowry. Mary had been willing to remain unmarried, but as reconciliation with her father was important, she conceded.* Her feelings towards Mrs Godwin, however, were unchanged: 'something very analogous to disgust'. Claire avoided the wedding to keep her pregnancy concealed. 'Very few inquiries have been made of you,' Shelley reassured her, 'and those not of a nature to show that their suspicions have been alarmed.'

Mary returned to Bath after the ceremony, dreaming of the house that Thomas Love Peacock had found for them which would finally put an end to their scuttling and exclusion, and above all, their long-term cohabitation with Claire. 'Be kind,' she told Shelley, when breaking the news, 'but make no promises and above all do not say a word that may imply any responsibility on your part for her future actions.' Shelley, meanwhile, remained in London to seek legal custody of his motherless children, Charles and Ianthe. Having trusted that all legal obstacles would have evaporated in the face of his respectable marriage, he found himself outflanked by the Westbrooks, who were determined that the children should have nothing to do with their father. Harriet's parents pre-emptively filed a Bill of Complaint, sending copies of Shelley's works to the Lord Chancellor along with a petition accusing him, in Shelley's words, of being an adulterer, 'REVOLUTIONIST, and an *Atheist*'.

---

* Over half a century later, Claire recalled the circumstances of the marriage as her mother had recounted them, although how accurate these are is impossible to determine: 'Mr Godwin and Shelley had an argument as to whether the latter would marry Mary. Mr Shelley repeated all his reasons against marriage and seemed determined not to perform the ceremony. Mary was sitting at another part of the room listening attentively – when there seemed no likelihood of either party agreeing, she rose and coming up to Shelley, put her hand on his shoulder and said – "Of course you are free to do what you please – and I am free to act as I like and I have to tell you, dear Shelley, if you do not marry me, I will not live – I will destroy myself and my child with me." Shelley turned a little pale, looked at her steadily and reading determination in her countenance, said "If such are your intentions of course I will marry you, but allow me to say, that your mode of action leaves me no liberty whatever. I will marry you – and let us drop the subject." The next morning Mr Godwin asked when the ceremony was to be performed.'

What had seemed at first straightforward took on a sinister aspect now that Chancery was invited to look into Shelley's conduct and beliefs, a process that, as Shelley was acutely aware given the repressive climate, could result in fines and imprisonment and even having William taken away. His one hope of defence lay in attacking Harriet, and here Godwin offered his support by claiming to possess evidence that she had been unfaithful to Shelley four months prior to his elopement with Mary in 1814. This 'evidence' suited Godwin a little too well, yet to his credit, Shelley refused to betray his principles to slander the dead, or even deny that the baby Harriet had carried was his. As the case looked set to drag on, her spectre haunted him.

In March, the Shelleys took up a twenty-one-year lease on Albion House, Marlow, a rough, white two-storey building on the edge of the Windsor Forest with a long lawn enclosed by high hedges, firs and apple trees, and nothing beyond it but open countryside and the gentle Thames. Shelley planned to live here as a recluse, going so far as to instruct his upholsterer to inform the locals that 'The coming family would associate with no one in the village, would never go to church, and would do as they chose in defiance of public opinion.' Rumours about him spread quickly, including one that said he kept a room hung completely in black for the reception of Lord Byron.

Shelley unpacked the boxes of books he had ordered from his publisher, Charles Ollier, to furnish a study that was large enough to host a ball, and in which he installed life-sized statues of Apollo and Venus recovered from an attic. But having taken such pains to set it up, he rarely used it, preferring instead to rise early, put on country clothes and take long walks in the countryside, where he worked on his poems while sitting on a hill in Bisham Wood. Although he spurned polite society, he maintained his philanthropic mission, visiting the sick, dispensing charity among the distressed lace makers of Marlow, and maintaining a list of pensioners to whom he provided a weekly allowance. As the sky reddened, he would return to the house for a meal of vegetables, his hat wreathed with bryony and 'his hand filled with bunches of wild-flowers plucked from the hedges as he passed'.

Shelley had always chosen to stand apart, but now his preference for solitude was leavened both with a sense of his uncertain career as a poet and guilt at the deaths of Fanny and Harriet. By now the 'Hermit of Marlow', as he would describe himself, was the author of two major poems, *Queen Mab* and *Alastor*, both long and allusive and not readily digested by his Regency audience. *Alastor*, subtitled *The Spirit of Solitude*, had been particularly baffling. Composed towards the end of 1815 while Claire was in Lynmouth and Mary was pregnant with William, this strange, beautiful and impressionistic poem, heir to Milton, Wordsworth and Coleridge, retreated from the combative Godwinism of *Queen Mab* to a place of far greater introspection. Written in the wake of William Lawrence's erroneous diagnosis of terminal lung disease, it recounts the wanderings of a young poet in awe of nature and the 'vast earth and ambient air'. Sustained by tranquillity and reflection, philosophy is his sole pleasure, until one night he is visited by a veiled poetess in an erotic dream, their 'frantic', 'breathless', 'dissolving' congress revealing to him the existence of another realm beyond the visible. Suddenly aware of what he lacks, the poet embarks on a small boat driven on a whirlpool into a cavern of the earth where he hopes to find the membrane dividing sleep from death. His senses darkening even as the perceptions of his mind expand to encompass a vivid world that flames about him, he becomes exhausted and dies by a solitary pine.

In his preface to the poem, Shelley described the theme of *Alastor* as man's search for a lover able to bring together all that is 'wonderful, or wise, or beautiful' in a perfect union, followed by the realisation that this is an unobtainable dream. A meditation on the disillusionment attendant to idealism, the poem concedes that the pursuit of transcendent love, such as that he had sought with Mary, is ultimately illusory, until 'blasted by his disappointment,' Shelley wrote, 'he descends to an untimely grave'. Critical disappointment followed its appearance in January 1816, published among a suite of poems that included the first two cantos of *Queen Mab* recast as *The Daemon of the World*. The *British Critic* called the volume 'nonsense', 'vastly unintelligible', the 'madness of a poetic mind' and, picking up on a reference to Alastor's 'thin hair', suggested that Shelley buy a wig. The *Monthly Review* wrote that 'We must candidly own that these poems are beyond our comprehension; and we did not obtain a clue to their sublime obscurity', a view mirrored by the *Eclectic Review,* which said, 'All is wild and specious, untangible and incoherent as a dream. We should be utterly at a loss to convey any distinct idea of the plan or purpose.'

Shelley had one ally in the journalist and poet, Leigh Hunt, editor of the liberal *Examiner* newspaper, with whom he had made friends after their return from Geneva. Shelley had long admired Hunt for the outspoken political views that had already landed him in Horsemonger Lane gaol on a charge of libelling the Prince Regent, and as a friend of Byron, the two men had a shared connection. That Hunt's family set-up was as unorthodox as Shelley's was another point on which the men found common ground. Hunt also struggling to confine his affections to one woman, and felt a particularly strong attraction to his wife's sister.

Hunt was the first critic to praise Shelley in the press, publishing his 'Hymn to Intellectual Beauty' in January 1817, and introducing him to the circle of friends who met around his home in Hampstead, including the artist Benjamin Robert Haydon, the young poet John Hamilton Reynolds, the critic William Hazlitt, as well as another of his *protégés*, John Keats. Keats and Shelley shared Hunt's table and walked together on Hampstead Heath, although Keats, ever aware of class, found Shelley condescending and prone to 'aristocratical sallies'.

Even with Hunt on his side, Shelley remained 'morbidly sensitive to what I esteem as the injustice of neglect'. 'I am an outcast from human society,' he told Hunt, 'my name is execrated by all who understand its entire import.' To Byron, whose prolific output made Shelley despair, he said, 'I still feel the burden of my own insignificance and impotence.' Despite these anxieties, 1817 proved a productive year as he returned to politics in a series of pamphlets aimed at repressive government, and spent the six months of summer and autumn composing the longest poem he would ever write. Consisting of twelve cantos and almost five thousand lines, written in the same Spenserian stanzas as Byron's *Childe Harold*, *Laon and Cythna; or, the Revolution of the Golden City: A Vision of the Nineteenth Century* was an epic romance describing the bloodless overthrow of the despotic sultanate of Argolis by the young lovers Laon and Cythna. Once more Shelley asserted the transformative power of love and the revolutionary potential of female excellence, basing his young heroine, Cythna, on his wife, Mary, and her mother, Mary Wollstonecraft. The brilliance of the poem lay in the manner Shelley knitted the metaphysical longing of *Alastor* to the revolutionary hunger of *Queen Mab* within a Byronesque narrative of passion and sacrifice. Its presentation to the public, however, was another misstep. Not only was the poem filled with his characteristic attacks on Christianity, calling God 'Some moon-struck sophist stood/Watching the shade from his own soul upthrown/Fill heaven and darken Earth,' but he had made the lovers Laon and Cythna brother and sister. Ollier, his publisher, was forced to pull the poem from sale, requiring

Shelley to hack pages from it before it could be published again under a new title, *The Revolt of Islam*.

With nowhere else to go, Claire arrived in Marlow in early April, performing the credulous virgin for the visiting Godwin the very next day while Alba remained in London with the Hunts. A week later they brought her down, with Marianne's sister Elizabeth, known as Bess, and their own four children. The Hunts had hosted Mary and Shelley while Albion House was being readied, and to return their hospitality, Shelley invited them to spend the summer in Marlow, an offer that Hunt readily accepted as, improvident, impractical and in constant need of money, he looked to economise.

With so many residents, Albion House in the summer of 1817 came very close to becoming the 'Association of philosophical people' Claire had dreamed of, its gardens buzzing with children as everybody partook of an atmosphere that, in Mary's words, was 'very political as well as poetical'. Hunt found a spot in the garden where he composed his weekly editorials, while Bess, a skilled botanist, sketched and studied the plants around her. Shelley remained deep in his thoughts, composing as his boat floated under beech groves, or while he wandered on the chalk hills. Mary, pregnant again, set up a desk for herself, made her final corrections to *Frankenstein* and began to plan her *History of a Six Weeks' Tour*, a compilation of the journals, poems and letters they had written while travelling in 1814 and 1816. Even Claire, when not busy with Alba, continued to scratch away at 'The Ideot'. When the work was done, there were long walks to Windsor Castle, Virginia Water and the Chiltern Hills, or boisterous upriver outings to Henley and Maidenhead. Godwin made regular visits (without his wife, who had declared Mary the 'greatest enemy she has in the world'), and by carefully shepherding the conversation, Mary was at last able to enjoy her father's company. Still unaware of the existence of Alba, and therefore the reason for Claire's frequent absences, he concluded that she was suffering from depression, an affliction Mrs Godwin ascribed to Mary's neglect.

Although happy to be reconciled with her father, Mary was less happy about the number of people who were constantly about. Far from being her 'little mousehole', Albion House had swollen to become a household of nine adults (including Elise, the nurse-maid, a cook called Milly Shields, and Harry, the gardener and general manservant), six small children (the eldest, Thornton Leigh Hunt, was just about to turn seven), and a local girl called Polly Rose, one of the strays Shelley liked to accumulate who came every day to take lessons from him and sometimes stayed overnight. In addition to those *in situ* could be counted Thomas Love Peacock, who lived nearby with his mother and appeared at dinner every day, uninvited, complained Mary, 'to drink his bottle', as well as weekly visits from Thomas Jefferson Hogg, towards whom her feelings had also changed – 'I do not like him,' she told Leigh Hunt, 'he is more disagreeable than ever.' With so much activity, she longed for simpler times far from the 'menagerie'. Reading the third canto of *Childe Harold* that summer, she was surprised at the force of the memories it recalled, finding herself pining for the 'dear lake', and the first time she had heard the verses as Shelley recited from the manuscript as they lay on their bed at Maison Chappuis. 'This time will soon also be a recollection,' she reflected, 'death will at length come and in the last moment all will be a dream.'

Claire, by contrast, was oblivious to the outside world, her life narrowing to a point that contained only the child whose breath-ing she listened to as she shared her bed, both her 'treasure' and the confirmation of her solitude. 'The little creature occupies all my thoughts, all my time and my feelings,' she wrote, 'when I hold her in my arms I think to myself – there is nothing else in the world that is of you or belongs to you – you are utterly a stranger to every one else: without this little being you would hold no relations with any single human being.' Shelley tried his best to bring her back to the fold, commissioning Hunt's friend, the organist and music publisher Vincent Novello, to find them a cabinet grand piano, and having obtained music and engaged a teacher, Claire played for them regularly. The music was a balm, and neither the ascending clarity of her voice nor the fact that she was maturing into a beautiful woman was lost on the men who frequented Albion House. One of these was Peacock, who joined her in duets and fell in love with her over the course of the summer, later using her as the model for the character of Stella in his novel *Nightmare Abbey*, a Wollstonecraft-quoting runaway described as 'a female form and countenance of dazzling grace and beauty, with long flowing hair of raven blackness, and large black eyes of almost oppressive brilliancy, which strikingly contrasted with a complexion of snowy whiteness'. Neither was her beauty lost on Shelley, who, like Byron before him, was transported on the liquid motion of her voice to a kind of erotic enervation that he set out in a poem entitled 'To Constantia':

> Thy voice, slow rising like a Spirit, lingers
> O'ershadowing me with soft and lulling wings;
> The blood and life within thy snowy fingers
> Teach witchcraft to the instrumental strings.
> My brain is wild, my breath comes quick,
> The blood is listening in my frame,
> And thronging shadows fast and thick

Fall on my overflowing eyes,
　My heart is quivering like a flame;
As morning dew, that in the sunbeam dies,
I am dissolved in these consuming ecstasies.

I have no life, Constantia, but in thee;
Whilst, like the world-surrounding air, thy song
Flows on, and fills all things with melody:
Now is thy voice a tempest, swift and strong,
　　On which, as one in trance, upborne
　　Secure o'er woods and waves I sweep
　　Rejoicing, like a cloud of morn:
　　Now 'tis the breath of summer's night
　　Which, where the starry waters sleep
Round western isles with incense-blossoms bright,
Lingering, suspends my soul in its voluptuous flight.

A deep and breathless awe, like the swift change
Of dreams unseen, but felt in youthful slumbers,
Wild, sweet, yet incommunicably strange,
Thou breathest now, in fast ascending numbers:
　　The cope of Heaven seems rent and cloven
　　By the enchantment of thy strain,
　　And o'er my shoulders wings are woven
　　To follow its sublime career,
　　Beyond the mighty moons that wane
Upon the verge of Nature's utmost sphere,
Till the world's shadowy walls are past, and disappear.

Cease, cease – for such wild lessons madmen learn:
Long thus to sink, – thus to be lost and die
Perhaps is death indeed – Constantia turn!

Yes! In thine eyes a power like light doth lie,
   Even though the sounds, its voice that were,
   Between thy lips are laid to sleep –
   Within my breath and on thy hair
   Like odour it is lingering yet –
   And from thy touch like fire doth leap:
Even when I write my burning cheeks are wet –
Such things the heart can feel and learn, but not forget!

Like her mother, Alba lacked the certainty of a single name. For the sake of appearances she was known in Marlow as 'Miss Auburn', the child of a friend in London sent out for country air. But when the Hunts left Marlow at the end of June, and their sprawling family were no longer able to offer a screen, it became much harder, in Shelley's words, to hide the enigmatic infant and 'temporise with our servants or our visitors'. The chief inquisitor appears to have been David Booth, husband of Mary's childhood friend Isabel Baxter, whose growing suspicions led to uncomfortable questions. Why, he asked Godwin, did Claire always stay in lodgings when she came to London, and not with them? 'An unconquerable fear of ghosts,' was the reply, a fear so incapacitating that she could not possibly sleep alone, but had always to stay with Shelley (a fear, it was noted, that did not apply in Marlow). Booth seems to have divined the meaning of the riddle well ahead of the rest, suggesting that if Godwin really wanted Claire to come home, 'I will advise him to ask Miss Auburn also.'

This was exactly the kind of poison that Mary was determined to keep from Marlow. 'We find it indispensable that Clare should reside with us,' Shelley had written to Byron shortly after Claire's arrival, 'and a perpetual danger of discovery that it is hers impends. Nothing would be easier than to own that it was hers, and that it is the offspring of a private marriage in France. But the wise heads suppose that such a tale would make people consider it as mine, and that the inhabitants of this most Christian country would not suffer me to dwell among them under such an imputation.' Claire, meanwhile, made a joke out of their double lives, pretending to Elise that there were two Miss Clairmonts, 'Madame Clairmont', the identity she assumed in Geneva and Bath, who was a pretty, ailing woman, abandoned by her cruel husband, and 'Mademoiselle Clairmont', her sister, who was gay and heartless, and cared nothing for her sister's death. By the middle of the summer the situation remained unchanged, and Shelley wrote to Byron again: 'We are somewhat embarrassed about her', he wrote of Alba, and, 'exposed to what remarks her existence is calculated to excite', proposed to place her with some ladies in the town.

'Little faithless' sent them no reply, although the silence was not entirely his fault. Letters to Italy usually took two weeks to arrive, but Shelley was still sending his via Hentsch-Chevrier in Geneva, which meant that it took a full four months for news of Alba's birth to reach Byron. By this time, he had settled in Venice (a fact that rankled with Claire, who assumed 'he is over head and ears in love with some Venetian'), having also spent close to a month in Rome, where, among other things, he had witnessed a triple guillotining and crossed paths with a Lady Lidell who had instinctively shouted to her daughter, 'Don't look at him, he is dangerous to look at.'

Having digested the news of the arrival, he passed it on to Augusta with the usual dose of staged disinterest. 'By the way,' he said, it seems that I have got another – a *daughter* – by that same lady you will recognise by what I said of her in former letters – I mean *her* who returned to England to become a Mamma incog. – and whom I pray the Gods to keep there . . . They tell me it is very pretty – with blue eyes and dark hair – although I never was attached nor pretended to attachment to the mother.

In mid-September, he wrote to Shelley asking that Alba be delivered to him in Venice, and though he confessed to being 'a little puzzled how to dispose of this new production', he had already given some thought as to why he would want her with him, envisaging how the baby might compensate for the loss of Ada in 'the eternal war and alienation' he foresaw with Lady Byron. 'I must love something in my old age,' he told Augusta, 'and probably circumstances will render this poor little creature a greater (and perhaps my only) comfort than any offspring from that misguided and artificial woman – who bears and disgraces my name.'

Mary was keen to send the child as soon as possible, having given birth to her own daughter, Clara, just a few weeks earlier, telling Shelley that 'I am not at peace until she is on her way to Italy.' Claire, however, was adamant that she would not hand over her child without first receiving assurances from Byron that he would send regular letters and accounts of her progress, an insistence that vexed Mary. 'Promises with Albé!' she complained. 'The first object that engaged his attention would put them all out of his head – and negotiated by letter also – why it is the labour of several months to get any kind of answer from him and then if he makes objections and you have to answer the child can never depart.'

Mary was exhausted. Clara was not feeding well, and she was constantly busy trying to write, manage the house and keep track of everybody's hats and coats. Shelley was often away, tackling his legal problems and tightening the knots on his chaotic financial transactions, while Claire she found 'forever wearying with her idle and childish complaints'. Autumn rains revealed the house's imperfections – mildewed rooms, indecent draughts, and the tall trees in the garden that made it cold and dark even when the sun was out. Looking haggard and dishevelled, she was easily crossed and had little patience with Claire's prevarications, which, she felt, might mean the difference between Alba enjoying all the protections of wealth and status or leading a life of scrambling uncertainty. Certain that Claire would 'instinctively place all kind of difficulties in the way', she urged Shelley to be decisive, 'For if by imprudent delay we find that the fair prospect of Alba's being brought up by her father is taken away how shall we reproach ourselves – Clare also will then see the extreme evil and distress of her situation and not easily forgive us for having destroyed her childs fortune by want of firmness.'

Finding a suitable chaperone to take Alba to Italy, however, proved difficult, and after Claire vetoed the hapless Hunts, Mary suggested that they take her themselves. The groundwork had already been laid by Shelley, whose health had bowed under the gruelling burden of the custody case, resulting in a recurrence of the lung condition he was convinced would eventually kill him, in addition to a case of ophthalmia he had contracted while visiting Marlow's poor. William Lawrence prescribed a healthful climate, but as they discussed the merits of various destinations, Shelley stalled, claiming that he might not survive a long journey and that he should clear Godwin's debts before he left. His reasons for doing so are uncertain, although he may have been loath to unmake the household, and may not have shared his wife's convictions regarding Alba's fate. 'I think Alba's remaining here exceedingly dangerous,' Mary countered, fretting at the delay in case Byron changed his mind or decided to move to Greece. Her sense of the infant as an agent of unrest was even projected onto her children: she told Shelley in October how William began to cry whenever Alba came near, while he 'kisses Clara – strokes her arms and feet and laughs to find them so soft and pretty'.

By the time Alba turned one in 1818, Shelley had been spared prison but resigned himself to losing custody of Charles and Ianthe after the Lord Chancellor had ruled that neither he nor the Westbrooks could raise them, and that they should placed in the care of a Hanwell doctor named Hume. With nothing to keep them in England, a plan to take Alba to Italy was agreed. Claire commemorated her daughter's first birthday by sending Byron a lock of her hair. 'My dear friend how I envy you,' she wrote to him, imagining the time when they should soon live together.

> You will have a little darling to crawl to your knees and pull you till you take her up – then she will sit on the crook of your arm and you will give her raisins out of your own plate and a little drop of wine from your own glass and she will think herself a little Queen in Creation. When she shall be older she will run about your house like a lapwing; if you are miserable her light careless voice will make you happy. But there is one delight above all this: if it shall please you, you may delight yourself in contemplating a creature growing under your own hands as it were. You may look at her and think 'this is my work.'

Claire could only sustain the vision temporarily before it collapsed to reveal her fears:

If you knew the extreme happiness I feel when she nestles closer to me, I could tear my flesh in twenty thousand different directions to ensure her good and when I fear for her residing with you it is not the dread I have to commence the long series of painful anxiety I know I shall have to endure it is lest I should behold her sickly and wasted with improper management lest I should live to hear you neglected her.

There was still a chance that things could work out differently. The thought of Claire's departure spurred Peacock into making her a proposal of marriage. He was her senior by thirteen years, yet generally considered to be handsome and, with his small income and growing reputation as an author of satirical novels, he was by no means an unfavourable prospect. But the proposition so embarrassed Claire that she took to hiding upstairs to avoid his calls, leaving Peacock to gaze at the soundless piano and lament to Hogg, 'Here's the harp she used to touch. Oh, how that touch enchanted.'

A week after Alba's birthday, the lease of Albion House was sold along with its furniture for a thousand pounds. An additional fourteen hundred went as a gift to Hunt, who had cemented his attachment to the family by naming his newest son Percy Bysshe Shelley Hunt. A little income balanced these outgoings as, after rejections from three publishers, including John Murray, *Frankenstein; or, the Modern Prometheus* was published on New Year's Day 1818, by Lackington's, the biggest bookseller in London, and a well-known purveyor of horror, magic and supernatural tales. The novel appeared anonymously in a three-volume edition, warmly dedicated to William Godwin, whose influence shone in every word, and with a short preface by Shelley that recounted the competition at Diodati but erased John Polidori and Claire from it entirely. Only five hundred copies were printed, and while it was favourably reviewed, most notably by Sir Walter Scott, who thought the work must be Shelley's, it would be several years before its real author became a household name. Yet even though the sale amounted to a mere £28 14s., it was still enough to make Mary the most commercially successful author in the house.

Ever competitive, Claire asked Shelley to offer Lackington 'The Ideot', which the publisher refused, although the disappointment did not prevent her taking considerable pride in her step-sister's achievement. An inscribed edition was sent to Byron, followed by a note in which Claire declared herself to be 'delighted' by the book, 'and whatever private feelings of envy I may have at not being able to do so well myself yet all yields when I consider that she is a woman and will prove in time an ornament to us and an argument in our favour. How I delight in a lovely woman of strong and cultivated intellect.'

From Marlow they decamped to London in lieu of their departure, staying briefly at the New Hummums Family Hotel in Covent Garden, before moving to lodgings in Great Russell Street. For the next few weeks, Claire studied Italian and joined the others as they visited Hogg and the Hunts, and a disappointed but generous Peacock, who offered his arm to escort her to opera and exhibitions. Byron, meanwhile, sent further instructions. As he told Kinnaird, he was happy to 'acknowledge and breed' the child himself, 'giving her the name of *Biron* (to distinguish her from little Legitimacy)' – Ada – and having provided her with a surname, he reserved the right to christen her as well, selecting the name 'Allegra', which, he said, 'is a Venetian name'. Claire agreed to the alteration without remark, and on 9 March 1818, at the church of St Giles in the Fields, Alba was christened Clara Allegra Byron (the 'Clara' a necessity required to conform to the Church's list of approved names), 'reputed' daughter of the Rt.

Hon. George Gordon, Lord Byron, peer, of 'No fixed residence, Travelling on the Continent'. Alba, Miss Auburn, Allegra – at just over a year old, the child was already a true de Vial, taking on her third identity. 'What is a name?' asks Stella in *Nightmare Abbey*, 'any name will serve the purpose of distinction.'

Two days later, Shelley packed his pistols and led them all to Dover, with Elise, the cook Milly Shields, and the three children, their third trip to the Continent in less than four years. Crossing the Channel aboard the *Lady Castlereagh*, mountainous waves swept them to Calais in just two hours and forty minutes. There, they bought a carriage (whose springs broke), and journeyed south, bypassing Paris to approach Italy via Lyon. There was a delay at the border between France and the Kingdom of Savoy while Shelley's books underwent examination by a local priest, a man with a reputation for burning Enlightenment works, and who would happily have done the same with Shelley's, were it not for the helpful appearance of an English cleric who happened to know his father.

Claire was delighted to be back in the mountains, which the spring thaw had turned into a cascade of rivers, but Milan moved her unlike any other place she had ever visited, walking in the public gardens with 'Itty Ba', revelling in the opera and admiring the buildings. 'I can conceive of no building that partakes more perfectly of the nature of air and heaven,' she wrote of Milan's cathedral, finding in that 'sensation of veneration' she felt on entering the building not the presence of God but a confirmation of her atheism and 'an hommage to the Works of Man'.

A letter that arrived from Byron on 21 April served to return her to reality: 'Nothing but Discomfort,' she wrote in her diary. She had continued to hope that relations between them might at least be cordial, if not exactly friendly, following the transfer of Allegra, but Byron's letter made it plain that, contrary to his promise, he expected her to renounce all claims to her child once the exchange had taken place. Shelley proposed that he come and spend the summer as their neighbour on Lake Como, hoping that some time spent together might help foster an understanding between them. Byron refused, claiming that it would only reignite the gossip about him and Claire – a claim Shelley refused to accept, arguing that as they were completely unknown in Como, 'I can see no loophole for calumny.' Claire, of course, was adamant that she would never surrender her daughter on such terms. 'Pardon me but I cannot part with my Child never to see her again,' she told him. 'Only write me one word of Consolation – Tell me that you will come and see Shelley in the Summer or that I may then be some where near her – Say this and I will send her instantly. I cannot describe to you the anguish with which I bring myself to contradict your expectations or in any manner to oppose your will but on this point I am firm – If you will not regard me as her mother, she shall never be divided from me.'

Even partial rapprochement was beyond Byron, and when Shelley submitted to Claire's plea to be allowed to see their correspondence, she found herself described by Byron as 'stupid' and hysterical, writing letters that were worse than 'bad German novels'. To ensure that Allegra might never be a cause of contact between them, Byron dispatched a 'mercantile acquaintance' from London to collect her. This was Francis Merryweather, an agent of Douglas Kinnaird charged with delivering the contracts from the sale of Byron's estate, Newstead Abbey. His instructions now included a trip to Milan to collect a child ('desire Shelley to pack it carefully', Byron said).

Once again, Shelley tried to intervene in what he called 'this painful controversy', planning to detain Byron's messenger until he and Claire had reached an agreement. 'It is not that I wish to make out a case for Clare,' he wrote to Byron, 'my *interest*, as you must be aware, is entirely on the opposite side. Nor have I in any manner influenced her', but he insisted that as a mother she had rights, and as a person should be treated with 'reassurance and tenderness'. The move angered Byron, who wrote to Hobhouse to inform him of the stalemate. 'I can't leave my quarters,' he claimed, 'and have "sworn an oath" – between Attorneys, – Clerks – and Whores – and wives – and children – and friends – my life is made a burthen – and it is all owing to *your* negligence and "want of memory".' If only he had remembered the condoms.

After a week of such exchanges, Byron finally made the concession that Claire desired. Allegra would be allowed to spend holidays with her mother on the condition that Claire and Byron never met. Claire agreed, although Shelley appears to have had another change of heart and, staying true to his belief in ideal community, he made one last, unsuccessful, appeal to have Allegra stay with them.

On 28 April 1818, the fifteen month-old Allegra was sent to Venice in the company of Elise. 'I have sent you my child because I love her to[o] well to keep her,' Claire wrote, her eyes filled with tears:

> With you who are powerful and noble and the admiration of the world she will be happy but I am a miserable and neglected dependant. Dearest and best I entreat you to think how wretched and lone I feel now she is gone, and to write word that she is well the darling bird . . . and besides I have one favour to beg of you. Send me the smallest quantity of your own dearest hair that I may put with some of Allegra's in a locket. Dearest friend, my dear Lord Byron do not refuse me this one favour. Never again shall you have to complain that I teize you. For the future you shall do as you please and

I will not even grieve. Pray think before you refuse the mother of your child this slight request. If I have been faulty I have suffered enough to redeem my error; my child was born in sorrow and after much suffering – then I love her with a passion that almost destroys my being she goes from me. My dear Lord Byron I most truly love my child. She never checked me – she loves me stretches out her arms to me and cooes for joy when I take her – Farewell my dearest friend. Pray tell me how your health is. I pray for your happiness and her's. I assure you I have wept so much to night that now my eyes seem to drop hot and burning blood. Remember that I am wretched how wretched and for the smallest word of kindness from you I will bless and honour you. My dearest Lord Byron best of human beings you are the father of my little girl and I cannot forget you.

It was Claire's twentieth birthday.

13

THE VAMPYRE

Even though he had almost died in a carriage accident, John grew impatient at the slowness of his recovery. As soon as he was able to walk, he tried to make up for lost time, sending a confused note to Murray to excuse himself for not sending him his Pisan journal, explaining that 'Before my fall from the gig, I had been attacked in my head in consequence of exposure to the sun when suffering under tooth ache so that for a long time back I have been incapable of doing anything.' He also asked for news of Byron, to whom, he told Murray, he had not written, 'in consequence of having heard that he has spoken harshly about me in his letters'. How John might have heard such a thing in Norwich is unclear, although it was, of course, entirely true. The reserves of *noblesse oblige* Byron had spared for him in the past had dried up, leaving only disdain. 'I am as sorry to hear of Dr Polidori's accident as one can be for a person for whom one has a dislike – and – something of contempt,' Byron had said to Murray upon hearing the news, adding, 'I fear the Doctor's Skill at Norwich/ Will hardly salt the Doctor's porridge.' Having intuited that his relationship with the poet was over, John, like Claire, begged for a memento: 'I have not a single piece of his handwriting,' he said to Murray, 'could you give me a piece?'

It was clear that the effects of concussion were more protracted than John had at first imagined. A deep depression enveloped him in which he reflected on the disappointment he felt 'in every pursuit – a vapid nullity in every object', which manifested itself in his speech, which had become clipped and abbreviated as he developed a habit of speaking in abrupt half-sentences. As 1817 slipped away in a convalescent fog, he made inconsistent efforts to get back on his feet, finally sending his Pisan journal to Murray in the new year, and asking if he might be engaged to write on a new periodical Murray was launching, while simultaneously working on a longer text that more honestly reflected his mood. This was a speculative treatise John entitled *An Essay Upon the Source of Positive Pleasure*, a text composed in the course of his recovery that sought to extend an observation made by the politician and philosopher Edmund Burke, who had claimed that instead of being a 'positive active feeling', pleasure was in fact a negative category best defined as 'the absence of pain' – as when the 'pleasure' of feeling full supplants the discomfort of hunger. 'Happiness,' John's text claimed, 'is not a reality but a vision', formed in a world of 'constant decay and irreparable destruction', where people are dogged by ceaseless suffering from cradle to grave. The sole respite from this bleak prospect was the faculty of the imagination, John argued, which permits us to escape the reality of life by flooding the mind with temulent illusions. 'If we seek present pleasure,' he wrote, 'we take to the bottle, to opium, to dancing, or yield to enthusiasm, the mere ravings of folly; all of which have but one action upon the mind – that of banishing reason, and letting the pictures of the imagination pass rapidly before us.' Memory was similarly prone to the 'colouring of imagination', he asserted, gilding recollections which, when viewed objectively, were of a much different hue. 'If indeed we were to raise up true pictures of the past,' he wrote, seemingly invoking regrets of his own, 'without a veil or colouring-glass to look upon our own actions, our friends' proofs of friendship, and our varying fortunes, we should look with disgust at the scenes of meanness, perfidy, and disappointed hope, which have formed the drama of our life.' Of these illusions, none was crueller than love, an emotion that feeds entirely from the imagination of the lover. 'Is it not another proof,' he wrote, 'that lovers discover in the objects of their affection, charms which others cannot see, and seldom remain lovers beyond the honey-moon?':

> We think the possession of beauty will make us happy, forgetting that even in the body, what is constantly stimulating us, at last produces a state in which we are incapable of receiving impressions from the same stimulus. We think that talents will give us pleasure, forgetting that a mother, a regulator of the household affairs of a family, can no longer waste her time in playing sonatas or writing sonnets, and that a good temper is, in fact, not the cause of pleasure, but a mere turn-key upon pain.

'Were we not as well when alone?' he asked. 'We had then no cause to fear that our secrets would be betrayed; we had then no intimates who tormented us by their pettishness, or fretted us with their caprices; and what can we expect more from a wife, than that she should not abuse the confidence we place in her, or show ill temper and caprice?'

John submitted his manifesto to the Norwich Philosophical Society in early 1818, where it was debated for three whole meetings. With a revised text planned for publication in June, he hoped to dedicate the piece to Lady Jerningham, but she declined, unwilling to have her name be associated with such a nihilistic tract. 'I should be very sorry to assist in depriving any one of the more pleasurable belief in real and substantial happiness,' she told him, adding that there is 'also something unpleasant in being named in a dedication to an "Essay *on Pleasure*".' With no patience for the piece whatsoever, she counselled him to buck up. 'I regret you are still blowing bubbles, and building castles,' she said, '[and] I cannot at *all* comprehend, how any man can be unoccupied, uninterested, and unhappy, whilst he has *parents friends Books* and the country and the town.'

If the rebuke had any effect on John, it was only to remind him of how much he cared for his reputation in the eyes of the world. When the *Essay* came to print he attempted to distance himself from the work, adding a preface in which he claimed that the entire text had come to him in a dream which he had merely sought to transcribe in 'the form of a speech'. 'I therefore trust that I shall not be made responsible for every sentiment in the book, so as to have it supposed, that any herein inserted are my own private opinions.' Yet, as Byron well knew, the reading public was not apt to draw neat distinctions between a writer and his work, and female readers in particular were angered by the *Essay*'s undisguised misogyny. 'What a tyger of a man he must be,' complained one young woman (a comment of which John seemed rather proud). Others accused him of posturing and, even worse, *faux*-Byronism, aping the mode of Byronic despair but with none of its redeeming lyrical sweetness. A verse appearing in the *Norfolk Chronicle*, for example, compared him to 'gifted Harold' but was brutal in its criticism:

> But thou – weak follower of a soulless school!
> Whose stoic feelings vacillate by rule,
> Doomed through a joyless wilderness to rove,
> Uncheered by friendship, and unwarmed by love.

Dull, satiate spirit! ere thy prime's begun,
Accurst with hating what thou canst not shun;
Man shall despise thee for thy vain attempt,
And woman spurn thee with deserved contempt;
Thy pride of apathy, thy folly see,
And what we hate in Harold – loathe in thee.

Its author was Aubrey Spencer, a newly ordained priest who would later become Archbishop of Newfoundland.

Gaetano also loathed John's *Essay*, telling him it was 'a bad use of your intellect', and urging him to return to medicine as quickly as possible: 'You might perhaps gain something by your profession,' he wrote, 'which is the only thing on which you can found your hopes; for if you flatter yourself upon making money by writing, you will soon find out your mistake. That is a beggarly trade.'

John had been imprudent with more than just his opinions, and Gaetano grew increasingly frustrated as he watched his son fritter away money in bootless pursuits. Travels abroad and well-to-do friends had accustomed him to living as a gentleman, but with no income and an expensive social life, he was desperately short of cash. At the beginning of 1818, he had written to his godfather, John Deagostini, to request a loan of five hundred pounds to buy a house in Norwich and keep a servant. When Gaetano heard of this, he took it as a personal affront. 'How much I have done for you you may perhaps forget,' he said to his son, 'how much I have suffered for you, and still suffer, cannot be comprehended by your imagination, tho' it is a poetical imagination.' Nothing was more disgraceful or vainglorious to Gaetano than living beyond one's means, and he berated John for his inability to maintain himself on '8 or 10 guineas a month in a provincial city', while squandering money on 'useless expenses'. 'I for my part cannot discover any slavery greater,' he concluded, 'or more repulsive and humiliating, than that of debts; and I grieve to see how much you are inclined to contract them.'

John still needed money, and an agreement was reached that if he would stick to his profession and rein in his expenses, Deagostini would advance him a hundred pounds at five per cent interest. This was in February, and by May the money was already gone, replaced by what a disappointed Deagostini called 'debts and embarrassment'. Gaetano conferred with the Jerninghams, who both agreed that John had changed since his accident. He implored his son to return to London, offering him the upstairs flat in the family home or, failing that, promising to pay the rent on somewhere nearby where he 'need incur little further cost, as you can come every day to breakfast and dinner with us. And here you can earn something, if not otherwise, at least by writing for some journal.'

What remained of 1818 was spent delaying the inevitable, but by January 1819 John had returned to London, reluctantly accepting his father's charity, although not his home. Instead he took rooms in Covent Garden Chambers, a singular red-brick building on the busy north-west corner of Covent Garden market that had once been home to the diplomat Sir Kenelm Digby, who had retired there in the reign of Charles II to perfect his 'powder of sympathy', a miraculous salve he claimed could cure wounds by being applied to the weapon that had caused them. Yet it was a subsequent lessee to whom the Chambers owed their odd appearance, the privateering sea lord Admiral Russell, who razed Digby's building and rebuilt the façade to resemble a ship's forecastle. Every day as he went to his rooms, John climbed the magnificent central staircase Russell had fashioned from the timbers of the

Britannia, the 100-gun ship-of-the-line he had commanded during the defeat of the French at La Hogue, its handsome newels carved with ropes and anchors. Nowadays the admiral's safe harbour was a scruffy lodging house tenanted by bachelors and artists like the marine painter John Serres, or Charles Kemble, actor brother of Gaetano's pupil John Philip. The ground floor housed a large coffee and dining room known as the Star for the many men of rank and influence who used it, although John wasted no money there, preferring to get his sustenance by walking over to Great Pulteney Street and eating the square meals served by his father's maid, Charlotte Reed.

John was determined to be a writer still and, moreover, to cure his unhappiness by attaining fame, but finding work proved difficult. He approached Murray again, asking to review for his journals and proposing a three-volume history of the popes, but received no reply. Opportunities should have been plentiful as never before had Britain enjoyed such a large and boisterous print culture, powered by the steam press and dominated by a central claque of magazines like the *Edinburgh Review*, the *Quarterly Review* and *Blackwood's Edinburgh Magazine*, whose pages sustained a debate on writers and their work that kept them constantly in the view of ordinary readers. As such, many of these magazines trafficked heavily in personalities, investing in the Romantic ideology of the creative genius and its attendant fascination with the lives of individuals. In its purest form, this produced writing that was searching, confessional and intimate, as in the personal essays of writers like William Hazlitt and Charles Lamb, whose work explored the varied moods of private life. In less exalted circumstances, it led to a prurient obsession with celebrities, where even 'the meanest insects', in Coleridge's words, 'are worshipped with a sort of Egyptian superstition'. Magazines elevated their favourites and dropped them just as quickly. 'By changing the object of our admiration,' wrote Hazlitt, 'we secretly persuade ourselves that there is no such thing as excellence. It is that which we hate above all things. This is the worm that gnaws us, that never dies.' It made for a feuding, belligerent culture, with writers and editors marshalling into aesthetic and political factions that traded rascally gossip and personal attacks giving many cause for concern. The 'ordinary business of life could not proceed if it became general', warned the *Scotsman.* 'We should have nothing but a perpetual round of cudgelling, duelling, and stabbing, if every weak, odd, or even vicious *private act* of every individual were to be published, with all the circumstances of name, time, and place, for the general amusement.'

When he eventually landed his first assignment with the *Eclectic Review,* a periodical for dissenting Evangelicals whose contributors were mainly curates and ministers, John wasted no time in finding his voice, attacking John Cam Hobhouse's *Historical Illustrations of the Fourth Canto of Childe Harold,* a book of notes and essays on Italian literature and history Hobhouse had compiled as a companion to the final instalment of Byron's poem. The text, as John took great pleasure in pointing out, had many deficiencies, and his review accused Hobhouse of 'great inaccuracy', the 'abuse of quotations', and embarrassing his readers with the 'rubbish of erudition'. Most egregious of all, John noted, was the condescending sneer with which Hobhouse dismissed better-credentialled authors than himself. Had Hobhouse been able to stop himself, John concluded, 'he might have rendered a service to the literary world'.

As satisfying as this might have been, within a month of his arrival in London, John was writing to his sister Frances to complain of low spirits and ill health. 'I still am very miserable,' he told her, 'I am so solitary [and] busy writing and fag like a horse uncertain whether I may not be wanting even of the power of fagging next day not from illness but the caprice of a book-seller.' With self-interest crouching in every corner and its churning spectacle serving only to affirm his friendlessness, London was to John a wasteland, 'worse than the deserts of Arabia'.

There were some successes. A relationship with the bookseller Thomas Longman bore fruit when Longman agreed to publish a revised version of his play 'Count Orlando', now titled *Ximenes*, along with a number of his poems entitled *The Wreath*. John was delighted with the collection, passing it proudly among his family and boasting to Frances that a lady of his acquaintance had learned parts of it by heart. He also asked her to show it to her friend, the opera singer Martha Dickons, 'as you know my great love for notoriety and fame'. What was more, the reviews were good – flattering even. The *Gentleman's Magazine* called him a 'writer of strong mind and powerful talents', and the *European Magazine* declared that his work showed 'much proof of an original genius'; while the April number of the *New Monthly Magazine*, reviewing his verse alongside the *Essay on the Source of Positive Pleasure*, pledged to observe John's future career with great interest, 'anxious,' it said, 'to examine how far a youthful and enthusiastic imagination would be effected by an intimacy with certainly, the greatest poet of the day'. On this count, John had been far more successful in escaping the oppressive influence of Byron, said the reviewer, than Hobhouse, whose own attempts at poetry he described as 'flat and artificial' and deserving of 'unqualified condemnation'. Rather, *Ximenes and The Wreath* possessed 'numerous beauties, and an individuality of spirit which breathes throughout, no less obvious, though of a very different complexion, than that of Lord Byron'.

Under normal circumstances, a flattering comparison to Byron combined with a pasting for Hobhouse would have pleased John immensely, yet the April edition of the *New Monthly Magazine* contained a second, more prominent, article that was too alarming to be ignored. Printed on the opening page, under the heading 'Original Communications', there was a piece entitled 'Extract of a Letter from Geneva'. It purportedly came from an English tourist, who described a recent visit to the Villa Diodati in the company of other curious English. They had traipsed over the villa's parquet floors and inspected its sconces 'with the same feelings of awe and respect as we did . . . those of Shakespeare's dwelling at Stratford'. Having made this first pilgrimage, the letter goes on to recount a tour of the environs in order to sniff out gossip about Byron's residence there, interviewing servants and locals only to receive repeated assertions of how private he had been. Just as he was on the brink of abandoning his enquiries, however, the correspondent had the good fortune to meet the Countess Breuss, who told him all about her parties at the Maison d'Abraham Gallatin, and the many 'excellent accounts' she had received from John Polidori 'of his Lordship's character'. While the specifics of these 'accounts' are omitted from the letter, the article lists a number of morsels that can only have come from John, matters so precise that even Byron had to admit their veracity. They included a detailed account of Shelley's hallucination during Byron's recitation of 'Christabel', and Shelley signing 'Atheist' in the album at Chamonix – the first accounts ever printed of either of these episodes – and accurate identifications of both Claire and Mary, who, it asserted, did not live in Byron's house as 'partakers of his revels', as the mythology upheld, but in a separate villa of their own. The letter also included an account of the Diodati ghost-story competition that differed from the one Shelley had told in his preface to *Frankenstein*, inasmuch as it omitted Shelley and added John as one of its participants. Furthermore, the letter said, the Countess Breuss had copies of all these stories, and had been kind enough to pass them on in order that they might be printed in the *New Monthly*, 'as I was assured you would feel as much curiosity as myself, to peruse the *ebauches* of so great a genius, and those immediately under his influence'. Appearing beneath the letter was a story entitled *The Vampyre; A Tale by Lord Byron.*

John was horrified. *The Vampyre* was not Byron's but his, a forgotten story written almost three years earlier for the entertainment of Breuss, and only loosely based on the outline Byron had abandoned in favour of taking Shelley on a tour of the lake. Not only had the *New Monthly Magazine* misattributed the work, it had also announced the imminent appearance of a separate edition to be published by the firm of Sherwood, Neely and Jones, who were calling it *The Vampyre; a tale, By the Right Honourable Lord Byron.*

Two problems presented themselves. The first was that John's work had appeared uncredited and without payment, and that his chances of receiving any money for it looked close to none. The vagaries of copyright law meant that stories in magazines were not subject to exclusive rights, so that anyone with the means to reprint them in book form could take the profits. Furthermore, books became subject to copyright only after they had been registered with Stationers' Hall and, as John soon discovered, the Sherwood edition had been recorded four days before the April issue of the *New Monthly Magazine* had appeared, thus making it impossible for him to publish his own edition at a later date.

His second predicament was even more scalding than lost revenue, and concerned the question of honour. A footnote in the 'Letter from Geneva' claimed that the magazine had in its possession 'the Tale of Dr _____ ', which, 'upon consulting with its author, we may, probably, hereafter give to our readers', a statement that, while ambiguous, clearly suggested a degree of friendly collusion between John and the magazine. Appalled by the implication that the misattribution was a fraud perpetrated with his full co-operation, John wrote to the magazine's proprietor, Henry Colburn, the man who had brought *Glenarvon* to the world, and who no doubt saw *The Vampyre* as a complementary tale. 'I received a copy of the magazine of last April,' John wrote, 'and am sorry to find that your Genevan correspondent has led you into a mistake with regard to the tale of *The Vampyre* – which is *not* Lord Byron's but was written *entirely* by me at the request of a lady.' Desiring that a correction be inserted in the next number, he then addressed the issue of remuneration. 'I shall not sit patiently by and see it taken without my consent, and appropriated by any person,' he wrote, adding that, 'I shall expect that you will account to me for the publishers . . . and demand either that a compensation be made me, or that its separate publication be instantly suppressed.' The following day, he wrote an even more forceful letter to Sherwood, Neely and Jones. 'I am deprived of all copyright therein and cannot any longer take advantage of my own work,' he told them.

> If I have not an immediate answer I shall immediately procure an injunction from Chancery to stop its further sale for I will not in any manner allow myself to be deprived of what is mine – I shall at the same time if the title page is not cancelled and my name inserted instead of Lord Byron, immediately publish it in all the papers that there is a mistake in the author.

To substantiate this final threat, he drafted a letter to the editor of the *Morning Chronicle* denouncing them all.

The Vampyre was published on a Thursday, John sent his letters on Friday and Saturday, and on Monday there appeared on his doorstep the emaciated figure of Henry Colburn, a man so diminutive he was said to wear boys' clothes. Colburn, along with John Murray and William Blackwood, was one of the most influential men in publishing, although his reputation in the industry was clear from the fact that even his highest-earning authors referred to him as a 'royal bastard'. Bribing reviewers and cheating rivals was his stock-in-trade, and it was claimed that he had even exploited the near-blindness of an elderly client to switch contracts on her so that she would sign over to him her entire literary property. Colburn, like John Murray, sought not only to commission works but to manipulate popular taste. Yet whereas Murray liked to feed the myth of his authors, Colburn literally cobbled books together in his office to react to the latest trends, and was roundly mocked for having instituted what he called a 'Publicity Department', dedicated to puffing his stock in his own magazines and paying people to talk them up at dinner parties.

Colburn arrived at John's rooms in Covent Garden Chambers with a contract, which, he claimed, would assure at least three hundred pounds in profits, along with the promise to pen a correction (what John called an '*amende honorable*'), as long the letter to the *Chronicle* was withdrawn. John agreed, but allowed Colburn to leave before anything could be signed due to the publisher's insistence that the contract was only a draft, and that if John 'might trust to his honour', he would return with a finalised one immediately. From that moment on, Colburn went to extensive lengths to avoid him completely – telling him that he had heard Byron *was* the true author, asking for time to investigate the matter properly, and dodging John's subsequent visits to his office by pretending never to be in. In the interim, the April number of the *New Monthly Magazine* sold out, as did the Sherwood, Neely and Jones edition of the *The Vampyre* published with an accompanying text by the unsavoury hack John Mitford entitled 'Lord Byron's Residence in the Island of Mitylene', a piece of pure fantasy purporting to be an account of Byron's travels through Greece, and an explanatory note on vampiric superstitions that quoted extensively from Byron's allusion to them in his 1813 poem, *The Giaour*.

> But first, on earth as Vampire sent,
> Thy corse shall from its tomb be rent;
> Then ghastly haunt thy native place,
> And suck the blood of all thy race,
> There from thy daughter, sister, wife,
> At midnight drain the stream of life;
> Yet loathe the banquet which perforce
> Must feed thy livid living corse;
> Thy victims ere they yet expire
> Shall know the daemon for their sire.

The Vampyre's success was both immediate and international, inspiring a wave of new editions in London, New York and Philadelphia, and translations into French, German, Spanish, Swedish and Italian.

The book had Colburn's market-massaging thumbprint all over it, but how he came to possess the text is a mystery. His claim was that the manuscript had been sent to him from Switzerland in the autumn of 1818, although the identity of the sender is unknown. Some point to the over-medicated Madame Gatelier, a member of Countess Breuss's household, while others suggest it was obtained by the author of the piece printed alongside the Sherwood edition of *The Vampyre*, John Mitford. However, given that Mitford was an alcoholic, said to be so derelict that he ate only cheese and onions, washed his clothes in a pond and spent his nights sleeping in an open field, it seems unlikely that he would have travelled abroad, much less been admitted into the presence of John's countess.

A third possibility arises from the testimony of the *New Monthly Magazine*'s young sub-editor Alaric Watts, who had taken himself to the offices of John Murray the moment the story appeared in order to 'exculpate himself from the baseness of the transaction'. Watts had originally prefaced the story with a note that presented it to the reader 'without pledging ourselves positively for its authenticity, as the production of Lord Byron' but at the last moment had found himself overruled by Colburn, who pulled this circumspect note and replaced it with an alternative, which stated only that the story had been written by a fascinating 'Individual' of 'erratic but transcendent genius'. Watts and Colburn quarrelled, the young journalist accusing his wily employer of 'deception and chicanery' before resigning his post and confessing all to Murray. In the process of excusing himself, Watts pushed hard for John Polidori's guilt, claiming that it was he who had approached them with the story, telling them that 'the whole plan of it' was Byron's, and that it had been 'merely written out by him'. It was '*quite impossible*', claimed Watts, that John 'should have been ignorant of the circumstances under which the Vampyre was published, as Mr. C informed me that he had applied to him for advice on a certain point connected with it'. John had given Watts 'his positive assurance upon the <u>honour</u> of <u>a gentleman</u> (which I had then no reason to disbelieve) that the tale had been <u>related</u> by Lord Byron to a <u>party at which he was present</u>; and, that he had committed it to paper from <u>recollection</u>!' Furthermore, said Watts, John was in possession of a second '*private* MS. of Lord Byron's', 'unscrupulously obtained', that he was presently trying to sell. This represented only a fraction of all he intended to publish, as, said Watts, 'this same specious physician', is preparing various MSS for publication (which he is pleased to term travels) the principal attraction of which he represents to Colburn, to be a detail of every <u>private occurrence</u> during his residence with Lord B. – the subjects of the noble Lord's conversations – accounts of his morning visits – mode of dressing – sleeping eating – travelling in fact from what I can find he promises to <u>masquerade</u> in the character of <u>Boswell</u>; and if one may judge from the bulk of his memoranda, he seems to have noticed every <u>mention</u> his master ever made during his stay with him!

Any denials that came from Polidori, concluded Watts, were made simply because the doctor was furious he had sold the story so cheaply after it had proved more popular than he ever could have imagined, and were intended to blackmail Colburn into paying him more.

Watts was young himself, only twenty-two, and clearly thinking of his own career as he curried favour with Murray while also avoiding public condemnation of his powerful former employer, yet the confidence with which he laid blame at John's feet suggests that Polidori may have been more than just a scapegoat. Was he guilty? The autumn of 1818 had seen him at his lowest ebb, recovering from concussion, suffering from depression, and incapable of supporting himself. In such circumstances, it is easy to envisage him sending a unique manuscript to Colburn in exchange for a quick return and a good review, a decision made all the easier by the appearance of *Frankenstein*, and its preface that deleted him from Diodati entirely and gave no credit for his contributions to the fireside conversations regarding 'whether man was thought to be merely an instrument' that had so inspired Mary. Still, the immediacy and earnestness with which John wrote to Colburn and Sherwood make it appear unlikely that this was just a bad deal gone wrong. That said, William Godwin had written to Sherwood on the same day as John to complain about 'the grossest and most unmanly reflections on my daughter' that had been published in the preface to the tale, and within days had managed to get Colburn to remove the paragraph that referred to the 'two sisters as the partakers of [Byron's] revels' from all subsequent printings. Colburn could, then, be reasonable and act swiftly to amend a wrong if need be. Perhaps John had suffered a change of heart and, feeling the need to undo what he had done, had distanced himself from his own work just as he had done in the preface to *An Essay on the Source of Positive Pleasure*. Perhaps he was as innocent as he claimed.

'Damn "*the Vampire*",' wrote Byron to Kinnaird, 'what do I know of Vampires?' Byron had moved to disown the story even before hearing the news from London, having seen an advertisement for it in *Galignani's Messenger*, an English-language newspaper published in Paris. 'I have a personal dislike to "Vampires",' he had written to the paper's editor, still oblivious of his ex-employee's role, 'and the little acquaintance I have with them would by no means induce me to divulge their secrets.' Shortly afterwards, Murray sent him the original, along with the news that the doctor was 'now preparing a sort of Boswell diary of your Lordships Life'. 'What do you mean by Polidori's *diary*?' Byron spluttered in response, in spite of having discussed with John the prospect of his journal as they had rumbled through Flanders three years earlier, 'why – I defy him to say any thing about me.'

Hobhouse, said Murray, 'has taken Polidori in hand'. Indeed, Byron's bulldog had written to John, demanding that he 'take some measures to put a stop to so dishonourable an artifice' and insisting that he apologise to Byron and drop the plan to publish his travels. 'That you should really have the intention of betraying the privacy of any man with whom you have lived in a confidential and professional footing,' steamed Hobhouse, 'is altogether incredible, and I trust you will favour me with a line contradicting so unpleasant a rumour.' John replied testily, maintaining that he had been misled 'by the means of a third person', and adding, 'As to the other point my travels I imagine you are aware that I pretend to the character and rank of a gentleman and therefore you must be aware that such a statement from whatever quarter it came must be absolutely false.' As for the matter of an apology, he refused: 'I certainly shall not do it, not for any reasons connected with the tale, but because I have heard from several quarters that he has written unkindly about me and cannot therefore feel any inclination to recommence a correspondence.' The exchange ended there, and when Hobhouse wrote the matter up for his friend, he laid the fault entirely at the doctor's door: 'a vile imposture and Dolly's whole and sole doing', he told Byron, mocking his claims to '*the rank and name of a gentleman*'. 'He is a sad scamp,' concluded Hobhouse, 'but you know I told you that you were wrong in taking him, you know I did.'

To put an end to the matter, Byron sent Murray the original leaves of his Diodati tale, dated 17 June 1816, with the instruction to publish it in *Blackwood's Edinburgh Magazine*, although, to his annoyance, the bookseller preferred to add it as an appendix to his forthcoming poem *Mazeppa*, without any note of explanation. The similarities between Byron's 'Augustus Darvell' fragment and Polidori's *Vampyre* are clear to see: both feature an older and a younger man travelling on the Continent, and both contain a sudden death and a vow extracted in eldritch circumstances. Yet whereas Byron's story exuded all his familiar Levantine musk,

Polidori's is a far more claustrophobic and pessimistic production, focusing almost entirely on the relationship between its two protagonists rather than the trappings of external magic. *The Vampyre* opens with the appearance in London of a pale and fascinating nobleman, 'more remarkable for his singularities, than for his rank', who incites interest among the fashionable ladies by virtue of his melancholy air and 'reputation of a winning tongue'. Known as Lord Ruthven (a name lifted directly from Caroline Lamb's *Glenarvon*), the stranger befriends a young gentleman named Aubrey, a rich but naïve orphan who brims with 'high romantic feeling of honour and candour' and believes that 'the dreams of poets were the realities of life'. When Ruthven is required to leave England on account of 'embarrassed' affairs, he invites Aubrey to accompany him on a journey into Greece. Aubrey accepts, but witnesses such cruelty and prodigality in a companion who delights in bringing men into financial ruin and reducing women to despair through his 'irresistible powers of seduction' that he decides to proceed alone. Arriving in Greece, Aubrey falls in love with Ianthe, a beautiful peasant who recounts the local legend of the vampire. The next day, he is caught in a violent thunderstorm and, searching for shelter, comes across a hut from which can be heard the dreadful shrieks of a woman 'mingling with the stifled, exultant mockery of a laugh'. He rushes to the woman's aid, only to find himself lifted up and flung to the ground 'by one whose strength seemed superhuman'. Regaining his senses, Aubrey finds Ianthe dead at his feet, her corpse painted with the blood that gushes from her neck.

Sickened by grief, the young man enters a delirium in which visions of his lover inexplicably mingle with those of Ruthven, who by that time has also arrived in Athens and come to attend the young man's sickbed. Ruthven having redeemed himself through his close attentions, the two men resume travelling through the Greek countryside, until their progress is one day halted by an attack of bandits. Ruthven is shot, and as his life drains away, he extracts a promise from Aubrey similar to that of Augustus Darvell – namely, that he will not announce the death to anyone for a year and a day. Aubrey swears, at which point Ruthven literally dies laughing. His corpse is left to rest in a nearby hovel, and by morning, it has disappeared.

Aubrey's homeward journey is as meandering and melancholy as his thoughts, and when he finally re-enters London society, he finds that the man who has died in his arms is vigorously alive and posing as the Earl of Marsden. 'Remember your oath,' whispers Ruthven, emerging from a fashionable throng and driving the young man so mad with fear that he flirts with the notion of suicide. Doctors are called and Aubrey is shut up in his home, wasting away in a near catatonic state while preparations are made for his eighteen-year-old sister, a plain, shy, sad girl with her thoughts fixed on a higher realm, to be married. Though he has yet to meet her intended, it dawns on Aubrey that the groom can only be Ruthven. Insane with impatience for the oath to expire, he writes to his sister, begging her to delay the wedding, but the note is impounded by his physician who reads it as a symptom of his madness. Dragging himself to the wedding chamber, he confronts Ruthven, who reminds him again of his promise and warns him of the dishonour that will descend upon his sister if he dares to utter a word. This so enrages Aubrey that he suffers a fatal aneurysm, yet in the moments before he dies, he is at last able to convince his guardians of his sister's peril. They rush to her aid, but are too late: 'Lord Ruthven had disappeared, and Aubrey's sister had glutted the thirst of a VAMPYRE!'

John Polidori's story holds a unique place in literary history for presenting the first fully realised vampire in English literature, having brought the feral, dirt-caked monster Byron had known from rural legend into the city, and transformed him into the mesmeric habitué of drawing rooms and gaming tables. But aside from remodelling the monster, in his presentation of Ruthven as the hit of the season, John's *Vampyre* can also be read as an attack on the cult of fame, castigating a jaded chattering class whose appetite for novelty makes them vulnerable to exploitation. More specifically, Ruthven's elevation to a position of celebrity affords the licence that allows him to pursue a career of seduction and predation that takes the form of a focused and rapacious misogyny. But while women are the victims of Ruthven's violence, they are also the instruments he uses to destroy another man; as such *The Vampyre* becomes a parable of resentful male intimacy. Although Ruthven's sexual frenzy annihilates the ideals of chastity and court-ship that Ianthe and Miss Aubrey represent, it is not their murders that assure his dominance over Aubrey, so much as his oath. In Byron's story of Augustus Darvell, the oath and its associated rituals are a gift suggesting induction into an occult world. In John's version, the oath is a gag, a means of binding Aubrey to a stifling confidentiality in which his mute helplessness is reinforced by Ruthven's belittling laughter, an idea sustained by the fact that when John set to revising the text for what he hoped would be his 'authorised' edition, one of the key amendments he made was to change the name Ruthven to 'Strongmore'. Emasculated by the stronger man, Aubrey hopes to find consolation in a feeling of ethical superiority that equates success with immorality, and pleasure with violence. The defence is weak, and, shamed by the loss of his voice, he becomes listless and ill until his anger triggers a fatal violence that he can deploy only against himself. On the brink of death and powerless to prevent his sister's murder, Aubrey is left with nothing but a prideful commitment to his word, and a faint consolation that his suffering is somehow virtuous.

14

SEA SODOM

For the first time since leaving London, Byron felt blessedly free of the 'infection' of the English. Eighteen months in Venice had revitalised him, affording him a sense of liberation and renewal in a place that shared his love of theatricality and masquerade, a feeling of rejuvenation that he hoped would never end. 'Here have I pitched my staff,' he told Samuel Rogers, 'and here do I propose to reside for the remainder of my life.'

The city was a tarnished jewel, passed from one invading hand to the next, with a dwindling population and suffocated commerce that struggled under a rate of Austrian taxation that had reached 60 per cent. Dereliction and abandonment smothered the majesty around him to create a floating ruin, which, in the words of Hobhouse, seemed to have belonged 'to better people in better times'. Yet the air of exhausted opulence made Byron love it all the more, its silent canals and 'gloomy gaiety' entirely in sympathy with his own disposition.

The change was reflected in his work as he put aside the introspective archaeology of *Childe Harold* with a fourth and final canto, and moved on to fleeter, more satirical works, such as the lasciviously playful *Beppo*, based on a Venetian tale about a seafaring husband, presumed dead, who returns from a long captivity to find his wife happily cavorting with her lover. The poem inaugurated a new style, one that he would continue to develop in his last great epic, *Don Juan*, which showed, Byron said, 'that I can write cheerfully, and repel the charge of monotony and mannerism'.

To live in Venice was cheap, but even so Byron had already managed to spend five thousand pounds, funded by the sale of Newstead Abbey and the generous proceeds of his writing, which had finally allowed him to begin the ascent from debt to wealth. Half of that sum had gone on the rent for a grand *palazzo* and summer villa staffed by fourteen servants in blue and white livery. The other half had been spent on women. Liberal attitudes to adultery combined with the recessionary economics of pandering and prostitution had transformed a city long synonymous with sophisticated libertinage into a veritable 'Sea Sodom', 'the seat of all dissoluteness', into which the poet had lowered himself with ease. Every Venetian was 'employed in the laudable practice of Lovemaking', he told a friend, and since instructing his piratical head gondolier, the large and evilly bearded Tita Falcieri, to procure any woman who caught his eye, he claimed to have slept with at least two hundred, preferring to take lovers from the 'middling and lower classes' on account of finding 'their amatory habits more universally diffused'. 'My hands are full,' he declared, 'what ever my Seminal vessels may be.'

Allegra and her nurse, Elise, entered this sensuous scene in May 1818. 'My Bastard came three days ago,' Byron wrote to Hobhouse, 'very like – healthy – noisy – and capricious', although he was some distance from being able to offer her a stable home. His principal mistress, Marianna Segati, had been dismissed in favour of involvements with Margherita Cogni, the illiterate wife of a baker known as 'La Fornarina' (the 'little oven'), and the opera singer Arpalice Taruscelli, 'the prettiest Bacchante in the world – and a piece to perish in . . . I have fucked her twice a day for the last six,' he boasted to Hobhouse of Arpalice, 'today is the seventh – but no Sabbath day – for we meet at Midnight at her Milliners.' As well as being between mistresses, Byron was also between homes, having resigned his accommodation in the Frezzaria to negotiate a lease on the considerably more sumptuous Gritti Palace.

While he made his arrangements, Allegra was placed in the care of the British consul to Venice, Richard Belgrave Hoppner and his Swiss wife, Isabelle. Hoppner, the son of the portrait painter and Royal Academician John Hoppner, was a talented painter in his own right. He had been a keen and solicitous friend to Byron, offering any help he could, in return for which the famous lord had stood as godfather to his baby son, John William Rizzo. Allegra and Elise stayed with the Hoppners for around six weeks as her father failed to secure the Gritti Palace and arranged instead a three-year lease on the Palazzo Mocenigo. In sight of the Piazza San Marco and the Rialto, this was the mansion into which she was noisily welcomed in mid-June, toddling through its high-ceilinged rooms and onto the broad stone balconies that overhung the Grand Canal, and exploring its wet basement where her father kept a fox, some monkeys and numerous cats and dogs. She was 'a very fine child', Byron told Hobhouse, 'much admired in the gardens and on the Piazza – and greatly caressed by the Venetians from the Governatrice downwards'.

Shortly after the move, La Fornarina abandoned her husband and proclaiming eternal devotion to her lover, invited herself to move in, asserting her claim by threatening to kill any woman who came near him, a promise supported by an imposing presence that led Byron to describe her as a 'Pythonness', who combined 'the strength of an Amazon with the temper of Medea'. Her installation caused havoc within the house as she adopted aristocratic airs, scared the wits out of Fletcher, and set the termagant cook and querulous servants at one another's throats. Allegra was treated like a doll, dressed up and stuffed with peculiar foods.

It was all too much for Elise. Byron rarely rose before three, and with poor English and no Italian, she found it impossible to negotiate between the warring factions who ruled over daytime. Trying to make sense of it all, she sent a series of alarming reports back to Claire, who was summering with the Shelleys in the spa town of Bagni di Lucca in the chestnut-wooded mountains behind Livorno.

Elise's letters convinced Claire that Allegra was in grave danger of neglect. She begged Shelley to take her to Venice, a long and difficult journey that required crossing the entire peninsula from coast to coast, and Shelley agreed: he had grown bored of their quiet excursions, daily baths, and the genteel entertainments of the narrow-minded locals, and the thought of seeing Byron and an adventure with Claire was greatly appealing. Leaving Mary behind with two servants and the infants William and Clara, Claire and Shelley crossed the Apennines, travelling sixty miles a day for three days in dust and stifling heat before arriving in Padua on 21 August. On the road they devised a plan: Claire would remain in Padua where Shelley would claim they were all living, thus providing him with an excuse for casually dropping in. But on arrival, Claire changed her mind, repelled by the threat of bedbugs and loneliness and, with night falling, insisted that they travel the final twenty miles to Venice together. They went by water, huddled on the couch of a covered gondola, lit like an amphibious hearse, listening as their gondolier, unprompted, recounted tales of an English '*nome stravagante*' who spent enormous sums of money and kept the company of countless women. They entered the lagoon at midnight just as a thunderstorm erupted, rain making glitter of the water, and the city revealing itself in silhouettes of domes and turrets as lightning split the sky.

They spent the night at an inn, where their waiter offered his own spontaneous accounts of Byron, before calling on the

Hoppners the following morning. The consul and his wife received Claire warmly, and were sorry to confirm Elise's stories, as well as confiding in Claire that Byron had frequently spoken of her 'with extreme horror'. Allegra was sent for, and arrived looking well, although much quieter than they remembered her and 'so grown you would hardly know her', Shelley reported to Mary. 'She is pale and has lost a good deal of her liveliness, but is as beautiful as ever though more mild.'

Leaving Claire and Allegra to spend some time together, Shelley went to call on Byron. With no idea what to expect of the friend he had not seen since Geneva, he found the signs of his excess worn on him like a slow erosion. While not quite the 'fat, fat-headed, middle-aged man, slovenly to the extreme, unkempt, with long, untied locks that hang down on his shoulders', reported by Lord Glenbervie, he appeared as weathered as the city, in old clothes, threadbare and ill-fitting from too many washes. His mood, however, bucked his appearance, and Shelley was disarmed at how cheerful and agreeable he had become, telling Thomas Love Peacock that his friend seemed to be 'the liveliest, and happiest looking man I ever met'. Affability animated their conversation as Byron issued declarations of enduring friendship and insisted that, if he had been in England, he would have done all he could to help Shelley keep his children and banish the Westbrooks. Even when the subject turned to Claire, Shelley was amazed at the readiness with which Byron acknowledged her maternal claims, even going so far as to say that Claire could keep Allegra if she really wanted her, only that it would ruin both the child's prospects and his own standing among the Venetians who had already marked him with 'the reputation of caprice'. This he accompanied with a proposal to let Shelley take Allegra to see her mother at Padua, even offering them his summer villa at nearby Este.

Shelley was desperate to share this wonderful news, but first

Byron insisted on taking him riding. They went across the lagoon to where he kept horses at the Lido – a further sign of his extravagance, as it was said there were only eight horses in the whole of Venice, four bronze ones over the cathedral of San Marco and four in Lord Byron's stable. As they galloped across the firm sands and towy weeds of the Adriatic, he regaled his friend with yet more 'histories of his wounded feelings'.

Both men enjoyed the meeting, and both were satisfied with its outcome – Shelley with Byron's concession, and Byron at having placated Claire without having to see her. 'Allegra is well,' he told Augusta, 'but her mother (whom the Devil confound) came prancing the other day over the Apennines – to see her *child*.' Congratulating himself on packing her off to Este before her presence could cause trouble with his mistresses, he remarked that he had 'declined seeing her for fear that the consequence might be an addition to the family'. 'Why might not the father and mother of a child whom both so tenderly love meet as friends?' Claire had asked him during the negotiations for Allegra's transfer, but his note to Augusta suggests that the answer lay partly in a fear that he could not trust himself not to sleep with her again. Certainly, she had made it clear that she remained available. 'Are you not the Sun to me?' she had asked him only two months before. 'I verily believe it for I have never known a hot moment since I left Geneva.'

Byron's villa, with its vine-trellised walks and views across the plain of Lombardy, was a deliciously cool haven in those dog days. Situated forty miles west of Venice on the southern tip of the Euganean hills, its long garden abutted onto a ruined castle that had once been the citadel of the Este family and was now home to a colony of owls and bats. It was a joy for Claire to be able to spend so long with her daughter, although for Mary, who was required to travel all the way from Bagni di Lucca with William, Clara and a servant named Paolo Foggi, the trip was a much harder ordeal. One-year-old Clara had been sick with dysentery when Mary received Shelley's hasty summons, and the heat and discomfort of the journey made the baby worse. She arrived at Byron's villa only to find that Claire and Shelley were also ill – Shelley with food poisoning and Claire with an undiagnosed ailment.

While no one was well, it was at least tranquil, as William and Allegra spent sun-dappled mornings beagling around the fruit trees and ruins while Mary and Shelley wrote and read and took excursions to see Petrarch's tomb. In late September, however, Clara's health suddenly worsened as she cut all her teeth at once and fell into a fever. The physician in Este was 'a stupid fellow', according to Mary, so she bundled Clara up and took her first to Padua, where Claire also wanted to see a doctor, and then on to Venice in search of better medical help.

It was Mary's first visit to a city she had been curious to see for months, but she took no pleasure in her arrival. At five in the morning on 24 September as she stepped from a gondola and entered an inn, Clara became convulsive. Shelley went to fetch the doctor, but returning alone, he found Mary in terrible distress, pacing the hall with the baby in her arms. Within an hour, Clara was dead.

The bereavement delayed Allegra's return to Venice. She was a companion for William, and with one child gone, Shelley was reluctant to snatch another from its mother. But Byron refused to extend her stay beyond October and recalled her to Mocenigo, sending Shelley into a rage. Unable to fathom how a man might prefer to have his daughter to live neglected on the margins of his debauchery rather than at the heart of a loving, idealistic community, he denounced Byron to Peacock, raging at the poet's 'insanity' and the putrescence of his consorts, 'the most ignorant the most disgusting, the most bigotted, the most filthy' in the world, he claimed, women who 'smell so of garlick that an ordinary Englishman cannot approach them . . . You may think how unwillingly *I* have left my little favourite Alba in a situation where she might fall again under his authority,' he said, his anger finding solace only in the knowledge that if Byron continued on his current path he would probably die. 'I hope,' he wrote, 'that his present career must end up soon by some violent circumstance which must reduce our situation with respect to Alba into its antient tie.'

Shelley's anger was justified. When Allegra did return to Venice, it was not to be reunited with her father, who had dismissed Elise and made no provision for another nurse, but to be placed into the care of the Hoppners, who continued to feed Claire a regular drip of unwelcome news. Allegra was listless and looked like an old lady, they said. Her speech was delayed, and she did not have half the vocabulary of John Rizzo, almost a year younger. Byron saw her only rarely, and when he did, it was to send her back with hands and feet raw from the cold of being left underdressed in the huge, damp *palazzo* where she competed for attention with her father's ever-growing menagerie.

But Claire was also unavailable, as she and the Shelleys spent eight months travelling between Rome and Naples on account of Shelley's health. No news of Allegra reached her until the spring of 1819, when Mrs Hoppner told her that an acquaintance of hers, a wealthy British widow named Mrs Vavassour, had offered to adopt the child on condition that her father renounce all claims. At last Claire let her frustration at Byron show. 'I have said nothing definitively because I knew what a very unnatural thing you would think it that I should interfere with my own child,' she wrote to him. 'It is impossible that you can live as you now do – therefore before you do any thing decided think and do not throw away the greatest treasure you have on strangers.'

Byron's circumstances were also about to change, as that spring he had discovered a new love – Teresa Guiccioli, a short, cherubic nineteen-year-old countess he described to Kinnaird as 'a sort of Italian Caroline Lamb, except that she is much prettier, and not so savage' – and even though his friends uniformly counselled him against it, his pursuit of her became all-consuming. The intensity of his feelings took even Byron by surprise, and it was clear that this would be no casual conquest. Teresa was married and had no intention of deceiving her husband, a rich, powerful and not entirely unsinister count forty years her senior whom she addressed as 'sir'. While she reciprocated Byron's passion, she refused to follow the straightforward path of clandestine meetings and secret adultery, requiring him instead to perform the ritual duties of a *cavalier servante*, the doting male companion whose supposedly platonic attentions made arranged marriages bearable. It was a role fully condoned by Italian society, but still, the disorientating civility with which Count Guiccioli treated Byron even as rumours of his cuckoldry began to circulate, made the poet especially uneasy, 'so that if I come away with a Stilleto in my gizzard some fine afternoon – I shall not be astonished'.

Drawn by love, Byron followed Teresa to her husband's home in Ravenna, leaving Allegra once more with the Hoppners, who themselves wished to be rid of her as they were going to Switzerland. When Byron refused their offer to settle her with a good Swiss family, the Hoppners simply left, committing her to the care of Mrs Martens, wife of the Danish consul. Mrs Martens in turn seems to have passed her on to the family of Hoppner's clerk, Richard Edgecombe, although Byron had specifically stated that she should not go near Mrs Edgecombe, whom he considered a 'foolish mad woman'. For about six weeks in the summer of 1819, no one – not

Claire, not Shelley, not Byron – was able to say exactly where Allegra was, or even if she had been adopted by Mrs Vavassour. At last, Byron managed to have her sent to him in Bologna, a commission that took more than two weeks to fulfil, as nobody seemed to be quite sure how this could be accomplished.

Allegra's return marked the beginning of a new project of domestication for Byron, and by the autumn, she was staying with Byron and Teresa at La Mira, Byron's new summer house on the banks of the Brenta near Venice. The project's success, however, was debatable, as Byron was troubled both by the 'degradation' of his life as the 'fan carrier of a woman' and his role as a father. Thomas Moore paid him a visit there, and records his friend gesturing in Allegra's direction and asking if he had 'any notion . . . of what they call the parental feeling? For myself, I have not the least.' Moore was baffled by the comment and, on reflection, decided it was a joke. Certainly, when Byron next wrote to Augusta to describe the progress of his 'very amiable and pretty' daughter, he sounded unreservedly proud. 'She is English,' he wrote:

> but speaks nothing but Venetian – 'Bon *di* papa' etc.
> etc. she is very droll – and has a good deal of the Byron
> – can't articulate the letter *r* at all – frowns and pouts
> quite in our way – blue eyes – light hair growing *darker*
> daily – and a dimple on the chin – a scowl on the brow
> – white skin – sweet voice – and a particular liking of
> Music – and of her own way in every thing – is not that
> B. all over?

It was also a creditable description of Claire.

Allegra's future would become increasingly tied to the fortunes of Byron's relationship with Teresa Guiccioli, two married people, one internationally famous, the other bound by strict social codes, whose love affair was always going to be difficult. Byron thrived on entanglements, but his relationship with Teresa was altogether of another order. The first sign of its complexity came when Teresa's father, the well-connected Count Ruggero Gamba, objected to the romance on the grounds of Byron's notoriety and began to exert pressure on Count Guiccioli to curb his young bride and recall her to Ravenna. A reluctant Byron counselled her to go back, aware that an elopement would not only ruin her own reputation but, in the unforgiving patriarchy of Italy, that of her five unmarried sisters. Teresa's obeisance left Byron bereft. 'Never again shall Sorrow be/A Vampire at my heart for thee,' he wrote. 'Yes! drop by drop and beat by beat/Ye wrung my bosom's blood, most Sweet!'

The extent of his feeling was unlike anything he had experienced as an adult. He was filled with jealousy and, admitting that he was 'lonely', pledged to abandon Italy for ever. He would return first to England where he meant to challenge and slay Henry Brougham (for the bad review of *Hours of Idleness*, for giving 'Fare Thee Well' to the press, and for spreading lies in Geneva), before crossing the Atlantic to settle with Allegra in Venezuela. 'I am not yet thirty two years of age,' he told Hobhouse, 'I might still be a decent citizen and found a *house* and a family, as good – or better than the former.'

Even as he gave the order to sell his fox, his gondola and his two silver coffee pots, Allegra fell sick, and while the doctors dosed her with Peruvian bark, Byron's plan of 'revenge first – and emigration afterwards' found itself 'lulled upon the feverish pillow of a sick infant'. By the time Allegra recovered, winter had set in, making a journey through the Alps impossible. Then, on Christmas

Eve 1819, hearing the news that Teresa had herself fallen ill, he gathered up Allegra and went straight to Ravenna to be at her bedside, there to be further mystified by the count who invited him and his court of cats, birds and monkeys to move into the Palazzo Guiccioli and occupy its second floor.

In Ravenna, Byron happily resumed the persona of *cavalier servante*, a role he found at once absurd and oddly satisfying as he made the rounds of the local *conversazioni* revelling in the almost total absence of English and the fond welcome he received from local society. Allegra also fitted in well, as Teresa took her for rides along the Corso and through the Roman pine forest, and gave her dolls to add to the fine collection she had already begun to amass. She was now three years old, in good health and 'as ravenous as a Vulture', Byron told Hoppner, growing steadily both 'in good looks and obstinacy', as she openly defied the servants and made her father laugh with her teasing imitation of Fletcher.

It was now the spring of 1820, and Claire had not seen her daughter for a year and a half. She had been travelling for almost the entire period, living in four different cities, at seven different addresses, and staying in upwards of thirty-five different inns and lodgings on the road. From Byron's villa in Este, Claire and the Shelleys had travelled to Rome and Naples, and back again to Rome, where they endured the tragic and unexpected death of three-year-old William from malaria. Having made their way north, they had settled first in Livorno, where they had become close with John and Maria Gisborne, English friends of the Godwins. The company of Maria Gisborne, in particular, was a great consolation to Mary, who was soon pregnant again, while Maria's son, Henry Reveley, persuaded Shelley to invest in his scheme to build a steamboat to ferry passengers between Livorno and Marseille, and may also have asked Claire for her hand in marriage. From

Livorno, they moved to nearby Montenero and then Florence so that Mary could find a good doctor to help deliver her baby, another little boy whom they named Percy Florence. With their new child, they settled at last in Pisa, attracted by its spring-like climate, cheap *palazzi,* and the relative benignity of the Tuscan government.

Life in Pisa gave them all some much-needed stability. For Claire especially it was the closest she had come to a settled home since her dawn flight from Skinner Street in the summer of 1814. She enjoyed full days of music and dancing lessons, and social calls facilitated by John Polidori's one-time mentor, Andrea Vaccà Berlinghieri. Yet the most important friend she made was another acquaintance of the Godwins, an author for the Juvenile Library and friend of her mother, known as Mrs Mason. 'Mason' was the assumed name of Margaret King Moore, Lady Mount Cashell, a tall, brawny Irish woman who had borne eight children before leaving her tyrannical husband for a life based on the emancipated precepts of her childhood tutor, Mary Wollstonecraft. Claire would come to look upon her as a second mother, and took tea with her regularly at Casa Silva, the house on the Via Mala Gonella that Lady Mount Cashell shared with her lover George Tighe, and their daughters Laura and Nerina. It was an exclusively female environment, as Tighe, a quiet and chivalrous Irishman, was absorbed in the mysteries of potatoes and rarely entered the drawing room, preferring to dedicate his time to agricultural experiments and refinements of cultivation that earned him the nickname 'Tatty'.

Once settled, Claire wrote to Byron hoping that Allegra might be allowed again to spend the hot summer months with her in Bagni di Lucca, sending the message through Hoppner, who delayed it, 'fearing to annoy you with it'. Byron ultimately refused, citing the deaths of Clara and William as his reason for keeping her near. 'I should look upon the Child as going into a hospital,' he said, of sending Allegra to be with them,

> Is it not so? Have they *reared* one? – Her health has hitherto been excellent – and her temper not bad – she is sometimes vain and obstinate – but always clean and cheerful – and as in a year or two I shall either send her to England – or put her in a Convent for education – these defects will be remedied as far as they can in human nature. – But the Child shall not quit me again – to perish of Starvation, and green fruit – or be taught to believe that there is no Deity.

The barb wounded Claire deeply, but she retained her composure, conscious that it was necessary if she were to have any hope of seeing her child again. Patiently, she sought to rebut his allegations one by one, promising to keep Allegra away from the Shelleys, feed her any diet he prescribed, and even to recant her own atheism. 'Your fears concerning the Child's religious principles are quite unnecessary,' she told him, 'as I should never allow her to be taught to disbelieve in what I myself believe, therefore you may be assured that in whatever way you desire, she shall be taught to worship God.'

As usual, Byron did not answer, but Claire was left in no doubt that he considered her an 'atheistical mother' and that Allegra would be best served by being placed in a convent. This idea had come to him even before he had met his daughter, telling Augusta in May 1817 that he planned to bring her up as 'a good Catholic – and (it may be) a Nun – being a character somewhat wanted in our family', a notion that had been reinforced in the course of his affair with the convent-educated Guiccioli. Teresa had entered the Dominican convent of Santo Stefano at the age of five, before moving to the convent of Santa Chiara in Faenza at the age of nine, remaining cloistered until seventeen, whence she emerged with exactly the degree of education required of women in Byron's opinion, before they curdled into rebarbative blue-stockings. She knew literature and history, and though he liked to mock the florid effusions of her 'convent' prose, she wrote wittily and well, and inhabited the world with such effortless grace that she appeared to him the quintessence of agreeable femininity. This was exactly what Claire feared most: 'I am willing to undergo any affliction rather than her whole life should be spoilt by a convent education', she said to him, imagining a curriculum of superstition and ignorance that would 'inflict the greatest of all evils on my child' and 'destroy every seed of virtue that she may have'.

Although Claire had no way of knowing, Byron had other considerations to take into account, most notably the difficulties of engaging an acceptable governess. Teresa found fault with almost everyone he employed, especially during the summer of 1820 while she stayed at her father's summer residence and Byron remained in Ravenna. Separated for months and threatened by his proximity to other women, she demanded that he take a servant who was personally loyal to her and then objected to each in turn. The first to go was Anna, 'that new woman of yours', followed by the daughter of a coachman, dismissed for lying. Annunziata, the third, was rejected because Teresa had heard she was 'very suited for causing disorder in families'. The fourth, an old employee named Fanny Silvestrini, presumptuously promoted herself to the role, sending both Teresa and Byron into fits. Send her a 'passport to Hell', Teresa said. Allegra, meanwhile, was in a third location, Villa Bacinetti, where she spent the summer alone with her servants, bed-ridden with intermittent fevers and issuing orders for birds to be killed and cooked.

Shelley tried again to keep the peace, urging Byron to 'forgive the weak', but Byron was flushed with resentment at what he called Claire's 'Bedlam behaviour'. 'Clare writes me the most insolent letters,' he complained to Hoppner. 'If [she] thinks she shall ever interfere with the child's morals or education – she mistakes – she never shall – The girl shall be a Christian and a married woman . . . To express it delicately,' he concluded, 'I think Madame Clare is a damned bitch.'

But Hoppner had already washed his hands of Claire, and no longer offered to pass on Byron's messages. Byron was curious to discover what had brought about such a sudden change of heart, to which Hoppner replied that Claire was not only a 'damned bitch', 'but any thing worse even that you can say of her'. Following their favourable first impressions, the Hoppners had become increasingly uneasy about Claire's relationship with Shelley, only to have their doubts confirmed by some very troubling reports they had heard via Elise, William and Allegra's former nurse, now married to another of the Shelleys' former servants, Paolo Foggi. Hoppner had initially thought to keep the rumours to himself, but in the midst of the fight over Allegra, he felt compelled to pass on everything he had heard 'as it will fortify you,' he told Byron, 'in the good resolution that you have already taken never to trust her again to her mother's care'.

What Elise had told him was this: when Claire and Shelley had come to visit Allegra in the summer of 1818, Claire was pregnant with Shelley's baby, a secret they had successfully concealed from Mary. After failing to kill the child with toxic abortifacients, Claire had given birth to it in Naples just after Christmas, bribing a midwife, Hoppner reported to Byron, to take the child to an orphanage 'half an hour after its birth, being obliged likewise to purchase the physician's silence with a considerable sum'. The delivery, like the pregnancy, took place without arousing the slightest suspicion in Mary, although having parted with the child,

Claire and Shelley subjected her to the vilest abuse – Shelley beating her while Claire threw insults and hectored Shelley to abandon her. 'Clare does not scruple to tell Mrs Shelley that she wishes her dead,' Hoppner said.

As disturbing as it sounds, the story was not without some foundation. A girl had been born in Naples on 27 December 1818 – although Claire was not its mother – whom Shelley had taken to be baptised on 27 February, 1819, naming her Elena Adelaide Shelley and listing himself and Mary as parents. The child's actual parents are impossible to ascertain, as is the extent of Mary's complicity, but the available evidence suggests that, in the haze of grief that followed the death of Clara and the return of Allegra, Shelley took the step of claiming an orphan as his own, leaving her in Naples and providing for her until she was old enough to be brought into the family proper. Given his history of taking children under his wing, this was perfectly in character, although the lengths to which he went to conceal the adoption, confiding only in the Gisbornes, who burned his letters and sent him money under an assumed name, indicate a deeper mystery. In June 1820, however, Elena Shelley contracted a fever and died, but not before Paolo Foggi, engaged at Bagni di Lucca but dismissed in Naples for being an inveterate cheat, had tried to extort them. The threat of a lawyer made Foggi retreat, and there they thought that the matter lay – until, that was, Foggi sought to exact his revenge via his wife.

'The Shiloh story is true, no doubt,' Byron replied to Hoppner, 'it is just like them.' Meanwhile, in London, William Godwin had finally learned of the existence of Allegra, and was telling the visiting Maria Gisborne that her real father was Shelley.

While yet ignorant of Elise's venom, the Shelley household was suffering as the accumulated difficulties of the previous year began to take their toll. The deaths of her children and Godwin's renewed demands for money – this time to settle years of unpaid back rent – along with his principled refusal to offer any emotional support to Mary had pushed her deeper into a depression. 'He heaps on her misery, still misery,' said Shelley of Godwin, calling him 'this solemn lie'. Shelley was preoccupied with his own poor health and failing to understand his wife's unhappiness or absorption in Percy, felt increasingly distant from her. They clashed constantly. 'Mary considers me as a portion of herself,' Shelley told the Gisbornes, 'and feels no more remorse in torturing me than in torturing her own mind.' Claire also fought with her, but was more inclined to see their battles as a continuation of the status quo. 'Heigh-ho the Clare and the Ma,' she wrote in her journal, 'find something to fight about every day.'

As happened in times of turmoil, the promise of future happiness was bound to the question of Claire. In an echo of her Lynmouth exile, a plan was considered to find her a job in Paris through connections in the expatriate community in Pisa, but this fell through after she displayed some unwelcome honesty about her background and political opinions. Lady Mount Cashell provided some temporary shelter at Casa Silva, counselling her on the need to become independent of the Shelleys, and encouraging her to write a volume of her travels. In the short term, Claire needed to earn money, and as she had no intention of marrying, the only available route that would make use of her linguistic and musical talents and maintain the comforts of her present lifestyle, was to become a governess.

A place for her was found in Florence as a paying guest in the house of Dr Antonio Bojti, the personal surgeon of Ferdinand III, Grand Duke of Tuscany, and Claire moved into their house opposite Duke Ferdinand's residence in the Pitti Palace that October. It was intended as an apprenticeship, a month's trial during which she would familiarise herself with the Bojti children, learn German from Bojti's German wife, and introduce herself to potential employers among the cream of Tuscan society. The days were filled with introductions and walks in the Boboli Gardens, and nights spent over Latin exercises and poems by John Keats. On one of those nights, Fletcher and Elise appeared to her in a dream and told her that Allegra was on her way to visit her.

It was lonely in Florence, and the frequent letters that came from Shelley only served to worsen Claire's condition. He had provided the money for her stay in Florence and even taken her to settle in, but had been against the move and, although unable to say as much in front of Mary, resented Lady Mount Cashell for advocating the untying of their bond. Mary might be his intellectual partner, but Claire was his accomplice, an ally whose loyalty and understanding could always be depended upon, and who stirred feelings in him which by his own admission had always been 'a source of disquietude to me'. Some of these letters had been written in secret to avoid being 'taxed' by Mary, who would censor their expressions of unhappiness, poor health and solitude. 'Cheerful conversation is of some use to me,' he wrote, 'but what would it be to your sweet consolation, my own Clare?' In others, he imagined their future escapades, telling her about his cousin, Thomas Medwin, whom Mary considered an outright bore, and his plans for an expedition to Egypt. Claire and Shelley would go too, 'and do not mention it in your letter to Mary'. When the trial month was due to end, he begged her to make her excuses and come back to Pisa, but Claire tried her hardest to live up to Lady Mount Cashell's expectations and fortify herself against him. 'Think of yourself as a stranger and a traveller on the earth,' she wrote in her journal, 'to whom none of the many affairs of this world belong and who has no permanent township on the globe.'

Thoughts of Byron and Allegra also filled the pages of that notebook, and she began to make sketches for a work she called 'Hints for Don Juan' about a deformed and monstrous poet driven mad by self-indulgence to commit acts of unspeakable evil. She also recorded ideas for a series of Gillray-esque cartoons about him. One lampooned his womanising, others his waxing and waning belief in God. Another revealed his recipe for writing poetry:

> He sitting drinking spirits, playing with his white moustachios. His mistress . . . opposite him Drinking coffee. Fumes coming from her mouth, over which is written 'garlich'; these curling direct themselves towards his English footman who is just then entering the room and he is knocked backward – Lord B. is writing he says, '*Imprimis*, to be a great pathetic poet. 1st Prepare a small colony, then dispatch the mother by worrying and cruelty to her grave afterwards to neglect and ill treat the children – to have as many dirty mistresses as can be found; from their embraces to catch horrible diseases, thus a tolerable quantity of discontent and remorse being prepared to give it vent on paper, and to remember particularly to rail against learned women.

'This,' says a self-satisfied Byron, 'is my infallible receipt by which I have made so much money.' Claire's final sketch would depict his death, 'extended on his bed, covered all but his breast, which many wigged doctors are cutting open to find out (as one may be saying) 'what was the extraordinary disease of which this great man died?' His heart laid bare, they find an immense capital "I" grown on its surface.'

She also prepared a sketch about Shelley: 'He looking very sweet and smiling. A little Jesus Christ playing about the room. He says, "I will quietly murder that little child."'

TORN CLOUDS BEFORE
THE HURRICANE

'Ambition,' John had written in the preface to *Ximenes*, 'is the most assuming of all passions. Its appetite, like that of the furnace, indeed, increases with the fuel thrown in, which but raises a greater flame.' By the spring of 1820, however, he wanted nothing more than to be absorbed back into the saltless anonymity he had so despised. Accused of being Colburn's indentured hack, shut up in a back room on seven shillings a day, he had seen himself ridiculed as a member of the 'Vampyre family', 'a knot of scribblers, male and female, with weak nerves, and disordered brains, from whom have sprung those disgusting compounds of unnatural conception, bad taste and absurdity'. Throughout 1819, the scandal had failed to abate as the magazines and journals chewed over the 'mysterious transaction so murderous to the literary name of the poor Doctor', and accused him of 'pilfering the pockets of the public', 'audacious and unprincipled forgery' and an 'accursed hunger [for] gold'.

In truth, John was poor. Having run out of money, he resigned his lodgings at Covent Garden Chambers and moved back into the family home a virtual outcast. His efforts to interest Longman in a second instalment of *The Vampyre* came to nothing, and the chances of prospering in a literary career seemed as remote as those of making his fortune as a physician. 'I must have something to engage my mind and I now find nothing to do,' he told Frances, his childhood impatience driving him to the point of distraction. In a final attempt to clear his name, he sent a long, self-pitying letter to the *Morning Chronicle* in an attempt to salvage his reputation ahead of the publication of the story he had truly begun as his contribution to the Diodati competition, an Alpine melodrama named *Ernestus Berchtold* that featured orphans, incest, spectral mothers, Asiatic bandits and a young hero whose only flaw is his love of 'public instead of private virtues'. It was an entertaining and not unworthy novel, which, under different circumstances might have passed as the respectable début of an apprentice novelist, despite its curious introduction promising that a 'prototype' of it had never appeared elsewhere before. Notoriety did not translate into sales. Only 199 copies were sold, and John saw his work condemned in Colburn's *Literary Gazette* as yet another example of the 'prose Byroniads which infect the times'. There was one last literary effort through the patronage of Chandos Leigh, a member of the Holland House set associated with Drury Lane. Leigh had promised to show *Ximenes* to the Lane's manager, Robert Elliston, but the offer went nowhere as Leigh, recently married and often away in the country, had little time for John's affairs.

That summer, the nation was consumed with the case of Caroline, the exiled princess John had courted in Milan, who had returned to London in June, determined to attain her rights as queen. Unable to divorce her due to his own reproachable conduct, the new king, George IV, attempted to have her tried according to a bill of 'Pains and Penalties' before the House of Lords, but the case soon became a focus for anti-government protesters who viewed his conduct as cruel and despotic. A second spectacle kept London in thrall that summer: on 9 August the English Opera House débuted a stage adaptation of *The Vampyre* to rapt audiences, among them William Godwin. It was a transfer from the Paris stage, where an adaptation at the Théâtre de la Porte-Saint-Martin had been such a success that it was emulated in six other productions across the French capital. Polidori did not receive a penny. 'I begin to despair,' he told Frances.

John had officially joined that cadre of writers Shelley referred to as 'the Academy of Disappointed Authors', wounded poets who peered up at the towering figures of Scott and Byron and saw only their own feeble obscurity. In an age where poetry was considered the intimate expression of interior worth, rejection was a devastating assessment of self. Byron had threatened to kill himself when he read his first bad review and still intended to kill its author, Henry Brougham. The genealogist Sir Egerton Brydges, a cousin of Chandos Leigh, remembered the indifferent reception of his first book of poems as the most painful blow of his life. 'I had looked up to the fame of a poet as something magical,' he wrote in his *Recollections*, until the experience of rejection,

> drove back the fire upon my heart, [where] it smouldered inwards for some years, consuming me with a black burning melancholy. I had no spirit; my faculties were shrivelled up, like dry scorched leaves, ready to fall into dust at a touch. I had no amusements . . . I sank in my own estimation down into helpless feebleness. My . . . shyness and reserve redoubled upon me; – and thus I lost the prime years of my youth from 23 to 28.

Brydges's candid confession to such shattered feelings is not simply evidence of his sincerity but also participates in a peculiar literary sub-culture that attributed a lack of success with the philistinism of industrial society. The sub-culture had its own laureate in Isaac

Gaetano Polidori in 1848, drawn by his grandson, the artist Daniel Gabriel Rossetti.

John's beloved sister Frances at the age of sixty-three, posing with her children, the painter Dante Gabriel Rossetti (far left), the poet Christina Rossetti, and the literary critic William Michael Rossetti (right). The photograph, taken in the Rossettis' garden in Cheyne Walk, London, is by Lewis Carroll, author of Alice in Wonderland.

William Godwin by James Northcote, 1802.

Mary Wollstonecraft by John Opie, c.1797, the portrait that hung in Godwin's study as Claire and Mary were growing up.

A view of the Simplon Pass, the feat of Napoleonic engineering that enabled rapid travel through the Alps, connecting Paris and Milan. John passed along it as he walked from Villa Diodati to the Italian border, a journey of two hundred and fifty miles in just twelve days.

Costessey Hall, Norfolk, four miles west of Norwich. The family seat of the Jerningham family, John spent a great deal of time here on his return from Italy, and was badly injured when his coach crashed in its park.

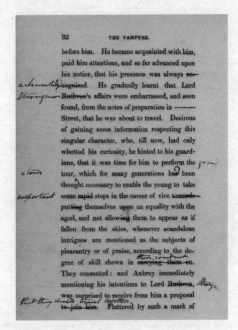

First print edition of The Vampyre *showing John's handwritten corrections. Here, 'Ruthven' is deleted and replaced with the name 'Strongmore'.*

Margaret King Moore, Lady Mount Cashell, the Irish aristocrat who befriended Claire in Pisa and encouraged her to break free from the influence of Shelley. This portrait was drawn by 'physionotrace', a complicated, booth-like apparatus designed to faithfully replicate a sitter's profile.

Palazzo Mocenigo on the Grand Canal in Venice, the home into which Byron welcomed his daughter, Allegra.

Two images of Allegra Byron, the daughter of Claire Clairmont and Lord Byron. Allegra was sixteen months old when she went to live with her father in Venice. This miniature was painted shortly thereafter.

Allegra, aged three or four, wearing a high-waisted muslin frock similar to the one she wore when Shelley last saw her. This miniature, along with a lock of hair, is the one that Byron sent to Claire following Allegra's death, and which Claire kept with her until her final days.

Byron's last love, Teresa Guiccioli. 'A sort of Italian Caroline Lamb', Byron told Douglas Kinnaird, 'except that she is much prettier, and not so savage'.

The convent of San Giovanni in the town of Bagnacavallo, twelve miles west of Ravenna, where Allegra went to live in early March 1821. 'This guiltless child of four years', wrote Claire, 'was treated by Lord Byron as if she were a criminal of the deepest dye, confined to a prison and left to die without one friend or relation near her'.

A view of Villa Magni, Shelley's last house on the bay of Spezia, along with the sailboat he shared with Edward Williams.

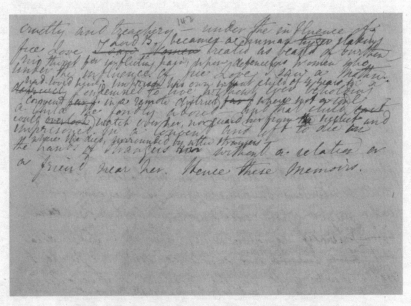

'Under the influence of free Love, Lord B— became a human tyger slaking his thirst for inflicting pain upon defenceless women who loved him.' Claire Clairmont's final denunciation of Lord Byron, written more than a half century after their affair in the summer of 1816.

D'Israeli, father of the future prime minister, Benjamin, and one of Byron's favourite authors. D'Israeli's hugely popular books *The Calamities of Authors* (1812), *The Quarrels of Authors* (1814) and *The Literary Character* (1818) chronicled the various feuds and disasters to which writers had been subject: of William Collins, driven mad by his 'poetical disappointments', of the poisonous envy of Horace Walpole, or the deadly impulses of Andrea del Catagno, who assassinated his teacher out of jealousy. Though D'Israeli's subjects belonged to an earlier era, the connection to the present was plain. 'We censure no man for loving fame, but only for showing us how much he is possessed by the passion,' wrote D'Israeli. 'Thus we allow him to create the appetite, but we deny him its aliment.'

If D'Israeli was failure's laureate, its patron saint was Thomas Chatterton, the seventeen-year-old poet whose death in 1770 was deemed suicide brought on by hopelessness. (In actuality, Chatterton's death may have been accidental, a result of his venereal medicine, arsenic, interacting with a recreational dose of laudanum.) Chatterton was a figure of great significance to the Romantics, the embodiment of the sacrifices demanded by artistic creation, of the fragility of beauty, and of how much is given for such uncertain reward. Coleridge's 'Monody' on his death was his first published work. Keats dedicated his *Endymion* to his memory, and after Keats's own death from tuberculosis in 1821, Shelley composed *Adonais* as an elegy to him, strongly echoing the Chattertonian theme of genius 'hooted from the stage of life' and rounding on the savages who had mauled Keats's poems in the *Quarterly Review*. Even John had a Chatterton poem, 'Chatterton to his Sister' that told of his hopes 'mock'd by all the world' and compares the flattery of men to the flapping of the 'vampire bat', its wings creating a lulling breeze even as it sucks its victim's blood. An awkward footnote to the poem acknowledges that Chatterton did not actually have a sister although, of course, John did.

The compound humiliations of that summer persuaded John to turn his back on literature and seek a different life. One thought was to study law at Lincoln's Inn, which meant an investment of four or five years at a cost of a hundred guineas per annum. Unlike the university, the Inns of Court offered virtually no instruction, expecting their students to read and study independently, their fees merely purchasing the right to sit the exams required to enter the profession. Not that John was eligible to become a barrister, as Catholics were still prohibited from the bar. Instead, he intended to practise conveyancing – the legal transfer of property – writing to Sir George Jerningham in the autumn of 1820 to ask if he might be recommended to the Jerningham family lawyer, Charles Butler, a prominent writer on Anglo-Catholic issues and one of the most successful conveyancers in London.

But the law was just a fallback plan. John's dearest wish was to return to Ampleforth. He had written to Thomas Burgess, an old classmate who was now the school's prior, asking leave to study for the priesthood. A reply had been long in coming, and when it did arrive, it was not encouraging. 'I must say that I think that our state of life is much too difficult for you now,' Burgess had written, adding that John's presence at the school would be less than desirable, in 'consequence of certain publications which I have seen and of which I must tell [you] as a friend, I wish you had not been the author'.

Utterly disillusioned, on 7 November 1820, John paid money he could ill afford to become a student at Lincoln's Inn and, sick of the trouble that attended being Polidori, he wrote a new name in the register, 'John Pierce'.

In February 1821 eleven thousand Austrian troops entered Florence, filling its ochre-stoned squares with baggage wagons, snorting horses and tall Hungarian infantrymen who towered over the intimidated locals. Troops marched out almost as quickly as they came in. In a single day, Claire witnessed thousands of soldiers marching away through the Roman gate, only to be replaced by thousands more arriving from the north-east. All of them would eventually move south, responding to the events of the previous summer when a group of armed insurrectionists inspired by a revolution in Spain had marched through Naples to depose King Ferdinand, who had fled to Florence where he was greeted with a hundred-and-one-gun salute. Ferdinand was safe, but revolution continued to threaten the south as the insurgency spread to Sicily, forcing the Austrians to mobilise if they were to restore the integrity of their empire.

Amid the rattle of war, Claire's life in Florence continued to evolve. She excelled at German, becoming so proficient that Shelley asked her to translate Goethe's *Aus Meinen Leben*, a commission he had received from Byron, who was fascinated with the German poet, and who read her work thinking that Shelley had commissioned it in Paris (Shelley had the manuscript copied to disguise Claire's handwriting). She made progress with those ladies who might deign to take an interest in her future career as a governess, moving chiefly among the Russian and Polish communities, while also making the acquaintance of the Neapolitan Princess Montemiletto, a friend of Lady Mount Cashell who had fled north in the wake of the insurrection. Yet for all her best efforts, Claire still retained a marked ambiguity towards the demands of her new role, refusing to bury the fact that she 'issued from the very den of freethinkers', and unwilling to lace herself into the dreaded stays, which earned her a reprimand from Lady Mount Cashell for 'affecting singularity in dress'.

Her health also wavered, requiring the gland in her neck to be bled on New Year's Day (an illness Andrea Vaccà Berlinghieri diagnosed as scrofula, and Shelley ascribed to 'dejection of spirits') and, for a while, she and Mary stopped speaking to one another, each blaming the other for the rift, even as Claire kept up her correspondence with Shelley by sending letters via Lady Mount Cashell. Byron plagued her solitary thoughts, appearing one moment as a cloven-footed demon whose lameness was a warning she had failed to heed, and another as a spent artist whose stunted vision revealed 'so much of leg and so much of thigh, hands feet &&c . . . without a sign of the lord and master of the mansion, the soul'.

While politics rarely intruded on Claire's shrinking world, Byron had become fully immersed in the revolutionary swell. Austrian spies had been watching him since his first entry into Milan, reading his correspondence. They had tolerated him in more stable times but, with trouble afoot, were eager to rid themselves of such an infamous liberal. Something of this appeared to motivate Count Guiccioli's new demand that the poet immediately cease his dalliance with Teresa. A violent scene followed, after which Teresa sought the protection of her father, who applied directly to Pope Pius VII for a legal separation on account of old Guiccioli's cruelty. The separation was granted in the summer of 1820, after which Byron became increasingly aligned with Teresa's family, the nationalist Count Gamba and his fiery son Pietro, who took Byron into their confidence, revealing themselves as members of a clandestine revolutionary society called the Carbonari, and passing on the theurgic words that inducted him into their fraternity.

Byron was in love with the idea of a free Italy, what he called 'the very *poetry* of politics', and as skirmishes were fought in the Kingdom of the Two Sicilies, he became more involved with the northern Carbonari. They began to organise, guided by the belief that Austrian intervention would inevitably mean weakened imperial positions in Piedmont and Lombardy. 'The king-times are fast finishing,' wrote Byron, in his private memoranda. 'There will be blood shed like water, and tears like mist.' Evidence of just how dangerous things were about to become appeared when a local military commander was assassinated in front of his house. Exposing himself to a second shot, Byron ran into the square and, with the help of his servants, carried the bleeding man into the Guiccioli Palace, where he was laid on Fletcher's bed to die. It was a contorted double plot, or so Byron believed, to implicate him in the murder and justify a wave of arrests. Undaunted, Byron armed the Carbonari with his private funds and, as the Austrian troops began their march, let them use his apartments as a magazine to store their weapons. Meanwhile, hidden in the woods, the Gambas formed themselves into detachments and made plans to ambush the artillery as it passed south.

The Austrians won their battles, while poor planning and broken allegiances saw to it that no uprising in Ravenna ever took place. Open to reprisals, Byron was warned by anonymous notes not to take his daily exercise lest he be shot. In such an uncertain atmosphere, he told Hoppner, he 'had no reason to look upon my personal safety as particularly insurable' and, feeling that Allegra was no safer, followed through on his plans and had her placed in the Capuchin convent of San Giovanni in the town of Bagnacavallo, twelve miles west. Claire was distraught, and even though she gave herself a week to compose her thoughts, her letter to Byron was cold with ferocity. 'This . . . with every advantage in your power, of wealth, of friends, is the education you have chosen for your daughter,' she wrote, 'condemned by her father to a life of ignorance and degradation.' Convent-educated women, she said, 'are bad wives and most unnatural mothers, licentious and ignorant they are the dishonour and unhappiness of society . . . This step will procure you an innumerable addition of enemies and of blame.'

Those enemies were not immediately forthcoming, as Shelley continued his policy of careful appeasement, not only reassuring Byron that he had done the right thing, but apologising for Claire's attack by blaming it on himself. 'Our solitary mode of life, and my abstracted manner of thinking, were very unfit for her,' he said, 'and have probably been the sources of all her errors. It is well, therefore, that I should intercede for their forgiveness.' Was Shelley the 'friend', to whom Claire would later allude, who 'in his calm voice and with the gentlest looks' explained that he would betray her, 'and that he expected I should submit without a murmur'?

But Claire did more than rage at Byron. She presented him with a proposal to take Allegra back and have her educated in an English boarding school at her own expense. It was a hopeless request, for Byron had taken steps two years earlier to ensure that Allegra should never be Anglicised, adding a codicil to his will which stated that her inheritance of five thousand pounds came 'on Condition she does not marry with a Native of Great Britain'. Once again, Byron sent Claire's letter to Hoppner as further evidence of her abuse, invoking the Neapolitan gossip as a means of releasing him from any obligation. 'You *know* (perhaps more than I do),' he wrote, 'that to allow the Child to be with her mother – and with *them* and their principles – would be absolute insanity – if not worse – that even her health would not be attended to properly – to say nothing of the Indecorum.' This time, the Hoppners were not able to offer easy reassurances and, fearing for Allegra's Protestant soul, tried again to persuade their friend to send his daughter to the family of 'any Swiss clergyman'. 'If I had but known yr. notion about Switzerland before,' Byron replied, somewhat curiously, 'I should have adopted it at once.' It was the last comment the Hoppners would make on the child's well-being, although they were not sorry to have no more to do with her. 'Allegra was not by any means an amiable child,' Hoppner would write some years later, 'nor was Mrs Hoppner or I particularly fond of her.'

Allegra arrived in the small town of Bagnacavallo on 1 March 1821, having travelled across the marshy plains of the Romagna in the company of Pellegrino Ghigi, her father's banker. San Giovanni stood behind the main square like a minor fortress, its blank stone walls rising thirty impenetrable feet before being topped with small crescent windows. The building had been home to religious communities for five centuries, although the order of Capuchin nuns who ran the school had arrived only recently, following the opening of a nearby hospital.

Byron had had some experience with Capuchins, having stayed in a small monastery at the foot of the Athenian Acropolis in 1810. Back then he had enjoyed a series of adventures among a game group of travellers and amorous washerwomen, enduring very little of the asceticism that defined the order. Capuchins were meant to subsist solely on alms and whatever money might be foraged by the missionaries they sent into the world, a duty the sisters of San Giovanni had circumvented by applying to the pope for permission to open a boarding school. The school consisted of thirty nuns overseeing almost eighty girls, all taken from local families of high rank. In most cases, pupils had to be between seven and twelve to be accepted for admission, yet, as Allegra was handed over to the care of the mother vicar, Sister Marianna Fabbri, along with a double pension from Ghigi to ensure her 'proper treatment and attention', she was only six weeks past her fourth birthday. As the child was shown around her new home and introduced to Padre Vicenzo, her spiritual guide, the servants unpacked the items she had been instructed to bring – a bed, a washstand, a chest of drawers, two chairs, eighteen chemises, and a dress of black woollen cloth. In her arms she carried one of her favourite dolls, dressed in hand-stitched clothes so beautifully made that the wife of the convent's carpenter used them to dress her own children. Later that day, as was customary, Allegra provided a dinner for the nuns, and would also provide a lamb on Easter Day and two capons for Christmas.

Almost as soon as Allegra arrived in Bagnacavallo, Byron's situation became more precarious. In July, the Gambas were expelled from Ravenna, forcing Teresa to accompany her father to Florence or – according to the terms of her separation – face being shut up in a convent of her own. On hearing the news of the expulsion, Shelley travelled to Byron in the hope of persuading him to let Allegra live with Lady Mount Cashell or some Swiss or English family. The two men talked long into the night, Byron telling his friend what he had heard of the Neapolitan gossip, offending Shelley deeply, although not because people might think that Claire was his mistress ('nothing new,' he wrote to Mary, 'all the world has heard so much and people may believe or not believe as they think good'), but because he hated the idea that they might imagine he could abandon a child.

Byron was at a loss. He was reluctant to join Teresa in Florence due to the city's large English contingent and the presence of Claire, who, Shelley agreed, was best avoided: 'Gunpowder and fire,' he told Mary, 'ought to be kept at a respectable distance from one another.' The Gambas were considering exile in Geneva, but after the misery he had suffered there, Byron could think of nothing worse and urged Shelley to dissuade Teresa from such a move, which he did by letter, even though he had never met her. The uncertainty worked in Shelley's favour, and pursuing his plan to 'lull him into security', he was able to convince Byron over the course of the week to move to Pisa and bring Allegra with him. Mary was instructed to search for suitable *palazzi*.

After spending eight days with Byron, Shelley visited Allegra in Bagnacavallo. She appeared to him dressed in white muslin with a black silk apron, shy at first, but becoming friendlier after he handed her a basket of sweetmeats and a gold chain. She led him on a tour of the convent, showing him her bed and chair, and the little carriage that she and her best friend Elettra Malagola used to pull each other along the paths in the covered garden. She seemed happy and well – taller and thinner than before, but as beautiful as when he had seen her last in Este three years earlier, with thick hair hanging in curls about her neck, and looking altogether 'a thing of finer race and higher order' than the other girls. He also found her manners much improved. At first, Allegra had treated the nuns like servants, but had slowly come to show them respect, demonstrating this new thoughtfulness by offering the sweetmeats to them before taking any for herself. When Shelley asked what message she would like to give to her mother, Allegra answered that she would blow her a kiss and ask for a nice dress. What kind of dress? asked Shelley. 'All of golden silk,' Allegra replied. When Shelley asked what message she had for her father, Allegra asked him to visit her and bring Mammina with him, 'a message,' said Shelley to Mary, 'which you may conjecture I was too discreet to deliver'.

Shelley was comforted by what he saw at San Giovanni. As a survivor of Eton's 'Long Chamber', a lawless, primitive dormitory into which fifty boys were locked at night without a master to supervise them, he had certainly seen worse. But while he was happy to find Allegra in such good health, his doubts about her education remained. 'Her intellect is not much cultivated here,' he told Mary,

> she knows certain orazioni by heart and talks and *dreams* of Paradise and angels and all sorts of things – and has a prodigious list of saints – and is always talking of the Bambino. This *fuora* will do her no harm – but the idea of bringing up so sweet a creature in the midst of such trash till sixteen!

Before he was allowed to leave, Allegra made Shelley run around the convent's central courtyard 'like a mad thing', sending the nuns still in their nightclothes scattering to hide themselves, and ringing the convent bell to the confusion of its occupants who thought they had been called to muster. It was a happy conclusion to a visit that remained entirely secret from Claire.

While Shelley was in Ravenna, John was in Brighton, enjoying all the fashionable diversions and youthful dissipations that a seaside resort could offer. His legal studies had failed to suppress his urge to write, and he had turned from the boredom of his textbooks to publish two more works in the last six months – a long heterodox poem entitled *The Fall of Angels*, and a text that accompanied a series of plates depicting travels in France and Italy. Both were published anonymously.

In Brighton, John behaved out of character, which is to say, exactly like most young men of his age, drinking and gaming. Who he caroused with is unknown, although given that six months earlier he had told Frances he had no friends in London at all, they may have been new acquaintances made at the Inns of Court.

Certainly, they were a different kind of group from those he had associated with before, as he gambled heavily and lost heavily too; 'having incurred a debt of honour which he had no present means of paying off', he left the coast and returned to London.

'Be sure that no happiness can be grounded upon vice or misconduct', Gaetano had once written in his 'Directions for John', but to lose money at the gaming tables was an almost scripted ruin. The hero of *Ernestus Berchtold* had been seduced into gambling by a courtesan hired to debauch him, just as the hero of Godwin's *St Leon* had sold his soul to recover the fortune he had lost at cards. Nevertheless, the losses affected John badly, and he was in poor spirits when he appeared at Great Pulteney Street on 20 August 1821, after three weeks away.

The house was empty as the rest of the family were away at their country cottage in Holmer Green, save for Mr Deagostini. It was a while before anyone noticed that John was behaving strangely. The maid, Charlotte Reed, thought he looked unwell and oddly agitated as he complained of pains in his side and spoke in short sentences abutting on incoherence, behaviour that continued when Deagostini invited him up to his apartment to dine with one of his friends. John looked haggard throughout the meal, ate little and spoke, according to his godfather, 'in a very harsh way', like one of 'deranged mind', causing particular consternation when, in the course of a discussion about the future state of Britain, he told Deagostini that 'I should see more than him.' Getting up to leave, he shook the hand of his godfather's friend so violently that the man was forced to kneel on the ground. That evening, John instructed Charlotte to leave a glass tumbler in his room, and told her not to wake him the next morning. A little later, he came back to sit with Deagostini but refused to utter a word.

At twenty-five years old, John Polidori had achieved more than most men three times his age. His novels were as promising as they were unique, and his intellectual gifts could have placed him in the higher reaches of any profession. Although Byron liked to joke about John's skill as a physician, he knew his trade, and just weeks before he had left for Brighton, had nursed his beloved sister Frances back to health from a severe case of scarlet fever. Yet a worm gnawed at his innards, and with a temperament unsuited to fellowship, and the conviction that his life had been a failure, his hopes gave over to despair.

At noon the next day, 24 August, Charlotte Reed went to open his blinds and found him lying dressed on his bed with a tumbler of liquid on the chair beside him. He was breathing but unconscious. Reed called up to Deagostini, who immediately sent her out to Golden Square to fetch a doctor. She returned with Thomas Copeland, who tried to make him vomit. By this time, a second doctor, William Davies, had arrived from nearby Poland Street, but even with both men attending, their efforts were in vain. Three hours later, Gaetano returned from his cottage to the news that his eldest son was dead.

An inquest was convened in the sitting room, presided over by John Gell and a jury of twenty-four neighbours, thirteen of them from the adjourning houses in Great Pulteney Street, among them Francis Novello, the brother of Vincent, friends of Shelley and Hunt. Everyone who knew him suspected that John had killed himself, most probably with the same bitter almond-scented solution of prussic acid he had mixed for himself at Diodati.

Prussic acid occurs in many things, including laurel leaves, the garland of the poets, as Shelley had once discovered having made himself sick after reading that chewing them stimulated poetic creativity. Its poison is swift, inducing a chemical asphyxiation that convulses the body and flushes the face bright pink, so for John to have been conscious when Copeland arrived some time before one o'clock (according to the evidence he gave the jury), he must have taken an imperfect dose only moments before the maid found him. Yet no trace of it was discovered in his room, a fact Copeland confirmed by taking a sip from the bedside tumbler to find it contained only water.

In the absence of any evidence, the coroner displayed a charitable unwillingness to declare the death suicide and thus deny a respected member of the community the chance to bury his son in sanctified ground. A verdict was returned by the end of the day: 'departed his life in a natural way by the visitation of God'. It was the sole notice of John's passing to be printed in the paper. 'Poor Polidori,' said Byron, when he heard the news, 'it seems that disappointment was the cause of this rash act. He had entertained too sanguine hopes of literary fame.'

Byron's imminent arrival in Pisa was signalled by a caravan of furniture led by his voluminous bed, its headrest carved with the family motto 'Trust Byron'. Claire, who was in the city visiting Lady Mount Cashell, took this as her cue to leave, relieved by Shelley's assurances that Allegra would soon be in Pisa with her father. She set off for Florence on 1 November, getting as far as Empoli before she saw the dark green of Byron's Napoleonic carriage trundling into view, its chipped paint and battered roof preceding an equally ramshackle train of animals in crates and cages. Claire and Byron were virtually face to face, but although their paths crossed for the first time since Geneva, she may not have seen him at all. Byron was now so averse to being looked at that he travelled everywhere with his blinds drawn.

His lordship ensconced himself in the Lanfranchi Palace, 'large enough for a garrison', on a silted bend of the Arno opposite Mary and Shelley's new apartments in Tre Palazzi di Chiesa. It

was like something summoned from the tired imagination of a
Gothic novelist, with dungeons below and bricked-up passages so
suggestive of haunting that Fletcher refused to sleep in his rooms
and even Byron believed he had been whispered to by a spectral
voice. As usual, he avoided the locals and confined himself to the
company of the Gambas, who had arrived before him, and the
small group of Shelley's expatriate friends, who now included his
cousin Thomas Medwin, the amenable pair Edward and Jane
Williams, and the amateur Irish poet, John Taaffe. Dubbing themselves the 'Pistol Club', the men went riding in the woods and
shot at targets, and were entertained every Wednesday with a large
dinner when they poked away at billiards and rinsed themselves
in claret.

Shelley told Claire that he despised the 'detested intimacy' that
compelled him to listen to Byron's slanders, especially about her.
Byron 'feared Claire', Mary would later claim, 'and did not spare
her' from the vilest insinuations. Yet Shelley's attraction to him
remained strong. He was drawn to him once more, at once basking
in the great 'worth' that he felt Byron's friendship bestowed upon
himself and Mary, and was impressed with his new-found political
commitment, sexual continence, and expanding poetic powers,
powers that pained Shelley with feelings of competition and inferiority. 'I despair of rivalling Lord Byron,' he told Mary, having
listened to him recite newly composed stanzas from *Don Juan*,
'and there is no other with whom it is worth contending.'

Allegra, however, did not follow her father to Pisa, and all
Shelley's enquiries were met with vague replies and the second-
hand updates he received from Byron's secretary, a defrocked
priest who had served Count Guiccioli, named Lega Zambelli.
Allegra's absence, Claire believed, was due to Teresa's jealousy,
although in February 1822 she was forced to consider a more
horrifying motive. It was then that Claire was visited by a repentant

Elise Duvillard, now serving with a family in Florence, who confessed everything she had told the Hoppners about the child baptised in Naples and Claire and Shelley's supposed affair. As Elise tearfully sought to make amends, a shocked and humiliated Claire resolved to leave Italy for ever, and wrote to Byron asking permission to say goodbye to her daughter. 'My dear Friend,' she wrote, 'I conjure you do not make the world dark to me, as if my Allegra were dead.' Mary pleaded with her to come to Pisa, where, with Lady Mount Cashell, she convinced her not to leave. But though Claire decided to remain in Florence, it was clear to her that Elise's defamation meant that Byron would never let her see her daughter again.

Claire began to obsess over Allegra's health, convinced that she would become sick in a convent that her imagination had transformed into a purgatorial sinkhole, 'dark as a prison', with 'gloomy, damp walls and almost bare of furniture', surrounded by impenetrable stone and infectious swamps. In Claire's mind the nuns were a horde of corvine devotees holding tyrannical dominion over 'the children of small shop keepers', making them go without fires or meat, and 'once a week at midnight in their chapel they scourge themselves with an iron chain'. Allegra haunted her dreams. Once Claire dreamed that Mr Tighe had rescued her from Bagnacavallo, in defiance of John Cam Hobhouse and a lady called Miss O'Neil. Another night, she dreamed she had received a letter telling her that her child was ill and unlikely to live.

Shelley tried dutifully to impress Claire's distress on Byron, who just shrugged and said, 'Women could not live without making scenes.' Driven to desperation, she devised a scheme to infiltrate the convent dressed as a pensioner and snatch Allegra away, and was dismayed that the Shelleys would not lend their support. Mary was pregnant again (she would miscarry in June), and wrapped up in her father's endless financial predicament, she tried patiently to talk her step-sister through the impracticalities of a rescue. Reminding her of the 'high walls and bolted doors' and the strict oversight of the children throughout the day, she attempted to ease Claire's fears about the child's health by telling her that 'the towns of Romagna . . . enjoy the best air in Italy'. 'Another thing I mention,' Mary added, 'which though sufficiently ridiculous may have some weight with you. Spring is our unlucky season. No spring has passed with out some piece of ill luck.'

Shelley similarly warned Claire against such a rash plan, calling it 'madness' and 'infamy', and arguing that if he should be seen to have aided her, Byron would have every right to challenge him, in which case he would certainly be slain. Mary also made much of Byron's capacity for vengeance. 'LB is at present a man of 12 or 15 thousand a year,' she wrote, 'he is on the spot, a man reck-less of the ill he does others, obstinate to desperation in the pursuance of his plans or his revenge. What then would you do – having A. on the outside of the convent walls? Wd you go to America?'

Were these the same people she had boarded a carriage with in 1814? Claire was especially disgusted with Shelley, who had only recently asked for her help in liberating the governor of Pisa's daughter, Teresa Viviani, from a convent, when this literate and beautiful young woman had become the object of one of his quixotic emancipation projects. As for Mary, it marked a funda-mental shift in their relationship that cut deeper than any that had gone before. 'Recollecting her conduct at Pisa,' Claire later wrote, 'I can never help feeling horror even in only looking at her. The instant she appears I feel not as if I had blood in my veins, but in its stead the sickening crawling motion of the Death Worm.'

In early April, the five-year-old Allegra caught a slight fever. After a few days without improvement, it was considered bad enough to require the attentions of two local doctors, a physician named Berardi and a surgeon named Enrico Marmani. She recovered quickly, but soon after succumbed to a second illness that prompted Sister Fabbri to call for Dr Rasi, Allegra's regular doctor in Ravenna, who diagnosed an 'attack to her chest', bled her and confined her to a diet of milk and water. Pellegrino Ghigi travelled to Bagnacavallo to check on her, sending his dispatches back to Lega Zambelli, who passed them on to Byron, who found himself 'dreadfully agitated' and requested that the nuns send to Bologna for the more expert advice of Dr Thomasini. Ghigi visited the child in the middle of April, finding her improved and asking for soft cheese, although still bed-ridden and surrounded by doctors and a retinue of nuns all eager to serve. 'It is now hoped that she can be kept out of danger,' Ghigi wrote to Zambelli. But even as he filed his report, Allegra suffered another convulsive attack in the career of a disease that turned out to be typhus. She was bled again, and cupped, at which point Sister Marianna wrote to Zambelli to assure him that 'Miss Allegrina's inflammation seems to have been overcome,' although 'there remain to be mastered some attacks of pangs, the trial of Children, and the weakness that has presented itself'. 'The young lady's situation is still dangerous,' she said,

> my distress, and that of all the sisters, is supreme, we do not cease to offer prayers to Heaven for the recovery of such a precious Child nor to attend her, as is our duty, and as her dear qualities deserve. She herself, informed that I am writing to her Papa, repeated to me many times that I send him her love, and to the Secretary as well. I do not know how to describe my anguish to you. Patience! I still hope.

Just after ten o'clock that evening, Allegra died.

When a messenger arrived in Pisa, Zambelli digested the news and passed it on to Teresa, who went directly to Lanfranchi to tell Byron. He did not cry, but rather sat motionless for an hour with a look of profound sorrow, before dismissing his mistress and spending a difficult night alone. When she saw him the next day, Teresa believed that a look of religious resignation hung about him. 'She is more fortunate than we are,' he told her, 'besides, her position in the world would scarcely have allowed her to be happy. It is God's will – let us mention it no more.'

Byron did not have the stomach to break the news to Shelley himself, and sent Teresa to do it, writing some lines later that day. 'I do not know that I have any thing to reproach in my conduct, and certainly nothing in my feelings and intentions toward the dead,' he told him. 'But it is a moment when we are apt to think that, if this or that had been done, such event might have been prevented.' Fearing what the news would do to her, Shelley was unable to tell Claire. By sheer coincidence, she had been in Pisa for a week, hiding herself away with Lady Mount Cashell and, on the day of Byron's letter, had been in the nearby coastal town of La Spezia, where she was helping the Shelleys look for a summer house. Determined to get her as far away as possible from Byron, Shelley sent Claire, with Mary, little Percy and their new friend Edward John Trelawny, ahead 'like a torrent', instructing Mary to take whatever house she could find and stay there. Harried and unable to secure anything remotely suitable, Mary leased the Casa Magni, a large, featureless villa outside the tiny village of San Terenzo. It could not have been more isolated, with a beach before it and cliffs behind, and nothing more than a rocky footpath to connect it to the world. Even the furniture had to be delivered by boat.

Shelley and the Williamses joined them a few days later, by

which time Claire was already keen to leave the draughty, uncharismatic house and return to her daily life in Florence. Shelley felt cornered into saying something, but when he gathered the others in Jane Williams's room to discuss how this might best be done, Claire walked in on their whispering huddle and immediately guessed what had happened. It was 2 May 1822, a day of storms and clouds reminiscent of Geneva.

The first bolt of grief left Claire sick and unsteady. Anger followed fast behind and she wrote to eviscerate Byron, a letter he returned in disgust, but which at last managed to puncture his indifference. He felt the loss 'bitterly', Mary told Maria Gisborne the following month, 'for he felt that he had acted against every body's councils and wishes, and death had stamped with truth the many and often urged prophecies of Claire'. 'While she lived,' Byron later told Lady Blessington, 'her existence never seemed necessary to my happiness; but no sooner did I lose her, than it appeared to me as if I could not live without her.'

Three nights after Claire learned of the death of her daughter, Shelley and Williams stood on the terrace of Casa Magni, looking out across the Bay of Spezia as the moon lay brightly on the waters. Clasping his companion's arm, Shelley pointed to something out at sea. 'There it is again!' he said. 'There!' A vision of Allegra had risen from the waves, smiled at him and clapped her hands with joy.

EPILOGUE

Mary Marshall was a stout woman with a strong Cockney accent and the ability to speak with the dead. From her home in Maida Vale, she had gained a reputation as London's most powerful medium, able to channel spirits by guiding a pencil across an alphabet, or rapping on a table that would levitate and glide across her living-room floor. She also took in washing.

William Rossetti stopped at Mrs Marshall's on a dark November afternoon in 1865 at the urging of a friend. His attendance there was entirely unplanned, and although the writer was a spiritual agnostic, what happened gave him pause. A séance was in progress, and when a gentleman at the circle asked if there were any spirits willing to speak with them, the answer was returned, 'Uncle John.'

'I had no uncle of that name,' said the man.

'Is it *my* uncle John?' asked Rossetti. The third child of Frances Polidori and her Italian husband, Rossetti had never met the uncle who had died nine years before he was born and whom it was forbidden to mention by order of his unsmiling grandfather, Gaetano. For him, Uncle John was just a name he had seen scratched on the flyleaves of the old books his Aunt Charlotte kept, or as a cameo in biographies of Byron. Even his gravesite was about to disappear as St Pancras Churchyard made way for the Midland Railway, the bones dug up and boxed for reburial at a municipal site overseen by a young architect and aspiring novelist named Thomas Hardy.

It came as some surprise, therefore, when the spirit answered, 'Yes.'

'Will you tell me truly how you died?' asked Rossetti.

'Yes,' said the spirit.

'How?'

'Killed.'

'Who killed you?'

'I.'

'There is a celebrated poet with whom you were connected,' said Rossetti. 'What was his name?'

Using the alphabet laid out on the table, Mrs Marshall twice wrote out the letters B-R-O, and on a third attempt, 'BYRON.'

'There was a certain book you wrote,' Rossetti said, 'attributed to Byron: can you give me its title?'

'Yes,' replied the spirit, but the medium failed repeatedly to catch it.

Abandoning the attempt, Rossetti asked his uncle, 'Are you happy?'

Two hard raps followed, meaning, 'Not exactly.'

The voices of the past could be ambiguous, Rossetti knew that. As a critic, editor and biographer, he had made a career from piecing together the traces of an earlier age and, shortly after the encounter with his ghostly Uncle John, found himself trying to do the same with the life of Percy Bysshe Shelley. Rossetti and his brother, the poet, painter and founder of the Pre-Raphaelite Brotherhood, Gabriel Dante Rossetti, had first read Shelley together in the summer of 1844, aged fifteen and sixteen respectively. It was a moment William long remembered as a time when he 'revelled in . . . glorious idealism'. The passion for Shelley endured, and by the late 1860s, he had decided to compile an edition of Shelley's works and write a biography. Certain facts about the poet's life, however, were proving difficult to clarify. Since his death in July 1822, drowned in the Bay of Spezia with Edward Williams and an eighteen-year-old sailor named Charles Vivian, Shelley's fleshless memory had become encrusted by legend – first by Mary, as she settled into respectable Victorian widowhood; and then, after Mary succumbed to a brain tumour in 1851, by her only surviving child, Sir Percy Florence Shelley, and his wife, Lady Jane Gibson.

Lady Jane could also speak with spirits, believing sometimes that her mother-in-law would manifest within her and communicate via automatic writing. Lady Jane not only venerated Shelley, she had sanitised his reputation and turned his memory into a cult, constructing at their home, Boscombe Manor, a shrine she called 'the Sanctum', a dark chamber, its domed ceiling lit with a sacerdotal red glow, where lay an array of relics under Roman satin: letters and portraits, locks of hair, the volume of Sophocles Shelley was carrying when he drowned, and the urn that held the ashes of his heart.

As the ostiary of this temple, Lady Jane granted entry only to the worshipful few, while fighting fiercely to discredit anyone who might seek to portray the poet in an unflattering light. Those who had known him as a man, real but imperfect, were the first to be banished, including Thomas Jefferson Hogg and Thomas Love Peacock. Both had written insufficiently respectful memoirs, with Peacock causing particular offence by contradicting Lady Jane's version of the events surrounding the poet's separation from Harriet. In her 1859 publication, *Memorials of Shelley*, Lady

Jane had claimed that Shelley and Harriet had mutually agreed to end their marriage at least forty days prior to his involvement with Mary, citing (without quoting) documents in her private collection that proved her point beyond all question. They were forty days that not only exonerated him from adultery, they indemnified him from all culpability in his first wife's death. 'Shelley had no more to do with it,' said Lady Jane, 'than Oliver Cromwell.' When Peacock's book made it clear that there had been neither consent nor a chaste intermission, the ghost of Mary Shelley appeared to Lady Jane and consoled her by telling her that Peacock only had a year to live.

Rossetti was also interested in the circumstances surrounding the end of Shelley's first marriage, but having determined to be 'outspoken as to the merits and demerits' of his subject, he decided to give Lady Jane a wide berth, even though it meant denying himself access to her archive of letters and diaries.

Then, in June 1869, just as his work was nearing completion, Rossetti had the good fortune to run into one of the last people alive who had known Shelley, Edward John Trelawny. At seventy-four years of age, Trelawny had the strength of an ox, taking an ice bath every morning, walking five miles a day, and refusing to wear underwear. 'Everything that old folks do, I do not,' he boasted, claiming to retain every ounce of the stamina that had helped him survive one shot between the shoulder blades and another in the jaw from an assassin's rifle in Greece and, as a confirmed teetotaller, the operation to remove the bullets without the aid of alcohol. These days, he preserved his strength for telling anecdotes, and was capable of talking about Byron and Shelley for up to nine hours straight.

Rossetti and Trelawny spent a long afternoon together, but as the old adventurer had met Shelley only six months before he died, he had no definitive answer regarding the separation from

Harriet. The only survivor who could possibly know was Claire Clairmont, said Trelawny, but unfortunately she was insane and living in an asylum in Pisa.

Claire and Trelawny had dined together on the night Allegra died. They became lovers shortly afterwards, although the affair was brief as both left Italy before the end of the year. In September 1822, Claire had gone to live with her brother Charles in Vienna, where she was watched by the secret police. In 1824, she travelled to Russia to become governess to the family of the Moscow senator Zakhar Nikolayevich Posnikov, the start of a long career that saw her work for several families across Europe. She suffered frequently from depression, but her language and literary skills, as well as her superb singing and piano playing made her services highly prized by families of distinction. All the while she kept her past a secret but, and though unable to show it, she remained loyal to the spirit of Wollstonecraft. 'I think I can with certainty affirm all the pupils I have ever had will be violent defenders of the Rights of Women,' she told Mary. 'I have taken great pains to sow the seeds of that doctrine wherever I could.'

Claire never married, nor had another child despite raising fifteen children who belonged to other people. She was courted and had a few lovers, men she appreciated but kept at arm's length. She had her brother and nieces and nephews, with whom she was close, but remained oblivious to the existence of the family of her biological father, Sir John Lethbridge, through whom she had a half-brother in Parliament, two half-sisters and a puddle of affluent relatives.

The memory of Byron cleaved to her. 'He lies like a porcupine in my way,' she wrote in her notebook, 'his prickles disturb at

every instant my feet as they wander thro' the flowery path.' Byron
had died in the marshes of Missolonghi in April 1824, almost two
years to the day after Allegra; like her, he had been sick with fever
and desiccated from incessant bleedings. He had gone there with
thoughts of leading the Greeks to a glorious independence from
the Ottoman Empire. Afterwards, Claire heard through Mary,
who had heard through Fletcher, that Byron had spoken of her
in his final hours, expressing remorse at his conduct. Claire
refused to believe it. 'This I always thought was a lie invented by
the tenderness of Fletcher's heart,' she said. 'I knew the man too
well.' Knowing Byron had destroyed a part of her. 'I am unhappily the victim of a *happy passion*,' she had written to Jane Williams
from Moscow in the winter of 1826,

> I had one like all things perfect in its kind, it was fleeting
> and mine only lasted ten minutes but these ten minutes
> have discomposed the rest of my life; The passion God
> knows for what cause, from no fault of mine however
> disappeared leaving no trace whatever behind it except
> my heart wasted and ruined as if it had been scorched
> by a thousand lightnings.

Byron's reputation only grew after his death, as he became the
embodiment of liberty, passion and individualism, leaving Claire
furious at the idiocy of a public who would make a hero of such
an 'impostor'. His legend flourished, but her own history was
deleted. This had begun as an act of kindness meant to protect
her livelihood, as when Mary asked Leigh Hunt to 'erase' all
mention of Claire from his memoirs, while also keeping her out
of Tom Moore's biography of Byron. Over time, however, these
early omissions made it much easier to scrub her from the story
entirely, especially when the long, feuding intimacy that

characterised her relationship with Mary eventually led to an irreconcilable break. 'She poisoned my life when young,' complained Mary, 'but as we never loved each other, why these eternal complaints of me?' After Mary's death, Sir Percy and Lady Shelley denied that Claire had ever known them well at all, describing her as a 'stranger in the Shelley family'. The deletion was complete when St Pancras Churchyard was emptied of its dead, and the Shelleys had the remains of Mary Wollstonecraft and William Godwin, who had been buried next to his first wife, removed to their family vault at Boscombe. The remains of Claire's mother, Mary Jane, which had also been laid to rest alongside her husband of forty years, did not make the trip, but were permitted to be reinterred in the same anonymous municipal grave as John Polidori's.

After his summer meeting with Rossetti in 1869, Trelawny wrote a speculative note to Claire, not knowing what answer, if any, he might receive. Almost half a century had passed since they had superintended the cremation of Shelley's blue, sea-scalded body on the beach near Viareggio, although to Trelawny's delight, Claire answered almost immediately. Talk of her mental illness proved to be untrue, and she was neither incarcerated nor in Pisa but living in a plain set of rooms in a wing of the Palazzo Orsini in Florence, on the same street where she had attended the birth of Percy Florence in 1819. She had become an attentive Catholic, and despite having spent much of her adult life abroad, was described as being 'very English'.

'Satisfy me by writing about Percy,' Trelawny had said, keen to learn details of Shelley's early life and introduction to Mary. Claire agreed, but asked in return for clarification regarding the death of Allegra. Claire had never seen her daughter's body: having arranged to view the coffin before it was shipped to England, she had allowed herself to be talked out of it by Shelley, who urged her to accept a portrait miniature and a lock of hair instead. This troubled Claire, and for years she clung to a rumour that Allegra had never died, but instead had been spirited away by her father, who had had a goat's body buried in her place.

It was a wild story, but there had been a great deal of confusion surrounding the child's burial, exacerbated by what Trelawny called Pisa's 'absurd quarantine laws' and Byron's refusal to pay the surgeon Enrico Marmani, who embalmed her, arguing that he had been charged for a full-grown body and that his bill should be reduced by two-thirds. There had also been 'A Goat with a broken leg' that Byron had abandoned to the care of Pellegrino Ghigi as he departed Pisa for good, along with 'two ugly old monkeys', a 'badger on a chain' and a bird 'which could only eat fish'. The confusion continued after Allegra's coffin arrived in Britain some five months after her death, delivered to John Murray's offices in Albemarle Street. Murray commissioned Palmer and Sons to take care of the arrangements, placing the leaden coffin that had arrived from Italy, containing two smaller packages – her body and internal organs – in an elm casket covered in black cloth with cherubim handles. Byron had asked that his daughter be buried under the pavement in the nave of Harrow Church, with a marble tablet placed on a wall above that read 'In memory of Allegra – daughter of G.G. Lord Byron – who died at Bagnacavallo in Italy April 20th 1822. aged five years and three months – "I shall go to her, but she shall not return to me"'. According to the *Morning Chronicle*, he had selected this spot because it was directly opposite the pew most favoured by his estranged wife, although this was pure mischief as Lady Byron never visited the church. The point was rendered moot, as the rector, Joseph William Cunningham, refused Byron's request on the grounds of propriety, citing the support of his parishioners, the most vocal of whom was the mother of the novelist Anthony Trollope.

In the end, Allegra was buried in the churchyard on the brow of the hill overlooking Windsor. 'The story of this Child's burial,' wrote Byron, 'is the epitome or miniature of the Story of my life.' A more prominent memorial was erected in the convent of Bagnacavallo, where 'the nuns', wrote Pellegrino Ghigi, 'to preserve the dear memory of a most lovable Child, had a small statue made that represents her, they dressed it with her very clothes, that is, a red dress, fur coat, and a gold chain around her neck', very possibly the chain Shelley had given her on his visit.

Fifty years on, Trelawny refused to dignify Claire's fantasy. 'You may be well in body,' he told Claire, 'but you have a bee in your bonnet – an insane idea has got into your brain regarding Allegra . . . What possible object could he have in feigning her death or in wishing it?' Trelawny had no great respect for Byron, but told Claire that the poet's affection for the child had been genuine, before concluding with a mocking rebuttal that he hoped would shake her free of her delusions: 'If I was in Italy I would cure you of your wild fancy regarding Allegra,' he wrote:

> I would go to the Convent – and select some plausible cranky old dried-up hanger-on . . . about the age your child would now be, fifty-two, with [a] story and documents properly drawn up, and bring her to you – she should follow you about like a feminine Frankenstein – I cannot conceive a greater horror than an old man or woman that I had never seen for forty-three years claiming me as Father – do you see any of that age or indeed any age that you should like to have as son or daughter? I have not.

Given the severity of Trelawny's remark, Claire's reply was markedly polite. 'No one admires more than I do your magnanimity,' she told him. 'I understand your feeling and respect it . . . however it is impossible for me to do so.' With that, she reached deep into the past and wrung all the bitterness she could from it, blaming Teresa Guiccioli for placing Allegra in Bagnacavallo, Shelley for standing idly by, and Byron for persecuting her with the vehemence of a devil. She had learned only one lesson from Byron and Shelley, she said, 'that a woman without rank, without riches, without male relatives to protect her, is looked upon by men as a thing only fit to have her feelings and her rights trampled on'.

But what had motivated Byron's cruelty? In 1826, Claire had told Jane Williams that it was a mystery, but now, in 1870, she believed she finally understood. It could all be traced back to a morning at the Villa Diodati in the summer of 1816, when Byron had approached her and asked if she believed him to be a bad person.

'No,' she recalled saying. 'Shelley says your imagination is over excited, so you see visions, and have hallucinations and cannot help romancing.'

'Oh! So Shelley is your oracle,' said Byron, 'but I will prove to you he is a goose.'

He went to his bureau and, unlocking it, spread over a table several letters from his half-sister Augusta Leigh. Making a point of showing his sister's signature on them, he invited Claire to read. 'The beginning paragraphs were ordinary enough,' Claire told Trelawny, 'common news of friends, of her children etc. etc. and then came long spaces written in cyphers which he said only he and she had the key of.' At this point, Byron asked her if she 'believed now', and while Claire was puzzling over what he could mean,

> he gathered up the letters, and on a sudden broke out
> fiercely, 'there is a letter missing and you have taken
> it.' He was much agitated. I begged him to remember
> I had not had any of the letters in my hand even. He
> looked over them again found the missing letter (they
> were all numbered on the outside) and made a sort of
> apology for grasping me by the arm so fiercely it gave
> me great pain.

While no other source corroborates Claire's story, Byron's own correspondence shows that he took great care over the safe-keeping of Augusta's letters. As he wrote to his sister at the end of that summer, 'Your confidential letter is safe, and all the others.' The issue of Augusta was raised only once more, at which time, said Claire, 'it was to make me promise never to mention to anyone, what he had revealed'. As she told Trelawny, 'he said that none knew that secret besides us, Lady Byron and Lady Caroline Lamb'.

Such was Claire's understanding of the past that she had learned the forbidden truth and earned Byron's eternal malefaction for it. Byron's 'secret' was, of course, the report that he had conducted an incestuous relationship with Augusta, and that he was the father of her daughter, Medora, born in April 1814. To know this, even when Byron had volunteered the information himself, was to become his mortal enemy. 'Now you know the reason why he hated and persecuted and infamously calumniated a certain person,' Claire wrote to Trelawny. 'He hated every body who possessed his secret, yet he was so weak in love that he could not help confiding it to the ladies of his affection for the moment.'

Claire's story elevated her to an exclusive group of spurned women, but it also found a pronounced literary parallel in William Godwin's most successful novel, *Caleb Williams*. Here, the young hero is presented with a mysterious trunk that contains the murderous secrets of his employer, and is hounded, victimised and broken for what he knows. Oddly, Annabella Milbanke had made the same allusion to her daughter, Ada, in 1841, something that Claire could never have known. Annabella had been the first to discover the mysterious 'marks' that passed between her husband and Augusta as she ransacked his writing desk searching for evidence of insanity. Byron confronted her and 'afterwards,' said Annabella, 'threatened me that if I sought to know his secrets, like Caleb in Godwin's novel, he would prove a Falkland to me and "persecute me for *ever*".' Like Annabella, Claire, it seems, was unable to unbind Byron from the literature that had interleaved her history. Had she ever been able to? 'Where there is mystery,' Byron had written in the fragment of 'Augustus Darvell', 'it is generally supposed there must be evil.'

The reconnection with Trelawny and the growing interest in Shelley throughout the literary world brought Claire to a realisation that the letters and mementoes she had long hung onto might be of some worth. Her apartments were draughty and crumbling and, looking to supplement her modest income, she courted her old friend as a potential buyer. In 1873, Trelawny sent William Rossetti to Florence to examine the papers. Claire, now seventy-five years old, had just had a fall and, unable to walk, received John Polidori's nephew in her bedroom. She was a 'slender, pallid old lady with thinned hair that had once been dark, and with dark and still expressive eyes', recalled Rossetti. She had a clear voice, although was 'more than moderately deaf'. Rossetti left empty-handed and a colony of vultures began to circle the Palazzo Orsini, alert to the existence of Claire's treasures and eager to pick over the remains of an ailing old lady who kept the company of ghosts. Among them were men of means, and hard-nosed book dealers and bibliophiles, although the most dogged was an American sailor from Salem, Massachusetts, who first appeared on Claire's doorstep in 1872.

This was Edward Silsbee, a man of middle age, cast in the same mould as Trelawny but with far more polished manners. Since retiring from the sea, he had turned his life over to the worship of Shelley, whom he called 'the Christ of Literature', and for four years lodged intermittently with Claire and her niece, Pauline, known as Plin, who had also come to share the *palazzo* as a paying guest with her illegitimate daughter, Georgina. Silsbee was hungry for information about Shelley, and drew Claire into long, one-sided conversations that he tried to keep in his head until he was able to run back to his room and transcribe them into a series of tiny notebooks. Proximity to Claire was to bask in the presence of one who had walked in his idol's footsteps and breathed the same air, but Silsbee was also playing a longer game. Wanting to own Shelley's papers but with nothing to offer except promissory notes, he burrowed deeper into the household, hoping to receive something as a gift. In the meantime Plin, a spirited and adventurous woman like her aunt, fell in love. He was 'so charming so tender so charitable Christlike,' Plin wrote of Silsbee in her journal, 'that one would like Magdalen sink down at his feet and admire him like a spirit soaring high above human imperfection'.

Silsbee slept with Plin, but he had no intention of marrying her, all the while feeding his need for Shelley as he drained the memories from Claire. Talk of his behaviour was picked up by Henry James, who used it for his novella, *The Aspern Papers*. It was a cruel and calculating game, but Claire enjoyed Silsbee's rapt attention, and flirted with him, playing the 'Gurli', or 'imbecile', in her niece's words. But his presence also seems to have inspired her to set to paper her most emphatic recollections yet. The result was an angry fragment, blotted and cross-written, that attacked the followers and consequences of 'free love', denouncing the 'evil passions' it aroused and the predatory instincts that fame and genius were permitted to indulge. 'Under the influence [of] the doctrine and belief in free Love,' Claire wrote,

> I saw the two first Poets [of] England perhaps of Europe, also men of high birth highly cultivated considered the most refined and honourable specimens of their age, become monsters of lying, meanness cruelty and treachery. Under the influence of free Love, I saw women treated as beasts of burthen. Under the influence of free Love, Lord B– became a human tyger slaking his thirst for inflicting pain, upon defenceless women who loved him; imprison his own infant child of 4 years in a convent in a remote district where not anyone could watch over her, nor guard her from the neglect and the hands of strangers without a relative or a friend near her. Under the influence of free Love, I saw a mother condemned to live without ever beholding a child she fondly adored – and that child imprisoned in a Convent where she died surrounded by utter strangers.

It was a harsh renunciation of convictions she had once held dear, presided over by the vampiric image of Byron 'slaking his thirst'. Had Claire finally broken a spell that had kept her in its thrall since the age of seventeen? Possibly. According to Plin, Claire had 'double ways', and could be 'mercurial . . . capricious, wilful . . . mercenary', at once the agent of her history and its victim. It was, she said, a '<u>Byronic</u> nature'.

Claire died on 19 March 1879, at the age of eighty. 'She went

out like a candle snuff,' said Plin. She was interred in the cemetery of Misericordia di Santa Maria d'Antella, beneath a headstone
whose inscription Claire had chosen herself: 'She passed her life
in sufferings, expiating not only her faults but also her virtues.'
To warm her endless sleep she was buried with a little shawl, a
gift from Shelley. That she chose it rather than Allegra's miniature
or lock of hair suggests that, even after the final repudiations and
all she had endured, he remained the strongest attachment of
her life.

But it was fame as much as Shelley that shaped Claire Clairmont's
destiny. Both she and John Polidori had sought proximity to it
but, once within its beam, found that what they hoped would
exalt them caused them only pain. Internalising the low-grade
fever that was the Romantic obsession with celebrity, its corrosive
pathogens steered their course, moulding them into archetypes
of grievance that would become increasingly familiar as the nineteenth century drew on – the female hysteric, the embittered
bourgeois. Once exposed to celebrity, it infected them for ever.
'He that embarks in the enterprizes of ambition,' Madame de
Staël had written, 'must burn the vessels which might transport
him back to a more tranquil state of life.'

There was a cure but, as Byron knew, it was fatal:

> Love, fame, ambition, avarice – 'tis the same,
> Each idle – and all ill – and none the worst –
> For all are meteors with a different name
> And Death the sable smoke where vanishes the flame.

ACKNOWLEDGEMENTS

Each country Book-club bows the knee to Baal,
And, hurling lawful Genius from the throne,
Erects a shrine and idol of its own;
Some leaden calf – but whom it matters not,
From soaring SOUTHEY, down to grovelling STOTT.

Byron: *English Bards and Scotch Reviewers*

A little grovelling is the least I can do, given all the magnificent people without whose generosity this book would never have seen the light of day. The New York Public Library looms especially large here, where I was fortunate enough to be a Fellow at the Cullman Centre for Scholars and Writers, and where most of the research was done. Jean Strouse, director of the Cullman Centre, offered a welcome and cultivated an atmosphere of creative collegiality that I shall always prize. Elizabeth Denlinger, curator of the Pforzheimer Collection of Shelley and His Circle, helped navigate the riches of its collection, sifted the evidence, offered brilliant suggestions to improve the draft and, most importantly, became a friend. The same is true of Doucet Devin Fischer, co-editor of *Shelley and His Circle*, whose encouragement was invaluable, whose erudition was humbling, and whose dedicated scrutiny of the manuscript spared my blushes on more than one occasion. To all, my sincerest thanks.

Thanks also to Peter Buse, who read the manuscript, offered his advice unalloyed, and who for almost twenty years has been improving my work with his friendship and acumen. To Vicki Parslow Stafford, the genealogist who uncovered Claire Clairmont's true parentage in the archives of the Somerset Heritage Centre; to Lindsay Efusia and Jerrold Frakes, who made skilled translations from the Italian; Leah Benedict who helped things run on time; and Hazel Orme, for her faultless copy-editing. Peter Cochran was kind enough to allow me to quote from his invaluable transcription of Hobhouse's diaries. Needless to say, none of the above would have happened without the galvanising industry of Ben Mason at Fox Mason, or the surgical skill of not one, but two editors, Nick Davies (now by happy coincidence in charge at John Murray), and Anya Serota at Canongate.

I am also grateful to the many archivists and librarians whose expertise any researcher relies on, most notably Sarah Romkey, archivist Rare Books and Special Collections, University of British Columbia Library; David McClay, curator, and Rachel Beattie, assistant curator of the John Murray archive at the National Library of Scotland; Christine Reynolds, assistant keeper of the Muniments at Westminster Abbey; James Maynard, associate curator, Poetry Collection, University at Buffalo, SUNY; and Charles Carter, bibliographer of the Pforzheimer Collection.

I also pay homage to the many scholars whose original work on the Byron-Shelley circle I have drawn on so heavily, noting in particular Marion Kingston Stocking, the scholar responsible for putting the letters and journals of Claire Clairmont before the world, and D. Lorne Macdonald, author of the fullest biography on John Polidori. Though I neither met nor corresponded with Professor Macdonald, I was saddened to hear of his passing while writing this book.

Last, but first always in my affections, is my wife, Josie. 'What is a work – any – or every work,' wrote Byron, 'but a desert with fountains and, perhaps, a grove or two, every day's journey?' How true this is, although I'd consider any writer lucky enough to find a grove a day to be blessed indeed. Fortunately, I had Josie with me at every step, urging me along even when the oasis felt very far away. Josie makes all things possible, and for this – and so much else – I shall love her for ever.

NOTES

List of Abbreviations

ARCHIVAL MATERIAL

Abinger: Oxford, Bodleian Library, MS. Abinger.

ADC: Angeli-Dennis Collection of Papers, Rare Books Library, University of British Columbia.

BL: British Library, London MS. Add 36456, 54226.

Berg: The Henry W. and Albert A. Berg Collection of English and American Literature, the New York Public Library.

Murray: The John Murray Archive at the National Library of Scotland, Edinburgh.

Pforz: The Carl H. Pforzheimer Collection of Shelley and His Circle, the New York Public Library, Astor, Lenox and Tilden Foundations, New York.

Vial: Letters relating to Mary Jane Vial, Somerset Heritage Centre, xx DD/DP 17/11.

WA: 'An Inquisition Indented, taken for our Sovereign Lord the King at the House of Gaetano Polidori . . .' Westminster Abbey Muniment Room and Library, Westminster Abbey, London.

PRINTED MATERIAL

BCPW: Jerome J. McGann (ed.), _Lord Byron: The Complete Poetical Works,_ 7 vols (Oxford: Oxford University Press, 1980–86)

BCMP: Andrew Nicholson (ed.), *Lord Byron: The Complete Miscellaneous Prose* (Oxford: Clarendon, 1991)

BLJ: Leslie A. Marchand (ed.), *Byron's Letters and Journals*, 13 vols (Cambridge, Mass.: Belknap, 1973–94)

CC: Marion Kingston Stocking (ed.), *The Clairmont Correspondence: Letters of Claire Clairmont, Charles Clairmont, and Fanny Imlay Godwin*, 2 vols (Baltimore and London: Johns Hopkins University Press, 1995)

CCJ: Marion Kingston Stocking (ed.), *The Journals of Claire Clairmont* (Cambridge, Mass.: Harvard University Press, 1968)

CFJWP: John William Polidori, *The Vampyre and Ernestus Berchtold; or, the Modern Oedipus: Collected Fiction of John William Polidori*, ed. D. L. Macdonald and Kathleen Scherf (Toronto: University of Toronto Press, 1994)

DJCH: *Diary of John Cam Hobhouse*, transcribed by Peter Cochran, http://petercochran.wordpress.com/hobhouses-diary/

Dowden: Edward Dowden, *The Life of Percy Bysshe Shelley*, 2 vols (London: Kegan Paul, 1886)

Frankenstein: Mary Shelley, *Frankenstein; or the Modern Prometheus*. In *The Original Frankenstein: Two New Versions – Mary Shelley's Earliest Draft and Percy Shelley's Revised Text*, ed. Charles Robinson (New York: Vintage, 2009)

Hogg: Thomas Jefferson Hogg, *The Life of Percy Bysshe Shelley*, 2 vols (London: 1858)

Letters MWS: Betty T. Bennett (ed.), *The Letters of Mary Wollstonecraft Shelley*, 3 vols (Baltimore: Johns Hopkins University Press, 1980–88)

Letters PBS: Frederick L. Jones (ed.), *Letters of Percy Bysshe Shelley*, 2 vols (Oxford: Clarendon, 1964)

MacCarthy: Fiona MacCarthy, *Byron: Life and Legend* (New York: Farrar, Straus and Giroux, 2002)

Macdonald: D. L. Macdonald, *Poor Polidori: A Critical Biography of the Author of* The Vampyre (Toronto: University of Toronto Press, 1991)

Marchand: Leslie A. Marchand, *Byron: A Biography*, 3 vols (New York: Knopf, 1957)

Medwin: Ernest B. Lovell (ed.), *Medwin's Conversations with Lord Byron* (Princeton: Princeton University Press, 1966)

Moore: Thomas Moore, *The Life, Letters and Journals of Lord Byron, Collected and Arranged with Notes,* new edition (London: 1860)

MWSJ: Paula R. Feldman and Diana Scott-Kilvert (eds), *The Journals of Mary Shelley,* 2 vols (Oxford: Clarendon, 1987)

PD: John William Polidori, *The Diary of John Polidori 1816: Relating to Byron, Shelley, etc.,* ed. William Michael Rossetti (London: Elkin Matthews, 1891)

Prothero: Rowland Edmund Prothero, *Works of Lord Byron,* 7 vols (New York: Octagon, 1966)

SC: Neil Cameron, Donald H. Reiman, Doucet Devin Fischer, et al. (eds), *Shelley and His Circle, 1773–1822,* 10 vols (Cambridge, Mass.: Harvard University Press, 1961–2002)

Voice: Ernest J. Lovell (ed.), *His Very Self and Voice: Collected Conversations of Lord Byron* (New York: Macmillan, 1954)

Prelude

1 *After a dinner at the Ship Inn:* PD, 98.

1 *Cow Lane:* PD, 27.

1 *'Here lie the remains of the celebrated Charles Churchill':* PD, 27; DJCH, 24 April 1816. The first three dates in Polidori's journal are ahead of Hobhouse's (correct) entries by a day.

1 *'What was he celebrated for?':* PD, p. 28.

2 *As the sun began to set:* DJCH, Wednesday, 24 April 1816.

2 *'What a lesson':* PD, p. 28.

1. St George's Day

3 *Hobhouse:* DJCH, 22 April 1816, fn. 341.

3 *Byron had stayed up writing letters:* BLJ, vol. 5, p. 68.

3 *The men rose at six:* BLJ, vol. 5, p. 71.

4 *'clump foot':* Morning Post, 23 April 1816.

4 *'all sorts of accidents':* DJCH, 23 April 1816.

4 *bailiffs:* DJCH, 25 April 1816.

4 *'Trust Byron':* DJCH, 23 April 1816. See also Judith Pascoe, *The Hummingbird Cabinet: A Rare and Curious History of Romantic Collectors* (Ithaca: Cornell University Press, 2005), p. 107.

5   *a host of monstrous rumours*: 'Caroline Lamb accused Byron of —. Poor fellow, the plot thickens against him.' *DJCH*, 9 February 1816.

5   '*lion of 1812*': *BLJ*, vol. 8, p. 29; Medwin, p. 214; *BLJ*, vol. 8, p. 27.

5   *concerned friends*: BCMP, p. 95; T. A. Burnett, *The Rise and Fall of a Regency Dandy: The Life and Times of Scrope Berdmore Davies* (Boston: Little Brown, 1981), p. 103.

5   '*awoke one morning and found myself famous*': Moore, 159. 'His fame,' said Moore, 'had not to wait for any of the ordinary gradations, but seemed to spring up, like the palace of a fairy tale, in a night.'

5   '*however the way to riches or Greatness lies*': *BLJ*, vol. 1, p. 49.

6   '*a Man whose works are praised*': *BLJ*, vol. 1, p. 130.

6   *savaged by the lawyer Henry Brougham*: Andrew Rutherford (ed.), *Byron: The Critical Heritage* (New York: Barnes and Noble, 1970), pp. 27, 31, 28; *BLJ*, vol. 3, p. 213.

6   *a long autobiographical poem*: Moore, p. 122.

7   *William Gifford*: For Gifford's role, and that of the *Quarterly Review*, see Jerome Christensen, *Lord Byron's Strength: Romantic Writing and Commercial Society* (Baltimore and London: Johns Hopkins University Press, 1993), pp. 146–7.

7   *Then, in March 1812*: Robert Dallas's discussion of the progress of *Childe Harold's Pilgrimage* through the press, including his own recommended edits, and those from Murray suggesting he cut both political and personal material, constitutes Chapter 7 of Dallas's *Recollections of the Life of Lord Byron from the Year 1808 to the End of 1814* (London: 1824).

7   *By charging fifty shillings*: For those who care to know, the quartos measured 11' x 5'. I know because I measured one.

7   '*circle of star-gazers*': *BLJ*, vol. 8, p. 29; Medwin, p. 214; Moore, p. 163.

7   '*This poem appears on every table*': BCH, p. 36. Essential studies on Byron's celebrity and the public life of Regency literary culture include Tom Mole, *Byron's Romantic Celebrity: Industrial Culture and the Hermeneutic of Intimacy* (Basingstoke: Palgrave Macmillan, 2007); Eric Eisner, *Nineteenth-Century Poetry and Literary Celebrity*

(Basingstoke: Palgrave Macmillan, 2009); Richard Cronin, *Paper Pellets: British Literary Culture after Waterloo* (Oxford: Oxford University Press, 2010); Frances Wilson (ed.), *Byromania: Portraits of the Artist in Nineteenth and Twentieth-Century Culture* (London: Macmillan, 1999); Ghislaine McDayter, *Byromania and the Birth of Celebrity Culture* (Albany: SUNY Press, 2009); and Tom Mole (ed.), *Romanticism and Celebrity Culture, 1750–1850* (Cambridge: Cambridge University Press, 2009).

7   '*The genius which the poem exhibited*': Samuel Rogers, *Recollections of the Table Talk of Samuel Rogers* (New York: Appleton, 1856), p. 229.

7   *Having made Byron fashionable:* See William St Clair, *The Reading Nation in the Romantic Period* (Cambridge: Cambridge University Press, 2004), Appendix 9, p. 586. As Peter J. Manning tells us, such milestones were not always to be trusted, as it was Murray's practice to announce new editions before the old ones had sold out in order to give an even greater impression of *Childe Harold* as a literary juggernaut than perhaps the facts allowed. Manning, '*Childe Harold* in the Marketplace: From Romaunt to Handbook', *Modern Language Quarterly*, 52:2 (1991), pp. 170–90: 184. The profits from the poem allowed Murray to move from his cramped office in Fleet Street to a more fashionable address in Albemarle Street, occupying the vacated rooms of one of the publishers who had been foolish enough to reject the poem (MacCarthy, p. 159). It should be noted that this was commerce from which Byron determined to remain aristocratically aloof, refusing to take a penny of profit for himself.

8   *a readership dispirited by war:* This was certainly the opinion of Thomas Moore, who credited Byron's popularity to the 'great struggle of that period', which had created 'in all minds, and in every walk of intellect, a taste for strong excitement, which the stimulants supplied from ordinary sources were insufficient to gratify', Moore, p. 158.

8   '*Yet oft-times*': *BCPW*, vol. 2, pp. 10–11.

8   '*the first poet who*': Quoted in Rutherford (ed.), *Byron: The Critical Heritage*, p. 138; *Voice*, 48. The implicit theatricality of the phrase

'before the public' is noted by Richard Cronin, *Paper Pellets*, p. 53.

9   '*Then bring me wine*': *BCPW*, vol. 1, p. 351.

9   *the career open to talent*: Not even Byron was immune to the power of celebrity. He had owned a bust of Bonaparte as a schoolboy, and as he grew into a keen follower of theatre and sport, he had asked his fencing master, Henry Angelo, to make him a screen with pictures of famous actors on one side and boxers on the other. Henry Angelo, *The Reminiscences of Henry Angelo*, 2 vols (New York and London: Blom, 1969), vol. 2, pp. 100–101.

10 *to see Byron in his creations*: See, for example, Corin Throsby, 'Flirting With Fame: Byron's Anonymous Female Fans', *Byron Journal*, 32:2 (2004), pp. 115–124: 117.

10 '*in some very trivial particulars*': *BCPW*, vol. 2, p. 4.

10 *anonymous cogs of industrialisation*: This point is heavily indebted to the work of Tom Mole, who notes that 'The growth of celebrity culture [in the early nineteenth century] . . . eased the sense of industrial alienation between readers and writers. The celebrity apparatus relied on the concealed use of new cultural technologies to construct an impression of unmediated contact. Instead of appearing as industrial productions competing for attention in a crowded market made up of increasingly estranged readers and writers, [Byron's] poems fostered a hermeneutic of intimacy.' Mole, *Byron's Romantic Celebrity*, pp. 22–3. See also Manning, '*Harold* in the Marketplace', p. 182.

10 '*state of almost savage torpor*': William Wordsworth and Samuel Taylor Coleridge, *Lyrical Ballads, with Other Poems*, 2 vols (London:1800), 'Preface', xiv.

11 '*somewhat cracked*': Henry Crabb Robinson, *Henry Crabb Robinson on Books and Their Writers*, ed. Edith J. Morley, 2 vols (London: Dent, 1938), pp. 93, 85.

11 '*Turdsworth*': Mark Brown, 'Lord Byron's Dig at William Turdsworth', Guardian.co.uk, 27 September 2009.

11 '*the impersonation of myself*': Medwin, p. 214.

11 *performing his moody solitude*: See Leo Braudy, *The Frenzy of Renown: Fame and Its History* (New York: Vintage Books, 1997), p. 404.

11 '*withdraw myself from myself*': *BLJ*, vol. 3, pp. 225, 179.

11 '*a very repulsive personage*': *BCPW*, vol. 3, p. 150; Moore, p. 159.

11 '*Everything by turns*': Ernest J. Lovell (ed.) *Lady Blessington's Conversations of Lord Byron* (Princeton: Princeton University Press, 1969), p. 47.

12 *in the privacy of his own home:* MacCarthy, p. 190; Henry Angelo, *Reminiscences*, vol. 2, p. 98.

12 '*absurdly courting him*': Quoted in Ethel Coburn Mayne, *The Life and Letters of Anne Isabella, Lady Noel Byron* (New York: Scribner's, 1929), p. 37.

12 '*to be an anything*': Quoted in Mayne, *Life and Letters*, p. 44.

13 '*never be able to pull with a woman*': Quoted in Donald Low, *That Sunny Dome: A Portrait of Regency England* (London: Dent, 1977), p. 103.

13 *really was a tortured soul:* James Solderholm, *Fantasy, Forgery, and the Byron Legend* (Lexington: University Press of Kentucky, 1996), p. 96.

13 '*the result of temporary solitude*': *BLJ*, vol. 4, p. 183.

13 *paroxysms of rage:* As Lady Byron testified in a statement to Stephen Lushington: 'He had for many months professed his intention of giving himself up either to women or drinking, and had asked me whether I gave him leave or not. Accordingly for about three months before my confinement he was accustomed to drink Brandy and other liquors to intoxication, which caused him to commit many outrageous acts, as breaking and burning several valuable articles, and brought on paroxysms of rage or frenzy – not only terrifying but dangerous to me in my then situation – and of this he was so well aware that he had asked me on occasions of extreme ill-usage, if the Child was dead. About two months before my confinement he took a Mistress, of which Circumstance I was ignorant till informed by himself . . . He studiously and maliciously informed me of the times of his visits to this other woman, and seemed to have a pleasure in alluding to the subject before me and others. He has at various times declared to me that he should have no scruple in connecting himself with any woman that came in his

way, and told me that if I were dissatisfied with his conduct in that respect I was perfectly at liberty to do the same . . .' Quoted in Malcolm Elwin, *Lord Byron's Wife* (New York: Harcourt, Brace and World, 1962), p. 328.

13 '*Murder was the idea*': Quoted in Elwin, *Lord Byron's Wife*, p. 340. While a 'deeper meaning' for Byron's hostile behaviour is impossible to ascertain, as Fiona MacCarthy has argued, Byron's continued allusions and promises one day to confess were most probably hints of the homosexual affairs he had pursued in his youth, sexual desires that continued both to torture and entice him throughout his life. See MacCarthy, p. 261.

14 '*grew cunning and mysterious about it after I seemed to detect it*': Quoted in Elwin, *Lord Byron's Wife*, p. 346.

14 *Justine*: John Cam Hobhouse, Lord Broughton, *Contemporary Account of the Separation of Lord and Lady Byron; Also of the Destruction of Lord Byron's Memoirs* (London: privately printed, 1870), p. 68. The assertion that the book, which Hobhouse describes as 'a volume which as a curiosity might be kept, but which was certainly not fit for an open library', is *Justine*, can be found in MacCarthy, p. 262.

14 '*strutting about*': DJCH, 12 February 1816. 'Mrs Leigh and George Byron tell me he forgets what he did and said – it is part of his disease.' Elwin, *Lord Byron's Wife*, p. 414. On the question of Byron feeling suicidal, see also Lovell (ed.), *Lady Blessington's Conversations*, pp. 41–2. Clearly, his adverse reactions to stress had been noted in the past. As he wrote in April 1814, a 'staid grave' physician who had examined him had asked 'many questions to me about *my mind*' and 'how I felt "when anything weighed upon my mind".' *BLJ*, vol. 4, p. 105.

14 '*lucky we had not all our throats cut*': Quoted in Burnett, *Rise and Fall*, p. 101.

15 '*could not be considered otherwise than disastrous*': Moore, p. 305. For the homophobic context of Byron's departure, see MacCarthy, p. 275, and Louis Crompton, *Byron and Greek Love: Homophobia in 19th-Century England* (Berkeley: University of California Press, 1985), p. 199.

15 *the pages of the* Champion: See *SC*, vol. 4, p. 643. Leigh Hunt called this his 'poetical power of assuming an imaginary position, and taking pity on himself in the shape of another man.' Leigh Hunt, *Lord Byron and Some of His Contemporaries, with Recollections of the Author's Life and of His Visit to Italy* (London: 1828), p. 7.

16 '*the greenest island*': *BLJ*, vol. 5, p. 129.

16 '*poor dear Bonaparte!!!*': *BLJ*, vol. 5, p. 73.

16 '*Childe Harolded himself*': John Gibson Lockhart, *Memoirs of the Life of Walter Scott*, 7 vols (Edinburgh: 1837), vol. 2, p. 15.

16 *teenaged girls sketched dreamily*: Harriet Martineau, *Autobiography, with Memorials by Maria Weston Chapman*, 3rd edition, 3 vols (London: 1877), vol. 1, p. 82.

17 *artistic dishevelment:* This was typical of studious young men of the period. John Keats's friend, Henry Stephens, remembered him as a medical student, going about with 'his neck nearly bare, à la Byron'. See Dorothy Hewlett, *A Life of John Keats*, 3rd edition (New York: Barnes and Noble, 1970), p. 41.

17 '*short and thick*': Medwin, p. 7.

17 '*water and a towel*': Hunt, *Lord Byron*, p. 109.

17 '*periodical headaches*': *BLJ*, vol. 11, p. 44. Byron's childhood dislike of doctors is alluded to in Pryse Lockhart Gordon's, *Personal Memoirs; or, Reminiscences of Men and Manners at Home and Abroad, During the Last Half Century*, 2 vols (London: Colburn and Bentley, 1830), vol. 2, p. 320. See also Medwin, p. 104.

17 *naval surgeon had treated him*: *BLJ*, vol. 2, p. 58; vol. 2, p. 161.

17 '*torpid liver*': *BLJ*, vol. 5, p. 33; *DJCH*, 12 February 1816. See also Wilma Paterson, 'Was Byron Anorexic?', *World Medicine* (15 May 1982), pp. 35–8; and J. H. Baron, 'Illnesses and creativity: Byron's Appetites, James Joyce's Gut, and Melba's Meals and *Mésalliances*', *British Medical Journal*, 315 (20 December 1997), pp. 1697–1703.

17 '*He was very ill*': Hunt, *Lord Byron*, pp. 4–5.

18 *facility with languages*: *BLJ*, vol. 5, p. 92. On 28 March 1816, Augusta Leigh wrote to the Rev. Francis Hodgson that 'B. talks of taking a young Physician recommended to him by Sr W. Knighton as a travelling companion' (quoted in Elwin, *Lord Byron's Wife*, p. 461). On the same day, Hobhouse records in his journal that 'Byron

is going abroad, and takes a young Dr Polidori with him' (*DJCH*, 28 March 1816). See also Robert R. Harson, 'A Clarification Concerning John Polidori, Lord Byron's Physician', *Keats-Shelley Journal*, vol. 21–2 (1972–3), pp. 38–40.

18 '*an odd dog*': Peter W. Graham (ed.), *Byron's Bulldog: The Letters of John Cam Hobhouse* (Columbus: Ohio State University Press, 1984), p. 270; *DJCH*, 17 April 1816.

18 '*inevitable*': *DJCH*, 28 March 1816.

18 '*a nearer inspection*': Marchand, vol. 2, p. 608.

18 '*feeling very awkward*': *PD*, 68.

18 '*light wines*': *BLJ*, vol. 5, p. 71.

19 '*wild Irishmen*': Moore, p. 28; *BLJ*, vol. 5, p. 192.

19 '*my ruffled spirits*': *PD*, 30.

19 '*a very absurd thing*': *PD*, 30. See also *DJCH*, 24 April 1816.

19 '*His attachment to reputation*': *DJCH*, 24 April 1816.

19 '*shall have the reputation*': *DJCH*, 24 April 1816.

2. Directions for John

20 *Soho's Golden Square*: William Michael Rossetti, *Dante Gabriel Rossetti: His Family-Letters with a Memoir*, 2 vols (London: 1895), vol. 1, p. 25. Gaetano's father, Agostino Polidori, penned a long poem entitled 'Osteology' detailing the exact position and purpose of every bone in the human body, and his brother Luigi composed heroic verses in the style of Ariosto.

20 '*moral tales*': Rossetti, *Family Letters*, vol. 1, p. 26. The local Italian literati included the publishers Luigi Nardini and the Molini brothers, and John Deagostini, a writer and editor with whom Gaetano established an intimate friendship, and who would become godfather to John. Gaetano Polidori and L. Nardini are first recorded as 'Booksellers' in the London Directory of 1797 (see *A London Directory, or Alphabetical Arrangement; Containing the Names and Residences of the Merchants, Manufacturers, and Principal Traders in the Metropolis and its Environs* [London, 1797]). Prior to that, Polidori's name as publisher appeared on his 1795 translation of *The Castle of Otranto* as 'Molini, Polidori, Molini and Co.'. Gaetano also used to describe himself with the phrase

'*maestro di lingua italiana*', as can be seen from the title page of his *Saggio di novelle e favole* (London, 1798). See also Helen Rossetti Angeli, 'Byron's Physician', ADC, Box 31, f. 4, p.1; 'Gaetano Polidori: Poète et Littérateur', ADC, Box 27, f. 3, p. 709. The title pages of Gaetano's works from the 1790s often feature the phrase 'Il Vendeno Presso L'Autore'.

20 *Anna Maria Pierce*: It was a good match, as teaching writing was lucrative enough at the end of the eighteenth century for Maria's father to keep a carriage and maintain a large household. See Rossetti, *Family-Letters*, vol. 1, p. 29.

21 *Another brother*: See the family note by Anna Maria Polidori, ADC, Box 27, f. 3. Margaret's nervous giggles are recorded in the 'Memoir by W. M. Rossetti' appended to Christina Rossetti's *Poetical Works* (1904), http://www.canamus.org/Enchiridion/Xtrs/rsetiwmr.htm (accessed 1 July 2010).

21 '*sworn enemy to pretence*': Rossetti, *Family-Letters*, vol. 1, p. 28.

21 *Napoleon had marched into Milan:* Christopher Duggan, *The Force of Destiny: A History of Italy Since 1796* (Boston: Houghton Mifflin, 2008), p. 12.

21 *a historical diet*: Autographed letter, signed [ALS], John Polidori to Gaetano Polidori, December 1813, ADC, Box 31, f. 5.

21 '*The Roman and Greek historians*': ALS, John Polidori to Gaetano Polidori, December, 1813, ADC, Box 31, f. 5.

21 '*a remarkable talent*': Gaetano Polidori, original undated MS, ADC, Box 27, f. 3. Translation by Jerrold Frakes.

22 '*Let us suppose*': Gaetano Polidori, original undated MS, ADC, Box 27, f. 3. Translation by Jerrold Frakes.

22 *settled by French refugees:* See William St Clair, *The Godwins and the Shelleys: The Biography of a Family* (New York: Norton, 1989), pp. 541–2, fn. 6.

22 '*out-of-the-world*': 'Memoir by W. M. Rossetti'.

23 '*bad company*': Gaetano Polidori, original undated MS, ADC, Box 27, f. 3. Translation by Jerrold Frakes; ALS, John Polidori to Gaetano Polidori, 28 December 281808, ADC, Box 31, f. 6.

23 '*My boy*': Gaetano Polidori, original undated MS, ADC, Box 27, f. 3. Translation by Jerrold Frakes. Marty was quoting the words

of Themistocles' tutor, *cf.* Plutarch, *Themistocles*, chapter 2, section 2.

23 *The school was desperately remote:* Dom Cuthbert Almond OSB, *The History of Ampleforth Abbey From the Foundation of St Lawrence's Dieulouard to the Present* (London: Washbourne, 1903), p. 269.

24 *twelve boys:* For the early history of the school, see Anselm Cramer, *Ampleforth: The Story of St Laurence's Abbey and College* (Ampleforth: Trustees of Ampleforth Abbey, 2001), Appendix L, p. 202; Anthony Marett-Crosby OSB, *A School of the Lord's Service* (Frome: Ampleforth Abbey Trustees, 2002); and Philip Smiley, 'Polidori at Ampleforth', *The Ampleforth Journal*, 97:2 (1992), pp. 34–43.

24 *Tuition . . . cost fifty:* See Andrew Motion, *Keats* (London: Faber and Faber, 1997), p. 22. For nineteenth-century British public schools, see John Chandos, *Boys Together: English Public Schools, 1800–1864* (London: Hutchinson, 1984). p. 23.

24 *Lessons were conducted in an outhouse:* Cramer, *Ampleforth*, p. 65.

24 *basil, carnations, Venus's looking-glass:* ALS, John Polidori to Gaetano Polidori, 8 June 1807, ADC, Box 31, f. 6.

24 *'It is wished that the parents would avoid':* Cramer, *Ampleforth*, p. 63.

24 *Chased from their European abbeys:* Cramer, *Ampleforth*, p. 49.

24 *'Directions for John':* Gaetano Polidori, 'Directions for John', n.d., ADC, Box 27.

24 *Asceticism was key:* Smiley, 'Polidori at Ampleforth', p. 36.

25 *'We heard a knock at the door':* ALS, John Polidori to Gaetano Polidori, 24 November 1804, ADC, Box 31, f. 6.

25 *'foolish':* ALS, Gaetano Polidori to John Polidori, n.d. [1804], ADC, Box 31, f. 6.

26 *'Now tell me!':* ALS, Gaetano Polidori to John Polidori, n.d. [1804], ADC, Box 31, f. 6.

26 *'for I have thought a great while':* ALS, John Polidori to Gaetano Polidori, 15 December [1806?], ADC, Box 31, f. 6.

27 *tropical illnesses:* See Martin Howard, *Wellington's Doctors: The British Army Medical Service in the Napoleonic Wars* (Staplehurst: Spellmount, 2002), p. 155.

27 *'I have learned':* ALS, John Polidori to Gaetano Polidori, 28 December 1808, ADC, Box 31, f. 6.

27 '*genius*': ALS, John Polidori to Gaetano Polidori, 28 December 1808, ADC, Box 31, f. 6. On Major Pierce's rift with the Polidoris, see ALS, John Polidori to Frances Polidori, 22 March 1815, ADC, Box 31, f. 6.

27 '*state of life*': ALS, John William Polidori to Gaetano Polidori, Ampleforth Lodge, 9 January 1809, ADC, Box 31, f. 6.

27 *This was hardly news*: As autocratic as it seems, it was not only commonplace for fathers to decide their son's future without consultation, it was considered a sign of great love and attention. As the educationalist and member of the distinguished Lunar Society Richard Lovell Edgeworth had written in his *Essays on Professional Education*, only those 'who feel that they are willing to take more than common care of the education of their children, should incur the responsibility of deciding early upon the choice of their professions, upon the fate of their future lives'. Richard Lovell Edgeworth, *Essays on Professional Education*, 2nd edition (London: 1812), p. 24.

28 '*infectious society*': ALS, John Polidori to Gaetano Polidori, 28 December 1808, ADC, Box 31, f. 6.

28 '*Ecclesiastical life*': ALS, John Polidori to Gaetano Polidori, 28 December 1808, ADC, Box 31, f. 6.

28 '*compared to that of a turtle*': Anon., *The Traveller's Guide Through Scotland and Its Islands*, 6th edition, 2 vols (Edinburgh: 1814), vol. 1, p. 11.

28 '*a confused heap of ancient houses*': Louis Simond, *Journal of a Tour and Residence in Great Britain, 1810 and 1811, by a French Traveller*, 2 vols (Edinburgh: 1815), vol. 1, p. 265.

28 '*dirty and detestable way*': Basil Cozens-Hardy (ed.), *The Diary of Sylas Neville, 1767–1788* (London: Oxford University Press, 1950), p. 140.

29 '*dull and unhealthy habitations*': Anon., *Traveller's Guide*, vol. 1, p. 25; Cozens-Hardy (ed.), *Diary of Sylas Neville*, p. 146.

29 *450 other young men*: Number of students taken from Edinburgh University's database 'Students of Medicine, 1762–1826': http://www.archives.lib.ed.ac.uk/students/search.php?view=advanced1. For the matriculation album, see Lisa Rosner, *Medical Education*

in the Age of Improvement: Edinburgh Students and Apprentices, 1760–1826 (Edinburgh: Edinburgh University Press, 1991), p. 44.

29 *did not prohibit Catholics*: Rosner, *Medical Education*, p. 16. See also 'Graduations at Edinburgh' in the *Edinburgh Medical and Surgical Journal*, vol. 9 (1813), p. 498–9; vol. 10 (1814), pp. 511–2; vol. 11 (1815), p. 533.

29 *Thomas Charles Hope*: Rosner, *Medical Education*, p. 50.

30 '*is to explain the principles*': J. Johnson, *A Guide for Gentlemen Studying Medicine at the University of Edinburgh* (London: 1792), p. 20.

30 *most influential medical educators*: John D. Comrie, *The History of Scottish Medicine*, 2nd edition, 2 vols (London: Wellcome Institute, 1932), vol. 2, p. 476. See also Sir Robert Christison, *The Life of Sir Robert Christison, Edited by His Sons*, 2 vols (Edinburgh and London: 1884), vol. 1, p. 78.

30 '*outrun*' *his fever*: Howard, *Wellington's Doctors*, p. 171.

30 *He learned phlebotomy:* Christison, *Life*, vol. 1, pp. 155, 156.

31 *students formed unruly 'shoals'*: Charles Lett Feltoe, *Memorials of John Flint South* (London: 1884), pp. 26–7.

31 '*goings round*': Feltoe, *Memorials*, p. 27.

31 *physicians were gentlemen*: See John Barnard, 'The Busy Time': Keats's Duties at Guy's Hospital from Autumn 1816 to March 1817', *Romanticism*, 3:3 (2007), pp. 199–218.

31 '*emanations . . . of the human "subject"*': Christison, *Life*, vol. 1, p. 67.

32 *a nepotistic age*: Comrie, *Scottish Medicine*, vol. 2, p. 473.

32 *Alexander Munro III*: Christison, *Life*, vol. 1, p. 68.

32 '*when I was a student in Leyden*': Comrie, *Scottish Medicine*, vol. 2, p. 493.

32 *a freelance anatomist:* Christison, *Life*, vol. 1, p. 68. Fyfe's incomparable knowledge had been acquired over forty years of dissections; he passed on his experience in the form of a bestselling textbook filled with plates he had drawn himself.

32 *Body-snatching:* Christison, *Life*, vol. 1, p. 175.

33 *at the leading edge of scientific innovation*: As Hermione De Almeida writes of John Keats's medical education, it was 'at least as good as the brief university educations of Coleridge, Byron and Shelley,

and it exceeded theirs in its philosophical and practical intensity. Indeed, when one realises that Wordsworth was trained for three years at a purportedly "scientific" university in later seventeenth and early eighteenth century thought and learning, Keats' medical education suddenly takes on a unique contemporaneity among British artists.' Hermione De Almeida, *Romantic Medicine and John Keats* (New York and Oxford: Oxford University Press, 1991), p. 8.

33 *In comparison with Byron's education*: Moore, p. 46–9. For Scott, see Prothero, vol. 3, p. 412.

34 '*College improves in everything but Learning*': *BLJ*, vol. 1, p. 80.

34 *Byron spent less than ten months in residence*: MacCarthy, p. 57.

34 *dallying in London*: G. M. Trevelyan, *Trinity College: An Historical Sketch* (Cambridge: Cambridge University Press, 1946), p. 90.

34 '*I am buried in an abyss of Sensuality*': *BLJ*, vol. 1, pp. 158–9.

35 *sober recreations*: A. J. Youngson, *The Making of Classical Edinburgh, 1750–1840* (Edinburgh: Edinburgh University Press, 1966), p. 208.

35 *Botanical Gardens*: Anon., *Traveller's Guide*, vol. 1, p. 24.

35 '*merely from curiosity*': Cozens-Hardy (ed.), *Diary of Sylas Neville*, p. 156.

35 '*They are automatons*': MS, John Polidori to Gaetano Polidori [?December], 1813, translation, ADC, Box 31, f. 5.

35 '*petty bickerings*': John William Polidori, *An Essay on the Source of Positive Pleasure* (London: 1818 [ADC, PR 10 N9 R6a 1818]), p. 22.

35 *preferring that of two Germans*: Although Polidori does not name his Germans, Thierens and Ziegler were the only two to have signed the matriculation album between 1811 and 1813. A third, Thomas Zuckerbecker, entered in 1814. There is no proof, however, that John's German friends were medical students, or even students at the University of Edinburgh.

35 '*I see that they feel*': MS, John Polidori to Gaetano Polidori [?December], 1813, translation, ADC, Box 31, f. 5.

36 *The heralds of war*: The dramatic numbers of battlefield wounds and amputations enabled military surgeons to learn more about

the process of tissue decay and regeneration than ever before. Similarly, the great numbers of troops living together provided invaluable insights into virology and the spread of disease. In 1806, Edinburgh instituted a professorship of military surgery.

36 '*No doctor ever acquired glory*': John Polidori to Gaetano Polidori, December 1813, translation, ADC, Box 31, f. 5.

36 '*Return to your reason*': Gaetano Polidori to John Polidori, 9 December 1813, translation, ADC, Box 31, f. 5.

36 '*would be a shame for the rest of my life*': Quoted in Macdonald, p. 31.

37 '*that more than heavenly lyre – poetry*': Polidori, *Positive Pleasure*, p. 22.

37 '*half literary, half bacchanalian*': Polidori, *Positive Pleasure*, p. 21.

37 '*marked disposition to melancholy*': Religious Tract Society, *Sketches of Eminent Medical Men* (London: Religious Tract Society, 18–), pp. 131, 180.

37 *a practice in Berners Street*: Religious Tract Society, *Sketches of Eminent Medical Men*, p. 136.

37 '*philosophical criticism*': Quoted in David Chandler, 'Taylor, William (1765–1836)', *Oxford Dictionary of National Biography*, Oxford University Press, 2004 [http://www.oxforddnb.com.gate.lib. buffalo.edu/view/article/27092, accessed 19 March 2013].

37 '*Speculative Society*': According to Taylor's friend, J. W. Robberds, there was at that time 'more mind afloat in Norwich than is usually found out of the literary circles of the metropolis' (J. W. Robberds, *A Memoir of the Life and Writings of the Late William Taylor of Norwich*, 2 vols [London: 1843], vol. 1, p. 44). Norwich intelligentsia at the time included Philip Meadows Martineau, an eminent surgeon and governor at the Norfolk and Norwich Hospital; Frank Sayers, an Edinburgh alumnus turned writer who had inherited a large amount of money, abandoned writing and became a hypochondriac; Henry Reeve, another alumnus, whose accounts of travels through Germany and Switzerland John might well have read in the *Edinburgh Medical and Surgical Journal*, and who practised medicine at the Bethel Hospital for Lunatics; James

Alderson, whose daughter was the novelist and poet Amelia Opie; and Edward Rigby, who balanced medicine with his role as mayor. Other notables included the religious and political writers John and Susanna Taylor (no relation to William); the dissenting minister Joseph Kinghorn; the natural philosopher the Rev. Dr Efield; the botanist and founder of the Linnaean Society Sir James Edward Smith; the writer and reviewer Thomas Starling Norgate; and the banking brothers Hudson and John Joseph Gurney, neither of whom seemed to have relished banking despite being extremely good at it. Hudson's sole ambition was to write 'one good poem', while John Joseph dropped out of polite society to become a Quaker, spending the rest of his life in a sincerely personal struggle concerning the compatibility of piety and wealth. Robberds, *Memoir of William Taylor*, vol. 1, pp. 46–8.

38 *much admired for his romantic good looks*: Martineau, *Autobiography*, vol. 1, p. 81.

38 '*Apollo here his every gift imparts*': ALS, William Taylor to John Polidori, 12 March 1815, ADC, Box 31, f. 5.

38 '*See how I must have caught them*': ALS, John Polidori to Frances Polidori, 22 March 1815, ADC, Box 31, f. 6.

38 '*ignorant and conceited young men*': Martineau, *Autobiography*, vol. 1, p. 301.

38 *Taylor baiting his sycophantic audience*: Martineau, *Autobiography*, vol. 1, p. 300. See also Robberds, *Memoir of William Taylor*, vol. 2, pp. 452–3.

38 '*handsome, harum-scarum young man*': Martineau, *Autobiography*, vol. 1, p. 82.

39 '*too convulsed*': ALS, William Taylor to John Polidori, 28 May 1815, ADC, Box 31, f. 6.

39 '*no interest to push me on*': ALS, John Polidori to Frances Polidori, 22 March 1815, ADC, Box 31, f. 6. John's landlady, Mrs McDowall, was a kinswoman of the Lord of Galloway, who had made his fortune importing sugar from St Kitts. Having been born in India herself, she knew and understood the profits that might come of a colonial life, telling John (as he recounted home) 'that it is a lucrative honourable station that in 17 years I may come

home with an independence and that while I am there I should feel myself very happy'. She may have also had in mind the career of John Fleming, who had left Edinburgh to become an assistant surgeon in Bengal and returned as president of the Medical Board, before retiring to a Middlesex estate with a fortune of £160,000.

39 '*I really see obstacles*': ALS, John Polidori to Frances Polidori, 22 March 1815, ADC, Box 31, f. 6.

39 *On 24 June 1815*: For a list of graduates see the *Edinburgh Medical and Surgical Journal*, vol. 11 (1815), pp. 531–3.

39 '*and was by the imposition of the velvet cap*': Polidori, 'An Account of My Passing Ye Trials', holograph memorandum, ADC, Box 3.

40 '*No man was allowed to practise*': ALS, Robert Gooch to John or Gaetano Polidori, 3 February 1816, ADC, Box 27, f. 3.

40 *candidates had to be at least twenty-six years of age*: ALS, Robert Gooch to John or Gaetano Polidori, 3 February 1816, ADC, Box 27, f. 3.

3. The Footing of an Equal

41 '*an ugly coast*': Philip Thicknesse, *Useful Hints to those who Travel into France or Flanders by the way of Dover, Margate, and Ostend* (London: 1782), p. 11; *BLJ*, vol. 5, p. 71.

41 *bad weather had run the* Sir William Curtis *aground*': Anon., *Billets in the Low Countries 1814 to 1817, in a Series of Letters* (London: 1818), p. 195; *The Times*, 10 November 1815.

41 '*be ready for them*': *DJCH*, 25 April 1816.

41 '*a presentiment*': *DJCH*, 25 April 1816.

42 '*God bless him*': *DJCH*, 25 April 1816.

42 '*last sight of my native soil*': *PD*, p. 31. 'This points pretty clearly to a love passage,' wrote William Rossetti in his edition of Polidori's *Diary*, although genuine candidates for a love interest are scarce. Rossetti suggests Eliza Arrow, a relative in India with whom John had corresponded at least once, though admits that the link is tenuous. Other suspects include Harriet Martineau's eldest sister, Elizabeth (Martineau, *Autobiography*, vol. 1, p. 82), or even his mother or female siblings. Alternatively, John might have made a promise to a woman at Dover.

42 *'the most beautiful moment'*: *PD*, p. 32.

42 *Byron was throwing up*: Byron had been in the vicinity of a 'Merchant of Bruges', who 'capsized his breakfast close by me – and made me sick by contagion'. *BLJ*, vol. 5, p. 71.

43 *green-uniformed Customs officials*: James Mitchell, *A Tour Through Belgium, Holland, Along the Rhine and Through the North of France in the Summer of 1816* (London: 1816), p. 9.

43 *'fell like a thunderbolt'*: *PD*, p. 33. This, at least, is how William Rossetti reconstructs the passage expunged in the original by his aunt (John's sister), Charlotte Polidori, who enthusiastically deleted a number of passages in the holograph diary of which she did not approve.

43 *'Don't forget the Cundums'*: *PD*, p. 32; *BLJ*, vol. 5, p. 71.

43 *'"atrabilious" man'*: MS, Gaetano Polidori to Luigi Polidori [?1818], trans. William Rossetti, ADC, Box 31, f. 6.

43 *John agreed*: *BLJ*, Supp. vol. X, p. 41.

43 *'his youthful fancy'*: MS Gaetano Polidori to Luigi Polidori [?1818], trans. William Rossetti, ADC, Box 31, f. 6.

43 *John drew up a will*: John William Polidori, 'My Wishes to be Fulfilled', ADC, Box 31, f. 6.

44 *secretary to the Italian tragedian*: Angeli, 'Byron's Physician', ADC, Box 31, f. 4, p. 1.

44 *Dogged by depression*: Edgar Alfred Bowring (ed.), *The Tragedies of Vittorio Alfieri*, 2 vols (Westport, CT: Greenwood, 1876, rpt 1970), vol. 1, pp. x–xi.

44 *'fine and speckless apparel'*: Rossetti, *Family Letters*, vol. 1, p. 27.

44 *The tragedian also fancied himself as a lover*: This story is recounted in Vittorio Alfieri, *Memoirs*, trans. Anon., revised E. R. Vincent (London: Oxford University Press, 1961), pp. 111–20. 'We fought for a considerable space of time,' recalled Alfieri, 'I always attacking and he defending, and I judge that he did not kill me because he did not want to, and that I did not kill him because I did not know how to!' (p. 113).

45 *firmness of his thighs*: *PD*, p. 200–201.

45 *'filthy sewer'*: Alfieri, *Tragedies*, p. xi.

45 *'ruins of the Bastille'*: Rossetti, *Family Letters*, p. 27.

45 *'so many points of resemblance'*: Lovell (ed.), *Lady Blessington's Conversations*, p. 64.

45 *Fridays brought ill-luck*: BLJ, vol. 5, p. 71; Hunt, *Lord Byron*, p. 84. Byron's superstition is also confirmed by Lovell (ed.), *Lady Blessington's Conversations*, pp. 30–31.

45 *'basking in the sun'*: PD, 33.

46 *a two-pound cannon*: PD, 34; Charles Campbell, *The Traveller's Complete Guide Through Belgium, Holland, and Germany* (London: 1815), p. 107.

46 *solitary bathing machine*: Henry Smithers, *Observations Made During a Tour in 1816 and 1817 Through that Part of the Netherlands, which comprises Ostend, Bruges, Ghent, Brussels, Malines and Antwerp* (Brussels: 1818), p. 6.

46 *'A few hours in Ostend'*: Anon., *A Hand-book for Travellers on the Continent* (London: 1836), p. 99.

46 *'banished among the Algerins'*: Anon., *Billets*, p. 187.

46 *'only not quite so filthy'*: PD, p. 33.

46 *'the most obscene nature'*: PD, p. 33.

46 *'while looking at her eyes'*: PD, p. 33.

46 *'half-a-dozen women'*: PD, p. 33.

46 *'Luckily for myself'*: PD, p. 33.

47 *'public Treason private Treachery'*: BCMP, p. 51.

47 *'no desire to view a degraded country'*: BLJ, vol. 5, p. 77. A hasty memo written in 1816, however, suggests that France remained a possibility – 'Swisserland – Flanders – Italy – & (perhaps) France. —' See 'Detail of Domestics and Intended Itinerary (1816)', BCMP, p. 219.

47 *less corrupt than the French*: Campbell, *Guide Through Belgium*, p. 3.

47 *'zielverkoopers'*: 'zielverkoopers' (literally, 'soul sellers') were in fact gangs who pressed unfortunate farmers into service on Dutch East Indiamen. Campbell's version appears to signal the existence of a vampiric urban myth. Campbell, *Guide Through Belgium*, p. 5, 19.

48 *'frais du grassage'*: Anon., *A Hand-book for Travellers*, p. xix; Campbell, *Guide Through Belgium*, p. 32.

48 *'the Flemish face'*: Campbell, *Guide Through Belgium*, p. 108; PD, p. 45; Anon., *Billets*, p. 173.

48 *Pretty villages*: PD, p. 35.

48 '*Country pleasure*': Campbell, *Guide Through Belgium*, p. 24.

48 *oddments of his profession*: See D. Cox, *Directions for Medicine Chests; with Remarks, etc., on Medicine and Surgery* (London, 1799).

48 '*every apparatus*': Gordon, *Personal Memoirs*, vol. 2, p. 329. See also the description of the Napoleonic original in John Theodore Tussaud, *The Romance of Madame Tussaud's* (New York: John Doran, 1920), pp. 127–38.

49 *toll booths placed every mile and a half*: PD, p. 46.

49 '*that a person may read, write, or even draw*': Campbell, *Guide Through Belgium*, p. 17.

49 '*or doing nothing at all*': Richard Edgcumbe (ed.), *The Diary of Frances, Lady Shelley* (New York: Scribner, 1912), pp. 176–7.

49 *forty or fifty windows*: Campbell, *Guide Through Belgium*, p. 108.

49 *converted into warehouses for corn*: Anon., *Billets*, p. 201.

49 '*heedless of the myriads*': PD, pp. 35–6.

50 '*manifestly consumptive*': PD, p. 36.

50 '*most rascally face*': PD, p. 34.

50 '*four or five well-armed people*': BLJ, vol. 5, pp. 72–3.

51 *John thought superior even to London*: PD, p. 38.

51 '*For slighter offences*': Smithers, *Observations Made During a Tour*, pp. 17, 24; Mitchell, *Tour*, pp. 32, 78.

51 '*Cupids*' Anon., *Billets*, p. 200.

52 *a notorious art-collecting cleric*: See John Scott, *Paris Revisited in 1815, by Way of Brussels*, 2nd edition (London: 1816), pp. 312–91.

52 *Catholic tinsel and Presbyterian sobriety*: Campbell, *Guide Through Belgium*, p. 18.

52 *that so disturbed Byron*: PD, p. 40.

52 *two statues of young Englishwomen*: PD, p. 42.

53 '*bed-gown, like the Scotch*': PD, p. 45.

53 '*not seen a pretty woman since I left Ostend*': PD, p. 43.

53 '*I dare say he is dead by now*': BLJ, vol. 5, p. 73.

53 *an article in the town's* Gazette: PD, p. 44.

53 '*all ugly without exception*': PD, p. 43.

53 *famous Rubens altarpieces*: Charlotte Eaton (née Waldie), *Waterloo*

Days: The Narrative of an Englishwoman Resident at Brussels in June, 1815, new edition (London: 1888), p. 106.

53 '*As for churches – and pictures*': *BLJ*, vol. 5, pp. 74–5.

54 '*yawn in admiration*': *PD*, p. 44.

54 '*abuse him like a pickpocket*': *BLJ*, vol. 5, p. 72.

54 '*I am very pleased with Lord Byron*': ALS, John Polidori to Frances Polidori, 1 May 1816, ADC, Box 31, f. 6.

54 '*He has not shown any passions*': ALS, John Polidori to Frances Polidori, 1 May 1816, ADC, Box 31, f. 6.

55 '*continue being a tragedian*': *PD*, p. 54.

55 '*always talking of Prussic acid*': Medwin, p. 104.

4. That Odd-headed Girl

56 *dainty and ill-provisioned post-chaise*: For further details on Shelley's carriage, see *SC*, vol. 3, pp.153–8. On its size specifically, see p. 163.

57 '*An utter stranger*': *CC*, vol. 1, p. 24.

57 '*If a woman*': *CC*, vol. 1, p. 25.

57 '*I hate to be tortured by suspense*': *CC*, vol. 1, p. 25.

57 '*E. Trefusis*': So much of Claire's desperation and loneliness is expressed in the use of this name. Through her (supposed) father, Charles Gaulis, Claire claimed kinship with Gaulis's sister Albertine, who had married the Devon landowner, Robert Cotton Trefusis and become Lady Clinton. That Claire should appropriate the Trefusis name for her first letter to Byron suggests that she certainly wished to present herself as his social equal, but also, in tune with her fairy-tale thinking, an orphaned heiress in need of rescue. *CC*, vol. 1, p. 26, fn. 4.

57 *The poem had resonated strongly with women*: Hobhouse, somewhat literal-mindedly, had to admit that the poem's 'great success' was due in part to 'the intimate knowledge which he has shown of the turns taken by the passion of women'. Quoted in Nicholas Mason, 'Building Brand Byron: Early-Nineteenth-Century Advertising and the Marketing of *Childe Harold's Pilgrimage*', *MLQ*, 63:4 (December 2002), p. 414.

57 '*upon perusing "Childe Harold"*': ALS, 'M:H' to Lord Byron, 21 October 1813, Murray. MS 43437.

58 '*make a woman fly into the arms of a* tiger': John A. Doyle (ed.), *Memoir and Correspondence of Susan Ferrier, 1782–1854* (London: 1898), p. 131.

58 '*Rosalie*': Quoted in Throsby, 'Flirting With Fame', p. 119.

58 '*leave the rest to Echo*': Quoted in Throsby, 'Flirting With Fame', p. 121.

58 *tear-stains*: See Murray, MS 43437.

58 '*an occasional place in your lordship's thoughts*': See Peter Quennell, 'Byron and Harriet Wilson', *Cornhill Magazine*, 151 (January–June 1935), pp. 415–26; ALS, 'M: H' to Lord Byron, 21 October 1813, Murray, MS 43437.

58 '*a lady to communicate with him on business*': *CC*, vol. 1, p. 26.

59 '*he will however be at home*': *BLJ*, vol. 5, p. 59.

59 '*utmost secrets*': *CC*, vol. 1, p. 27.

59 '*a string of pearls*': Pforz, Cl.Cl.26, p. 97. In their *Claire Clairmont and the Shelleys* (Oxford: Oxford University Press, 1992), p. 27, Robert Gittings and Jo Manton suggest that Claire 'visited him [Byron] in his green room at Drury Lane'. While there is no evidence for this (besides the fact that there was only one green room, reserved for performers, and not private ones as the sentence seems to imply), it remains a possibility.

59 '*There be none of Beauty's daughters*': *BCPW*, vol. 3, p. 379, and commentary, p. 493. The MS of this poem is in Byron's hand, but below it, in John Murray's, is written 'Recd March 28, 1816', from which is derived the conjecture that this poem is addressed to, or inspired by, Claire. Marchand disputes the date, preferring to read the subject as John Edleston, also a singer, and the subject of Byron's 'Thyrza' poems. Jerome McGann, however, considers Murray's dating of the poem authoritative, and sees no reason to doubt that the addressee is Claire.

60 '*May I beg of you*': *CC*, vol. 1, p. 27.

60 '*The Ideot*': Claire makes her first reference to 'The Ideot' on 10 September 1814. *CCJ*, p. 40.

61 '*the ill humour I feel for every thing*': *CC*, vol. 1, p. 27.

61 *Byron, however, declined the invitation*: Claire would later claim that

Byron made her look 'foolish' when discussing 'that hateful novel thing I wrote'. *CC*, vol. 1, p. 92.

61 *she openly declared her feelings*: *CC*, vol. 1, p. 36.

61 *'I do not expect you to love me'*: *CC*, vol. 1, p. 36.

61 *'If you stand in need of amusement'*: *CC*, vol. 1, p. 38.

62 *'God bless you – I never was so happy'*: *CC*, vol. 1, p. 36.

62 *rescheduling their assignation*: *BLJ*, vol. 5, p. 59.

62 *'little fiend'*: *CC*, vol. 1, p. 38.

63 *London's principal sewer*. See Ford K. Brown, 'Notes on 41 Skinner Street', *Modern Language Notes*, 54:5 (May 1939), pp. 326–32.

63 *witness the hanging*: Andrew Knapp and William Baldwin, *The Newgate Calendar*, 4 vols (London: 1825), vol. 3, pp. 443–5.

63 *'crazy and ill-built house'*: Hogg, vol. 2, p. 537.

63 *crept out of bed to sit on the stairs*: Emily W. Sunstein, *Mary Shelley: Romance and Reality* (Baltimore: Johns Hopkins University Press, 1989), p. 40.

64 *Although now somewhat anonymous*: By 1800, Hazlitt would write that 'Mr Godwin's person is not known, he is not pointed out in the street, his conversation is not courted, his opinions are not asked, he is at the head of no cabal, he belongs to no party in the State, he has no train of admirers, no one thinks it worth his while even to traduce to vilify him, he has scarcely friend or foe, the world makes a point . . . of taking no more notice of him than if such an individual had never existed.' Quoted in *SC*, vol. 1, p. 13.

64 *'a species of government unavoidably corrupt'*: William Godwin, *An Enquiry Concerning Political Justice and its Influence on General Virtue and Happiness* (London: 1793), vol. 1, p. viii; vol. 2, p. 423.

65 *'never to endure a life of dependence'*: Janet Todd (ed.), *The Collected Letters of Mary Wollstonecraft* (New York: Columbia, 2003), p. 357.

65 *'lend me a bit of indian rubber'*: Wollstonecraft, *Letters*, p. 399.

65 *'What say you'*: Wollstonecraft, *Letters*, p. 396.

65 *'Seldom have I seen such live fire'*: Wollstonecraft, *Letters*, p. 375.

65 *'I am in the most natural state'*: Wollstonecraft, *Letters*, p. 437.

66 *coached him in how to give her a biscuit*: See, for example, Wollstonecraft, *Letters*, p. 402.

66 '*cadaverous silence*': Earl Leslie Griggs (ed.), *Collected Letters of Samuel Taylor Coleridge*, 6 vols (Oxford: Clarendon, 1956–71), vol. 1, p. 553.

66 '*handsome, fantastic woman*': ALS, Anna Maria Porter to Jane Porter, *c*.1804, Huntington Library, POR 46. Porter had seen Godwin and his family at a performance of *The Mourning Bride*. I am extremely grateful to Devoney Looser for providing this reference.

66 '*you great Being*': Maud Rolleston, *Talks with Lady Shelley* (London: Harrap, 1925), pp. 35–6.

66 *by December they were married*: Victoria Myers, David O'Shaughnessy and Mark Philp (eds), *The Diary of William Godwin* (Oxford: Oxford Digital Library, 2010), http://godwindiary.bodleian. ox.ac.uk, 4 June 1802.

66 *Gaulis died*: The familial complications arising from Mary Jane Clairmont's fabrications are laid out in St Clair, *Godwins and Shelleys*, pp. 247–54, and *CC*, vol. 1, pp. 42–3, fn. 2 (aggregating research undertaken by Herbert Huscher, published as 'The Clairmont Enigma', *Keats-Shelley Memorial Bulletin*, 11 [1960], pp. 13–20). All have been superseded by the researches of Vicki Parslow Stafford in the Somerset Heritage Centre, who in 2010 uncovered a series of letters between Mary Jane Vial, John Lethbridge and their representatives that prove Lethbridge's paternity beyond doubt. I am extremely grateful for her help in navigating these materials. Transcripts of the letters, along with a family tree, chronology, and narrative account, may be found at her website: http://sites.google.com/site/maryjanesdaughter/

67 '*I have the means of concealing my Engagements*': ALS, John Lethbridge to Robert Beadon, 15 February 1799, Vial.

67 '*I will not be* bullied': ALS, John Lethbridge to Robert Beadon, 15 January 1799, Vial. See also ALS, Mary Jane Vial to James Bryant, January 1799, Vial.

68 '*I ever saw a Child like a Father*': ALS, W. L. White to Robert Beadon, 22 November 1799, Vial.

68 '*I am ready to keep her on certain conditions*': ALS, Mary Jane Vial to John Lethbridge, 19 January 1799, Vial.

68 '*If some step of this kind is not taken*': ALS, John Lethbridge to Robert Beadon, 15 February 1799, Vial.

68 '*I had no business to have anything to do with her*': ALS, John Lethbridge to Robert Beadon, 11 June 1799, Vial.

68 '*in the literary line*': ALS, M. J. Vial to Robert Beadon, 5 September 1799, Vial.

69 '*infernal bitch*': Lamb to Wordsworth, 29 January 1807, quoted in Sunstein, *Romance and Reality*, p. 30; Janet Todd, *Death and the Maidens: Fanny Wollstonecraft and the Shelley Circle* (Berkeley: Counterpoint, 2007), p. 151; Dorothy and Thomas Hoobler, *The Monsters: Mary Shelley and the Curse of Frankenstein* (New York: Back Bay Books, 2007), p. 44.

69 *cast-off convict*: For the rumour that Mary Jane had spent time in debtor's prison, see Henry Crabb Robinson, *Diary, Reminiscences and Correspondence of Henry Crabb Robinson*, ed. Thomas Sadler, 2 vols (Boston: 1871), vol. 1, p. 298.

69 *dual wedding ceremonies*: *CCJ*, p. 14; St Clair, *Godwins and Shelleys*, p. 248.

70 '*The influence of governments on the character of a people*': Matthew L. Lewis (ed.), *The Private Journal of Aaron Burr During His Residence of Four Years in Europe*, 2 vols (New York: 1838), vol. 2, p. 307.

70 '*All the family worked hard*': *CC*, vol. 2, pp. 617–8.

70 '*toy of man*': Mary Wollstonecraft, *A Vindication of the Rights and Women* and *A Vindication of the Rights of Men*, ed. Janet Todd (Oxford: Oxford World's Classics, 2008), p. 100.

70 *use as a sitting room to entertain friends*: Sunstein, *Romance and Reality*, p. 48.

70 *lessons in geography, mathematics and chemistry*: Miranda Seymour, *Mary Shelley* (New York: Grove Press, 2000), p. 54; Sunstein, *Romance and Reality*, p. 48.

70 *Fanny and Mary also learned to draw*: Pforz Cl.Cl.26 81; ALS, Mary Jane Godwin to Robert Beadon, 8 February 1811, Vial.

71 '*I can neither walk, nor read, nor write*': *CC*, vol. 1, p. 15.

72 '*my feet are on the edge of a precipice*': William Godwin, *St Leon*,

ed. Pamela Clemit (Oxford: Oxford World's Classics, 1994), p. 175.

72 '*to bring us up in respect for all conventionalities*': *CC*, vol. 2, p. 627.

72 '*liberal passion*': William Godwin, *Memoirs of Mary Wollstonecraft* (London, 1798), p. 2. A further indication of Godwin's preoccupation with posterity might be found in his 'Essay on Sepulchers', which advocates the widespread erection of memorials to great men and women, and the maintenance of a national catalogue of the 'Illustrious Departed': 'Virtue is virtue still,' he argued, 'though a thousand years should have passed away since it was alive.' See William Godwin, 'Essay on Sepulchres', in *Political and Philosophical Writings of William Godwin*, ed. Mark Philp, 7 vols (London: William Pickering, 1993), vol. 6, pp. 3–30, 17. On the critical praise for Godwin's *Caleb Williams*, see *SC*, vol. 1, pp.11–12.

72 '*I was nursed and fed with a love of glory*': Mary Wollstonecraft Shelley, 'Life of William Godwin' fragment of a draft, n.d., MS Abinger c. 61, f. 42; Lady Jane Shelley (ed.), *Shelley and Mary*, 4 vols (printed for private circulation, 1882), vol. 4, p. 1218; *CC*, vol. 1, p. 295.

72 '*Of the two persons to whom your enquiries relate*': C. Kegan Paul, *William Godwin: His Friends and Contemporaries*, 2 vols (London: Henry King, 1876), vol. 2, p. 214.

73 *both were intelligent, engaging and lively*: Todd, *Death and the Maidens*, p. 69.

73 '*calm, grey eyes*': *CCJ*, p. 431. See also Edward John Trelawny, *Recollections of the Last Days of Shelley and Byron* (London: 1858), p. 20. For many years it was believed that Mary's first publication was a comic poem entitled *Mounseer Nongtongpaw; or, the Discoveries of John Bull in a Trip to Paris*, published by the Juvenile Library in 1808, when Mary was ten. The poem elaborated a song by the impresario of Sadler's Wells, Charles Dibdin, and revolved around John Bull making a series of enquiries about French habits and innovations to which the uniform answer was '*Monsieur, je ne n'entend pas*' ('Sir, I don't understand you'). Through his lack of comprehension, Bull is convinced that a

certain Mr 'Nongtongpaw' is behind everything, and must surely be the most wealthy and innovative man in France. The poem was de-attributed to Mary in 1996. See Nora Crook (ed.), *The Novels and Selected Works of Mary Shelley*, 8 vols (London: Pickering and Chatto, 1996), vol. 8.

73 '*blessed Switzerland*': ALS, M. J. Godwin to Robert Beadon, 8 May 1811, Vial; ALS, W. L. White to Robert Beadon, 17 December 1813, Vial; *CC*, vol. 1, p. 42.

73 '*pleasure in contemplating the daughter of Mary Wollstonecraft*': Lewis (ed.), *Private Journal of Aaron Burr*, vol. 2, p. 257.

74 '*detest*': *Letters MWS*, vol. 1, p. 3. According to family tradition, Mrs Godwin was jealous of Mary, who treated her like a fairy-tale evil step-mother. 'Jane might be well educated,' said Lady Shelley, years later, 'but Mary could stay at home and mend the stockings.' Rolleston, *Talks with Lady Shelley*, pp. 33–4.

74 '*Clairmont style*': Paul, *William Godwin*, vol. 2, p. 250; *MWSJ*, vol. 1, p. 70. In their quarrels, said Mrs Godwin, Mary called Claire 'stupid . . . because she had not such first rate abilities as her own'. Pforz, Cl.Cl.26, p. 88.

75 *It was the first in a series of exiles*: Seymour, *Mary Shelley*, p. 60.

5. Here is a Man

76 '*pork and sausages*': Quoted in Oswald Doughty, *Perturbed Spirit: The Life and Personality of Samuel Taylor Coleridge* (Rutherford: Farleigh Dickinson University Press, 1981), p. 367.

76 '*the worst and most degrading of Slaveries*': Griggs (ed.), *Letters of Coleridge*, vol. 4, p. 626.

76 '*immethodical rhapsody*': Griggs (ed.), *Letters of Coleridge*, vol. 4, p. 627; Robinson, *Diary, Reminiscences*, vol. 1, p. 227.

77 '*a dissertation on incest*': Robinson, *Diary, Reminiscences*, vol. 1, p. 225. At another performance, Godwin had heard Coleridge claim that Shakespeare never intended his plays for the stage. See Frederick L. Jones (ed.), *Maria Gisborne and Edward E. Williams, Shelley's Friends: Their Letters and Journals* (Norman: University of Oklahoma Press, 1951), p. 43.

77 *would have seen Byron*: Myers, O'Shaughnessy and Philp (eds),

Diary of William Godwin, 20 January 1812; Robinson, *Diary, Reminiscences*, vol. 1, p. 238.

77 '*Here is a man*': *Letters PBS*, vol. 1, p. 219, fn. 10.

77 '*sold himself to the Court*': Dowden, vol. 2, p. 156.

78 '*I am young*': *Letters PBS*, vol. 1, p. 220; vol. 1, p. 229.

78 '*an evil of primary magnitude*': *Letters PBS*, vol. 1, p. 228. 'Never read a book, Johnnie,' Sir Timothy reportedly told Shelley's younger brother, John, 'and you will be a rich man.' Rolleston, *Talks with Lady Shelley*, pp. 95–6.

78 '*I did not truly think and feel*': *Letters PBS*, vol. 1, p. 303.

78 '*heir by entail to an estate*': *Letters PBS*, vol. 1, p. 228.

79 '*no right to dispose of a shilling*': Godwin, *Political Justice*, vol. 1, p. 88.

79 '*You cannot imagine how much all the females of my family*': *Letters PBS*, vol. 1, p. 270, fn. 6.

79 '*Mad Shelley*': James Bieri, *Percy Bysshe Shelley: A Biography* (Baltimore: Johns Hopkins University Press, 2008), p. 58. In some versions, the fork is a pen-knife. See Thomas Love Peacock, *Peacock's Memoirs of Shelley*, ed. F. B. Brett-Smith (London: Henry Frowde, 1909), p. 13; *Letters MWS*, vol. 1, p. 475.

79 '*tricks, conundrums, and queer things*': Dowden, vol. 1, p. 32.

79 '*books of Chemistry and Magic*': *Letters PBS*, vol. 1, p. 227.

80 '*the voracious appetite of a famished man*': Hogg, vol. 2, p. 56, vol. 1, p. 260.

80 *The Necessity of Atheism*: Hogg, vol. 1, p. 260; *Letters PBS*, vol. 1, p. 228. Thomas Jefferson Hogg's *Life of Percy Bysshe Shelley* has been largely dismissed in Shelley circles, thanks to many failings of the author and the condemnatory efforts of Lady Shelley, who sought to cast it as slanderous and self-serving. It is in fact a humorous, affectionate and ironic portrait – the reminiscence of someone happy to represent himself as a naïve and gullible youth. In this it is entirely in keeping with the Victorian tradition of 'table-talk', a convivial and anecdotal reminiscence characteristic of literary and theatrical figures with no pretence to critical or scholarly authority. That it contains errors, lacks objectivity and seeks to distort and justify Hogg's own actions is

self-evident, yet it nevertheless represents the testimony of someone who knew Shelley intimately during his formative years, and from a position that resists much of the subsequent hagiography.

80 *six languages*: They were: English, French, Italian, German, Greek and Latin (he would later learn Spanish in Italy).

80 *'You are preparing a scene of blood'*: *Letters PBS*, vol. 1, p. 270, fn. 6.

81 *'a woman of great fortitude'*: *Letters PBS*, vol. 1, p. 327, fn. 8.

81 *boarding school in Walham Green*: See Godwin, *Diary*, 12 October 1812; Thomas Faulkner, *Historical and Topographical Account of Fulham, including the Hamlet of Hammersmith* (London: 1813), p. 329; Gittings and Manton, *Claire Clairmont and the Shelleys*, p. 9.

82 *'The harmony and happiness of man'*: Percy Bysshe Shelley, *The Major Works*, ed. Zachary Leader and Michael O'Neill (Oxford: Oxford University Press, 2009), p. 40.

83 *'catch the aristocrats'*: *Letters PBS*, vol. 1, p. 361.

83 *'very plain'*: *Letters PBS*, vol. 1, p. 327, fn. 8.

83 *'all persons younger than himself'*: *Letters PBS*, vol. 1, p. 350, fn. 2.

84 *'the most admirable specimen of a human being'*: *Letters PBS*, vol. 2, p. 92.

84 *'nakedism'*: St Clair, *Godwins and Shelleys*, p. 263.

84 *'the primate of all vegetables'*: St Clair, *Godwins and Shelleys*, p. 263.

85 *'the worst of all laws'*: See *On the Vegetable System of Diet*, in E. B. Murray (ed.), *The Prose Works of Percy Bysshe Shelley* (Oxford: Clarendon, 1993), pp. 146–55; Godwin, *Political Justice*, vol. 2, p. 849–50.

85 *'the happiest of my life'*: *Letters PBS*, vol. 1, p. 401.

86 *perpetually underdressed*: Hogg, vol. 2, p. 417.

86 *sexless beauty of a Miltonic angel*: Hogg, vol. 2, p. 407.

86 *'looks and sighs'*: Pforz, Cl.Cl.26, p. 68.

86 *settled back into a house that she had not lived in:* Sunstein, *Romance and Reality*, p. 62.

87 *'Everyone who knows me must know'*: Peacock, *Memoir*, p. 48. Shelley's dedicatory stanzas to Mary in his poem *Laon and Cythna* (later revised as *The Revolt of Islam*) stress the importance he placed on her auspicious birth:

They say that thou wert lovely from thy birth,
Of glorious parents, thou aspiring Child!
I wonder not – for One then left this earth
Whose life was like a setting planet mild,
Which clothed thee in the radiance undefiled
Of its departing glory; still her fame
Shines on thee, through the tempests dark and wild
Which shake these latter days; and thou canst claim
The shelter, from thy Sire, of an immortal name.

87 *Mrs Godwin raised the alarm*: Paul, *William Godwin*, vol. 2, pp. 215–16.

87 *'They always sent me to walk at some distance from them'*: Pforz Cl.Cl. 26 54–5.

87 *declared their mutual love*: As Godwin wrote to his friend John Taylor on 27 August 1814: 'On Sunday June 26th, [Shelley] accompanied Mary, and her sister . . . to the tomb of Mary's Mother, one mile distant from London; and there, it seems, the impious idea first occurred to him of seducing her, playing the traitor to me and deserting his wife.' *MWSJ*, vol. 1, p. 1.

88 *'return to virtue'*: *MWSJ*, vol. 1, p.1.

88 *'the tyranny which has been exercised upon her'*: *Letters PBS*, vol. 1, p. 390.

88 *fallen in love with Mrs Boinville's daughter*: *SC*, vol. 3, p. 278.

88 *'fair prey to a kind of sweet melancholy'*: Hogg, vol. 2, p. 381.

88 *'The contemplation of female excellence'*: *Letters PBS*, vol. 1, p. 401.

89 *'Death shall unite us'*: Pforz, Cl.Cl.26, p. 71.

89 *using laudanum heavily*: Peacock, *Memoir*, p. 48.

89 *not have been the first time Shelley had poisoned himself for love*: Hogg, vol. 2, p. 332.

89 *pass illicit notes*: Pforz, Cl.Cl.26, p. 56.

89 *they should take an early walk*: Pforz, Cl.Cl.26, p. 57.

90 *'they should be ruined and discovered and lost'*: Pforz, Cl.Cl.26, p. 86.

90 *'outstrip pursuit'*: *MWSJ*, vol. 1, p. 6.

90 *both she and Mary carried bundles of clothes*: *CCJ*, p. 31; Pforz, Cl.Cl.26, p. 56. The letters in Claire's hand, purporting to be from Mary

Godwin to Lady Mount Cashell, in the Pforzheimer Collection relate that 'In the morning they disappeared Mary awoke [Claire] at four with a remark on the beauty of the weather and asked her to take an early walk. She consented and quite ignorant of their intended flight, took their way up Holborn Hill to gain Marylebone fields. At the corner of Hatton Garden they found Mr Shelley in a Post Chaise and they said they were going to run away to France and she must come with them as she spoke French which they could not. She resisted and wanted to return home, but Mr S said they should be ruined and discovered and lost if she made them lose a moment and bewildered she entered the chaise – the whole scene occupied five minutes she thinks. Away they drove. Neither of them spoke a word more to her.' Pforz, Cl.Cl.26, pp. 85–6.

90 *'village after village'*: *Letters PBS*, vol. 1, p. 392.

90 *famished and inhospitable peasants*: *Letters PBS*, vol. 1, p. 392.

91 *'wild and entire solitude'*: *CCJ*, p. 30.

91 *'By rising above the habitation of men'*: Jean-Jacques Rousseau, *Julie; or, The New Héloïse*, trans. Philip Stewart and Jean Vaché (Hanover, New Hampshire: Dartmouth University Press, 1997), p. 64.

91 *'immoderately stupid and almost ugly to deformity'*: *CCJ*, p. 30.

92 *'Most laughable'*: *CCJ*, p. 31.

92 *'horrors'*: *MWSJ*, vol. 1, p. 20.

92 *'acting a novel, being an incarnate romance'*: *CCJ*, Appendix A, p. 442.

92 *'Nothing, but that her name was Mary'*: Peacock, *Memoir*, p. 49.

92 *'This is a vampire'*: *Letters PBS*, vol. 1, p. 421, fn. 2.

6. An Empire's Dust

93 *'an eternity of* pavement': *BLJ*, vol. 5, p. 75.

93 *'It must be up hill or down'*: *BLJ*, vol. 5, p. 75.

93 *stray bulldogs, and raw sewage*: Smithers, *Observations Made During a Tour*, p. 31.

93 *a goat harnessed to a baby's pram*: *PD*, p. 61.

93 *'and still worse'*: Smithers, *Observations Made During a Tour*, p. 148; *PD*, p. 59.

94 *'like a base pig'*: *PD*, 60.

94 *Brussels had a strong Anglophone presence*: Gordon, *Personal Memoirs*, vol. 2, p. 266. The expatriate ladies were proud of their origins, and dressed in Brussels as if they were in London, and in London as if they were in Paris. *PD*, p. 58.

94 *Having conducted a survey of faces*: *PD*, p. 34. Clearly Polidori never came across '*La belle Belge*', a fifteen-year-old beauty said to be the most attractive woman in Flanders. She had 'a blush, which looks as if she had been "fed on roses", and a bosom on which even lilies might gather whiteness', according to one British officer who saw her (Anon., *Billets*, p. 172).

94 '*one uninterrupted peal of thunder*': Robert Southey, *The Poet's Pilgrimage to Waterloo* (London: 1816), p. 206.

94 '*of each sex and every age*': Eaton Stannard Barrett, *The Talents Run Mad; or, Eighteen Hundred and Sixteen* (London: 1816), p. 18 fn; John Scott, *Paris Revisited*, pp. 39–40.

95 *this list already included*: See Stuart Semmel, 'Reading the Tangible Past: British Tourism, Collecting, and Memory after Waterloo', *Representations*, 69 (Winter, 2000), p. 11; and Janet Todd, 'The Anxiety of Emma', *Persuasions*, 29 (2007), pp. 15–25.

95 *John and Byron visited on the morning of 4 May*: *PD*, p. 61.

95 '*hoofs, and even limbs*': James Simpson, *A Visit to Flanders in July 1815*, 8th edition (Edinburgh: 1815), p. 63.

95 '*take me with you*': Eaton, *Waterloo Days*, p. 137.

95 *a few brick buildings*: Jacques Logie, *Waterloo: The Campaign of 1815* (Stroud: Spellmount, 2006), p. 77.

96 '*every day there still arrive on the battlefield*': Logie, *Waterloo*, p. 77.

96 '*books, and letters of the dead*': Simpson, *Visit to Flanders*, p. 132.

96 *a book of French songs saturated in blood*: Gordon, *Personal Memoirs*, vol. 2, p. 336.

96 '*it would outlast twelve natural teeth*': Robinson, *Diary, Reminiscences*, vol. 1, p. 327.

96 '*I know one honest gentleman*': Barrett, *The Talents Run Mad*, p. 19 fn.

96 *a business worth up to four thousand francs a year*: Gordon, *Personal Memoirs*, vol. 2, pp. 334–5.

96 *less of a man than a franchise*: Mitchell, *Tour*, pp. 89–90.

97 '*as if the field had been covered with crows*': Simpson, *Visit to Flanders*,

p. 48. 'At first there was a great preponderance of British slain,' wrote Simpson, on viewing the battlefield, 'which looked very ill; but more in advance, the revenge made itself dreadfully marked, for ten French lay dead for one British. The field was so much covered with blood, that it appeared as if it had been completely flooded with it; dead horses seemed innumerable, and the peasantry employed in burying the dead, generally stript the bodies first. Of course these people got a vast booty, when they ventured out the neighbouring wood, after the battle; many of them made some hundred pounds. A great quantity of cap plates, cuirasses, and other articles, were collected by them, and sold as relics.'

97 *the importunity of boys*: *PD*, p. 62; see also Mitchell, *Tour*, p. 93; and Thomas Raffles, *Letters During a Tour Through Some Parts of France, Savoy, Switzerland, Germany, and the Netherlands in the Summer of 1817*, 2nd edition (Liverpool: 1819), p. 329.

97 *Lord Uxbridge's hastily amputated leg*: *PD*, p. 62.

97 *Jesus whose toes had been burned off*: Mitchell, *Tour*, p. 89.

97 *Five hundred British soldiers had died there*: Mitchell, *Tour*, p. 90.

97 *asking only after the resting places of the dead*: Gordon, *Personal Memoirs*, vol. 2, p. 322.

97 *'Perhaps there is something of prejudice in this'*: *BLJ*, vol. 5, p. 76.

98 *'the best of his race'*: *BLJ*, vol. 4, p. 302.

98 *a Turkish song on a Cossack steed*: *BLJ*, vol. 5, p. 76; *PD*, p. 65.

98 *'marked with bullets, lance, and sabre-cuts'*: *PD*, p. 63; Mitchell, *Tour*, p. 90.

98 *'pantalon de tricot'*: Murray, MS 43545.

98 *'By Lord Byron's desire'*: ALS, John William Polidori to John Murray, Brussels, 6 May 1816, Murray, MS 43528.

98 *the coachmaker he had bought it from refused to take it back*: *PD*, 66.

99 *whose legs or arms had been amputated in the field*: Gordon, *Personal Memoirs*, vol. 2, pp. 280–81.

99 *lain naked on the battlefield*: Gordon, *Personal Memoirs*, vol. 2, pp. 277, 281, 284–5, 288; Semmel, 'Reading the Tangible Past', p. 9.

100 *famous poets and untrustworthy liberals*: Pryse Lockhart Gordon,

'Sketches from the Portfolio of a Sexagenarian', *New Monthly Magazine and Literary Journal*, 26 (1829), p. 195.

100 *obsequious bows before a chair*: Gordon, *Personal Memoirs*, vol. 2, p. 329.

100 *loathed above all to watch women eat*: When Byron went to Samuel Rogers's house for dinner, he refused soup, fish, mutton and wine, and when asked what he *did* eat, replied, 'Nothing but hard biscuits and soda-water.' (Rogers eventually served him potatoes 'bruised down on his plate and drenched with vinegar'.) A few days later, when Rogers bumped into Hobhouse, he asked him how long Byron intended to continue with his diet. 'Just as long as you continue to notice it,' was the reply. Rogers, *Table Talk*, pp. 228–9.

100 *Mrs Gordon's album*: Gordon, *Personal Memoirs*, vol. 2, p. 325.

100 *'a tassel on the purse of merit'*: PD, p. 70.

100 *'venomous Bat'*: Gordon, 'Sketches', p. 197.

101 *'eternity of pavement'*: BLJ, vol. 5, p. 75.

101 *'more squalid misery than I have seen anywhere'*: PD, p. 73.

101 *'Monsieur le Général en chef'*: PD, pp. 74, 214.

101 *'cela pour Napoleon'*: PD, p. 46; Mitchell, *Tour*, p. 83.

101 *'beggars, beggars'*: PD, p. 74; Anon., *Billets*, p. 196.

101 *'Why can't they keep their manufactures to themselves'*: Charles Edward Dodd, *An Autumn Near the Rhine; or, Sketches of Courts, Society, Scenery, etc., in Some of the German States Bordering on the Rhine* (London: 1818), pp. 469–70.

102 *'not very clean-looking'*: PD, p. 75.

102 *destination and route in a police book*: Dodd, *Autumn Near the Rhine*, pp. 475, 487.

103 *'a luxury known only in palaces'*: BLJ, vol. 5, p. 96; Dodd, *Autumn Near the Rhine*, p. 437.

103 *'the dupe of a bedfellow'*: Campbell, *Guide Through Belgium*, p. 11.

103 *'venture upon her carnally'*: BLJ, vol. 5, p. 76–7.

103 *'the dirtiest and most gloomy city of its size in Europe'*: Dodd, *Autumn Near the Rhine*, pp. 471, 472.

104 *'Kept countenance amazingly well'*: PD, p. 77.

104 *they might finally be considered beautiful*: PD, pp. 75–6.

104 '*a fine mass of water*': *PD*, p. 81.

105 *enormous floats of timber*: Dodd, *Autumn Near the Rhine*, pp. 449–50.

105 '*floating island*': Ann Radcliffe, 'Curious Description of the Timber Floats on the Rhine', in Rev. John Adams, *The Flowers of Modern Travels; Being Elegant, Entertaining, and Instructive Extracts, Selected from the Works of the Most Celebrated Travellers*, 3 vols (London: 1799), vol. 3, p. 217.

105 '*one of the finest scenes, I imagine, in the world*': *PD*, p. 82.

105 *prominent palace converted into stables and a guardroom*: Dodd, *Autumn Near the Rhine*, p. 443.

105 '*so proud there was no speaking to them*': Dodd, *Autumn Near the Rhine*, p. 503.

105 '*The French knew how to spend their money*': Dodd, *Autumn Near the Rhine*, pp. 5–6.

106 '*fifty yards from their original situation*': *PD*, p. 85.

106 '*the best town we have seen since Ghent*': *PD*, p. 86.

106 '*Poor Polidori is devilish ill*': *BLJ*, vol. 5, p. 76.

107 '*his stomach returning rapidly to its natural state*': *PD*, p. 213.

107 '*Once more upon the waters!*': *BCPW*, vol. 2, p. 77.

107 *twenty-six stanzas*: *PD*, p. 66; *BCPW*, vol. 2, p. 82.

108 *proud, ambitious, emotionally isolate*: See Simon Bainbridge, *Napoleon and English Romanticism* (Cambridge: Cambridge University Press, 1995) 177–82.

108 '*The loftiest peaks most wrapt in clouds and snow*': *BCPW*, vol. 2, p. 92.

109 '*a damned good thrashing*': This, one of several versions of this particular story, can be found in Frederick L. Jones (ed.), *Maria Gisborne and Edward E. Williams, Shelley's Friends: Their Journals and Letters* (Norman: University of Oklahoma Press, 1951), p. 122. A version may also be found in Medwin, p. 214.

7. Young Tahitians

110 '*So far am I on my journey*': *CC*, vol. 1, p. 43.

110 *Although they had left London*: Percy Bysshe Shelley and Mary Shelley, *History of a Six Weeks' Tour Through a Part of France, Switzerland, Germany and Holland; with Letters Descriptive of A Sail*

Round the Lake of Geneva and of the Glaciers of Chamouni (London: 1817), p. 86.

110 '*You will I dare say fall in love with her*': *CC*, vol. 1, p. 43.

110 '*Madame Clairville*': *CC*, vol. 1, p. 43.

111 '*How different from what I expected*': *CC*, vol. 1, p. 40.

111 '*I almost fear to think of you reading this stupid letter*': *CC*, vol. 1, p. 44.

111 *malignancy of Mrs Godwin*: As Mary wrote to Shelley on 28 October 1814, 'Why will not Godwin follow the obvious bent of his affections and be reconciled to us – no his prejudices the world and she – do you not hate her my love . . .' *Letters MWS*, vol. 1, p. 3. See also *MWSJ*, vol. 1, p. 44.

111 '*so beautiful it was a pity he was so wicked*': *MWSJ*, vol. 1, p. 72.

111 *ruined by a married man*: *SC*, vol. 5, p. 334.

112 '*Claire for seven hundred*': Pforz Cl.Cl.26 79; *Letters MWS*, vol. 1, p. 4.

112 *locked in a convent*: *MWSJ*, vol. 1, p.26.

112 '*in all situations openly proclaim and earnestly support*': *CC*, vol. 1, p. 80; *MWSJ*, vol. 1, p. 35; *CCJ*, p. 55, fn. 8.

112 '*a more ardent asserter of truth and virtue*': *Letters PBS*, vol. 1, p. 403. Edward John Trelawny, *Records of Shelley, Byron, and the Author* (New York: New York Review of Books, 2000), p. 66. According to Mrs Godwin, Shelley did not hold back when setting Claire assignments. 'She has to translate from the French Etienne de la Beætie's treatise on Voluntary Servitude,' she wrote, 'also a page every day from Davangati's Italian translation of Tacitus, and every morning she must learn four verses from Dante, and every evening read Gibbon's Decline and Fall.' Pforz, Cl.Cl.26, p. 88.

112 '*for her transparency*': *CC*, vol. 1, pp. 29–30, fn. 4. As Rousseau wrote in his *Confessions*: 'I imagined two female friends, rather than two of my own sex, because if an instance of such friendship is rarer, it is at the same time more amiable. I bestowed upon them two analogous, but different, characters . . . I made one dark, the other fair; one lively, the other gentle; one prudent, the other weak, but with so touching a weakness, that

virtue seemed to gain by it. I gave to one a lover, whose tender friend the other was, and even something more; but I admitted no rivalry, no quarrelling, no jealousy, because it is difficult for me to imagine painful feelings, and I did not wish to mar this charming picture by anything which degraded Nature. Smitten by my two charming models, I identified myself with the lover and friend.' See Deirdre Coleman, 'Claire Clairmont and Mary Shelley: Identification and Rivalry Within the "tribe of the Otaheite philosopher's" *Women's Writing*, 6:3 (1999), p. 313.

113 *'Otaheite philosophers'*: *CC*, vol. 1, p. 43–4, fn. 1.

113 *'An association of philosophical people'*: *CCJ*, p. 48.

113 *'the Elfin Knight'*: *SC*, vol. 3, p. 431.

113 *'my superintending mind'*: *Letters PBS*, vol. 1, pp. 391–2, 396.

114 *'I was an idiot to expect greatness'*: *Letters PBS*, vol. 1, p. 397.

114 *'I am united to another'*: *Letters PBS*, vol. 1, p. 399.

114 *trying to seduce her husband*: See *Letters PBS*, vol. 1, p. 331, fn. 3; *SC*, vol. 3, p. 429.

114 *'abandoned wife'*: See *MWSJ*, vol. 1, p. 45; *CC*, vol. 1, p. 11, fn. 3.

115 *'lawyer's holes'*: Dowden, vol. 1, p. 478.

115 *Claire, like Fanny, was in love with Shelley*: In 1820, Maria Gisborne wrote in her journal: 'Mr G[odwin] told me that the three girls were all equally in love with ____.' See *MWSJ*, vol. 1, p. 139, fn. 2.

115 *'the man whom I have loved'*: *Letters PBS*, vol. 2, p. 367; Todd, *Death and the Maidens*, p. 112; *CC*, vol. 1, p. 38.

115 *'two wives'*: *CCJ*, 'Introduction', p. 22; Pforz, Cl.Cl.26, p. 88; Todd, *Death and the Maidens*, p. 166; *CCJ*, p. 59. The friends included Leigh Hunt, who used Shelley as an inspiration as he considered seducing his own sister-in-law, and Jefferson Hogg, who was also interested in exploring polygamy.

115 *'though she is nearly sixteen'*: Pforz, Cl.Cl.26, p. 69.

115 *Shelley forbade it*: 'He will not let her go on with music and singing, so she will forget all she has learned.' Pforz, Cl. Cl.26, p. 88.

115 *'What shall poor Cordelia do'*: *CCJ*, p. 31.

116 *'Very philosophical way of spending the day'*: *CCJ*, p. 58.

116 '*horrible to feel the silence of night*': *MWSJ*, vol. 1, p. 32.

116 '*deep and melancholy awe*': *CCJ*, p. 48; *MWSJ*, vol. 1, p. 32.

116 '*wild and starting*': *MWSJ*, vol. 1, p. 33.

116 '*Just as the dawn was struggling with moonlight*': *MWSJ*, vol. 1, p. 33.

117 '*thinking of ghosts*': *CCJ*, p. 49.

117 '*the bitterness of disappointment*': *CCJ*, p. 51.

117 '*never suffer more than one even to approach*': *MWSJ*, vol. 1, p. 35.

117 '*groaned horribly*': *MWSJ*, vol. 1, p. 36.

117 *bad-tempered and depressed*: *MWSJ*, vol. 1, pp. 43–4; vol. 1, p. 48.

117 '*I weep yet never know why*': *CCJ*, p. 51.

117 '*indisciplinable wanderings of passion*': Shelley, *Major Works*, p. 76.

118 '*prejudiced*': *Letters PBS*, vol. 1, p. 184.

118 '*crying bitterly*': *CC*, vol. 1, p. 11, fn. 3.

118 '*My affection for you although it is not now exactly as you would wish*': *Letters MWS*, vol. 1, p. 8.

118 '*common treasure*': *SC*, vol. 3, p. 470.

118 '*Find my baby dead*': *MWSJ*, vol. 1, p. 68.

118 '*Dream that my little baby came to life*': *MWSJ*, vol. 1, p. 70.

119 *lead to his imminent death*: *SC*, vol. 3, p. 483.

119 *Their patrimonial games*: *SC*, vol. 4, p. 605–9 for a detailed account of the settlement.

119 '*Here are we three persons always going about*': *MWSJ*, vol. 1, p. 81.

120 '*Talk about Clara's going away*': *MWSJ*, vol. 1, p. 69.

120 '*This is, indeed, hard to bear*': *MWSJ*, vol. 1, p. 69.

120 '*An English young LADY*': *CC*, vol. 1, p. 12, fn. 3.

120 '*the lady*': *MWSJ*, vol. 1, p. 78.

121 '*A table spoonful of the spirit of aniseed*': *MWSJ*, vol. 1, p. 80.

121 '*our regeneration*': *MWSJ*, vol. 1, p. 79.

121 '*Mr Shelley's clutches*': Letters in the Pforzheimer Collection, purported by Claire to be copies of letters from Mary Jane Godwin to Lady Mount Cashell, state that it was Mrs Godwin's idea to send Claire to Lynmouth, where she arranged to have her stay with a sister of hers, although this is untrue. 'I thought it a pity to leave such a girl uncultivated,' Mrs Godwin writes, 'Mr Godwin has a most clear judgment, and he bid me observe that my first object ought to be to separate her as much as

possible from Mr Shelley and Mary, which a home in London would not do, neither would it cure Mary of her jealousy. I saw how advisable it was she should be placed at a distance. Three years ago I visited my sister at a little village called Lynmouth on the sea coast of Devonshire and I there made acquaintance with Mrs Bicknall the widow of an Indian officer who resides there. I wrote to Mrs B— saying my daughter was in want of country air would she receive her. She assented and my dear girl had been with her now two months and writes to me she is in love with the sea and with a valley full of Rocks a little way off and with some walks in the woods there. You may think my dear friend, how I rejoiced to get her out of Mr Shelley's clutches and what hopes I now entertain that a respectable career may open for the poor girl who has incurred such a stain without any fault of her own. My satisfaction would be complete if down there she meets with a good husband and gets settled for life. I understand that Mr S— was vexed at her leaving them and that he charged her not to let her mind get corrupted by the world, and above all not to eat any meat and that he only consented to her departure because C— wished it extremely.' This strange lie only deepens the mystery of Claire's residence there. Pforz, Cl.Cl.26, pp. 97–8.

121 '*nervous disorder*': *CC*, vol. 1, p. 38.

121 *She may even have been pregnant*: See Janet Todd's sensible conjecture, *Death and the Maidens*, p. 167.

121 '*After so much discontent*': *CC*, vol. 1, p. 9–10.

122 '*concentre round the soul*': *CC*, vol. 1, p. 10.

122 *Claire wrote no more*: The full story of Claire's residence in Lynmouth is a little more complicated than I allow here, as while Charles Clairmont wrote to his sister in September, saying that he had not heard from her for a long time, and assuming she was angry with him (*CC*, vol. 1, p. 13), he later made contact with her, and in October 1815, brother and sister travelled to Ireland where he was investigating a distillery in Enniscorthy with a view possibly to setting himself up in a business. Though Godwin was keen for him to learn the publishing trade, with

an eye to putting the Juvenile Library on a steady footing, Charles Clairmont, like his sister, was keen to escape the confines of Skinner Street. Shelley, who continued to oversee Claire's fortunes, paid for the trip, sending her ten pounds for expenses. *Letters PBS*, vol. 1, p. 434.

122 '*Pray is Clary with you?*': *Letters MWS*, vol. 1, p. 15.

122 '*odious curtains*': *Letters PBS*, vol. 1, p. 354.

122 *an idyllic spot*: *CC*, vol. 1, p. 13–17.

122 '*driven from all I loved*': *CC*, vol. 2, p. 319.

123 '*vex*': Half a century later, Claire would tell the Shelley fanatic and relic-hunter Edward Silsbee that she had pursued Byron with the deliberate intention of vexing the Shelleys. See *CC*, vol. 1, p. 25, fn. 1.

123 '*the object upon which every solitary moment led me to muse*': *CC*, vol. 1, p. 36.

123 *Godwin's financial difficulties*: *BLJ*, vol. 5, p. 16; Robinson, *Diary, Reminiscences*, vol. 1, p. 183.

123 *entered Switzerland through the mountain pass at Nion*: Shelley, *History of a Six Weeks' Tour*, p. 92.

123 *roadside poles*: Louis Simond, *Switzerland; Or, a Journal of a Tour and Residence in that Country, in the Years 1817, 1818, and 1819*, 2 vols (London: 1822), vol. 1, p. 17.

124 '*one of the best inns on the continent*': M. Reichard, *The Descriptive Road Book of France* (London: 1829), p. 352; M. J. Jousiffe, *A Road Book For Switzerland and Chamounix and the Route over the Simplon to Milan* (London: Hatchard, 1839), p. 285.

124 '*The house is not only à l'Anglais*': J. G. Lemaistre, *Travels After the Peace of Amiens Through Parts of France, Switzerland, Italy and Germany*, 3 vols (London: 1806), vol. 1, pp. 20–21.

125 *Despite its imported inconveniences*: Shelley, *History of A Six Weeks' Tour*, p. 94.

125 *Geneva was a fortified city*: Simond, *Switzerland*, vol. 1, pp. 242, 247.

125 '*offals and wood*': *DJCH*, 3 September 1816.

125 *preponderance of domed arcades*: Simond, *Switzerland*, vol. 1, p. 241.

125 *A botanical garden*: Simond, *Switzerland*, vol. 1, p. 241.

126 'far from interesting': Letters PBS, vol. 1, p. 356.

126 'moutons': K. Baedeker, Switzerland, and the Adjacent Portions of
     Italy, Savoy, and the Tyrol: Handbook for Travellers (London: 1883),
     p. 209–10.

126 'Give me here an orchard': Quoted in Thomas Hookham, A Walk
     Through Switzerland in September 1816 (London: 1818), pp. 30–31.

126 monogamous Chamois: Samuel Miller Waring, The Traveller's Fire-
     side: A Series of Papers on Switzerland and the Alps (London: 1819),
     p. 96.

126 bases turned a rich violet: This description of sunset on the Alps
     comes from Fanny Broadley's MS travel diaries (1842), Pforz,
     MISC 4024, 1:53.

126 'balsamic': Wollstonecraft, Letters, p. 352.

126 'happy as a new-fledged bird': Shelley, History of a Six Weeks' Tour,
     pp. 96–7. Fanny was the recipient of these letters, although no
     addressee is given in Mary's published version.

126 'first stepped out from childhood': Mary Shelley, Rambles in Germany
     and Italy in 1840, 1842, and 1843, 2 vols (London: 1844), vol.
     1, p. 139.

127 'purposely deceived her': CC, vol. 1, p. 42; CC, vol. 1, p. 46.

8. A Star in the Halo of the Moon

128 'a little experience will make him a very good traveller': BLJ, vol. 1,
     pp. 78–9.

128 'To the right, beautiful': PD, p. 91.

128 'a leg and a wing': BLJ, vol. 5, p. 78.

129 'heaped promiscuously': PD, p. 94.

129 'worthy of a novel': PD, p. 97.

129 'I suspected you were 200': CC, vol. 1, p. 46.

130 'I rode first with LB': PD, p. 98.

130 'not at home': PD, p. 98; BLJ, vol. 5, p. 207.

130 'How can you be so very unkind': CC, vol. 1, p. 47.

131 'They tell a strange adventure': Francis Bickley (ed.), The Diaries of
     Sylvester Douglas, 2 vols (London: Constable, 1928), vol. 2, p.
     160.

131 number of British visitors: Bickley (ed.), The Diaries of Sylvester

Douglas, vol. 2, p. 160. Lady Frances Shelley put the number in a broader region between Geneva and Lausanne at 1,100. Edgcumbe (ed.), *The Diary of Lady Shelley*, p. 231.

131 *'and not the best of all classes either'*: Simond, *Switzerland*, p. 256.

131 *New detachments disembarked*: M. J. G. Ebel, *The Traveller's Guide Through Switzerland* (London: 1820), p. 52. The mid-week arrivals are noted by Polidori, *PD*, p. 151.

131 *'at the sound of the fiddle'*: Simond, *Switzerland*, p. 255.

131 *'quantities of English'*: *PD*, 119.

131 *There were a few, like the Rawdons*: *BLJ*, vol. 5, pp. 79–80.

132 *'the discordant and unceasing cries'*: ALS, John Cam Hobhouse to Lady Melbourne, Geneva, 4 September 1816, Murray, MS 43472.

132 *first appointment to view a house*: For a description of Bellerive, see Frederic Schoberl, *Picturesque Tour from Geneva to Milan, By Way of the Simplon: Illustrated with Thirty Six Coloured Views* (London: 1820), p. 6.

132 *'How handsome he was'*: *CC*, vol. 1, p. 51, fn. 2.

133 *'and there lay my length, letting the boat go its way'*: *PD*, p. 99. John's melancholy drift is reminiscent of that of Victor Frankenstein, following the deaths of his brother, William, and Justine Moritz. Dogged by despair, he launches his boat from Bellerive out onto Lac Léman late at night: 'Sometimes, after rowing into the middle of the lake, I left the boat to pursue its own course and gave way to my own miserable reflections. I was often tempted – when all was at peace around me and I the only unquiet thing that wandered restless in a scene so beautiful and heavenly, if I except alone some bat or the frogs, whose harsh and inter-rupted croaking was heard only when I approached the shore – often, I say, I was tempted to plunge into the silent lake that the waters might close over me and my calamities for ever.' *Frankenstein*, p. 115.

133 *'Keeps two daughters of Godwin'*: *PD*, p. 101.

133 *'paid Godwin's debts'*: *PD*, p. 107.

133 *'no meretricious appearance'*: *PD*, p. 107.

134 *'Published at fourteen a novel'*: *PD*, p. 107. It should be noted that these numbers seem highly unlikely.

134 '*a frank, warm-hearted, very gentlemanly young man*': Peacock, *Memoir*, p. 46. Joachim Baptista Pereira graduated with an MD in 1815, see 'University of Edinburgh', *Caledonian Mercury*, 3 August 1815.

134 '*The more I read his Queen Mab*': *PD*, p. 107.

135 '*tea'd together*': *PD*, p. 110.

135 *taking baby William to be vaccinated*: *PD*, p. 116.

135 '*until the ladies' brains whizzed*': *PD*, p. 121.

136 '*a wild Eastern melody*': Moore, p. 316.

136 '*capricious, fascinating*': *MWSJ*, vol. 2, p. 478.

137 '*After a moment*': Moore, pp. 318–9.

137 '*drowning men catch at straws*': Moore, p. 318.

137 '*Pains in my loins*': *PD*, p. 120.

137 *The cottage, hidden from the road:* H. W. Häusermann, *The Genevese Background: Studies of Shelley, Francis Danby, Maria Edgeworth, Ruskin, Meredith, and Joseph Conrad (With Hitherto Unpublished Letters)* (London: Routledge and Kegan Paul, 1952), p. 2.

137 *His stock, said John Murray*: Graham (ed.), *Byron's Bulldog*, p. 225.

138 '*that phantom which passes for yourself*': Graham (ed.), *Byron's Bulldog*, p. 228.

138 '*prattling ignorance*': Graham (ed.), *Byron's Bulldog*, p. 228.

138 '*his Satanic Majesty*': *BLJ*, vol. 5, p. 93; Medwin, p. 12, 11.

138 '*wife to the man who keeps the Mount Coffee-house*': Bickley (ed.), *Diaries of Sylvester Douglas*, vol. 2, p. 160.

138 '*Lord Byron is living near here*': Edgcumbe (ed.), *Diary of Lady Shelley*, p. 231.

138 '*League of Incest*': *BCMP*, p. 100.

138 *The true culprit was Henry Brougham:* That Brougham was also going around Geneva transmitting details of the poet's debts, see *BCMP*, pp. 364–5, fn. 62, and *BLJ*, vol. 6, p. 76. On the lurid gossip surrounding Byron in Geneva more generally, see Marchand, vol. 2, p. 613, and Herbert Maxwell (ed.), *The Creevey Papers: A Selection from the Correspondence and Diaries of the Late Thomas Creevey, M.P.*, 2nd edition, 2 vols (London: John Murray, 1904), vol. 1, p. 249.

139 *John Milton:* A popular misconception has it that the poet John

Milton had also lived in the Villa Diodati at one time, and that this somehow connects the events of 1816 to the author of *Paradise Lost*. Milton had certainly been in Geneva while visiting Jean Diodati in 1639 – the young Milton was a friend of his nephew – yet Diodati was then living in the centre of Geneva and the house that Byron knew was not built until 1751. See William S. Clark, 'Milton and the Villa Diodati', *Review of English Studies*, 11:41 (January 1935), pp. 51–7.

139 *Hentsch arranged a six-month lease*: Marchand, vol. 2, p. 623, fn. 7.

139 '*petticoats*': John Cam Hobhouse to Augusta Leigh, 9 September 1816, quoted in Prothero, vol. 3, p. 347, fn. 1; see also ALS, John Cam Hobhouse to Lady Melbourne, Geneva, 4 September 1816, Murray MS 43472.

139 *a glass of kirsch*: Bickley (ed.), *Diaries of Sylvester Douglas*, vol. 2, p. 166.

139 *the snow-capped wall of the Jura*: Schoberl, *Picturesque Tour*, p. 6.

140 *heavy shutters and parquet floors*: Sir Egerton Brydges, *Recollections of Foreign Travel, On Life, Literature, and Self-Knowledge*, 2 vols (London: 1825), vol. 2, p. 216; Anon, 'Extract of a Letter from Geneva', *New Monthly Magazine*, 11:63, April (London: 1819), pp. 193–5.

140 *Less than ten minutes away*: Moore, p. 319.

140 '*Albé*': See *CC*, vol. 1, p. 72, fn. 8.

140 '*I breathe lead*': *BLJ*, vol. 5, p. 91.

140 *suppressing his appetite*: *BLJ*, vol. 8, p. 42.

140 *a vain little Swiss named Maurice*: *Voice*, p. 184.

141 '*without a pair of pistols*': Moore, p. 319, fn. 3; *CC*, vol. 1, p. 71; 'Extract of a Letter from Geneva', p. 193.

141 '*linen and plate*': *PD*, 89.

141 '*common red tooth powder from Waithe*': ALS, John William Polidori to John Murray, Villa Diodati, 18 June 1816, Murray, MS 43528.

141 '*now sends you thrice repeated*': ALS, John William Polidori to John Murray, Villa Diodati, 18 June 1816, Murray, MS 43528.

141 *leave John to himself*: *BCMP*, p. 100.

141 *'like a star in the halo of the moon'*: *PD*, p. 105.

141 *'What a strange person!'*: *BLJ*, vol. 6, p. 127; Edgcumbe (ed.), *Diary of Lady Shelley*, p. 236.

142 *leading Genevan professionals*: Marianne Baillie, *First Impressions on a Tour Upon the Continent in the Summer of 1811, Through Parts of France, Italy, Switzerland, The Borders of Germany, and a Part of French Flanders* (London: 1818), p. 254.

142 *'a good, old, toothless, chatty, easy-believing man'*: *PD*, p. 151.

142 *expert on public health*: Henry R. Viets, 'The London Editions of Polidori's *The Vampyre*', *Bibliographical Society of America, Papers*, 63 (1969), 88–9, fn. 15.

142 *'shrewd, quick, manly-minded'*: *PD*, pp. 122, 105. By English or Italian standards, Genevan society appears to have been old-fashioned and unmodishly pure, although John did enjoy the custom of asking ladies to dance without the need for a prior introduction. At Odier's house one evening he danced waltzes, cotillions, and French and English country-dances with a number of beautiful and willing partners, none of them English; his compatriots had all refused on the grounds of impropriety.

142 *coming home from the city*: John's nephew, William Rossetti, writes of Charlotte's censoring of her brother's journal, 'The other statement which my aunt excluded came somewhat further on, when Dr Polidori was staying near Geneva. He gave some account of a visit of his to some haunt of the local Venus Pandemos. I think the police took some notice of it. The performance was not decorous, but was related without any verbal impropriety.' *PD*, p. 33.

143 *'Such stupid mists – fogs – rains'*: *BLJ*, vol. 5, p. 86.

143 *40 degrees by May*: Henry Stommel and Elizabeth Stommel, *Volcano Weather: The Story of 1816, the Year Without a Summer* (Newport: Seven Seas, 1983), p. 41. See also the *Star*, 20 April 1816: 'The heavy and continued rain throughout Friday se'nnight, occasioned a great flood in many of the upland districts, to the injury, in some places, of the farmer and grazier. At Casterton, near Stamford, one person lost 26 sheep by the sudden swell of the river. The weight of water broke the river Glen, at Bourn,

and drowned all the neighbouring fen on the Bourn side. The waters are also much out on the lands on each side up the river Witham. There has not been such a flow of water in that river since 1802.'

143 *lower slopes of the Jura*: Bickley (ed.), *Diaries of Sylvester Douglas*, vol. 2, p. 164.

143 *'an almost perpetual rain'*: *Letters MWS*, vol. 1, p. 20.

143 *'How the lit lake shines'*: *BCPW*, vol. 2, p. 111.

143 *the lake and the Rhône to rise*: *SC*, vol. 7, p. 34.

143 *From the steps of the Hôtel de la Couronne*: John Clubbe, 'The Tempest-toss'd Summer of 1816: Mary Shelley's *Frankenstein*', *Byron Journal*, 19 (1991), p. 28. Should you be in the market for a pamphlet that compares 1816 to a nuclear winter with a Russian translation of Byron's 'Darkness' in the middle of it, you could do worse than consider Anthony Rudolf's, *Byron's Darkness: Lost Summer and Nuclear Winter* (London: Menard Press, 1984).

144 *'Now, you who wish to be gallant'*: Moore, p. 319.

144 *'Mrs S. called me her brother'*: *PD*, p. 127.

144 *'In spite of the jealous watch kept upon every countenance'*: Moore, pp. 317–8.

144 *unfortunate [. . .] goitre*: On Swiss goitres, see (for example), John Sheppard, *Letters Descriptive of a Tour Through Some Parts of France, Italy, Switzerland and Germany in 1816: With Incidental Reflections on Some Topics Concerned with Religion* (London: 1817), pp. 166–7.

145 *'talked of my play, etc.'*: *PD*, p. 123.

145 *'a conversation about principles'*: *PD*, p. 123.

145 *'we will each write a story'*: *Frankenstein*, p. 439.

145 *'really began to talk ghostly'*: *PD*, p. 128.

146 *'who feed upon him'*: *PD*, p. 128.

146 *torn from an old account book*: *BLJ*, vol. 6, p. 126.

146 *'deeply initiated into what is called the world'*: *BCMP*, p. 59.

147 *'A shovel of his ashes took'*: See *Frankenstein*, p. 439. It should be noted that while others have conjectured that the verse represents Shelley's contribution to the competition, Michael Ekelenz,

who edited the notebook in which it appears, prefers to date this as being composed around two weeks later, in early July 1816. See Michael Ekelenz (ed.), *The Geneva Notebook of Percy Bysshe Shelley: Bodleian MS. Shelley adds. e. 16 and MS. Shelley adds. c. 4, Folios 63, 65, 71, and 72, A Facsimile Edition with Transcriptions and Textual Notes*, (New York: Garland, 1992), p. 141.

147 *Byron felt an affinity for Rousseau*: *BLJ*, vol. 1, p. 49; Moore, p. 72.

147 *building a trap-door in his study*: Robert Darnton, *The Great Cat Massacre and Other Episodes in French Cultural History* (New York: Vintage, 1985), p. 234.

148 *Shelley was an acolyte*: Shelley knew almost all of Byron's work, and had not only written Mary his own love poems based on 'Thyrza' but had plagiarised some of Byron's verses as early as 1810. See Charles E. Robinson, *Shelley and Byron: The Snake and Eagle Wreathed in Fight* (Baltimore: Johns Hopkins University Press, 1976), p. 241.

148 '*it infinitely surpasses any poem he has yet published*': *SC*, vol. 4, p. 719.

148 *Boatmen were hired*: The exact dates of the Byron-Shelley lake tour have been much discussed, but I follow *SC*, vol. 4, p. 698.

148 '*intemperate remonstrances*': Moore, p. 318.

148 '*the greatest man the world has produced*': *SC*, vol. 4, p. 719.

148 *first illicit kiss*: Rousseau, *Julie*, p. 52.

149 '*A sense of the existence of love*': *BCPW*, vol. 2, p. 312.

149 '*even until the darkness of night had swallowed up*': *Letters PBS*, vol. 1, p. 486.

149 '*Polidori is not here*': Moore, p. 320.

9. Fog of the Jura

150 '*cross unkind things*': *CC*, vol. 1, p. 70, 77.

150 '*How contemptuously you used sometimes to speak of me*': *CC*, vol. 1, p. 92.

151 '*quip and crank*': Hunt, *Lord Byron*, p. 90.

151 '*My will is law*': *CC*, vol. 2, p. 606.

151 '*dark despairing modes of thought*': *CC*, vol. 2, p. 606.

151 '*One evening*': Pforz, Cl.Cl.26, p. 39, quotation silently modified. Unmodified text reads: 'He always talked of himself and

related deeds [illegible] of his which if true indicated a savage nature not averse to deeds of darkness and one evening, when we were all three with him he told us quite unexpectedly that at Constantinople he had sewn a mistress who was unfaithful to him up in a sack, and had her carried by two Greeks in the dead of the night (he walking with them) and thrown into the Bosphorus. Mary asked – did she not shriek and alarm the neighbourhood – he said – no, she was perfectly quiet and reconciled to her fate, as women expect no better treatment in that city.' This represents a draft version of manuscript Pforz, Cl.Cl.6, 'My Recollections of Lord Byron', subsequently published as Letter 210 in Stocking's *Clairmont Correspondence*.

152 *She had committed suicide*: *CC*, vol. 2, pp. 606–7.

152 '*for shaking the prejudices of society*': *CC*, vol. 2, p. 607.

152 '*adored Genius*': Pforz, Cl.Cl.26, p. 50.

152 *Byron might even have interceded in a similar event*: John Cam Hobhouse, *A Journey Through Albania, and Other Provinces of Turkey in Europe and Asia, to Constantinople During the Years 1809 and 1810*, 2 vols (London: 1813), vol. 2, p. 111. See also notes to *The Giaour*, *BCPW*, vol. 3, pp. 414, 422–3.

152 '*mad, bad, and dangerous to know*': Paul Douglass, *Lady Caroline Lamb: A Biography* (Basingstoke: Palgrave Macmillan, 2004), p. 104.

153 '*That beautiful pale face is my fate*': Clara Tuite, 'Tainted Love and Romantic Literary Celebrity', *ELH*, 74 (2007), p. 63.

153 '*the Nonsense-mania*': Quoted in Mayne, *Life and Letters*, p. 37.

153 '*Genio maligno*': *BLJ*, vol. 7, p. 37, vol. 2, p. 170.

153 '*heated by novel reading*': Medwin, p. 216; Tuite, 'Tainted Love', p. 63.

153 '*wild antelope*': See Tuite, 'Tainted Love', p. 59.

154 '*marvellous and grievous things*': Egerton Castle (ed.), *The Jerningham Letters (1780–1843): Being Excerpts from the Correspondence and Diaries of the Honourable Lady Jerningham*, 2 vols (London: Bentley, 1896), vol. 2, p. 111.

154 '*Such a monster as that*': *BLJ*, vol. 5, p. 93.

154 *thinly veiled portraits*: Tuite, 'Tainted Love', pp. 66, 72; *BLJ*, vol. 5, pp. 85, 86.

154 *'spirit of evil'*: Lady Caroline Lamb, *Glenarvon*, ed. Deborah Lutz (Kansas City: Valancourt, 2007), p. 145.

155 *'The hand of Heaven'*: Lamb, *Glenarvon*, pp. 118, 150.

155 *'I like to see your tears'*: Lamb, *Glenarvon*, pp. 197, 188.

155 *'When he was savage and unkind'*: Pforz, Cl.Cl.26, pp. 51–3.

155 *'My love is death'*: Lamb, *Glenarvon*, p. 224.

156 *'A man is a man'*: *BLJ*, vol. 5, p.162.

156 *'very impertinent way of looking in a person's face'*: *CC*, vol. 1, p. 83.

156 *concealed from Polidori*: Thomas Medwin, in his *Life of Percy Bysshe Shelley*, edited by Buxton Forman (London: Humphrey Milford/ Oxford University Press, 1913), goes even further, writing that, 'I have reason to believe, however, that this intrigue was carried on with the greatest secrecy; and that neither the Shelleys nor Polidori were for a long time privy to it' (vol. 1, p. 283).

156 *'so extremely suspicious'*: *CC*, vol. 1, p. 51.

156 *'skinless in sensibility'*: *Voice*, p. 57.

156 *'a little of the Scotch accent'*: Moore, p. 12.

156 *'family complaint of suspicion and defence'*: *CC*, vol. 1, p. 73.

156 *'Were I to float by your window drowned'*: *CC*, vol. 1, pp. 44, 47.

156 *'creations of our own mind'*: 'We had always been taught that to be just to others, or to judge them at all fairly,' Claire wrote, 'it was necessary we should love them: that it was a duty to extenuate the faults of others, to believe rather that these very faults were creations of our own mind and had no real existence! Nothing could be more refined and amiable than the doctrines instilled into us, only they were utterly erroneous. They unfitted us entirely for intercourse with vicious characters – we were certain to become and did become their dupes and their victims. By indulgence and a benevolent feeling we were to embellish every thing we looked upon by loving it like the sun that gilds every object with its rays.' Pforz, Cl.Cl.26, p. 109.

157 *a journal she ultimately destroyed*: *SC*, vol. 5, p. 460.

157 *'soliloquy'*: *PD*, p. 134.

157 *Byron and Shelley returned on 30 June*: Robinson, *Shelley and Byron*, p. 24.

157 '*amusing herself*': *CC*, vol. 1, pp. 52, fn. 1, 92; *SC*, vol. 4, p. 694.

158 *a loyal clerk making daily devotions*: See Sunstein, *Romance and Reality*, p. 121; *BLJ*, vol. 5, p. 83; vol. 6, p. 125.

158 '*If you want me*': *CC*, vol. 1, pp. 51–2.

158 *a fit of irrepressible anger*: Moore, p. 319.

158 '*Had a long explanation*': *PD*, p. 135.

158 '*Lord Byron is an exceedingly interesting person*': *SC*, vol. 7, p. 28.

159 *Shelley planned another trip*: *BLJ*, vol. 5, p. 86.

159 '*It is said that you expressed yourself so decisively last Evening*': *CC*, vol. 1, p. 52.

160 '*I never imagined what mountains were before*': *Letters PBS*, vol. 1, p. 497.

160 '*palaces of death and frost*': *Letters PBS*, vol. 1, p. 499.

160 '*another Keswick*': *Letters PBS*, vol. 1, p. 500–501.

160 '*atheists one and all*': Gavin de Beer, 'An Atheist in the Alps', *Keats-Shelley Memorial Bulletin*, IX (1958), pp. 6–7.

161 '*democrat, lover of mankind*': de Beer, 'Atheist in the Alps', pp. 8, 5.

161 '*These mountains are molehills*': de Beer, 'Atheist in the Alps', p. 11.

161 '*the very vilest specimen*': *Letters PBS*, vol. 1, p. 499, vol. 1, p. 501.

161 '*fatigued to death*': *MWSJ*, vol. 1, p. 115.

161 '*Clare sends her love*': *Letters PBS*, vol. 1, p. 495.

161 *Claire's pregnancy was beginning to show*: *SC*, vol. 4, p. 712.

162 *intended for her unborn child*: *SC*, vol. 4, p. 713.

162 '*Lord Byron did not seem to wish it*': *MWSJ*, vol. 1, p. 122.

162 *Byron withdrew*: As Shelley would later complain to Leigh Hunt, 'Lord Byron has made me bitterly feel the inferiority which the world has presumed to place between us.' *Letters PBS*, vol. 2, p. 405.

162 *guilt and responsibility for Claire*: As the editors of *Shelley and his Circle* suggest (*SC*, vol. 4, p. 714), lines in Shelley's allegorical poem *Epipsychidion* may allude to feelings of guilt over his own relationship with Claire, and her subsequent pursuit of Byron:

Thou too, O Comet beautiful and fierce,
Who drew the heart of this frail Universe
Towards thine own; till, wrecked in that convulsion,
Alternating attraction and repulsion,
Thine went astray and that was rent in twain.

162 *paternity might more properly be laid at Shelley's door*: *SC*, vol. 4, p. 713. In time, Byron accepted the child as his, but there is a suggestion that more than a shadow of doubt remained in his mind. When revealing the pregnancy to Douglas Kinnaird, he assumed the child was his, while also taking as read that Claire and Shelley had been lovers in the past, saying, 'That she had *not lived* with S during the time of our acquaintance – and that she had a good deal of that same with me' (*BLJ*, vol. 5, p.162). In the late 1860s/early 1870s, Claire told Trelawny that Elise (the nurse) had told her that she had heard Byron denying the child as his: 'She is no child of mine,' Claire reports Elise hearing him say. 'She is Mr Shelley's child.' *CC*, vol. 2, p. 603.

162 *'a Child always wanted a parent's care'*: *CC*, vol. 2, p. 603.

162 *Byron capitulated*: See *CC*, vol. 1, p. 163.

163 *'in that character I could see it and watch over it'*: *CC*, vol. 2, p. 603.

163 *the right to name the child*: *CC*, vol. 1, p. 92.

163 *Harriet, Charles and Ianthe*: *SC*, vol. 4, p. 748.

163 *'very bad spirits'*: *MWSJ*, vol. 1, p. 122.

163 *'a fixed, settled, eternal home'*: *SC*, vol. 7, p. 28.

163 *fair copies of his poems*: For Claire's transcriptions, see the commentary in *BCPW*, vol. 2, p. 298 and vol. 4, p. 449 *passim*.

164 *'War'*: *MWSJ*, vol. 1, p. 125.

164 *'fitted the taste of the audience'*: William Hazlitt, 'My First Acquaintance with Poets', in Duncan Wu (ed.), *Romanticism: An Anthology*, 2nd edn. (Blackwell: Malden, 1998), pp. 600–610, 608.

164 *Lewis's first-hand experience*: *SC*, vol. 5, pp. 365–6.

164 *told five ghost stories*: *MWSJ*, vol. 1, pp. 126–9; Marchand, vol. 2, p. 644.

165 *'Luigi'*: *SC*, vol. 3, p. 476.

165 *'heart preserved in a box'*: Baillie, *First Impressions on a Tour*, p. 246.

165 *extracted a promise that he would write*: CC, vol. 1, p. 69.

165 *followed much the same route as Byron*: Marchand, vol. 2, p. 645.

165 *Hobhouse brought provisions*: Graham (ed.), *Byron's Bulldog*, p. 228.

165 *'lean and feeble'*: Marchand, vol. 2, p. 624, fn. 8.

166 *William's nursemaid, Elise, came too*: See *MWSJ*, vol. 1, p. 201, fn. 1.

166 *They travelled through France*: *MWSJ*, vol. 1, p. 134; SC, vol. 4, p. 701.

166 *'I feel as if we parted ill friends'*: CC, vol. 1, p. 69.

166 *'Lord help me'*: BLJ, vol. 5, p. 92.

167 *'Farewell then dearest'*: CC, vol. 1, p. 69–70.

10. To Die of Joy

168 *'neglect and dissipation'*: PD, p. 135.

168 *Permission de Séjour*: Polidori's Swiss passport is held in ADC 31, f. 64; PD, p. 149.

168 *a priest called Evans*: PD, p. 145.

169 *live within forty leagues of Paris*: Ebel, *Guide Through Switzerland*, p. 185.

169 *'a strange sprinkling'*: DJCH, 12 September 1816; BLJ, vol. 3, p. 231.

169 *Albert Jean de Rocca*: BLJ, vol. 5, p. 94.

169 *Their marriage was supposedly a secret*: PD, p. 146.

170 *'some outlandish beast'*: Medwin, p. 12.

170 *scream and faint as he came in*: PD, p. 147.

170 *replied with a low bow*: Medwin, p. 12.

170 *'all snow and sophistry'*: BLJ, vol. 3, p. 244.

170 *permanent state of chaos*: Brydges, *Recollections*, vol. 2, p. 213.

170 *'writes octavos, and talks folios'*: BLJ, vol. 3, p. 207, 160.

170 *a whalebone busk*: Lovell, (ed.), *Lady Blessington's Conversations*, p. 23.

170 *'a beautiful, dirty-skinned woman'*: PD, p. 146; DJCH, 12 September 1816.

171 'agrémens de la Société': Anon., 'Extract of a Letter from Geneva', p. 194.

171 *testing the sexual technique of her mistress's prospective lovers*: See Giacomo Casanova, *History of My Life*, trans. Willard R. Trask, 12 vols (Baltimore and London: Johns Hopkins University Press, 1997), vol. 10, p. 355, fn. 64.

171 *an elegant woman in her early forties*: This age is surmised from Robert K. Massie's, *Catherine the Great: Portrait of a Woman* (New York: Random House, 2011), p. 458.

171 *amateur theatricals*: PD, p. 141.

172 'whilst the storms were raging': Anon., 'Extract of a Letter from Geneva', p. 194.

172 *played charades and games of forfeit*: PD, p. 141.

172 'excites love in every man's breast': PD, p. 145.

172 'In love with her': PD, pp. 145–6. The lady's identity remains unknown, although she may have been local – there was a George Brelaz living in Lausanne in the late nineteenth century.

172 'two fools': PD, p. 146.

172 'would-be scientific gentleman': PD, p. 145.

173 'Pray if you can send M. Polidori': CC, vol. 1, p. 51.

173 'Call me cold-hearted': Moore, p. 321.

173 *tried his employer's patience*: Moore, p. 318; PD, p. 135.

173 'As you asked these guests yourself': Medwin, p. 13, fn. 26; see also Moore, p. 318.

174 *Lloyd joined the fight*: PD, p. 150–51.

174 'in a fuss': BLJ, vol. 5, p. 81. 'My digestion is weak,' Byron told Medwin, 'I am too bilious.' Medwin, p. 9.

174 'collared him': PD, p. 136.

174 'cassée ses lunettes et fait tomber son chapeau': MWSJ, vol. 1, p. 124.

174 'Gained my cause': ALS, John William Polidori to William Taylor of Norwich, 3 September 1816. ADC, 31, f. 6.

175 'destroyed whatever scruples you might have felt': Letters PBS, vol. 1, p. 504–5.

175 *Bernese Oberland*: DJCH, 31 August 1816.

175 '*service*': John Cam Hobhouse, *Recollections of A Long Life*, 2 vols (New York: Scribner, 1909), vol. 2, p. 9.

176 *it was Claire's name only*: de Beer, 'Atheist in the Alps', p. 8.

176 '*vertical strata*': *DJCH*, 29 August 1816.

176 '*declared himself for both*': *DJCH*, 1 September 1816.

176 '*Dr Polidori says they are caused*': *DJCH*, 31 August 1816.

176 '*no great harm of him*': *BLJ*, vol. 5, p. 121.

176 '*not upon any quarrel*': *PD*, p. 152.

177 *making them all wait before they could sit down*: *DJCH*, 3 September 1816.

177 '*I shall die of apoplexy*': *DJCH*, 4 September 1816.

177 '*LB's conduct to me has been kind liberal and gentlemanly*': ALS, John Polidori to William Taylor of Norwich, 3 September 1816. *ADC*, Box 31, f. 6.

177 '*not even had a bickering*': *DJCH*, 5 September 1816.

177 *With Scrope went Byron's servant*: MacCarthy, p. 307.

178 '*paid away a great deal*': *PD*, p. 152.

178 '*Poor fellow!!*': *DJCH*, 15 September 1816.

178 '*I am sure you will be very sorry to hear*': *CC*, vol. 1, p. 71. When Claire heard of Polidori being sent away, she said he was 'never useful to you but what can you do without any physician at all'. *CC*, vol. 1, p. 89.

179 '*no companions but the ghosts of old remembrances*': *SC*, vol. 4, p. 746.

179 *in Bath when his romance with Mary had first begun*: See Louise Schutz Boas, *Harriet Shelley: Five Long Years* (London: Oxford University Press, 1962), p. 188.

180 '*putting his <u>heel</u> with great composure into my <u>eye</u>*': *CC*, vol. 1, pp. 74, 73.

180 '*I love you more and more every day*': *CC*, vol. 1, p. 77.

180 '*I am sure I should die of joy*': *CC*, vol. 1, p. 71.

180 '*very industrious in spreading false reports*': *CC*, vol. 1, p. 81.

180 *Fanny, the true orphan of Skinner Street*: Fanny's father, Gilbert Imlay, did not die until 1828, so while Fanny was not technically an orphan, he had no contact with her and showed no interest in her welfare whatsoever.

180 '*the minutest particulars*': *CC*, vol. 1, p. 56.

180 'laughing stock': CC, vol. 1, p. 49.

181 Mary simply laid the letter aside: MWSJ, vol. 1, p. 138.

181 'an Atheist and Murderer': CC, vol. 1, p. 78.

181 'every word of it true': CC, vol. 1, p. 77.

181 'the great Poet is coming': CC, vol. 1, pp. 83, 77.

181 'My dearest Albe might be the most contented of creatures': CC, vol. 1, p. 77.

181 'dull and heavy': CC, vol. 1, pp. 78, 92.

181 'I am melancholy': CC, vol. 1, p. 71.

182 'consoling letter': CC, vol. 1, p. 71.

182 'You might be ill or you might be dead': CC, vol. 1, p. 83.

182 'This above all makes me the most miserable of human Beings': CC, vol. 1, p. 84.

183 'perpetually lamenting the past and struggling with dread': CC, vol. 1, p. 84.

183 Her body was discovered the following morning: See Paul, William Godwin, vol. 2, pp. 241–4.

183 'Go not to Swansea': Dowden, vol. 2, p. 58.

183 Not even Charles Clairmont: Dowden, vol. 2, p. 58.

184 'From the fatal day of Mary's elopement': MWSJ, vol. 1, p. 140, fn. 2.

184 weighed his food: MWSJ, vol. 1, p. 142.

184 Mary buried herself in her story: Letters MWS. vol. 1, p. 22.

184 'I had so great an affection for her': CC, vol. 1, p. 92.

184 'I would do any thing': CC, vol. 1, p. 90.

184 'Write me a nice letter': CC, vol. 1, p. 90.

184 'send me some kind message to her': Letters PBS, vol. 1, p. 513.

184 'impertinent and nauseous': CC, vol. 1, p. 71.

184 'absentia Clariæ': Letters MWS, vol. 1, p. 22.

184 representing her step-sister as a crescent moon: MWSJ, vol. 1, p. 144. This is a common assertion, although Mary's cipher has never been satisfactorily decoded.

185 'My hopes are therefore over': CC, vol. 1, p. 92.

185 'I don't think I am made to inspire love': SC, vol. 4, p. 788.

185 'she killed herself': Letters PBS, vol. 1, p. 521.

185 'I could never refuse you': Letters PBS, vol. 1, p. 520.

11. The Hero of Milan

186 *kissed the hand of Countess Breuss*: ALS, John William Polidori to Lord Byron, Milan, 1 October 1816, Murray, MS 43528; PD, p. 152.

186 *'Wished nobody good-bye'*: PD, p. 152.

186 *dog started vomiting*: PD, p. 155–6.

187 *'We saluted'*: PD, p. 158; BLJ, vol. 5, p. 101.

187 *'The best advice to authors'*: Samuel Johnson, *The Lives of the English Poets: and A Criticism on Their Works*, 3 vols (Dublin, 1780–81), vol. 2, p. 170.

187 *'I am not accustomed to have a master'*: PD, pp. 215–6.

187 *Lady Westmorland*: PD, p. 216.

187 *'For assure yourself'*: PD, p. 216.

188 *'as smooth as the walk of a garden'*: Schoberl, *Picturesque Tour*, Preface, n.p.

188 *'where the grease might be scraped from the floor'*: PD, p. 164.

188 *bandits in the foothills*: Richard Boyle Bernard, *A Tour Through Some Parts of France, Switzerland, Savoy, Germany and Belgium, During the Summer and Autumn of 1814* (London: 1815), p. 117.

188 *'not gallant cavaliers'*: ALS, John William Polidori to Lord Byron, Milan, 1 October 1816, Murray MS 43528.

188 *Milan was a large city by Italian standards*: Mariana Starke, *Travels on the Continent, Written for the Use and Particular Information of Travellers* (London: 1820), p. 87.

189 *ex-almoner to Napoleon's brother-in-law*: PD, p. 176.

189 *best administered by police and censorship offices*: See Wilfred S. Dowden, 'Byron and the Austrian Censorship', *Keats-Shelley Journal*, 4 (Winter 1955), p. 68. While the rhetoric of post-Napoleonic politics liked to claim that Europe had been restored to the peaceful security of the old order prior to the madness of the French Revolution, in fact many states under the Bourbon Restoration had preserved their centralised Napoleonic governments intact, and simply handed them over to the aristocratic and ecclesiastical classes who wielded them as despotic instruments. See Marco Meriggi, 'State and Society in Post-Napoleonic

Italy', in David Laven and Lucy Riall (eds), *Napoleon's Legacy: Problems of Government in Restoration Europe* (Oxford and New York: Berg, 2000), pp. 53–4.

189 '*subject to no religious or moral principle*': Prothero, vol. 4, p. 461.

190 '*Must go to Mass every day*': Stendhal, *The Charterhouse of Parma*, trans. Richard Howard (New York: Modern Library, 2000), p. 88.

190 '*two kisses and apparent joy*': *PD*, p. 166.

190 '*hater of all Austrians*': *PD*, p. 146.

191 '*gratifies me more than any attentions*': *PD*, p. 176.

191 *curtains that could be drawn on occasions*: Lemaistre, *Travels*, p. 259.

191 '*without the slightest chance of receiving an insult*': Starke, *Travels on the Continent*, p. 92.

191 *still thought them the greatest he had ever seen*: *PD*, p. 169.

192 *self-exiled Frenchman*: *PD*, p. 177.

192 *cursing the detested Schlegel*: *DJCH*, 14 October 1816.

192 '*vilest slaves of Europe*': Stendhal, *Charterhouse of Parma*, p. 27; *PD*, p. 178.

192 '*a fat lascivious man*': *PD*, p. 177; *DJCH*, 28 October 1816.

192 *freely confiding Byron's work habits*: *PD*, p. 177; Prothero, vol. 3, p. 439.

192 '*an excellent pimp*': Quoted in Macdonald, p. 118.

193 '*blown my brains out*': Moore, p. 338.

193 '*air of a man who finds he has to repulse an intrusion*': *Voice*, p. 197.

193 *left the box in a rage*: *Voice*, pp. 196, 202; Prothero, vol. 3, pp. 438, 441.

193 *travelled hundreds of miles*: Prothero, vol. 3, p. 440.

193 '*the stage like a hero*': Medwin, p. 185.

193 '*owes you an infinity of thanks*': Prothero, vol. 3, p. 442.

193 '*a blockhead or a monster*': Prothero, vol. 4, p. 451.

194 '*worked off his legs*': *PD*, p. 182.

194 *life-threatening blisters*: *PD*, p. 181.

194 *the disgraced Princess of Wales*: Thea Holme, *Caroline: A Biography of Caroline of Brunswick* (New York: Atheneum, 1980), p. 161.

195 *drank porter like a man*: *DJCH*, 16 and 19 October 1816.

195 *A less lurid interpretation*: Holme, *Caroline*, pp. 178–9.

195 '*This night wrote a letter for Polidori*': *DJCH*, 16 October 1816.

195 '*all very civil*': *DJCH*, 19 October 1816.

195 *It came to nothing*: *PD*, p. 218.

195 '*Your letter produced in me*': ALS, Gaetano Polidori to John Polidori, 30 September 1816, trans. W. M. Rossetti, ADC, Box 31, f. 6.

196 '*Yes, I wish it*': *PD*, p. 186.

196 '*you are not equal to the last of Austrian soldiers in the house*': *PD*, p. 187.

197 '*quietly staring at the ballet*': *BLJ*, vol. 5, p. 121; Prothero, vol. 3, p. 441.

197 '*begirt with grenadiers*': *BLJ*, vol. 5, p. 121; Prothero, vol. 3, p. 441.

197 *leaving only Byron*: *DJCH*, 28 October 1816. Beyle claimed that Breme's brother was also present in the guardhouse, as well as their associate, the Count Confalonieri (Prothero, vol. 3, p. 441).

197 '*You must be off in four-and-twenty hours*': *PD*, p. 188.

197 '*bagatelle*': *PD*, p. 188.

198 '*his squabbles may be set down to me*': *BLJ*, vol. 5, p. 122.

198 '*having begun a row for row's sake*': *BLJ*, vol. 5, pp. 124, 121; quoted in Macdonald, p. 123.

198 '*Polidori must have been talking foolishly*': *DJCH*, 28 October 1816.

198 '*I was never more disgusted with any human production*': *BLJ*, vol. 5, p. 240.

198 '*foaming with rage*': Prothero, vol. 3, p. 441.

199 *bloody revenge*: *PD*, p. 193.

199 '*though she is hardly worth it*': *PD*, p. 201.

199 *King of Prussia*: *PD*, p. 199, 201.

199 *advances in the treatment of typhus*: ALS, Gaetano Polidori to the editor of the *Sun*, London, n.d., ADC, Box 27, f. 3.

199 *happily reunited with his dog*: *PD*, p. 203.

200 '*he maintained much calmness*': MS Letter, Luigi Polidori to Gaetano Polidori, 14 November 1816, trans. W. M. Rossetti, ADC, Box 27, f. 3. An alternative translation appears in *PD*, p. 219.

200 '*queen of the Pisan salons*': Seymour, *Mary Shelley*, p. 251.

200 '*more usefull than a book to me*': ALS, John William Polidori to Lord Byron, Pisa, 11 January 1817, Murray, MS 43528.

201 *John became doubly miserable*. ALS, Gaetano Polidori to John Polidori, London, 17 December 1816, trans. W. M. Rossetti, ADC, Box 31, f. 6.

201 '*Cytherean complaints*': ALS, John William Polidori to Lord Byron, Pisa, 11 January 1817, Murray, MS 43528.

201 '*I fear I shall have to struggle it out without hope*': ALS, John William Polidori to Lord Byron, Pisa, 11 January 1817, Murray, MS 43528.

202 '*I have arranged the observations I made*': ALS, John William Polidori to Lord Byron, Pisa, 17 January 1817, Murray, MS 43528.

202 '*I know no great harm of him*': *BLJ*, vol. 5, p. 163–4; Byron's further recommendations can be found at *BLJ*, vol. 5, pp. 212, 240 and 241.

203 '*He has also a tragedy*': *BLJ*, vol. 5, p. 164.

203 '*all the patients he had in Italy are dead*': *BLJ*, vol. 5, p. 241.

203 '*I think he would suit her*': *BLJ*, vol. 5, pp. 215, 241.

203 '*perambulating humbugger*': *BLJ*, vol. 5, p. 199.

204 *called at Byron's* palazzo *every day*. Marchand, vol. 2, p. 688.

204 '*The Doctor Polidori is here*': *BLJ*, vol. 11, p. 164.

204 '*I make love but with one woman*': *BLJ*, vol. 11, p. 165.

204 '*The said Doctor has had several invalids*': *BLJ*, vol. 11, pp. 164–5.

206 '*romanced amazingly about him*': Rossetti, *Life and Letters*, vol. 1, p. 3; Martineau, *Autobiography*, vol. 1, p. 82.

206 *prominent members of the Catholic gentry*. John's certificate, enrolling him in Freemasonry, can be seen in ADC, Box 31, f. 6.

206 '*blissfully happy*': Medwin, *Shelley*, pp. 151–2.

207 *stood over him in prayers*. Medwin also says he may have broken a leg, although this is not verified elsewhere.

207 '*they had given you up for dead*': Gaetano Polidori to John William Polidori, 16 October 1817, trans. W. M. Rossetti, ADC, Box 31, f. 6.

207 '*he would have remained a hero*': Martineau, *Autobiography*, vol. 1, p. 82.

12. Household Gods

208 '*dawn*': *Letters PBS*, vol. 1, p. 539.

208 '*little square chin divided in the middle*': *CC*, vol. 1, p. 109.

208 '*young "it and I"*': *BLJ*, vol. 5, p. 143.

209 '*I found her with Shelley and her sister at Geneva*': *BLJ*, vol. 5, p. 162.

209 *Mary and Shelley had married*: *Letters PBS*, vol. 1, p. 525.

209 '*a measure of convenience*': *Letters PBS*, vol. 1, p. 540.

209 *an exceptional match*: See *MWSJ*, vol. 1, p. 152, fn. 1.

209 *Mary had been willing to remain unmarried*: *SC*, vol. 5, p. 391.

210 '*something very analogous to disgust*': *Letters MWS*, vol. 1, p. 43. Mrs Godwin had been happy to report that 'We are now endeavouring to forget preceding sorrows and to enjoy the flattering prospects which seem to present themselves.' *SC*, vol. 5, p. 33.

210 '*Very few inquiries have been made of you*': *Letters PBS*, vol. 1, p. 525.

210 '*be kind*': *Letters MWS*, vol. 1, p. 28.

210 '*REVOLUTIONIST*': *Letters PBS*, vol. 1, pp. 527, 530; see also Dowden, vol. 2, pp. 76–95; *SC*, vol. 5, pp. 84–5.

211 *Chancery was invited to look into Shelley's conduct*: See *SC*, vol. 5, p. 245.

211 *claiming to possess evidence that she had been unfaithful*: *Letters PBS*, vol. 1, p. 528, and fn. 6.

211 *Shelley refused to betray his principles*: See Seymour, *Mary Shelley*, p. 175.

211 *Albion House, Marlow*: Peacock, *Memoir*, p. 61; *Letters MWS*, vol. 1, p. 45; *Letters PBS*, vol. 1, p. 540.

211 '*would do as they chose in defiance of public opinion*': *SC*, vol. 5, p. 392.

211 *Apollo and Venus*: Peacock, *Memoir*, p. 61; *Letters MWS*, vol. 1, p. 36, fn. 2.

212 '*his hand filled with bunches of wild-flowers*': T. L. Hunt, 'Shelley, by One Who Knew Him', *Atlantic Monthly* (February 1863), p. 187; Peacock, *Memoir*, pp. 68, 61; Hunt, *Lord Byron*, pp. 186–7, 191; Elizabeth Kent, *Flora Domestica, or the Portable Flower-Garden; With Directions for the Treatment of Plants in Pots; and Illustrations from the Works of the Poets*, 2nd edition (London: 1825) xix. For

a rich account of the Shelleys' lives in Marlow, see Daisy Hay, *Young Romantics: The Shelleys, Byron, and Other Tangled Lives* (London: Bloomsbury, 2010).

213 '*we must candidly own*': Dowden, vol. 2, p. 59.

214 '*aristocratical sallies*': On the relationship between Keats and Shelley, see *SC*, vol. 5, pp. 309–427. The remark is actually a comment regarding Shelley that Hunt shared with John and Maria Gisborne, quoted in *SC*, vol. 10, p. 696.

214 '*the injustice of neglect*': *Letters PBS*, vol. 1, p. 517.

214 '*I am an outcast from human society*': *Letters PBS*, vol. 1, p. 517.

214 '*insignificance and impotence*': *Letters PBS*, vol. 1, p. 530.

215 *he looked to economise*: *SC*, vol. 5, p. 229.

215 '*very political as well as poetical*': *Letters MWS*, vol. 1, p. 29.

215 *Windsor Castle, Virginia Water and the Chiltern hills*: Peacock, *Memoir*, p. 62.

216 '*greatest enemy she has in the world*': Jones (ed.), *Gisborne and Williams*, p. 39.

216 *a local girl called Polly Rose*: T. L. Hunt, 'Shelley', p. 187; Dowden, vol. 2, pp. 123–4.

216 '*he is more disagreeable than ever*': *Letters MWS*, vol. 1, pp. 41, 35.

216 '*menagerie*': Quoted in *SC*, vol. 5, p. 492.

216 '*death will at length come*': *MWSJ*, vol. 1, p. 172.

217 '*The little creature occupies all my thoughts*': *CC*, vol. 1, p. 110.

217 *Vincent Novello*: *SC*, vol. 5, p. 267; *CCJ*, p. 78; Peacock, *Memoir*, p. 66.

217 '*a female form and countenance of dazzling grace*': Thomas Love Peacock, *Nightmare Abbey/Crotchet Castle*, ed. Raymond Wright (Harmondsworth: Penguin, 1986), p. 91.

219 '*Miss Auburn*': *SC*, vol. 5, p. 391.

219 '*temporise with our servants*': *Letters PBS*, vol. 1, p. 539, vol. 1, p. 546.

219 '*An unconquerable fear of ghosts*': *SC*, vol. 5, p. 392.

219 '*ask Miss Auburn also*': *SC*, vol. 5, p. 392.

219 '*We find it indispensable that Clare should reside with us*': *Letters PBS*, vol. 1, p. 540.

220 '*Mademoiselle Clairmont*': *Letters MWS*, vol. 1, p. 46, and fn. 3.

220 '*remarks her existence is calculated to excite*': *Letters PBS*, vol. 1, p. 546.

220 *four months for news of Alba's birth to reach Byron*: *SC*, vol. 5, p. 84.

220 '*Don't look at him, he is dangerous to look at*': *Letters PBS*, vol. 1, p. 544; Marchand, vol. 2, p. 694; Ralph Milbanke Lovelace, *Astarte: A Fragment of Truth Concerning George Gordon Byron, Sixth Lord Byron* (London: Christophers, 1921), p. 17.

220 '*By the way – it seems that I have got another*': *BLJ*, vol. 5, p. 228.

221 '*I am not at peace until she is on her way to Italy*': *Letters MWS*, vol. 1, p. 50.

221 *regular letters and accounts of her progress*: *Letters MWS*, vol. 1, p. 48.

221 '*Promises with Albé!*': *Letters MWS*, vol. 1, p. 49.

221 *Clara was not feeding well*: *Letters MWS*, vol. 1, p. 46.

222 '*forever wearying with her idle and childish complaints*': *Letters MWS*, vol. 1, p. 56.

222 *the house's imperfections*: *Letters MWS*, vol. 1, p. 45; Bieri, *Shelley*, p. 381.

222 *looking haggard and dishevelled*: T. L. Hunt, 'Shelley', 189; Bieri, *Shelley*, p. 382.

222 '*if by imprudent delay*': *Letters MWS*, vol. 1, p. 49.

222 *a case of ophthalmia*: *MWSJ*, vol. 1, p. 189, fn. 2.

222 '*I think Alba's remaining here extremely dangerous*': *Letters MWS*, vol. 1, p. 57.

223 '*kisses Clara – strokes her arms and feet and laughs*': *Letters MWS*, vol. 1, p. 53.

223 '*My dear friend how I envy you*': *CC*, vol. 1, p. 109.

224 '*If you knew the extreme happiness I feel*': *CC*, vol. 1, p. 110.

224 '*Here's the harp she used to touch*': *CCJ*, p. 81; Nicholas Joukovsky (ed.), *The Letters of Thomas Love Peacock*, 2 vols (Oxford: Clarendon, 2001), vol. 1, p. 119 (Hogg was quoting Moore's poem 'Here's the Bower'). See also Neville Rogers, 'Music at Marlow', *Keats-Shelley Memorial Bulletin*, 5 (1953), p. 22.

224 *Percy Bysshe Shelley Hunt*: Hunt, *Lord Byron*, p. 192.

224 *a short preface by Shelley*: Shelley's 1818 preface to *Frankenstein* (written in the voice of Mary) claims that: 'Two other friends

(a tale from the pen of one of whom would be far more accept-able to the public than any thing I can ever hope to produce) and myself agreed to write each a story founded on some super-natural occurrence. The weather, however, suddenly became serene; and my two friends left me on a journey among the Alps, and lost, in the magnificent scenes which they present, all memory of their ghostly visions.' *Frankenstein*, p. 433.

225 *five hundred copies were printed*: *SC*, vol. 5, pp. 397–8; St Clair, *The Reading Nation*, pp. 359–60.

225 *which the publisher refused*: *Letters PBS*, vol. 1, p. 561.

225 *'How I delight in a lovely woman of strong and cultivated intellect'*: *CC*, vol. 1, p. 110. This signed edition of *Frankenstein*, recently discovered, was first displayed to the public at the New York Public Library's exhibition 'Shelley's Ghost: The Afterlife of a Poet', 24 February–24 June 2012.

225 *'Allegra'*: *BLJ*, vol. 6, p. 7.

226 *'No fixed residence'*: Continuing the Shelleys' recent tactic of legitimising their family ties to stave off legal harassment, William Shelley and his sister, Clara Everine Shelley, were also baptised. *MWSJ*, vol. 1, pp. 196–7, fn. 5.

226 *'What is a name?'*: Peacock, *Nightmare Abbey*, p. 93.

226 *Shelley packed his pistols*: T. L. Hunt, 'Shelley', p. 189.

226 *(whose springs broke)*: *MWSJ*, vol. 1, p. 199.

226 *Shelley's books underwent examination*: *MWSJ*, vol. 1, p. 200.

226 *'Itty Ba'*: *CCJ*, p. 92.

226 *'an hommage to the Works of Man'*: *CCJ*, p. 90; *SC*, vol. 5, p. 452.

226 *'Nothing but Discomfort'*: *CCJ*, p. 92.

227 *'I can see no loophole for calumny'*: *Letters PBS*, vol. 2, p. 11.

227 *'Only write me one word of Consolation'*: *CC*, vol. 1, p. 113.

227 *'bad German novels'*: *CC*, vol. 1, pp. 116, 115.

227 *'mercantile acquaintance'*: *CC*, vol. 1, p. 113.

227 *'desire Shelley to pack it carefully'*: *SC*, vol. 10, p. 747; *BLJ*, vol. 6, p. 25.

227 *'this painful controversy'*: *Letters PBS*, vol. 2, p. 11.

227 *'It is not that I wish to make out a case for Claire'*: *Letters PBS*, vol. 2, p. 10.

228 *'I can't leave my quarters'*: BLJ, vol. 6, p. 37.

228 *Shelley appears to have had another change of heart*: Letters PBS, vol. 2, p. 400.

228 *'I have sent you my child because I love her'*: CC, vol. 1, p. 115.

13. The Vampyre

230 *'Before my fall from the gig'*: ALS, John William Polidori to John Murray, Norwich, 19 October 1817, Murray, MS 43528.

230 *'the Doctor's Skill at Norwich'*: BLJ, vol. 5, p. 272.

230 *'I have not a single piece of his handwriting'*: ALS, John William Polidori to John Murray, Norwich, 19 October 1817, Murray, MS 43528.

231 *'Vapid nullity'*: Polidori, *Positive Pleasure*, p. 4. See also Henry Viets, '"By the Visitation of God": The Death of John William Polidori, M.D., in 1821', *British Medical Journal*, 2:5269 (December 1961), p. 1774.

231 *Pisan journal to Murray*: ALS, John William Polidori to John Murray, Norwich, 7 January 1818, Murray, MS 43528.

231 *'the absence of pain'*: See Macdonald, p. 153.

231 *'constant decay and irreparable destruction'*: Polidori, *Positive Pleasure*, pp. 37, 16.

231 *'we take to the bottle'*: Polidori, *Positive Pleasure*, p. 25.

232 *'we should look with disgust'*: Polidori, *Positive Pleasure*, pp. 43, 23.

232 *'We think the possession of beauty'*: Polidori, *Positive Pleasure*, p. 34.

232 *'Were we not as well when alone?'*: Polidori, *Positive Pleasure*, p. 35.

233 *'I should be very sorry to assist'*: Polidori, *Positive Pleasure*, holograph end papers, ADC, PR 10 N9 R6a 1818.

233 *'I regret you are still blowing bubbles'*: Polidori, *Positive Pleasure*, holograph end papers, ADC, PR 10 N9 R6a 1818.

233 *'I shall not be made responsible'*: Polidori, *Positive Pleasure*, p. ii.

233 *female readers in particular were angered*: See Macdonald, p. 166.

233 *'What a tyger of a man'*: Polidori, *Positive Pleasure*, holograph end papers, ADC PR 10 N9 R6a 1818.

233 *'But thou – weak follower of a soulless school'*: Thomas Medwin, *The Life of Percy Bysshe Shelley*, ed. H. Buxton Forman (London: Humphrey Milford/Oxford University Press, 1913), p. 150. See

also Polidori, *Positive Pleasure*, holograph end papers: 'The London Literary Gazette or Journal of Belles Lettres Arts and Sciences for Saturday Aug. 8th reviewed it – against. The Norfolk Chronicle for the 14th Nov:1818 had a letter to the Editor signed S.A. and some verses against it. The same paper for the 28th Nove: had an answer signed Vuiax attacking S.A. by Charles Austen. A Lady of Yarmouth asked Ed. Finch if he knew me – "what a tyger of a man he must be". The Monthly Review for Sept. 1819 cutting up.'

234 '*You might perhaps gain something by your profession*': MS Letter, Gaetano Polidori to John William Polidori, 27 January 1818, trans. W. M. Rossetti, ADC, Box 31, f. 6.

235 '*cannot discover any slavery greater*': MS Letter, Gaetano Polidori to John William Polidori, 27 January 1818, trans. W. M. Rossetti, ADC, Box 31, f. 6.

235 '*debts and embarrassment*': ALS John Deagostini to John William Polidori, 19 August 1818, ADC, Box 31, f. 6.

235 '*little further cost*': MS Letter, Gaetano Polidori to John William Polidori, 14 May 1818, trans. W. M. Rossetti, ADC, Box 31, f. 6.

235 *the magnificent central staircase*: John Timbs, *Walks and Talks About London* (London: 1865), p. 171.

236 *John was determined to be a writer still*: ALS, John William Polidori to John Murray, London, Wednesday, 13 January 1819, Murray, MS 43528.

236 *a large and boisterous print culture*: See David Minden, *Romantic Genius and the Literary Magazine: Biography, Celebrity and Politics* (Abingdon and New York: Routledge, 2005), pp. 6–10.

236 '*the meanest insects*': Samuel Taylor Coleridge, 'On the Errors of Party Spirit: Or Extremes Meet', in *The Complete Works of Samuel Taylor Coleridge*, ed. W. G. T. Shedd, 7 vols (New York: 1884), vol. 2, p. 192.

237 '*the worm that gnaws us*': William Hazlitt, 'On Envy (A Dialogue)', in *The Plain Speaker: Opinions on Books, Men, and Things*, 2 vols (London: 1826), vol. 1, pp. 229–54, 251.

237 '*We should have nothing but a perpetual round of cudgelling*': *Scotsman*, 24 February 1821, quoted in Richard Cronin, *Paper Pellets*, p. 39.

237 *'great inaccuracy'*: John William Polidori, Review of John Cam Hobhouse, *Historical Illustrations of the Fourth Canto of Childe Harold, Eclectic Review*, vol.10 (July–December 1818), pp. 328, 324, 325.

237 *'he might have rendered a service to the literary world'*: Polidori, *Review*, p. 336. But not only was John settling a personal vendetta, he was also standing up for his Milanese mentor, Ludovico di Breme, whose work Hobhouse had derided in his long essay on Italian letters.

238 *'worse than the deserts of Arabia'*: ALS, John William Polidori to Frances Polidori, London, 6 February 1819, ADC, Box 31, f. 6.

238 *'as you know my great love for notoriety and fame'*: ALS, John William Polidori to Frances Polidori, London, 6 February 1819, ADC, Box 31, f. 6.

238 *'writer of strong mind and powerful talents'*: Review of *An Essay Upon the Source of Positive Pleasure* and *Ximenes, the Wreath, and Other Poems*, in *Gentleman's Magazine and Historical Chronicle from January to June, 1819*, vol. 125 (London: 1819), p. 552; Review of *Ximenes, the Wreath, and Other Poems*, *European Magazine*, vol. 75, March (London: 1819), pp. 250–51, 250; Review of *An Essay Upon the Source of Positive Pleasure* and *Ximenes, the Wreath, and Other Poems*, in *New Monthly Magazine*, 11;63, April (London: 1819), pp. 246–250, 246.

238 *'flat and artificial'*: *New Monthly Magazine*, April (1819), p. 247.

238 *'numerous beauties'*: *New Monthly Magazine*, April (1819), p.247.

239 *'excellent accounts'*: Anon., 'Extract of a Letter from Geneva', p. 194.

239 *even Byron had to admit their veracity*: BLJ, vol. 6, pp. 125–7.

239 *The letter also included an account of the Diodati ghost-story competition*: Shelley did not actually name Byron in his 1818 preface to *Frankenstein*, but rather alluded to him as a writer 'a tale from the pen . . . whom would be far more acceptable to the public than any thing I can ever hope to produce', *Frankenstein*, p. 433.

240 *'you would feel as much curiosity as myself'*: Anon., 'Extract of a Letter from Geneva', p. 195.

240 '*the Tale of Dr* _____': Anon., 'Extract of a Letter from Geneva', p. 195.

241 '*which is* not *Lord Byron's*': *PD*, p. 15.

241 '*I shall not sit patiently by*': *PD*, p. 16.

241 '*I shall immediately procure an injunction*': ALS, John William Polidori, n.d. [1819], ADC, Box 31, f. 6.

242 *he was said to wear boys' clothes*: John Sutherland, 'Henry Colburn, Publisher', *Publishing History*, 19 (1986), p. 59.

242 '*royal bastard*': Sutherland, 'Henry Colburn', p. 59.

242 *sign over to him her entire literary property*: Sutherland, 'Henry Colburn', p. 59.

242 '*amende honorable*': *CFJWP*, 52, fn.

242 '*might trust to his honour*': ALS, John William Polidori to James Perry (editor of the *Morning Chronicle*), n.d. (24 September), ADC, Box 31, f. 6.

243 '*But first, on earth as Vampire sent*': *BCPW*, vol. 2, p. 64.

243 *London, New York, and Philadelphia*: Viets, 'Editions of the Vampyre', pp. 91, 98.

243 *the over-medicated Madame Gatelier*: Madame Gatelier is W. M. Rossetti's candidate for transmitter of the text, although on what grounds is unclear. See *PD*, p. 13.

244 *it seems unlikely he would have travelled abroad*: See James Reiger, 'Dr. Polidori and the Genesis of *Frankenstein*', in *Studies in English Literature, 1500–1900*, 3:4 (Autumn, 1963), p. 462, and Macdonald, p. 178, who derives the attribution from the catalogue of the Houghton Library, Harvard; Anon., *Sketches of Obscure Poets, with Specimens of their Writings* (London: 1833), p. 93.

244 '*exculpate himself from the baseness of the transaction*': Murray, *Letters*, p. 269.

244 '*erratic but transcendent genius*': Anon., 'Extract of A Letter From Geneva' (First state), ADC, Box 31, f. 6. 'We may, however, observe that it bears strong internal evidence of having been conceived by him,' continued Watts's note, 'though from the occasional inaccuracies, probably the result of haste, which occur throughout the whole, we should suppose it to have been committed to paper rather from the recital of a third person

than under the immediate direction of its noble author.'
Colburn's note read: 'We received several private letters in the
course of last autumn from a friend travelling on the Continent,
and among others the following, which we give to the public
on account of its containing anecdotes of an Individual,
concerning whom the most trifling circumstance, if they tend
to mark even the minor features of his mind, cannot fail of
being considered important and valuable by those who know
how to appreciate his erratic but transcendent genius.' Anon.,
'Extract of A Letter from Geneva', p. 193.

244 '*deception and chicanery*': Viets, 'Editions of the Vampyre', p. 91.

244 '*the whole plan of it*': Murray, *Letters*, p. 269.

244 '*should have been ignorant of the circumstances*': Macdonald, p. 183.

244 '*the honour of a gentleman*': ALS, A. A. Watts to John Murray, London, Tuesday [April 1819]. Murray, MS 42290.

244 'private *MS. of Lord Byron's*': See Macdonald, p. 183; ALS, A. A. Watts to John Murray, London, Tuesday [April 1819], Murray MS, 42290.

245 *intended to blackmail Colburn*: Murray, *Letters*, p. 270.

246 '*the grossest and most unmanly reflections*': *SC*, vol. 6, pp. 777–81.

246 '*Damn "the Vampire"*': *BLJ*, vol. 6, p. 114.

246 '*I have a personal dislike to "Vampires"*': *BLJ*, vol. 6, p. 119.

246 '*a sort of Boswell diary of your Lordships life*': Murray, *Letters*, p. 271.

246 '*I defy him to say any thing about me*': *BLJ*, vol. 6, p.127. Murray claimed this was completely new to him, which may have been true, although, on 28 April 1816, John had written in his diary to say that Murray had offered '£500 for my tour' (*PD*, p. 44). It is unclear why the commercially averse Byron should extend such an offer instead of Murray himself and, in his own excitement, it is entirely possible that John caught the wrong end of the stick.

246 '*taken Polidori in hand*': Murray, *Letters*, p. 270.

247 '*the intention of betraying the privacy of any man*': ALS, John Cam Hobhouse to John William Polidori, Whitton Park, Hounslow, 29 April 1819, Murray, MS 42990.

247 '*I pretend to the character and rank of a gentleman*': ALS, John

William Polidori to John Cam Hobhouse, n.d., Murray, MS 42290.

247 '*I certainly shall not do it*': ALS, John William Polidori to John Cam Hobhouse, Covent Garden Chambers, 'Saturday Morning' [1819], Murray, MS 42290.

247 'the rank and name of a gentleman': Graham (ed.), *Byron's Bulldog*, p. 270.

247 '*He is a sad scamp*': Graham (ed.), *Byron's Bulldog*, pp. 270–71.

247 *Byron sent Murray the original leaves*: BLJ, vol. 7, p. 58. See also *BCMP*, p. 331.

248 '*high romantic feeling of honour and candour*': [John William Polidori], *The Vampyre: A Tale* (London: Sherwood, Neely and Jones, 1819), p. 30.

248 *on account of 'embarrassed' affairs*: [Polidori] *Vampyre*, p. 32.

248 '*irresistible powers of seduction*': [Polidori], *The Vampyre*, p. 37.

248 '*the stifled, exultant mockery of a laugh*': [Polidori], *The Vampyre*, p. 46.

248 '*whose strength seemed superhuman*': [Polidori], *The Vampyre*, p. 47.

250 *the oath and its associated rituals*: The fact that Ruthven's vampirism is not virulent, infecting its victims with vampirism of their own, also suggests his selfish, walled-off nature.

14. Sea Sodom

251 '*infection*': BLJ, vol. 6, p. 65

251 '*Here have I pitched my staff*': BLJ, vol. 6, p. 16.

251 *rate of Austrian taxation*: Letters PBS, vol. 2, p. 43; see also *SC*, vol. 7, p. 168–9.

251 '*better people in better times*': DJCH, 10 November 1816.

251 '*gloomy gaiety*': BLJ, vol. 5, p. 132.

252 '*I can write cheerfully*': BLJ, vol. 6, p. 25.

252 *the ascent from debt to wealth*: BLJ, vol. 5, p. 132. The sale of Newstead was concluded on 10 December 1817. The purchase price was £94,500, and the purchaser, his school friend, Major Thomas Wildman – he of the friend with the knocking 'feet in rattattat'. See Marchand, vol. 2, p. 718, n.

252 *spent on women*: BLJ, vol. 6, pp. 43, 65–6.

252 '*seat of all dissoluteness*': BCMP, vol. 4, p. 127.

252 '*laudable practice of Lovemaking*': *BLJ*, vol. 6, pp. 44, 66; *MWSJ*, vol. 1, p. 213.

252 '*my hands are full*': *BLJ*, vol. 6, p. 40. 'LB is familiar with the lowest sort of these women, the people his gondolieri pick up in the streets,' wrote Shelley. 'He allows fathers and mothers to bargain with him for their daughters, and though this is common enough in Italy, yet for an Englishman to encourage such vice is a melancholy thing.' *Letters PBS*, vol. 2, p. 58.

252 '*My Bastard came three days ago*': *BLJ*, vol. 6, p. 39.

252 '*I have fucked her twice a day*': *BLJ*, vol. 6, p. 40.

253 '*a very fine child*': *BLJ*, vol. 6, p. 41.

253 '*Pythonness*': *BLJ*, vol. 6, pp. 69, 195.

254 *Bagni di Lucca*: *MWSJ*, vol. 1, p. 222.

254 'nome stravagante': *Letters PBS*, vol. 2, p. 35.

254 *just as a thunderstorm erupted*: *Letters PBS*, vol. 2, p. 35.

255 '*with extreme horror*': *Letters PBS*, vol. 2, p. 36.

255 '*She is pale*': *Letters PBS*, vol. 2, p. 36. Shelley left his impressions of Allegra in poetic form also, representing her as the daughter of Count Maddalo in *Julian and Maddalo*, the poem he composed following their visit:

A lovelier toy sweet Nature never made,
A serious, subtle, wild, yet gentle being,
Graceful without design and unforeseeing,
With eyes – oh speak not of her eyes! – which seem
Twin mirrors of Italian Heaven, yet gleam
With such deep meaning, as we never see
But in the human countenance: with me
She was a special favourite. I had nursed
Her fine and feeble limbs when she came first
To this bleak world; and yet she seemed to know
On second sight her ancient playfellow,
Less changed than she was by six months or so;
For after her first shyness was worn out
We sate there, rolling billiard balls about.

At the end of that poem, the narrator meets her again many years later. By this time she has grown into 'a wonder of this earth . . . Like one of Shakespeare's women'.

255 '*fat, fat-headed, middle-aged*': Bickley (ed.), *Diaries of Sylvester Douglas*, vol. 2, p. 329.

255 '*liveliest and happiest looking man I ever met*': *Letters PBS*, vol. 2, p. 42.

255 '*the reputation of caprice*': *Letters PBS*, vol. 2, p. 36.

256 '*histories of his wounded feelings*': See Marchand, vol. 2, p. 717, fn. 4; *Letters PBS*, vol. 2, p. 36.

256 '*an addition to the family*': *BLJ*, vol. 6, p. 69.

256 '*Are you not the Sun to me?*': *CC*, vol. 1, p. 117.

257 '*stupid fellow*': *Letters MWS*, vol. 1, p. 79.

257 *Clara became convulsive*: *Letters PBS*, vol. 2, p. 40.

258 '*smell so of garlick*': *Letters PBS*, vol. 2, p. 58.

258 '*must end up soon by some violent circumstance*': *Letters PBS*, vol. 2, p. 58. This also appeared to be the view of the Hoppners, at least for a while. See *CC*, vol. 1, p. 148, fn. 2.

258 *send her back with hands and feet raw from the cold*: Iris Origo, *A Measure of Love* (London: Jonathan Cape, 1957), p. 39.

258 *eight months travelling between Rome and Naples*: See *CC*, vol. 1, p. 146.

258 *on condition that her father renounce all claims*: *Letters MWS*, vol. 1, p. 106; *CC*, vol. 1, p. 129, fn. 4.

259 '*do not throw away the greatest treasure you have*': *CC*, vol. 1, p. 127.

259 '*a sort of Italian Caroline Lamb*': *BLJ*, vol. 6, p. 115; Marchand, vol. 2, pp. 784–5.

259 '*if I come away with a Stilleto in my gizzard*': Medwin, p. 22; Marchand, vol. 2, p. 805; *BLJ*, vol. 6, p. 163.

259 *committing her to the care of Mrs Martens*: ALS, Richard Belgrave Hoppner to Lord Byron, Venice, 29 June 1819, Murray MS 43448.

259 '*foolish mad woman*': Marchand, vol. 2, p. 803; *BLJ*, vol. 6, p. 213.

259 *For about six weeks in the summer of 1819*: *Letters PBS*, vol. 2, p. 129.

260 *At last, Byron managed to have her sent to him in Bologna*: *BLJ*, vol. 6, pp. 198, 218.

260 *a new project of domestication*: *BLJ*, vol. 6, p. 230.

260 *'fan carrier of a woman'*: *BLJ*, vol. 6, p. 226.

260 *'of what they call the parental feeling?'*: Moore, p. 422.

260 *'She is English'*: *BLJ*, vol. 6, p. 223.

261 *Byron counselled her to go back*: *BLJ*, vol. 6, pp. 244, 248; *SC*, vol. 7, p. 379, fn. 13.

261 *'Never again shall Sorrow be'*: *BCPW*, vol. 4, p. 240.

261 *the extent of his feeling*: See *BLJ*, vol. 6, pp. 228, 244, 241–2. 'I will say no more,' he wrote to Hobhouse, 'except that it has been as bitter a cut up for me – as that of leaving England.' *BLJ*, vol. 6, p. 245.

261 *'I am not yet thirty two years of age'*: *BLJ*, vol. 6, p. 226.

261 *'revenge first – and emigration afterwards'*: *BLJ*, vol. 6, pp. 255, 245–6.

262 *court of cats, birds and monkeys*: Untitled transcription, translated, typed, of original Italian MS (BL), n.d., detailing Pellegrino Ghigi's claim for expenses from the Estate of Lord Byron, Murray, MS 43547.

262 *Teresa took her for rides*: *SC*, vol. 7, p. 423.

262 *'as ravenous as a Vulture'*: *BLJ*, vol. 7, pp. 78, 66.

262 *Claire had not seen her daughter for a year and a half*: *CC*, vol. 1, p. 140.

262 *living in four different cities*: These figures come courtesy of Doucet Devin Fisher, one of the editors of *Shelley and His Circle*, who with great generosity reconstructed Claire's movements for me from the time she left Este on 5 November 1819, to her arrival in Pisa on 26 or 29 January 1820.

262 *asked Claire for her hand in marriage*: *CCJ*, Appendix C, p. 469.

263 *Lady Mount Cashell*: See Elizabeth Denlinger, *Before Victoria: Extraordinary Women of the British Romantic Era* (New York: New York Public Library/Columbia University Press, 2005), pp. 44–9.

263 *'fearing to annoy you with it'*: *SC*, vol. 10, p. 965, fn. 1; ALS, Richard Belgrave Hoppner to Lord Byron, Venice, 15 April 1820, Murray, MS 43448.

264 '*I should look upon the Child as going into a hospital*': BLJ, vol. 7, p. 80.

264 *even to recant her own atheism*: CC, vol. 1, p. 144.

264 '*she shall be taught to worship God*': CC, vol. 1, pp. 144–5.

264 '*atheistical mother*': BLJ, vol. 7, p. 174.

264 '*a good Catholic*': BLJ, vol. 5, p. 228.

265 *exactly the degree of education required of women*: SC, vol. 7, p. 378.

265 *the quintessence of agreeable femininity*: SC, vol. 7, p. 417.

265 '*inflict the greatest of all evils on my child*': CC, vol. 1, p. 147.

265 '*that new woman of yours*': SC, vol. 10, p. 631.

265 '*very suited for causing disorder in families*': SC, vol. 10, p. 847.

265 '*passport to Hell*': SC, vol. 10, p. 951.

265 *issuing orders for birds to be killed and cooked*: SC, vol. 10, p. 681.

266 '*Bedlam behaviour*': Letters PBS, vol. 2, p. 198.

266 '*I think Madame Clare is a damned bitch*': BLJ, vol. 7, pp. 174–5.

266 *Hoppner had already washed his hands of Claire*: ALS, Richard Belgrave Hoppner to Lord Byron, Venice, n.d. [May 1820], Murray, MS 43448.

266 '*any thing worse even that you can say of her*': Letters PBS, vol. 2, p. 318, fn. 5.

266 *troubling reports they had heard*: CC, vol. 2, Appendix B, p. 645.

266 '*never to trust her again to her mother's care*': Letters PBS, vol. 2, p. 318, fn. 5.

266 '*purchase the physician's silence*': Letters PBS, vol. 2, pp. 318, fn. 5, 319.

267 '*Clare does not scruple to tell Mrs Shelley*': Letters PBS, vol. 2, p. 318, fn. 5.

267 '*The Shiloh story is true no doubt*': BLJ, vol. 7, p. 191.

267 *that her real father was Shelley*: Jones (ed.), *Gisborne and Williams*, p. 48. See also SC, vol. 10, p. 974.

268 '*He heaps on her misery*': Letters PBS, vol. 2, p. 109.

268 *Shelley was preoccupied*: Letters MWS, vol. 2, p. 241.

268 '*Mary considers me as a portion of herself*': David M. Stocking and Marion Kingston Stocking, 'New Shelley Letters in a John Gisborne Notebook', *Keats-Shelley Memorial Association Bulletin*, 31 (1980), p. 3.

268 '*Heigh-ho*': *CCJ*, p. 153.

268 *a plan was considered to find her a job in Paris*: See *Letters MWS*, vol. 1, p. 158, fn. 13; *CC*, vol. 1, p. 170, fn. 2.

268 *to become a governess*: *SC*, vol. 10, p. 965.

269 *Fletcher and Elise appeared to her in a dream*: *CCJ*, p. 176.

269 *resented Lady Mount Cashell*: *Letters PBS*, vol. 2, p. 241.

269 '*a source of disquietude*': *Letters PBS*, vol. 2, p. 367.

269 '*what would it be to your sweet consolation, my own Clare?*': *Letters PBS*, vol. 2, p. 242.

269 *an expedition to Egypt*: Dowden, vol. 2, p. 365.

269 '*do not mention it*': *Letters PBS*, vol. 2, p. 243.

269 *he begged her to make her excuses*: *Letters PBS*, vol. 2, pp. 247–50.

269 '*Think of yourself as a stranger*': *CCJ*, p. 180.

270 '*Hints for Don Juan*': *CCJ*, p. 193.

270 '*He sitting drinking spirits*': *CCJ*, pp. 183–4, punctuation modified.

271 '*I will quietly murder that little child*': *CCJ*, p. 184, punctuation modified.

15. Torn Clouds before the Hurricane

272 '*Ambition*': John William Polidori, *Ximenes, the Wreath and Other Poems* (London: 1819), p. ii.

272 '*Vampyre family*': *Blackwood's Edinburgh Magazine*, v (July), p. 416.

272 '*murderous to the literary name*': *Edinburgh Magazine and Literary Miscellany*, v (August 1819), p. 159; *Blackwood's Edinburgh Magazine*, v (August, 1819), p. 432; 'accursed hunger' is a translation from the Latin verse in the *Edinburgh Magazine*, p. 159.

273 '*I must have something to engage my mind*': ALS, John William Polidori to Frances Polidori, London, 10 November 1819, ADC, Box 31, f. 6.

273 '*public instead of private virtues*': *CFJWP*, p. 56.

273 '*prototype*': *CFJWP*, p. 52.

273 *Only 199 copies were sold*: *CFJWP*, p. 26; Review of *Ernestus Berchtold*, in *Literary Gazette and Journal of Belles Lettres, Arts, Sciences, Etc.* (1819), p. 546.

274 *a stage adaptation of* The Vampyre: Viets, 'Editions of the Vampyre', p. 100.

274 '*I begin to despair*': ALS, John William Polidori to Frances Polidori, London, 10 November 1819, ADC, Box 31, f. 6.

274 '*the Academy of Disappointed Authors*': *Letters PBS*, vol. 2, p. 290.

274 '*looked up to the fame of a poet as something magical*': Brydges, *Recollections*, vol. 2, p. 20.

274 *the philistinism of industrial society*: See David Higgins, *Romantic Genius and the Literary Magazine: Biography, Celebrity, Politics* (London and New York: Routledge, 2005), p. 12.

275 '*poetical disappointments*': Isaac D'Israeli, *Miscellanies of Literature*, revised edition (London: 1840), pp. 401, 431.

275 '*we allow him to create the appetite*': D'Israeli, *Miscellanies*, p. 434.

275 *Chatterton's death may have been accidental*: According to Nick Groom, the author of his entry in the *Oxford Dictionary of National Biography*, Chatterton was enjoying a period of critical and financial success, and had no obvious motive for suicide. See Nick Groom, 'Chatterton, Thomas (1752–1770)', *Oxford Dictionary of National Biography*, Oxford University Press, 2004 [http://www.oxforddnb.com.gate.lib.buffalo.edu/view/article/5189, accessed 19 March 2013].

275 '*vampire bat*': Polidori, *Ximenes*, pp. 136, 138.

276 *offered virtually no instruction*: Macdonald, p. 174.

276 '*our state of life is much too difficult for you now*': ALS, Thomas Burgess to John William Polidori, Ampleforth College, 13 September 1820, ADC, Box 31, f. 6.

276 '*John Pierce*': Macdonald, p. 176.

277 *hundred-and-one-gun salute*: CCJ, p. 215, fn. 38.

277 *asked her to translate*: CCJ, p. 278, fn. 99.

277 *Princess Montemiletto*: CCJ, p. 203, fn. 2.

277 '*affecting singularity in dress*': CCJ, pp. 402, 255.

278 '*dejection of spirits*': CCJ, p. 201, fn. 98; *Letters PBS*, vol. 2, p. 301; Bieri, *Shelley*, p. 595.

278 *lameness was a warning she had failed to heed*: 'The deformity of your mind,' Claire had written, 'surpasses all that may be imagined monstrous but already in your birth Nature had set her warning mark upon you, unheeding that, by my own blindness have I fallen.' *CCJ*, p. 193.

278 '*so much of leg and so much of thigh*': *CCJ*, p. 225. Claire wrote a
long critique of Byron's work, seemingly influenced by conversations with Shelley, who was then composing his 'Defence of
Poetry'. The full critique is as follows:

'He ne'er is crown'd/With immortality who fears to follow/
Where airy voices lead'. It is for this reason that I think
L.B.'s poetry will not immortalise him; it is so entirely
divested of any thing pertainable to the aerial voice of
imagination, so sensual, so tangible that like every thing
corporeal, it must die. His song is woven of the commonest
and grossest elements of our Nature; desire, hatred,
revenge, a proneness to mischief spoilation and cruelty,
the description of these animal appetites, interspersed here
and there with an appeal to freedom which however a
marked animosity to philosophy and virtue renders null
and void from both the groundwork and superstructure
of this Poets works. They are pictures of animal life of the
sensations which belong to the robust body of a savage
whose senses bear a most immoderate preponderance in
the sum total of his being. It is a measurement of the body
of Man; there is so much of leg and so much of thigh,
hands feet &&c in proportion without a sign of the lord
and master of the mansion, the soul. This poet's hand
seems to[o] heavy to paint the subtle motions of the invisible inhabitant whose etherial emanations create the grace
and poetry of life. Again we repeat his poetry is the poetry
of the body and the poetry of the body is to the poesy of
the soul, what prose is by the side of poetry. Prose is the
language of every day life: it is used by lawyer, cooks,
dancing masters and courtiers: it expresses our wants, our
sicknesses, our crimes and our follies: it is dedicated to
the service of that part of us which is destined to the grave.
Poetry however has been throughout the long age of the
world, the ornament, the song, the music of humanity: it
has more particularly been the handmaid of the immortal

sojourner on Earth the soul, waiting to celebrate the inspirations of this mysterious power which to become visible to man assume the shapes of noble actions, as the mute Eolian strings wait for the breathing wind ere they swell into music; so poetry bursts into harmony inspired by mental perfection. Nature which is the unsubstantial food on which the soul feeds is as equally neglected by this poet: except one or two passages in a style so totally different that we wonder how they came there; he looks upon her fair adorned breast, not as if it were the bosom of beauty, the pillow upon which the golden locks of poetry should reposes, but as so much space alloted [*sic*] for the completion of his desires. Religion too with him becomes earthly: she bears him not to the heavenly spaces informing them with beneficence and promises of eternal happiness: he turns her into a demon; the fit companion of his savage heroes, bending to all their purposes; the Jack Ketch of the Almighty blowing the last trump as a signal to to [*sic*] execute an eternal doom of suffering upon criminal myriads: such are his praise offerings to the Creator of Beauty and Goodness: the possessor of never ending beneficence. (*CCJ*, pp. 225–6.)

278 *Austrian spies*: *SC*, vol. 10, p. 709.
278 *They began to organise*: See *BLJ*, vol. 8, pp. 40, 47, 45–6.
279 '*The king-times are fast finishing*': *BLJ*, vol. 8, p. 26.
279 *a contorted double plot*: Medwin, p. 26.
279 *and made plans to ambush the artillery*: *BLJ*, vol. 8, p. 43.
279 '*no reason to look upon my personal safety as particularly insurable*': *BLJ*, vol. 8, p. 97. It seems that Teresa suggested that Allegra might also be placed with an 'elderly lady' of her acquaintance. *BLJ*, vol. 8, p. 33.
279 '*a life of ignorance and degradation*': *CC*, vol. 1, p. 163.
279 '*bad wives and most unnatural mothers*': *CC*, vol. 1, p.163.
280 '*Our solitary mode of life*': *Letters PBS*, vol. 2, p. 283; vol. 2, p. 291.
280 '*calm voice and with the gentlest looks*': *CC*, vol. 1, p. 309.

280 '*not marry with a Native of Great Britain*': 'Codicil to the Last Will and Testament of the Right Honourable George Gordon, Lord Byron.' Signed Byron, Newton Hanson, and William Fletcher, Venice, 17 November 1818, Murray, MS 43547. 'It is besides my wish that She should be a Rm *Catholic*,' he told Hoppner, 'which I look upon as the best religion as it is assuredly the oldest of the various branches of Christianity.' *BLJ*, vol. 8, p. 98.

280 '*that to allow the Child to be with her mother*': *BLJ*, vol. 8, p. 98.

280 '*any Swiss clergyman*': 'If you were willing to place Allegra on the family of any Swiss clergyman,' wrote Hoppner, 'where she would be brought up according to any ideas for the future establishments you may suggest, I can only say, that as we propose visiting Switzerland in the course of the month, we will most willingly take charge of her, and place her in such a situation as both you and her Mother cannot fail to be satisfied with, and which will still have you the means of establishing her in the continent as you propose, without being liable to the objection made by Claira [*sic*] "of the ignorance and profligacy of Italian women all pupils of convents". – Should this idea meet with your convenience, it would not be difficult for you to send Allegra to us, and from what Clara proposes in regard to the childs establishment in a boarding school I conceive there will be no difficulty in obtaining from her a promise not to interfere directly or indirectly with her, nor ever to attempt seeing her contrary to any stipulation you may deem is proper to make. In submitting this proposal to your consideration I have only further to remark that if there is any truth in the objections suggested by Clara; of the affair in the manner she describes, such a plan must remove them.' ALS, Richard Hoppner to Lord Byron, Venice, 2 May 1821, Murray, MS 43448.

280 '*If I had but known yr. notion*': *BLJ*, vol. 8, p. 112.

281 '*Allegra was not by any means an amiable child*': Quoted in Marchand, vol. 2, p. 747.

281 *Byron had had some experience of Capuchins*: *BLJ*, vol. 2, pp. 12–13.

281 *subsist solely on alms*: *CC*, vol. 2, p. 612;

281 *'proper treatment and attention'*: *CC*, vol. 1, p. 164. There is some disagreement over the exact date of Allegra's entry into the convent at Bagnacavallo, and while Stocking (*CC*, vol. 1, p. xlii), puts her date of admission at 10 March 1821, the bill presented to Byron following his daughter's death states her date of admission as 1 March. Murray, MS 43547.

282 *the items she had been instructed to bring*: Origo, *Measure of Love*, p. 54.

282 *a dinner for the nuns*: Origo, *Measure of Love*, p. 54.

282 *face being shut up in a convent of her own*: *Letters PBS*, vol. 2, p. 316.

282 *Shelley travelled to Byron*: *Letters PBS*, vol. 2, p. 316.

282 *'nothing new'*: Shelley's account of the gossip to Mary can be found at *Letters PBS*, vol. 2, pp. 317–9. The letter Shelley asked Mary to write to Mrs Hoppner can be found at *Letters MWS*, vol. 1, pp. 205–9.

282 *'Gunpowder and fire'*: *Letters PBS*, vol. 2, p. 323.

283 *'lull him into security'*: *Letters PBS*, vol. 2, p. 399.

283 *bring Allegra with him*: That Byron agreed to bring Allegra to Pisa is intimated in *CC*, vol. 1, p. 169, and more explicitly in Pforz, Cl.Cl.26, p. 6. That he saw Allegra's residence at Bagnacavallo as only temporary is expressed in *BLJ*, vol. 8, p. 103.

283 *Mary was instructed to search for suitable* palazzi: *Letters PBS*, vol. 2, p. 331.

283 *a tour of the convent*: *Letters PBS*, vol. 2, p. 334; Origo, *Measure of Love*, p. 83.

283 *'a thing of finer race and higher order'*: *Letters PBS*, vol. 2, p. 334.

283 *'All of golden silk'*: *Letters PBS*, vol. 2, p. 334.

283 *'a message'*: *Letters PBS*, vol. 2, p. 334.

283 *'Long Chamber'*: Chandos, *Boys Together*, p. 87.

284 *'Her intellect is not much cultivated here'*: *Letters PBS*, vol. 2, pp. 334–5.

285 *'having incurred a debt of honour'*: Rossetti, *Family Letters*, vol. 1, p. 33.

285 *country cottage in Holmer Green*: Rossetti, *Family Letters*, vol. 1, p. 79.

285 *complained of pains in his side*: WA f. 4. See also Viets, 'By the Visitation of God', 1774.

285 '*deranged mind*': WA f. 5.

286 *had nursed his beloved sister Frances back to health*: Macdonald, p. 238.

286 *Everyone . . . suspected John had killed himself*: Rossetti, *Family Letters*, vol. 1, p. 33.

286 *chewing them stimulated poetic creativity*: See Nora Crook and Derek Guiton, *Shelley's Venomed Melody* (Cambridge: Cambridge University Press, 1986), pp. 75–6.

287 '*the visitation of God*': WA f. 1.

287 '*too sanguine hopes of literary fame*': Medwin, p. 105. Byron would later tell Lady Blessington a peculiar story that seemed to contain a small memory of Polidori, albeit in an oddly transposed form. It concerned an Italian princess who was said to be so in love with Vittorio Alfieri that she ran to see him on hearing the news that he was due to pass within fifty miles of her house. Arriving at his inn, the lady ran up to his room and, finding there a man sitting at a desk writing, thrust herself upon him, showering him with kisses. At this point, Alfieri entered the room to discover the lady in his secretary's lap, and stormed out, highly offended that his secretary could ever be mistaken for a man as great as he. See Lovell (ed.), *Lady Blessington's Conversations*, 64–5.

287 '*Trust Byron*': Bieri, *Shelley*, p. 592.

287 *so averse to being looked at*: Moore, p. 566.

288 *whispered to by a spectral voice*: BLJ, vol. 9, p. 74–5.

288 '*detested intimacy*': *Letters MWS*, vol. 2, pp. 143–4.

288 *Shelley's attraction to him remained strong*: See *CC*, vol. 1, p.172; *Letters PBS*, vol. 2, p. 399.

288 *He was drawn to him once more*: *Letters PBS*, vol. 2, p. 338.

288 '*I despair of rivalling Lord Byron*': *Letters PBS*, vol. 2, p. 323.

288 *all Shelley's enquiries*: See *Letters PBS*, vol. 2, p. 309; *CC*, vol. 1, p. 169; Pforz Cl.Cl.26 6.

288 *due to Teresa's jealousy*: Pforz, Cl.Cl.26, p. 103.

289 *shocked and humiliated*: See *CCJ*, pp. 274–8.

289 *'as if my Allegra were dead'*: CC, vol. 1, p. 170.

289 *'the children of small shop keepers'*: Pforz, Cl.Cl.26, p. 6. In her 1869/70 correspondence with Edward John Trelawny, Claire claimed to have sent Mr Tighe on a fact-finding mission to uncover the truth about Bagnacavallo and Teresa Guiccioli, a trip that remained secret to all except Lady Mount Cashell and herself.

289 *had rescued her from Bagnacavallo*: Claire said to Shelley, 'Now she shall never go back again.' CCJ, p. 228.

289 *she dreamed she had received a letter*: CCJ, p. 235.

289 *'Women could not live without making scenes'*: Pforz, Cl.Cl.26, p. 6.

289 *devised a scheme to infiltrate the convent*: In the 1870s, Edward Silsbee recorded a conversation with Claire in which she had said that she 'shd go to the convent to stay there as a pensioner boarder'. CC, vol. 2, p. 658.

290 *'high walls and bolted doors'*: Letters MWS, vol. 1, p. 225.

290 *'No spring has passed with out some piece of ill luck'*: Letters MWS, vol. 1, p. 226.

290 *'madness'*: Letters PBS, vol. 2, p. 399, 400.

290 *'Wd you go to America?'*: Letters MWS, vol. 1, pp. 225–6.

290 *Teresa Viviani*: Letters PBS, vol. 2, p. 267.

290 *'crawling motion of the Death Worm'*: CCJ, pp. 432–3. 'What would one say,' the passage continues, 'of a Woman . . . how would [one] feel towards her who should go and gaze upon the spectacle of a Child led to the scaffold, one would turn from her in horror – yet she did so, she looked coolly on, rejoiced in the comfortable place she had got in the shew, chatted with her neighbours . . . never winced during the exhibition and after all was over went up and claimed acquaintance with the executioner and shook hands with him.'

291 *'dreadfully agitated'*: Moore, p. 567; Marchand, vol. 3, p. 991.

291 *'It is now hoped that she can be kept out of danger'*: Marchand, vol. 3, p. 991.

291 *'The young lady's situation is still dangerous'*: ALS, Marianna Fabbri to Lega Zambelli, Bagnacavallo, 20 April 1822, BL MS Add 46873. Translation by Lindsay Eufusia.

292 *'She is more fortunate than we are'*: Moore, p. 568.

292 *Byron did not have the stomach*: See Teresa Guiccioli, *Lord Byron's Life in Italy*, ed. Peter Cochrane, trans. Michael Rees (Newark: University of Delaware Press, 2005), p. 443.

292 '*I do not know that I have any thing to reproach in my conduct*': *BLJ*, vol. 9, p. 147.

292 '*like a torrent*': *Letters MWS*, vol. 1, p. 236.

293 *immediately guessed*: Jones (ed.), *Gisborne and Williams*, p. 146.

293 *she wrote to eviscerate Byron*: This letter is lost, but Shelley alludes to it in *Letters PBS*, vol. 2, p. 416.

293 '*death had stamped with truth*': *Letters MWS*, vol. 1, p. 235.

293 '*While she lived*': Lovell (ed.), *Lady Blessington's Conversations*, p. 50.

293 '*There it is again!*': Jones (ed.), *Gisborne and Williams*, p. 147.

Epilogue

294 '*Uncle John*': William Michael Rossetti, *Rossetti Papers, 1862–1870* (New York: Scribner's, 1903), p. 159.

296 '*glorious idealism*': William Michael Rossetti, *Some Reminiscences of William Michael Rossetti*, 2 vols (New York: Scribner's, 1906), vol. 1, pp. 57–8.

296 '*the Sanctum*': See Stephen Hebron, 'The Shelley Sanctum,' in Stephen Hebron and Elizabeth Denlinger, *Shelley's Ghost: Reshaping the Image of a Literary Family* (Oxford: Bodleian Library, 2010), pp. 137–59.

297 '*Shelley had no more to do with it*': Lady Shelley to R. Garnett, 6 October 1859, quoted in William Richard Thurman, Jr, 'Letters About Shelley from the Richard Garnett Papers, University of Texas', unpublished doctoral dissertation (University of Texas at Austin, 1972), p. 36. See also Lady Jane Shelley (ed.), *Shelley Memorials From Authentic Sources* (London: 1875), pp. 64–5. Some had made bold to counter this view, specifically Thomas Love Peacock, although he, too, was dead by the time Rossetti came to compose his work. 'There was no estrangement, no shadow of a thought of separation,' wrote Peacock in 1860, 'till Shelley became acquainted . . . with the lady who was subsequently his second wife.' Peacock, *Memoirs of Shelley*, p. 50.

297 *the ghost of Mary Shelley appeared*: Hebron, 'Shelley Sanctum', p. 152.

297 '*outspoken as to the merits and demerits*': Rossetti, *Reminiscences*, vol. 2, p. 363.

297 *Edward John Trelawny*: R. S. Garnett (ed.), *Letters About Shelley Interchanged by Three Friends: Edward Dowden, Richard Garnett and W. M. Rossetti* (London: Hodder and Stoughton, 1917), p. 25. Claire and Trelawny were not the sole survivors of the group. Jane Williams was still alive, having outlived Thomas Jefferson Hogg, with whom she had lived in a common-law marriage since the death of Edward Williams, who had drowned alongside Shelley.

297 '*Everything that old folks do, I do not*': Edward John Trelawny, *Letters of Edward John Trelawny*, ed. H. Buxton Forman (London: Frowde, 1910), p. 228.

297 *talking about Byron and Shelley for up to nine hours straight*: Garnett (ed.), *Letters About Shelley*, p. 42. On 14 January 1872, Rossetti wrote: 'I saw Trelawny last Sunday, and am to see him again tomorrow. He continues highly vigorous, and kept up any amount of talk about Shelley etc. for 9 continuous hours. He has been writing down various supplementary reminiscences, and Miss Clairmont continues writing to him, and has some idea of publishing.'

298 *insane and living in an asylum*: As Rossetti told Richard Garnett: 'Trelawny tells me that Miss Clairmont is mad, and in an asylum.' *CC*, vol. 2, p. 601, fn. 1. Trelawny had said the same to the painter Seymour Kirkup, who lived in Florence, been a friend to Keats and had known Trelawny since the 1820s. See Garnett (ed.), *Letters About Shelley*, p. 25.

298 *They had become lovers*: Jones (ed.), *Gisborne and Williams*, p. 144; *CCJ*, p. 284.

298 '*violent defenders of the Rights of Women*': *CC*, vol. 2, p. 323.

298 '*He lies like a porcupine in my way*': *CCJ*, leaflet appendix, undated.

299 '*This I always thought was a lie*': Quoted in Gittings and Manton, *Clairmont and the Shelleys*, p. 112.

299 '*I am unhappily the victim of a* happy passion': *CC*, vol. 1, pp. 240–41.

299 ' *"erase" all mention of Claire*': Letters MWS, vol. 1, pp. 475–6.

300 '*She poisoned my life when young*': Letters MWS, vol. 2, p. 271.

300 '*stranger in the Shelley family*': Quoted in R. Glyn Grylls, *Claire Clairmont: Mother of Byron's Allegra* (London: John Murray, 1939), p. 211. This appears to have happened around 1875, as Clairmont was using Robert Browning as an intermediary to help her sell some Shelley letters.

300 '*very English*': CC, vol. 2, p. 601, fn. 1.

301 *Claire had never seen her daughter's body*: PBS Letters, vol. 2, pp. 415–6.

301 *a goat's body buried in her place*: As a hastily scribbled memo in Edward Silsbee's notebook tells us, in her later life Claire clung to the remote possibility that her daughter was still alive and living in the convent: 'Allegra was buried in England, says a story was that she did not die, but a goats body was substituted and sent there.' CC, vol. 2, p. 608, fn. 2.

301 '*absurd quarantine laws*': Trelawny, *Letters*, p. 218. See ALS, Enrico Marmani to Pellegrino Ghigi, Bagnacavallo, 24 May 1822, BL MS Add 46873. Translation by Lindsay Eufusia. The disagreement was not sorted out for many months. When Byron left Pisa the following year, he left Ghigi in charge of all his animals: 'A Goat with a broken leg (sold for 1 sc. 80), An ugly country Dog, A Bird which could only eat Fish, A Badger on a Chain, Two ugly old Monkeys.' Typed translation of original Italian MS, n.d. Murray, MS 43448.

301 '*A Goat with a broken leg*': Typed translation of original Italian MS, no date. Murray MS 43448.

301 *Palmer and Sons*: 'For the Funeral of Allegra Daughter of G.G. Lord Byron, performed by B. Palmer and Sons', 10 September 1822, Murray, MS 43448.

301 '*I shall go to her*': BLJ, vol. 9, pp. 163–4.

302 *mother of the novelist Anthony Trollope*: R. Glyn Grylls, 'Lines Written by a Celebrated Authoress on the Burial of the Daughter of a Celebrated Author', *Keats-Shelley Memorial Association*, 27 (1976), pp. 10–13.

302 '*The story of this Child's burial*': BLJ, vol. 10, p. 55.

302 '*had a small statue made*': 'Effects that belonged to Miss Byron, still existing', BL MS Add 46873. Translation by Lindsay Eufusia.

302 '*I would cure you of your wild fancy*': Trelawny, *Letters*, pp. 220, 222–3.

303 '*I understand your feeling and respect it*': Pforz, Cl.CL.26, p. 2.

303 '*that a woman without rank, without riches*': *CC*, vol. 2, p. 628.

304 '*Your confidential letter is safe*': *BLJ*, vol. 5, p. 88.

304 '*none knew that secret besides us*': Pforz, Cl.Cl.26, pp. 51–3.

304 *to become his mortal enemy*: According to a letter Claire wrote to her sister-in-law, Antonia, *c.*1869, 'In the year 1816 [Byron] told the Shelleys, that his sister was his mistress and her daughter Medora whom he called Little Do was his child and he shewed them letters from his sister with great spaces in them written in cyphers.' Pforz, Cl.Cl.26, p. 108. The issue of sexual propriety within the group had been raised by the publication in 1869 of C. Mackay's *Medora Leigh: A History and Autobiography*, and Harriet Beecher Stowe's 'The True Story of Lady Byron's Life', two works that claimed Byron had had an incestuous affair with his sister Augusta Leigh and fathered a child by her in 1814. Claire and Trelawny discussed the scandal in their correspondence, and in 'My Recollections of Lord Byron' she tells him that Byron confirmed it one evening in Geneva 'by saying that his sister Augusta was his mistress and little Do (Medora) was his and her child'. Pforz, Cl.Cl.26, pp. 39–40.

304 '*Now you know the reason why*': Pforz, Cl.Cl.26, p. 105.

305 '*persecute me for* ever': Doris Langley Moore, *Ada, Countess of Lovelace: Byron's Legitimate Daughter* (London: John Murray, 1977), p. 372. See also Marchand, vol. 2, pp. 616–7, 638–9.

305 '*Where there is a mystery*': Byron, 'Augustus Darvell', p. 450.

305 '*slender, pallid old lady*': Rossetti, *Reminiscences*, vol. 2, p. 353.

306 *Plin*: *CC*, vol. 2, p. 654.

306 '*so charming so tender so charitable*': *CC*, vol. 2, p. 655.

306 '<u>*Gurli*</u>': *CC*, vol. 2, p. 654. It has been conjectured that the fragment was composed in response to an 1875 letter from Trelawny that urged Claire to commit her memories to paper before it was too late – 'There is time for you to do it but not time to

shilly shally' – a request she rebuffed by pleading age and ill health (Trelawny, *Letters*, p. 247). However, close examination of both handwriting and paper stock leads me to believe that this memoir was written several years earlier as, while they are undated, they were composed on the same paper Claire had used to transcribe letters of her mother that she sent to Trelawny in 1870. The leaves used are exercise-book-style sheets, lined, folded once, and cross-written with a clear 'G.C.' watermark. The handwriting on both the memoir and the letters is also much thicker than on Claire's later correspondence. While this hardly constitutes proof, it might at least give some credence to the idea that both the Mary Jane Godwin letters and the memoir were produced around the same time. As Trelawny was showing the Mary Jane Godwin letters around London in 1872, they, at least, had been written before 1875.

307 *The result was an angry fragment*: Pforz, Cl.Cl.26, pp. 140–41.

307 '*Under the influence [of]the doctrine and belief in free Love*': Pforz, Cl.Cl.26, pp. 139–42. The overlapping, over-written draft paragraphs have been separated and reassembled by myself. A full transcript is forthcoming in a future volume of *Shelley and His Circle*.

307 '*Byronic nature*': *CC*, vol. 2, p. 658.

308 '*She passed her life in sufferings*': *CC*, vol. 2, p. 641.

308 '*Love, fame, ambition*': *BCPW*, vol. 2, p. 165.

BIBLIOGRAPHY

Adams, Rev. John, *The Flowers of Modern Travels; Being Elegant, Entertaining, and Instructive Extracts, Selected from the Works of the Most Celebrated Travellers*, 3 vols (London, 1799)

Alfieri, Vittorio, *Memoirs*, trans. Anon., revised E. R. Vincent (London: Oxford University Press, 1961)

Almeida, Hermione De, *Romantic Medicine and John Keats* (New York and Oxford: Oxford University Press, 1991)

Almond, Dom Cuthbert, *The History of Ampleforth Abbey From the Foundation of St Lawrence's Dieulouard to the Present* (London: Washbourne, 1903)

Altick, Richard, *The Shows of London* (Cambridge, Mass.: Belknap, 1978)

Angelo, Henry, *The Reminiscences of Henry Angelo*, 2 vols (New York and London: Blom, 1969)

Anon., *The Art of Puffing: An Inaugural Oration* (Edinburgh: 1765)

Anon., *Billets in the Low Countries 1814 to 1817, in a Series of Letters* (London: 1818)

Anon., 'Extract of a Letter from Geneva', *New Monthly Magazine*, 11:63, April (London: 1819), pp. 193–5

Anon., *A London Directory, or Alphabetical Arrangement; Containing the Names and Residences of the Merchants, Manufacturers, and Principal Traders in the Metropolis and its Environs* (London: 1797)

Anon., *A Hand-book for Travellers on the Continent* (London: 1836)

Anon., *List of the Graduates in Medicine in the University of Edinburgh from MDCCV to MDCCCLXVI* (Edinburgh: 1867)

Anon., *Sketches of Obscure Poets, with Specimens of their Writings* (London: 1833)

Anon., *The Traveller's Guide Through Scotland and Its Islands*, 6th edition, 2 vols (Edinburgh: 1814)

Baedeker, K. *Switzerland, and the Adjacent Portions of Italy, Savoy, and the Tyrol: Handbook for Travellers* (London: 1883)

Baillie, Marianne, *First Impressions on a Tour Upon the Continent in the Summer of 1181, Through Parts of France, Italy, Switzerland, The Borders of Germany, and a Part of French Flanders* (London: 1818)

Bainbridge, Simon, *Napoleon and English Romanticism* (Cambridge: Cambridge University Press, 1995)

Barnard, John, '"The Busy Time": Keats's Duties at Guy's Hospital from Autumn 1816 to March 1817', *Romanticism*, 3:3 (2007), pp. 199–218

Baron, J. H., 'Illnesses and Creativity: Byron's Appetites, James Joyce's Gut, and Melba's Meals and *Mésalliances*', *British Medical Journal*, 315 (20 December 1997), 1697–1703.

Barrett, Eaton Stannard, *The Talents Run Mad; or, Eighteen Hundred and Sixteen* (London: 1816)

Beer, Gavin de, 'An Atheist in the Alps', *Keats-Shelley Memorial Bulletin*, IX (1958), pp. 1–15

— 'Byron's French Passport', *Keats-Shelley Memorial Bulletin*, XX (1969), pp. 31–36

Bernard, Richard Boyle, *A Tour Through Some Parts of France, Switzerland, Savoy, Germany and Belgium, During the Summer and Autumn of 1814* (London: 1815)

Bickley, Francis (ed.), *The Diaries of Sylvester Douglas*, 2 vols (London: Constable, 1928)

Bieri, James, *Percy Bysshe Shelley: A Biography* (Baltimore: 2008)

Boas, Louise Schutz, *Harriet Shelley: Five Long Years* (London: Oxford University Press, 1962)

Bone, Drummond (ed.), *The Cambridge Companion to Byron* (Cambridge: Cambridge University Press, 2004)

Bowring, Edgar Alfred (ed.), *The Tragedies of Vittorio Alfieri*, 2 vols (Westport, Conn.: Greenwood, 1876, reprint 1970)

Braudy, Leo, *The Frenzy of Renown: Fame and Its History* (New York: Vintage Books, 1997)

Broman, Thomas H., 'The Medical Sciences', *The Cambridge History of Science*, 7 vols, vol. 4, pp. 463–84 (Cambridge: Cambridge University Press, 2008)

Brown, Ford K. 'Notes on 41 Skinner Street', *Modern Language Notes*, 54:5 (May 1939), pp. 326–32

Brydges, Sir Egerton, *Recollections of Foreign Travel, On Life, Literature, and Self-Knowledge*, 2 vols (London: 1825)

Burnctt, T. A., *The Rise and Fall of a Regency Dandy: The Life and Times of Scrope Berdmore Davies* (Boston: Little, Brown, 1981)

Campbell, Charles, *The Traveller's Complete Guide Through Belgium, Holland, and Germany* (London: 1815)

Casanova, Giacomo, *History of My Life*, trans. Willard R. Trask, 12 vols (Baltimore and London: Johns Hopkins University Press, 1997)

Castle, Egerton (ed.), *The Jerningham Letters (1780–1843): Being Excerpts from the Correspondence and Diaries of the Honourable Lady Jerningham*, 2 vols (London: 1896)

Chandos, John, *Boys Together: English Public Schools, 1800–1864* (London: Hutchinson, 1984)

Chew, Samuel, *Byron in England: His Fame and After-Fame* (New York: Russell and Russell, 1965)

Christensen, Jerome, *Lord Byron's Strength: Romantic Writing and Commercial Society* (Baltimore and London: Johns Hopkins University Press, 1993)

Christison, Sir Robert, *The Life of Sir Robert Christison, Edited by His Sons*, 2 vols (Edinburgh and London: 1884)

Clark, William S., 'Milton and the Villa Diodati', *Review of English Studies*, 11:41 (January 1935), pp. 51–7

Clubbe, John, 'The Tempest-toss'd Summer of 1816: Mary Shelley's *Frankenstein*', *Byron Journal*, 19 (1991), pp. 26–40

Coleman, Deirdre, 'Claire Clairmont and Mary Shelley: Identification and Rivalry Within the "tribe of the Otaheite philosopher's"', *Women's Writing*, 6:3 (1999), pp. 309–28

Coleridge, Samuel Taylor, *The Collected Letters of Samuel Taylor Coleridge*, ed. Earl Leslie Griggs. 6 vols (Oxford: Clarendon, 1959)

— 'On the Errors of Party Spirit: Or Extremes Meet', *The Complete Works of Samuel Taylor Coleridge*, ed. W. G. T. Shedd, 7 vols, vol. 2, pp. 187–202 (New York, Harper Bros, 1884)

Comrie, John D., *The History of Scottish Medicine*. 2nd edition, 2 vols (London: Wellcome Institute, 1932)

Cox, D., *Directions for Medicine Chests; with Remarks, etc., on Medicine and Surgery* (London: 1799)

Cozens-Hardy, Basil (ed.), *The Diary of Sylas Neville, 1767–1788* (London: Oxford University Press, 1950)

Cramer, Anselm, *Ampleforth: The Story of St Laurence's Abbey and College* (Ampleforth: Trustees of Ampleforth Abbey, 2001)

Crompton, Louis, *Byron and Greek Love: Homophobia in 19th-Century England* (Berkeley: University of California Press, 1985)

Cronin, Richard, *Paper Pellets: British Literary Culture after Waterloo* (Oxford: Oxford University Press, 2010)

Crook, Nora (ed.), *The Novels and Selected Works of Mary Shelley*, 8 vols (London: Pickering and Chatto, 1996)

— and Derek Guiton, *Shelley's Venomed Melody* (Cambridge: Cambridge University Press, 1986)

Dallas, Robert Charles, *Recollections of the Life of Lord Byron from the Year 1808 to the End of 1814* (London: 1824)

Darnton, Robert, *The Great Cat Massacre and Other Episodes in French Cultural History* (New York: Vintage, 1985)

Denlinger, Elizabeth, *Before Victoria: Extraordinary Women of the British Romantic Era* (New York: New York Public Library/Columbia University Press, 2005)

D'Israeli, Isaac, *Miscellanies of Literature*, revised edition (London: 1840)

Dodd, Charles Edward, *An Autumn Near the Rhine; or, Sketches of Courts, Society, Scenery, etc., in Some of the German States Bordering on the Rhine* (London: 1818)

Doughty, Oswald, *Perturbed Spirit: The Life and Personality of Samuel Taylor Coleridge* (Rutherford: Farleigh Dickinson University Press, 1981)

Doyle, John A. (ed.), *Memoir and Correspondence of Susan Ferrier, 1782–1854* (London: 1898)

Duggan, Christopher, *The Force of Destiny: A History of Italy Since 1796* (Boston: Houghton Mifflin, 2008)

Douglass, Paul, *Lady Caroline Lamb: A Biography* (Basingstoke: Palgrave Macmillan, 2004)

Dowden, Wilfred S., 'Byron and the Austrian Censorship', *Keats-Shelley Journal* 4 (Winter 1955), pp. 67–75

Eaton, Charlotte, *Waterloo Days: The Narrative of an Englishwoman Resident at Brussels in June, 1815*, new edition (London: 1888)

Ebel, M. J. G., *The Traveller's Guide Through Switzerland*, (London: 1820)

Edgcumbe, Richard (ed.), *The Diary of Frances, Lady Shelley* (New York: Scribner, 1912)

Edgeworth, Richard Lovell, *Essays on Professional Education*, 2nd edition (London: 1812)

Eisner, Eric, *Nineteenth-Century Poetry and Literary Celebrity* (Basingstoke: Palgrave Macmillan, 2009)

Ellis, David, *Byron in Geneva: That Summer of 1816* (Liverpool: Liverpool University Press, 2011)

Elwin, Malcolm, *Lord Byron's Wife* (New York: Harcourt, Brace & World, 1962)

Ekelenz, Michael (ed.), *The Geneva Notebook of Percy Bysshe Shelley: Bodleian MS. Shelley adds. e. 16 and MS. Shelley adds. c. 4, Folios 63, 65, 71, and 72, A Facsimile Edition with Transcriptions and Textual Notes* (New York: Garland, 1992)

Faulkner, Thomas, *Historical and Topographical Account of Fulham, including the Hamlet of Hammersmith* (London: 1813)

Feltoe, Charles Lett, *Memorials of John Flint South* (London: 1884)

Garnett, R. S. (ed.), *Letters About Shelley Interchanged by Three Friends: Edward Dowden, Richard Garnett and W. M. Rossetti* (London: Hodder and Stoughton, 1917)

Gaull, Marilyn, *English Romanticism: The Human Context* (New York: Norton, 1988)

Genest, John, *Some Account of the English Stage From 1660–830*, 10 vols (Bath: 1832)

Gittings, Robert, and Jo Manton, *Claire Clairmont and the Shelleys* (Oxford: Oxford University Press, 1992)

Godwin, William, *The Diary of William Godwin*, ed. Victoria Myers, David O'Shaughnessy and Mark Philp (Oxford: Oxford Digital Library, 2010) http://godwindiary.bodleian.ox.ac.uk.

— *An Enquiry Concerning Political Justice and its Influence on General Virtue and Happiness* (London: 1793)

— 'Essay on Sepulchres', *Political and Philosophical Writings of William Godwin*, ed. Mark Philp, 7 vols, vol. 6, pp. 3–30 (London: William Pickering, 1993)

— *Memoirs of Mary Wollstonecraft* (London: 1798)

— *St Leon*, ed. Pamela Clemit (Oxford: Oxford World's Classics, 1994)

Gordon, Pryse Lockhart, *Personal Memoirs; or, Reminiscences of Men and Manners at Home and Abroad, During the Last Half Century*, 2 vols (London: 1830)

— 'Sketches from the Portfolio of a Sexagenarian', *New Monthly Magazine and Literary Journal*, 26 (1829), pp. 191–200.

Graham, Peter W. (ed.), *Byron's Bulldog: The Letters of John Cam Hobhouse* (Columbus: Ohio State University Press, 1984)

Grylls, R. Glyn, *Claire Clairmont: Mother of Byron's Allegra* (London: John Murray, 1939)

— 'Lines Written by a Celebrated Authoress on the Burial of the Daughter of a Celebrated Author', *Keats-Shelley Memorial Association*, 27 (1976), pp. 10–13.

Guiccioli, Teresa, *Lord Byron's Life in Italy*, ed. Peter Cochrane, trans. Michael Rees (Newark: University of Delaware Press, 2005)

Harson, Robert R., 'A Clarification Concerning John Polidori, Lord Byron's Physician', *Keats-Shelley Journal*, 21–22 (1972–3), pp. 38–40

Häusermann, H. W., *The Genevese Background: Studies of Shelley, Francis Danby, Maria Edgeworth, Ruskin, Meredith, and Joseph Conrad (With Hitherto Unpublished Letters)* (London: Routledge and Kegan Paul, 1952)

Hay, Daisy, *Young Romantics: The Shelleys, Byron, and Other Tangled Lives* (London: Bloomsbury, 2010)

Haydon, Benjamin Robert, *Life of Benjamin Robert Haydon*, ed. Tom Taylor, 3 vols (London: 1853)

Hazlitt, William, 'On Envy (A Dialogue)', *The Plain Speaker: Opinions on Books, Men, and Things*, 2 vols (London: Colburn, 1826), vol. 1, pp. 229–54

— 'My First Acquaintance with Poets', Duncan Wu (ed.), *Romanticism: An Anthology*, 2nd edition (Blackwell: Malden, 1998), pp. 600–610

Hebron, Stephen, and Elizabeth Denlinger, *Shelley's Ghost: Reshaping the Image of a Literary Family* (Oxford: Bodleian Library, 2010)

Hewlett, Dorothy, *A Life of John Keats*, 3rd edition (New York: Barnes and Noble, 1970)

Hibbert, Christopher (ed.), *Captain Gronow: His Reminiscences of Regency and Victorian life, 1810–60* (London: Kyle Cathie, 1991)

Higgins, David, *Romantic Genius and the Literary Magazine: Biography, Celebrity, Politics* (London and New York: Routledge, 2005)

Hobhouse, John Cam, Lord Broughton, *A Journey Through Albania, and Other Provinces of Turkey in Europe and Asia, to Constantinople During the Years 1809 and 1810*, 2 vols (London: 1813)

— *Contemporary Account of the Separation of Lord and Lady Byron; Also of the Destruction of Lord Byron's Memoirs* (London: privately printed, 1870)

— *Recollections of A Long Life*, 2 vols (New York: Scribner, 1909)

Hogg, Thomas Jefferson. *The Life of Percy Bysshe Shelley*. 2 vols (London: 1858)

Holme, Thea, *Caroline: A Biography of Caroline of Brunswick* (New York: Atheneum, 1980)

Hoobler, Dorothy and Thomas, *The Monsters: Mary Shelley and the Curse of Frankenstein* (New York: Back Bay Books, 2007)

Hookham, Thomas, *A Walk Through Switzerland in September 1816* (London: 1818)

Howard, Martin, *Wellington's Doctors: The British Army Medical Service in the Napoleonic Wars* (Staplehurst: Spellmount, 2002)

Hunt, Leigh, *Lord Byron and Some of His Contemporaries, with Recollections of the Author's Life and of His Visit to Italy* (London: 1828)

Hunt, Thornton Leigh. 'Shelley, by One Who Knew Him', *Atlantic Monthly* (February 1863), pp. 184–204

Huscher, Herbert, 'The Clairmont Enigma', *Keats-Shelley Memorial Bulletin*, 11 (1960), pp. 13–20

Johnson, J., *A Guide for Gentlemen Studying Medicine at the University of Edinburgh* (London: 1792)

Johnson, Samuel, *The Lives of the English Poets: and A Criticism on Their Works*, 3 vols (Dublin: 1780–81)

Jones, Frederick L. (ed.), *Maria Gisborne and Edward E. Williams, Shelley's Friends: Their Journals and Letters* (Norman: University of Oklahoma Press, 1951)

Joukovsky, Nicholas (ed.), *The Letters of Thomas Love Peacock*, 2 vols (Oxford: Clarendon, 2001)

Jousiffe, M. J., *A Road Book For Switzerland and Chamounix and the Route over the Simplon to Milan* (London: 1839)

Keats, John, *Selected Letters of John Keats*, ed. Grant F. Scott, revised edition (Cambridge, Mass.: Harvard University Press, 2002)

Kent, Elizabeth, *Flora Domestica, or the Portable Flower-Garden; With Directions for the Treatment of Plants in Pots; and Ilustrations from the Works of the Poets*, 2nd edition (London: 1825)

Knapp, Andrew, and William Baldwin, *The Newgate Calendar*, 4 vols (London: 1825)

Lamb, Lady Caroline, *Glenarvon*, ed. Deborah Lutz (Kansas City: Valancourt, 2007)

Leighton, Alexander, *The Court of Caucus; or, the Story of Burke and Hare* (Edinburgh: 1861)

Lewis, Matthew L. (ed.), *The Private Journal of Aaron Burr During His Residence of Four Years in Europe*, 2 vols (New York: 1838)

Lemaistre, J. G., *Travels After the Peace of Amiens Through Parts of France, Switzerland, Italy and Germany*, 3 vols (London: 1806)

Lockhart, John Gibson, *Memoirs of the Life of Walter Scott*, 7 vols (Edinburgh: 1837)

Logie, Jacques, *Waterloo: The Campaign of 1815* (Stroud: Spellmount, 2006)

Low, Donald, *That Sunny Dome: A Portrait of Regency England* (London: Dent, 1977)

Lovell, Ernest J. (ed.), *Medwin's Conversations of Lord Byron*, (Princeton: Princeton University Press, 1966)

— (ed.), *Lady Blessington's Conversations of Lord Byron* (Princeton: Princeton University Press, 1969)

MacCarthy, Fiona, *Byron: Life and Legend* (New York: Farrar, Strauss and Giroux, 2002)

Manning, Peter J., '*Childe Harold* in the Marketplace: From Romaunt to Handbook', *Modern Language Quarterly*, 52:2 (1991), pp. 170–90

Marett-Crosby, Anthony, *A School of the Lord's Service* (Frome: Ampleforth Abbey Trustees, 2002)

Martineau, Harriet, *Autobiography, with Memorials by Maria Weston Chapman*, 3rd edition, 3 vols (London: 1877)

Mason, Nicholas, 'Building Brand Byron: Early-Nineteenth-Century Advertising and the Marketing of *Childe Harold's Pilgrimage*', *Modern Language Quarterly*, 63:4 (December 2002), pp. 411–40

Massie, Robert K., *Catherine the Great: Portrait of a Woman* (New York: Random House, 2011)

Maxwell, Herbert (ed.), *The Creevey Papers: A Selection from the Correspondence and Diaries of the Late Thomas Creevey, M.P.*, 2nd edition, 2 vols (London: John Murray, 1904)

Mayne, Ethel Coburn, *The Life and Letters of Anne Isabella, Lady Noel Byron* (New York: Scribner's, 1929)

McCann, Justin, and Columba Cary-Elwes (eds), *Ampleforth and Its Origins: Essays on a Living Tradition by Members of the Ampleforth Community* (London: Burns, Oates, and Washbourne, 1952)

McDayter, Ghislaine, *Byromania and the Birth of Celebrity Culture* (Albany: SUNY Press, 2009)

Medwin, Thomas, *The Angler in Wales; or, Days and Nights of Sportsmen*, 2 vols (London: 1834)

— *The Life of Percy Bysshe Shelley*, ed. Buxton Forman (London: Humphrey Milford/Oxford University Press 1913)

Meriggi, Marco, 'State and Society in Post-Napoleonic Italy', *Napoleon's Legacy: Problems of Government in Restoration Europe*, ed. David Laven and Lucy Riall (Oxford and New York: Berg, 2000), pp. 49–63.

Lovelace, Ralph Milbanke, *Astarte: A Fragment of Truth Concerning George Gordon Byron, Sixth Lord Byron* (London: Christophers, 1921)

Minden, David, *Romantic Genius and the Literary Magazine: Biography, Celebrity and Politics* (Abingdon and New York: Routledge, 2005)

Mitchell, James, *A Tour Through Belgium, Holland, Along the Rhine and Through the North of France in the Summer of 1816* (London: 1816)

Mole, Tom, *Byron's Romantic Celebrity: Industrial Culture and the Hermeneutic of Intimacy* (Basingstoke: Palgrave Macmillan, 2007)

— (ed.), *Romanticism and Celebrity Culture, 1750–1850* (Cambridge: Cambridge University Press, 2009)

Moore, Doris Langley, *Ada, Countess of Lovelace: Byron's Legitimate Daughter* (London: John Murray, 1977)

Motion, Andrew, *Keats* (London: Faber and Faber, 1997)

Murray, E. B. (ed.), *The Prose Works of Percy Bysshe Shelley* (Oxford: Clarendon, 1993)

Mylius, W. F., *The First Book of Poetry. For the Use of Schools. Intended as Reading Lessons for the Younger Classes* (London: 1811)

Newton, John Frank, *The Return to Nature; or a Defence of the Vegetable Regime* (London: 1811)

Nicholson, Andrew (ed.), *The Letters of John Murray to Lord Byron* (Liverpool: Liverpool University Press, 2007)

Origo, Iris, *A Measure of Love* (London: Jonathan Cape, 1957)

Palmer, Susan, *The Soanes at Home: Domestic Life at Lincoln's Inn Fields* (Nottingham: Sir John Soane Museum, 2002)

Pascoe, Judith, *The Hummingbird Cabinet: A Rare and Curious History of Romantic Collectors* (Ithaca and London: Cornell University Press, 2006)

Paterson, Wilma, 'Was Byron Anorexic?' *World Medicine* (15 May 1982), pp. 35–8

Paul, C. Kegan, *William Godwin: His Friends and Contemporaries*, 2 vols (London: 1876)

Peacock, Thomas Love, *Peacock's Memoirs of Shelley*, ed. H. F. B Brett-Smith (London: Henry Frowde, 1909)

— *Nightmare Abbey/Crochet Castle*, ed. Raymond Wright (Harmondsworth: Penguin, 1986)

Philp, Mark, *Godwin's Political Justice* (London: Duckworth, 1986)

Pinkerton, John (ed.), *A General Collection of the Best and Most Interesting Voyages and Travels in All Parts of the World*, 17 vols (London: 1808–14)

Piozzi, Hester Lynch, *British Synonymy; or, An Attempt at Regulating the Choice of Words in Familiar Conversation*, 2 vols (London: 1794)

Polidori, John William, 'On the Punishment of Death', *Pamphleteer*, XV:VIII (1816), pp. 282–304

— *An Essay on the Source of Positive Pleasure* (London: 1818)

— Review of John Cam Hobhouse, *Historical Illustrations of the Fourth Canto of Childe Harold*, *Eclectic Review*, 10 (July–December 1818), pp. 323–36

— *Ximenes, the Wreath and Other Poems* (London: 1819)

— *The Vampyre: A Tale*, published without attribution (London: Sherwood, Neely and Jones, 1819)

— *The Vampyre and Ernestus Berchtold; or, the Modern Oedipus: Collected Fiction of John William Polidori*, ed. D. L. Macdonald and Kathleen Scherf (Toronto: University of Toronto Press, 1994)

Quennell, Peter, 'Byron and Harriet Wilson', *Cornhill Magazine*, 151 (January–June 1935), pp. 415–26

Raffles, Thomas, *Letters During a Tour Through Some Parts of France, Savoy, Switzerland, Germany, and the Netherlands in the Summer of 1817*, 2nd edition (Liverpool: 1819)

Reichard, M., *The Descriptive Road Book of France* (London: 1829)

Reiger, James, 'Dr. Polidori and the Genesis of *Frankenstein*', *Studies in English Literature, 1500–1900*, 3:4 (Autumn 1963), pp. 461–72

Religious Tract Society, *Sketches of Eminent Medical Men* (London: Religious Tract Society, 18–)

Robberds, J. W., *A Memoir of the Life and Writings of the Late William Taylor of Norwich*, 2 vols (London: John Murray, 1843)

Robinson, Charles E., *Shelley and Byron: The Snake and Eagle Wreathed in Fight* (Baltimore: Johns Hopkins University Press, 1976)

Robinson, Henry Crabb, *Diary, Reminiscences and Correspondence of Henry Crabb Robinson*, ed. Thomas Sadler, 2 vols (Boston: 1871)

— *Henry Crabb Robinson on Books and Their Writers*, ed. Edith J. Morley, 2 vols (London: Dent, 1938)

Rogers, Neville, 'Music at Marlow', *Keats-Shelley Memorial Bulletin*, 5 (1953), pp. 20–25

Rogers, Samuel, *Byron's Life, Letters, and Journals In One Volume* (London: John Murray, 1908)

— *Recollections of the Table Talk of Samuel Rogers* (New York: 1856)

Rolleston, Maud, *Talks with Lady Shelley* (London: Harrap, 1925)

Rosner, Lisa, *Medical Education in the Age of Improvement: Edinburgh Students and Apprentices, 1760–1826* (Edinburgh: Edinburgh University Press, 1991)

Rossetti, William Michael, *Dante Gabriel Rossetti: His Family-Letters with a Memoir*, 2 vols (London: 1895)

— *Memoir of Percy Bysshe Shelley* (London: 1886)

— *Rossetti Papers, 1862–1870* (New York: Scribner's, 1903)

— *Some Reminiscences of William Michael Rossetti*, 2 vols (New York: Scribner's, 1906)

Rousseau, Jean-Jacques, *Julie or The New Héloïse: Letters of Two Lovers Who Live in a Small Town at the Foot of the Alps*, trans. Philip Stewart and Jean Vaché (Hanover: Dartmouth College Press, 1997)

Rubinstein, William D., *Who Were the Rich?: A Biographical Directory of British Wealth Holders, Volume One, 1809–1839* (London: Social Affairs Unit, 2009)

Rudolf, Anthony, *Byron's Darkness: Lost Summer and Nuclear Winter* (London: Menard Press, 1984)

Rutherford, Andrew (ed.), *Byron: The Critical Heritage* (New York: Barnes and Noble, 1970)

St Clair, William, *The Godwins and the Shelleys: The Biography of a Family* (New York: Norton, 1989)

— *The Reading Nation in the Romantic Period* (Cambridge: Cambridge University Press, 2004)

Schoberl, Frederic, *Picturesque Tour from Geneva to Milan, By Way of the Simplon: Illustrated with Thirty Six Coloured Views* (London: 1820)

Scott, John, *Paris Revisited in 1815, by Way of Brussels*, 2nd edition (London: 1816)

Selincourt, Ernest de (ed.), *The Letters of William and Dorothy Wordsworth*, 2nd edition, 7 vols (Oxford: Clarendon, 1970)

Semmel, Stuart, 'Reading the Tangible Past: British Tourism, Collecting, and Memory after Waterloo', *Representations*, 69 (Winter, 2000), pp. 9–37.

Seymour, Miranda, *Mary Shelley* (New York: Grove Press, 2000)

Shelley, Lady Jane (ed.), *Shelley and Mary*, 4 vols (printed for private circulation, 1882)

— (ed.), *Shelley Memorials From Authentic Sources* (London: 1875)

Shelley, Mary, *Rambles in Germany and Italy in 1840, 1842, and 1843*, 2 vols (London: Edward Moxon, 1844)

Shelley, Percy Bysshe, and Mary Shelley, *History of a Six Weeks' Tour Through a Part of France, Switzerland, Germany and Holland; with Letters Descriptive of A Sail Round the Lake of Geneva and of the Glaciers of Chamouni* (London: 1817)

— *The Major Works*, ed. Zachary Leader and Michael O'Neill (Oxford: Oxford University Press, 2009)

Sheppard, John, *Letters Descriptive of a Tour Through Some Parts of France, Italy, Switzerland and Germany in 1816: With Incidental Reflections on Some Topics Concerned With Religion* (London: 1817)

Sheridan, Richard Brinsley, *The Critic; or, A Tragedy Rehearsed* (London: 1797)

Simond, Louis, *Journal of a Tour and Residence in Great Britain, 1810 and 1811, by a French Traveller*, 2 vols (Edinburgh: 1815)

— *Switzerland; Or, a Journal of a Tour and Residence in that Country, in the Years 1817, 1818, and 1819*, 2 vols (London: 1822)

Simpson, James, *A Visit to Flanders in July 1815*, 8th edition (Edinburgh: 1815)

Smiley, Philip, 'Polidori at Ampleforth', *Ampleforth Journal*, 97:2 (1992), pp. 34–43.

Smithers, Henry, *Observations Made During a Tour in 1816 and 1817 Through that Part of the Netherlands, which comprises Ostend, Bruges, Ghent, Brussels, Malines and Antwerp* (Brussels: 1818)

Solderholm, James, *Fantasy, Forgery, and the Byron Legend* (Lexington: University Press of Kentucky, 1996)

Southey, Robert, *The Poet's Pilgrimage to Waterloo* (London: 1816)

Starke, Mariana, *Travels on the Continent, Written for the Use and Particular Information of Travellers* (London: 1820)

Stendhal, *The Charterhouse of Parma*. trans. Richard Howard (New York: Modern Library, 2000)

Stocking, David M., and Marion Kingston Stocking, 'New Shelley

Letters in a John Gisborne Notebook', *Keats-Shelley Memorial Association Bulletin*, 31 (1980), pp. 1–9

Stommel, Henry, and Elizabeth Stommel, *Volcano Weather: The Story of 1816, the Year Without a Summer* (Newport: Seven Seas, 1983)

Sunstein, Emily W., *Mary Shelley: Romance and Reality* (Baltimore: Johns Hopkins University Press, 1989)

Sutherland, John, 'Henry Colburn, Publisher', *Publishing History*, 19 (1986), pp. 59–84

Thicknesse, Philip, *Useful Hints to those who Travel into France or Flanders by the way of Dover, Margate, and Ostend* (London: 1782)

Throsby, Corin, 'Flirting With Fame: Byron's Anonymous Female Fans', *Byron Journal*, 32:2 (2004), pp. 115–23

Thurman, William Richard, Jr, ('Letters About Shelley from the Richard Garnett Papers, University of Texas'). Unpublished doctoral dissertation, University of Texas at Austin, 1972

Timbs, John, *Walks and Talks About London* (London: 1865)

Todd, Janet, *Death and the Maidens: Fanny Wollstonecraft and the Shelley Circle* (Berkeley: Counterpoint, 2007)

— (ed.), *The Collected Letters of Mary Wollstonecraft* (New York: Columbia, 2003)

— 'The Anxiety of Emma', *Persuasions*, 29 (2007), pp. 15–25

Trelawny, Edward John, *Recollections of the Last Days of Shelley and Byron* (London: 1858)

— *Letters of Edward John Trelawny*, ed. H. Buxton Forman (London: Frowde, 1910)

— *Records of Shelley, Byron, and the Author* (New York: New York Review of Books, 2000)

Trevelyan, G. M., *Trinity College: An Historical Sketch* (Cambridge: Cambridge University Press, 1946)

Tuite, Clara, 'Tainted Love and Romantic Literary Celebrity', *English Literary History*, 74 (2007), pp. 59–88.

Tussaud, John Theodore, *The Romance of Madame Tussaud's* (New York: John Doran, 1920)

Viets, Henry R., '"By the Visitation of God": The Death of John William Polidori, M.D., in 1821', *British Medical Journal*, 2:5269 (December 1961), pp. 1773–5.

— 'The London Editions of Polidori's *The Vampyre*', *Bibliographical Society of America, Papers*, 63 (1969), pp. 83–103.

Waring, Samuel Miller, *The Traveller's Fire-side: A Series of Papers on Switzerland and the Alps* (London: 1819)

Wilson, Frances (ed.), *Byromania: Portraits of the Artist in Nineteenth and Twentieth-Century Culture* (London: Macmillan, 1999)

Wollstonecraft, Mary, *A Vindication of the Rights and Women* and *A Vindication of the Rights of Men*, ed. Janet Todd (Oxford: Oxford World's Classics, 2008)

Woolf, Stuart, *A History of Italy, 1700–1860: The Social Constraints of Political Change* (London: Methuen, 1979)

Wordsworth, William, and Samuel Taylor Coleridge, *Lyrical Ballads, with Other Poems*, 2 vols (London: 1800)

Young, Edward, *Conjectures on Composition* (London: 1759)

Youngson, A. J., *The Making of Classical Edinburgh, 1750–1840* (Edinburgh: Edinburgh University Press, 1966)

INDEX